BEING RAM DASS

BEING RAM DASS

Ram Dass
with Rameshwar Das

Sounds True
Boulder, CO 80306

© 2021 Love Serve Remember Foundation

Foreword © 2021 Anne Lamott

Sounds True is a trademark of Sounds True, Inc.

Published 2021

Book design by Karen Polaski

Cover image © Rameshwar Das

Printed in the United States of America

Library of Congress Cataloging-in-Publication Data
Names: Ram Dass, author. | Das, Rameshwar, author.
Title: Being Ram Dass / by Ram Dass with Rameshwar Das.
Description: Boulder, CO : Sounds True, 2021.
Identifiers: LCCN 2020013806 (print) | LCCN 2020013807 (ebook) |
    ISBN 9781683646280 (hardback) | ISBN 9781683646297 (ebook)
Subjects: LCSH: Ram Dass. | Yogis—United States—Biography. | Hindus—
    United States—Biography. | Psychologists—United States—Biography.
Classification: LCC BL1175.R25165 A33 2021 (print) |
    LCC BL1175.R25165 (ebook) | DDC 204.092 [B]—dc23
LC record available at https://lccn.loc.gov/2020013806
LC ebook record available at https://lccn.loc.gov/2020013807

10 9 8 7 6 5 4 3 2 1

Dedicated to

MAHARAJ-JI,

remover of darkness

Wrapped in a blanket of this world,
you are a homing beacon of the heart,
one foot in form, one in the formless,
to you it's all one.

Your love is like the sun.

CONTENTS

FOREWORD

The 14th-century Christian mystic Meister Eckhart wrote that if the soul could have known God without the world, God would never have created the world. And oh! What a world She done create—the earth and the stars, astral planes, otters, a little boy in Boston named Richard Alpert. And it was good.

The short version is that he grew up in a rich, uptight Jewish family, extraordinarily gifted academically, tormented and chubby, to become an imposing and articulate man with a wild sense of compassion and humor. He became the water boy to a playful enlightened teacher in India and then brought Eastern truth back to America, where he filled the niche of a spiritual superstar, loved by the multitudes and even finally himself.

Yet he freely admits he never overcame a single one of his many neuroses; thank You, Jesus, because this is why I loved him so much— he made those familiar struggles with ego and delusion so touching and hilarious that I helplessly fell for him, forty-five years ago, at the age of twenty. I trusted and delighted in him when I first read *Be Here Now*, and again with every new book. Now, delving into the book you hold in your hands, it all came back—the wisdom, the exciting and calming joy of his company.

Being Ram Dass is the longer, definitive story of his evolution, his journey, his immersion in Maharaj-ji's teachings of love, freedom from ego, living in the heart, service as the path to fulfillment. It is radical stuff, this love business, soul and awakening, feeding everyone, Christ consciousness, and where it all begins—being here, now, as is. As is!

When I first read his statement in *Be Here Now* at age twenty, "You are loved just for being who you are, just for existing. You don't have to do anything to earn it," I thought, Wait, *what?* People seemed to have forgotten to mention this to me when I was growing up, but I instantly, instinctively, trusted this dear neurotic, funny soul.

Love and the transformation from the mind to the vast ocean of consciousness deep inside were always his themes, what the baby chick of soul might discover if she pecked a hole in the eggshell. She might find the truth. The truth was soul, love, breath, God, oneness, life writ large and infinite. One does not pray to have all one's illusions and comforts stripped away, to give up all one has accrued—I want my Maypo!—even as we Christians live by Saint Luke's words, "Give and it shall be given unto you; good measure, pressed down and shaken together and running over." Wanting with the expectation of getting was the problem. Kathleen Norris wrote, "Prayer is not asking for what you think you want, but asking to be changed in ways you can't imagine," and this happened for Ram Dass when he left for India. What he wanted radically changed.

This is what happened for me when I first read *The Only Dance There Is* at twenty-one. I found the book by my boyfriend's bed after a romantic night with him, although what I didn't know was that the other woman, the one he was falling in love with, had given it to him. My mind was blown by Ram Dass's stories of higher consciousness, love as the only reality, suffering and pain as portals. "Everything in your life is there as a vehicle for your Transformation. Use it!" He made me laugh, and his words filled me with the grace of both satiation and hunger.

Then the boyfriend told me sheepishly that, after a shower, he would be heading over to see her and would be gone all day, and night. I faked nonchalance—hey, we're all grown-ups here—and kept it together until he closed the bathroom door. Then I fell to pieces in his lovely bed, in his traitorous house, ambushed and rejected.

He left, and I read till early evening. And that was the day my baby chick pecked a hole in the shell of my prison.

Grace always meets us exactly where we are and does not leave us where it found us. I lost the boyfriend but became a serious seeker, the best deal of my life. The message of *The Only Dance There Is*, and of all his books, was love: he wrote, "Love until you and the beloved become one." Love it all—the mess, pain, and suffering, along with the sunsets and the rain, the darkness in your psyche as well as the angelic, Caspar Weinberger as well as a baby, a deer, an orchid. Love the best you can at any moment. Don't harsh yourself—it can be tricky for *everyone* having this dual citizenship, of the biographical and the divine. You're not alone; we are in this together, connected, all one.

It was all grist for the mill of awakening, toward union with eternal.

We all have our favorite lines from his earlier work—"You need to remember your Buddha nature and your social security number" is mine, along with "We're all just walking each other home." And one need not go any further than *Be Here Now* to have a lifetime owner's manual for the soul.

But he adds dozens more amazing lines and thoughts in this new book, as he takes us through each chapter of his life in words that manage to be profound and welcoming, familiar and new, mind-blowing and simple: "Nowadays the mantra I give everyone is 'I Am Loving Awareness,' which is my own simple practice. The love is bhakti, the awareness is Buddhism: awareness and love, wisdom and compassion, formless and form, consciousness and love." Ram Dass taught it with feeling and charm, the esoteric and private, accessible to lifelong devotees or regular old grown-ups who might not actively be in the market for wonder. He helps us get back what we had as children: awe, curiosity, now-ness. My young Sunday school kids feel it when we study nautilus shells and when they roll down grassy hills. They know it when the rains come and the grass turns green again. This is the teaching: Pay attention. Be here now.

If you have followed his life and work for any time at all, you already know the basics of his origin story, but in this book he takes a deeper dive into the details of his family life growing up, his parents, brothers, friends, high school, his guru, his *satsang*, his lovers, and then in his seventies, a son. We've read many times of his great academic successes and soul sickness, his acclaimed work as a psychology student, his furtive shame around his sexuality, and then—*drum roll*—meeting Tim Leary at Harvard. But we've never heard those told in such depth, along with new stories and insight.

Being Ram Dass begins with his love of crazy speed and adrenaline, and this love was the same thing inside that later propelled him to God. Psychology studies as a graduate student gave him the awareness of his shame and fear, his drive for power and achievement, and these gave him the first inklings of soul. The psilocybin experiments with Leary eventually led him to India, where he met his guru, the love of his life, Neem Karoli Baba, his soul mirror. After that, no matter what was going on—personal turmoil or Vietnam, humiliation or adulation—he knew, "I was carrying what felt like a jewel, Maharaj-ji's presence and the spiritual path." Love, serve, remember; rinse, repeat.

This book is chock-full of new stories about crazy moments in ashrams and basements, relationships and loneliness and paradise, an amazing reflection on Muktananda and Sai Baba duking it out, the giving and taking and healing, the pain, the ecstasy. He writes of all the power trips he witnessed, his own and those of the holy men and women along the way, and how they led him to a life of service, of his cofounding the international relief organization Seva to help alleviate suffering in the world. He never brags (well, rarely). He writes about service as another kind of jewel: "Since I must act, I do the best I can to act consciously and compassionately. I try to make every action an exercise in liberation. Because the truth that comes from freedom, the power that comes from freedom, and the love and compassion that come from freedom are the jewels I can offer to my fellow sentient beings to relieve their suffering." He wrote extensively about service as the path to joy in *How Can I Help?* Death was his path to greater living: he had been immersed in the field and appreciation of conscious dying much of his life, serving anyone nearing death—the Dying Center in Santa Fe that he'd opened was the first residential facility in the US to approach death in an open, graceful way, as a spiritual rite of passage.

He was on the same page as Mother Teresa, who said to her new recruits, "Find the joy here, or go home." He found the joy, the gratitude, and in those he found himself.

Twenty years after I read *The Only Dance There Is* at that wayward boyfriend's house in Marin County, I stopped by a Christian general store in the next town over, where as it turns out Ram Dass was living at the time. I was seeking a way to integrate the Eastern ways with my own Christian faith. I wanted a guided Christian meditation or instruction.

I asked the elderly woman at the cash register where I might find a CD of Christian meditation, and she all but recoiled, retorting, "Christians don't meditate," as if I'd asked to see a poster of Jesus in a thong.

Well, they do, and many have the sense to know that stillness of mind is the way home, to the heart. So when I got back to my house, I decided to call Ram Dass. I looked him up in the phone book. (You younger people can google "phone book.") He was not listed under Ram Dass. I looked under Alpert, Richard, but he was not there. Finally, I looked up Dass, Ram, and there he was with a listed number.

Heart in my throat, I called him. He picked up and said, "Hi!"

We chatted for a while. He was very dear, the most ordinary person. I told him I was looking for help with specifically Christian meditation, and he suggested the Eastern Orthodox church's mantra, "Lord Jesus Christ, son of God, have mercy on me," which I have repeated hundreds of times a day ever since.

He had a massive stroke some years later in that very house and lost his faith in Maharaj-ji. But as the Hebrew Bible tells us, through grace God will restore what the locusts have carried off, and through grace and love his faith returned, pressed down, shaken together, and running over. And he would so need this in his last years.

He grew old on the island of Maui in a lot of pain, surrounded by indescribable love and beauty, and both brought him closer to God and inspired him as he continued to share the teachings with the rest of us. "In the '60s, I was an uncle for a movement," he said years ago. "I was always showing people where they could go. I went east, and then there was a big movement east." Now, he said, "the baby boomers are getting old—and I'm learning how to get old for them. That's my role." Then he got *very* old.

I saw a bumper sticker recently that said, "If you lived in your heart, you'd be home now," and this is the guidebook. Open these pages, read the map, meet or reacquaint yourself with this gentle and funny madman of love: from the chubby little boy in Boston to the old man as he finished this book, immersed in birdsong, ocean, and sky; and to the friend who has now passed on to the other side of eternity, reabsorbed, and yet is as here, now, and alive as ever.

Anne Lamott
Fairfax, California
July 2020

INTRODUCTION

'**ve always loved things that go fast. I've owned an MG sports car, a Mercedes coupe, a Plymouth convertible, two Jaguars, and a Dodge Dart. In graduate school, I bought a Triumph motorcycle and a small Harley. I loved to roar up the hills in California at ninety-five miles an hour, the wind rushing in my ears. Racing upward, climbing faster and faster, I'd hit the throttle until I reached a moment when the adrenaline, the shiver of danger, and the roar of the engine created such a feeling of bliss that I felt suspended in time, the atoms of my being vibrating with joy.

It lasted all of a split second, but I craved that moment. After that, I took flying lessons. I had the motorcycle and the sports car, but I wanted a plane too. I'm not sure why—I didn't really have anywhere to go—except that I loved that adrenaline rush, that thrill that always brought me completely into the present.

I've always had this penchant for risk taking. There is a part of me that is impulsive, leaping into the moment without regard for consequences. In the airplane, I was often awestruck by the view, seeing the cloud formations and the patterns of the earth below. Sometimes I was so overcome that I would forget to look at my instruments. But for me, flying had more to do with power than with beauty. It was about pushing my limits. It was about reaching for something beyond myself.

This adventurer side—the curiosity, the impulsivity, the optimism— has defined my life. In many ways, this drive also thrust me into the position of cultural trailblazer for a changing America. In the 1960s, when I was still Richard Alpert, a professor of psychology at Harvard, I met Timothy Leary, with whom I first tried psychedelic drugs. These substances, which were completely legal at the time, promised such a transformative view of reality that we felt as if we'd stumbled onto a key to enlightenment. Suddenly I realized there was more to my existence than my professorial self. Underlying it all was a vast ocean of consciousness.

For a materialist like me, this was a cataclysmic shift. Wanting to understand the potential of psychedelics, especially their creative and therapeutic power, Tim and I famously designed experiments to explore human consciousness. Besides giving these chemicals to others, we ingested them ourselves. We were opening doors to unconscious and spiritual dimensions of the human psyche, with no real idea how to navigate. The insights were profound, though by also using ourselves as subjects, we risked being biased by our own conceptions. As scientists, it was like skydiving without knowing if the parachute would open.

News headlines at the time were about the space race and the first astronauts circling the globe. We thought of ourselves as intranauts, exploring the unmapped worlds of inner space.

Eventually our experiments, the attendant publicity, and a certain cavalier attitude on our part got us kicked out of Harvard. Psychedelics came under intense government scrutiny, and a backlash began. Tim and I, however, were not done exploring. We set up our own scientific community at an estate in New York called Millbrook. We met others in the field: Ken Kesey and the Merry Pranksters, the chemist Owsley Stanley. We continued our experiments. Tim preached on the value of psychedelics to the masses. I distributed LSD as a sideline to lecturing.

Amid all this hoopla, I realized psychedelics had their limitations. Like my motorcycle and my airplane, it turned out that drugs were a vehicle. After a trip into unknown dimensions of consciousness and deep cosmic unity, I still had to land. I tried bigger or more frequent doses, pushing the limits, but the bliss was temporary. I could not hold on to it. The motorcycle, the airplane, the drugs: they all gave me a taste of something I was searching for, but they were not enough.

I wanted to know more. This is how I ended up in India in 1967 and how I came to meet the being I now call my guru. Neem Karoli Baba

was an older Indian man who was called simply Maharaj-ji, a frequent honorific that means "great king." At first glimpse, he looked ordinary. He sat wrapped in a plaid blanket and seemed kind. But at his feet, I had an experience more powerful than any I'd had with psychedelics. He saw me as a soul with a love outside of place and time that stirred me to my core.

I stayed in India for six months, training as a yogi, before Maharaj-ji sent me back to America with a new name: Ram Dass. Back in the US I found that I was a pioneer of an entirely different sort. In the chaos and churning conflict of the late 1960s and early '70s—the assassinations of Bobby Kennedy and Martin Luther King Jr., the war in Vietnam, the Watergate scandal, the Kent State shootings—young Americans were searching for spiritual answers. I was carrying what felt like a jewel, Maharaj-ji's presence and the spiritual path.

Turning toward Eastern spirituality was not just my inner evolution but part of a major cultural shift. In my role as guide I found myself also leading other reconnaissance missions. I was involved in innovative prison programs, the emerging hospice movement, caring for the homeless and people with AIDS, making a commitment to planetary survival. As I aged and baby boomers did too, my own body provided a reason to explore yet another uncharted area: conscious aging. Sometimes I felt like my friends were letting me do all the work!

Helping others is a two-way gift. Over the years, my work as teacher, as lecturer, and as guide has brought me into contact with a truly inspiring cast of characters from many different fields. I've been a small pebble in a big pond. Some of the ideas I helped bring to the fore—psychedelic research, yoga and meditation, prison and hospice care—are still spreading. There are yoga studios in every community. Hospice is standard medical care. Research on therapeutic uses of psychedelics is reviving.

That's the outer view. None of my adventuring would have taken place without an inner aspiration, the drive to push my own internal limits. The true risk taking, the search that has really defined my life, has been about identity and inner truth. When I look back on my life, I can track those risks: choosing a psychology degree instead of medical school, taking drugs whose effects I didn't know, taking chances with my love life, and, most of all, becoming a yogi, serving as a mouthpiece for Maharaj-ji, a guru from another culture.

To be sure, these choices broke me out of the cultural box of my upbringing. Only after meeting Maharaj-ji did I really understand this impulse. I wasn't just an ambitious ex-professor, straining against expectations. I am a soul on a journey. My constant reaching for the edge is really a creative act, an existential push to break through to another level, to find that place in myself that answers the question, Who am I, really?

This book is about the internal journey. Who I *am* is awareness and deep love, a presence beyond experience within a temporal, changing form. Who I am is a soul, a soul without a name, address, Social Security number, or biography, who isn't born and doesn't die. I *am*.

I see this life as an incarnation, as an evolutionary progression of the soul, a journey not just in this life but through many lives. As westerners, we're taught to bookend our lives with birth and death. However, from my experiences with death and sitting with dying people, I find this to be a limited view. Reincarnation resonates for me because it connects my consciousness and spirit to the cycle of birth and death. It's not so much about bookends or beginnings and endings. Life and death are a continuum.

All traditional cultures have this sense of spiritual continuity. They live with ancestors and rituals. They honor the unseen mystery of where the life-force comes from and where consciousness goes. In India, with its thousands of years of layered civilizations, this continuum is thought of as a wheel of births and deaths, of lives linked by karma and punctuated by reincarnation. Birth and death, birth and death are propelled by the subtle thread of past actions and desires toward a fulfillment that is variously described as realization, liberation, unconditional love, and Oneness.

I am one of those evolving souls. From my birth in 1931 as Richard Alpert to Ram Dass as I am now, a spiritual seeker whose aging body is nearing death, this incarnation has been a journey of awakening. My life has been a succession of openings, accompanied by profound changes in point of view, how I identify who I am, how I see myself. At times, I feel like I'm on a spiral staircase, looking back at my former selves on the landings below, while above I am the witness, ensconced in my soul, watching myself traverse the steps of this incarnation.

Maharaj-ji's unconditioned love has radiated and reverberated through my life. Through his eyes I see everything in my life as an orchestrated play, each person and situation and desire a potential ingredient in the recipe for awakening. My sweep of years seems like a series of adventures, none of them coincidences. They are populated by an extraordinary panorama of friends straight from central casting. My fellow performers in the dance of love are, as I am, working out their own karma and sliding in and out of the embrace of the One. My life is part of a unified field, an interconnected whole, of which you, dear reader, are a part.

As a teacher, I always use my life experiences as a lesson plan—often as an example of what *not* to do. I am reminded of when I was flying my airplane with Tim Leary. I was circling the airfield in Mexico City where we were to land. I meant to follow the tower's instructions for landing, but with my inadequate Spanish I flew right into the path of a big Aeronaves de México airliner. The other pilot had to abort his landing and pull up in a hurry to avoid a crash. When I finally landed, our plane was surrounded by grim-looking *federales*. Everyone was furious. Tim, in his charming and inimitable way, knew how to get out of the jam. He said, "This is going to cost us about twenty dollars." It did, and we went out to lunch.

My high flying and risk taking have sometimes been destructive. A lot of things don't just go away with twenty dollars. But it's important to me to share as truthfully as I can. Some of the story that follows you may find familiar. I am nearing ninety now, and behind me lie decades of talks, books, and recordings. I hope putting these experiences together in the context of this incarnation will be helpful to you, as it is to me. After all, we are fellow souls. We are on the same journey home to the heart.

This is a story of awakening from feeling separate and alienated toward living in oneness and love. May this look back at my incarnation encourage you in yours.

Ram Dass
Maui, Hawaii
December 2019

PART I

LEARNING AND UNLEARNING

See everything
in the universe
for the good.

MAHARAJ-JI

CHAPTER 1

FIRED—AND FREE

id you give drugs to an undergraduate?"

It was May 14, 1963, and I was in the office of Harvard University president Nathan M. Pusey. A youthful-looking man with a patrician air, Pusey was known for both his low-key manner and his outspoken commitment to academic freedom. Early in his tenure, he'd tangled with Senator Joseph McCarthy and won great praise for resisting the demagogue's attempt to get several Harvard professors fired for being supposed Communists. Now he was staring at me from across his desk. He wanted an answer. Perhaps I had pushed the boundary of academic freedom too far.

His question wasn't that crazy. As an assistant professor in clinical psychology and education, I'd spent two years working with my colleague Timothy Leary, a lecturer in clinical psychology, on research projects involving psychedelic drugs. Tim and I were hardly the first to take an interest; research into LSD and mescaline was already happening in Canada and England. Harvard itself had conducted experiments in the 1950s on the mind-altering effects of LSD. Later it was revealed that this research was sponsored by the Central Intelligence Agency, as part of its MK-Ultra project.

By this point psychedelics had also captured the public imagination. In May 1957, *Life* magazine published a cover story titled "Seeking the Magic Mushrooms." It was a first-person account by a New York banker named R. Gordon Wasson, who had ingested a handful of "divine" wild mushrooms in the mountains of Mexico and reported visions "more real to me than anything I had ever seen with my own eyes."

But a lot of the early research focus had been on the drugs' psychotomimetic qualities, their potential to mimic psychosis. The CIA was interested in mind control and in some instances gave LSD to people without their knowledge or consent. Tim and I saw a potential in psychedelics not for psychosis, but for therapy, creativity, and spiritual growth. Some researchers, like the British psychiatrist Humphry Osmond, were already exploring this therapeutic approach. (He coined the term *psychedelic*, meaning "mind manifesting.") Osmond was successfully using psychedelics to treat conditions like alcoholism and depression.

Our own first experiences of psychedelics were overwhelmingly positive—and profound. Six months after Tim tried wild mushrooms in Mexico, a hallucinogenic trip that sent him down "the cellular time tunnel," as he put it, he facilitated my journey one night back in Cambridge with a dose of psilocybin, the synthetic version of the mushrooms.

I was twenty-nine at the time, an academic up-and-comer. I had a PhD from Stanford University, as well as research contracts at Stanford and Yale. I'd landed the assistant professorship at Harvard just a year earlier. As the son of the president of the New York, New Haven and Hartford Railroad, I was comfortable with Boston's elite and had all the trappings of academic success: a path to tenure, a corner office, two secretaries, dozens of research assistants, a Cambridge apartment full of antiques, a Mercedes-Benz, a Triumph motorcycle, an MG sports car, even a Cessna airplane.

Psilocybin turned my up-and-coming world upside-down. For the first time I saw myself from *outside* myself. Who I *thought* I was—a son, a professor, a psychologist—was not who I *actually* was. I thought my physical and psychological identity was everything. Psychedelics showed me I was a soul. There were planes of pure being beyond my achievements, prestige, and rational understanding. The realization was cataclysmic. It made me feel, as I would refer to it for many years afterward, that I was finally home, home in my heart.

Changed by our experiences, Tim and I embarked on a series of experiments to explore the creative and therapeutic potential of psychedelics. Under the auspices of Harvard's Center for Research in Personality, we administered psilocybin and later LSD to volunteer graduate students, artists, poets, writers, religious scholars, even prisoners. We amassed more than four hundred reports detailing psychedelic journeys, a growing compendium of successful and provocative research.

The research was perhaps *too* successful. Graduate students signed up in droves to participate in our studies, and our projects—such as the Concord Prison Experiment, which sought to discover whether psychedelics could lower recidivism rates—began to attract attention in the press. Some of our Harvard colleagues started raising eyebrows. As their projects lost graduate assistants gravitating to our work and as our research continued to expand, they began to voice concerns.

They argued our methodology was not rigorous or scientific. Moreover, the reports we were collecting from individuals included subjective feelings and sensations and mystical insights, not exactly the kind of hard data that behavioral psychologists typically collected. Our peers loved their rat mazes, graphs, and questionnaires. They wanted quantifiable metrics.

But how exactly does one quantify consciousness? At faculty meetings, Tim and I argued that we *were* being methodical and scientific; the challenge was that there were no categories yet for these sorts of mind-altering, beyond-words experiences. We took the psychedelics ourselves because it was impossible to understand our subjects' experiences otherwise—and because our participation, it appeared, influenced outcomes in a way that we wanted to understand. As we saw it, our research fell well within Harvard's scientific tradition. The psychologist and philosopher William James, one of the university's eminent professors, revered as a father of psychology, had created the field of introspective psychology after experimenting with drugs and consciousness at Harvard in the late 1800s.

The skittish administration made Tim and me promise we would not test our drugs with undergraduates. We gladly agreed. We had no need for undergrads in our research.

But psychedelics were not difficult to procure back then—they were still new, unregulated, and legal. Students on campus were experimenting with them on their own. Before long the press took notice, and so did the Massachusetts Department of Public Health, the FBI, and the Federal Bureau of Narcotics.

The university asked us to turn over our supply of drugs for safekeeping. We shouldn't have been surprised. Tim and I *were* provocative. "What is in question is the freedom or control of consciousness, the limiting or expanding of man's awareness," he declared in an editorial in the school newspaper, the *Harvard Crimson*, after our drugs were put under lock and key. I shocked psychologists at an international conference by announcing that a psychedelic trip could be a pathway to growth and love. We weren't exactly academic wallflowers.

What was lost in the media hoopla was our serious effort to develop conceptual models for consciousness itself. Psychology was meant to study the mysteries of the mind. But as psychologists, our professional toolbox was too limited to describe these intangible states. My own training, in personality development and human motivation, did not explain the heart connection our subjects felt on psychedelics. Tim, whose background was in game theory, saw that psychedelics could take one beyond social roles, offering hope for human problems.

We saw ourselves as pioneers, explorers on a quest to chart the unmapped worlds of human consciousness. This was the stuff of discovery. The obstacles seemed trivial compared to the magnitude of potential benefits.

"Did you give drugs to an undergraduate?"

I considered the question. Tim and I had actually been quite careful in our research to make sure we honored our promise to the university. If curious undergrads stopped by our offices, we dutifully sent them on their way—including a freshman named Andrew Weil, who was interested in psychoactive plants, especially mescaline.

Then I met Ronnie Winston. I was invited to a party for graduate students, and at some point he introduced himself: a brilliant young man studying chemistry and English literature at Harvard and also doing research in rocket propulsion at the Massachusetts Institute of Technology. I did not know he was an undergraduate. Though the son of Harry Winston, the Fifth Avenue jeweler and diamond king, Ronnie was self-effacing, funny, and self-possessed. He talked as if he was knowledgeable about psychedelics.

It didn't occur to me he might not be a graduate student. I enjoyed our conversation and invited him to lunch the next day. When he asked about trying psilocybin, I agreed without hesitation.

Psilocybin helped me discover something about myself, about the universe, about love, about the ineffable. We had such a quick and easy friendship, it felt natural to share the experience. I was also attracted to him.

I turned him on with psilocybin a few days after the party, and after that, I introduced him to LSD. This fell outside any formal research experiment. I was using my personal supply of psilocybin, in a social setting, and not even on campus. I didn't think university rules applied.

Ronnie and I made plans to fly to the Berkshires for lunch at a restaurant. I often flew out of Hanscom Field, near Bedford, Massachusetts. Before going, we both ingested LSD. Soon after we took off, the acid came on, and the ground started swirling around below. I couldn't tell whether it was the plane moving or the earth rotating. Of course, it was the drugs taking effect, spinning me on the inside. I quickly realized this was a bad idea. Somehow, I managed to land the plane in one piece.

Admittedly, I did not exercise the greatest judgment with Ronnie. It turned out Ronnie *was* an undergraduate. He was also roommates with Andy Weil, the undergraduate student Tim had turned away. Andy was not pleased to discover Ronnie had received psilocybin after he had been denied. I suspect he was attracted to Ronnie too. Andy was also a reporter for the *Crimson*, and he wrote an article that reached President Pusey.

University officials sent Andy to New York to speak to Ronnie's father, the diamond king, to pressure Ronnie to squeal. When Andy told Harry Winston that a faculty member was giving his son drugs, he called Ronnie right away. "If you don't tell the administration, I'm cutting you off."

Ronnie went in to speak with Pusey. "Did Professor Alpert give you psychedelics?" the president asked him. Ronnie didn't skip a beat. "Yes, and it was the greatest educational experience I have had."

"I don't care," Pusey told him. "I just want to know whether he gave them to you."

I didn't fully appreciate the collision course Tim and I were on with Harvard. First, there was the growing public furor over our work, which was causing even friends of ours, like author and philosopher Aldous Huxley, to urge caution. When the *Harvard Review* dedicated the spring issue to psychedelics, Tim and I contributed a provocative essay. We argued for the freedom to expand one's consciousness. "Trust your internal machinery," we urged our readers. "Be entertained by the social game you play. Remember, man's natural state is ecstatic wonder, ecstatic intuition, ecstatic accurate movement. Don't settle for less."

Tim embraced the publicity. He liked to tell reporters, "LSD is a strange drug that produces fear in people who don't take it."

Now Pusey's question hung in the air.

Staring at his silver-flecked hair, his impassive face, I realized the university was looking for a way to get rid of me. Under Pusey, Harvard's endowment and budget had quadrupled, enrollment was up, and new buildings were springing up all over campus. An assistant professor flouting scientific convention and attracting controversial press was a liability, not an asset.

Tim, my partner in scientific excess, had left for Los Angeles a few weeks earlier to do research. Problem was, he hadn't told anybody he was going. As soon as Pusey found out, he simply took Tim off the payroll.

My situation was trickier. My appointment in the Department of Social Relations would expire that year, but I'd received a new appointment in the Graduate School of Education.

I took a deep breath.

"Yes," I replied. I had given drugs to an undergraduate. But I'd been unaware of his status, and my actions fell outside the confines of the university—not part of any experiment, not part of any study. I'd abided by our agreement.

Pusey was, of course, unpersuaded.

"You broke a promise to the dean," he said. "We can't have that."

He had a meeting scheduled with the university's executive board. He planned to bring up my termination.

In retrospect, I was living in a bubble. Institutions are deeply threatened by expanded consciousness. Twelve days later, I was back in Pusey's office. I was fired, he said. I was to pack up my things immediately.

Suddenly, Harvard felt very small. I wasn't on any drugs that day, but inside I felt an incongruous sense of liberation. All my life, I had done what was expected of me, and now here I was, not doing what anybody expected—and very publicly. As a member of a family and community driven by achievement, I might as well have died. My Jewish parents would sit shiva for my career. But inside, I felt free, maybe for the first time since I'd been a child. I thought, "Did I blow it? Or did I just win the lottery? What just happened?"

Looking at Pusey, I saw a mind caught in a box delimited by his own projections. From my psychedelic-bedazzled mind, I felt a wave of compassion. Both of us were immersed in the great ocean of consciousness, but he wasn't going to find his way home to the heart, to love. Not this round.

I nodded, told Pusey good-bye, and headed to pack up my office. If Harvard wasn't interested, Tim and I would take our research elsewhere. We were freed from academic strictures. We wouldn't stop.

When I left Pusey's office that day in May, I felt mostly numb. But as I walked across campus to go pack my office, the green lawn starting to sparkle in the spring sun, I felt a distinct thrill. Harvard had just kicked me out—because of politics and shortsightedness. Psychedelics would teach me something I would never find in academia.

Drugs had changed me from a selfish, striving academic in search of recognition and power to someone who was aware of the soul. Psychedelics had introduced me to compassion, to recognizing and feeling love for others. Harvard seemed trivial by comparison.

Pusey issued a press release announcing my firing. My ouster and Tim's made national headlines. Over the next few months, our names appeared in the *New York Times*, the *Boston Globe*, *Newsweek*, *Time*, *Esquire*, and even *Ladies' Home Journal*. I was the first faculty member to be fired under Pusey and the first to be asked to leave campus since Ralph Waldo Emerson was banished from Harvard more than one hundred years earlier. In a commencement speech,

Emerson dared to argue for man's intuitive spiritual experience. Sounded familiar.

Tim and I would head in new directions. We were explorers, and so explore we would—though, as it would turn out, in wildly different ways. Tim would become a psychedelic prophet, promoting a social revolution summoned by his famous "Turn on, tune in, drop out" slogan, before ending up in jail. Meanwhile, I would find my way to India and a being who would change my life and identity even more drastically than drugs: a guru named Neem Karoli Baba. He would show me planes of consciousness I hadn't dreamed of, transform my heart and mind, and rename me Ram Dass.

Standing in Pusey's office I knew none of this. What I did know was that this part of my life was over and another was just beginning. On the one hand, I was angry at the Harvard administration and faculty for being too chicken to support our groundbreaking research. On the other, I knew how psychologists thought. I talked to academics every day whose entire world was psychology, and I knew why they were scared. Psychedelics opened up a new and unknown frontier. It was threatening. Before my experiences on psilocybin and LSD, I would have been scared too.

This was infuriating, but it was also a relief. I'd just lost everything I'd worked for: my career, my tenure, my reputation. But as I walked out the door and into Harvard Yard, I also felt an inexplicable lightness.

"I'm free!" I thought to myself. "I'm free, I'm free!"

CHAPTER 2

POWER AND LOVE

y mother wanted a girl.

But she was diagnosed with severe anemia, and doctors told her she'd be better off having a hysterectomy. She'd carried a couple of babies already—her two boys, William and Leonard, were eight and four at the time—and the strain of another pregnancy might be too much on her body.

But my mother loved babies, and she was used to getting what she wanted. Gertrude Levin was the eldest daughter of a wealthy, connected Jewish family in Roxbury, Massachusetts. Her father, a Russian immigrant, had gotten rich in the carpet business with Louis B. Mayer—the same Mayer who later founded MGM Studios and became a Hollywood mogul. Gertrude grew up in a mansion with stately pillars, and at age fourteen, she was allowed to drive her father's seven-passenger luxury Hupmobile. She had impeccable taste and enjoyed being generous, helping to furnish houses for others in need and using her connections to assist friends.

Though Gertrude was the oldest of five, when she'd married my father, George Alpert, in 1922, their shared joke was that she was "just eleven," as in "just a Levin." Perhaps the humor alleviated a sense of inferiority in my father, given that Gertrude was socially out of his league. Her three brothers would go into the carpet business too. Her youngest sister, Edna, became a social worker and therapist.

George, by contrast, had grown up poor in a tenement apartment in Boston, the oldest of six. Unlike his bride's upbringing, his had been defined by striving. His father, a Jewish immigrant from Poland, was an antiques "picker" who traveled around New England in an old Ford truck, buying up furniture pieces he sold to a dealer in Boston. Handsome and athletic, George joined the US Navy and served in World War I. But if he'd had any hopes of striking out on his own, they were derailed one day in 1918, when his father's truck, heavy with antiques, stalled on railroad tracks in New Hampshire, and the senior Alpert was killed by an oncoming train. It was a strange twist of fate, given that his son would one day run a railroad.

It fell to George, then twenty, to support his mother and siblings. Desperate to create a more prosperous life, he worked his way through Boston University School of Law. He was determined to achieve not only material security but also social respectability. After marrying my mother, he struggled to provide at first, moving her into a small Roxbury apartment that was, as if to underscore the contrast, just blocks from her parents' dignified home. Both the apartment and their finances would feel even more squeezed with the birth of Billy, in 1923, and then Len, almost four years later.

Despite their differences, my mother and father recognized a drive in each other. They were both firstborns and both second-generation Jewish immigrants, a people who had defied adversity for centuries. They were actually second cousins. They began to build a life that would take them into Boston's higher strata. Mother's father used his connections to get George a job at a big law firm, and at twenty-six my father landed a position as assistant district attorney. After a few years prosecuting high-profile cases and making a name for himself among the Boston Irish establishment, my father opened a law firm with his brother Herbert: Alpert & Alpert.

Then the stock market crashed in 1929, ushering in the Great Depression. Though my parents and brothers experienced some scarcity, my father's initial success and my mother's inherited wealth insulated the family from its worst effects. By the time I came along, my parents were able to buy a house for their growing family, moving from Roxbury to the suburb of Newton.

My mother was disappointed when I made my appearance on April 6, 1931—I was not the girl she had so wanted. But, maybe because

I was born against medical advice, I quickly became a golden child, the baby who brought new joy, cherished for my giggles and blond ringlets. Already in school, my brothers were protective and affectionate, especially Billy, who liked to hold me down and kiss me until I shrieked with laughter. They saw their playful kid brother as the family mascot, and I continued to get kisses from Billy even as I grew older—a fact that got me in trouble at age eleven, when he kissed me, smelled cigarettes on my breath, and ratted me out to Mother. I and my friends from grade school—Amy, from across the street, Doris, Weezie, and Peter—had been secretly smoking in the clubhouse we'd created in the back of my family's garage. Smoking was still cool.

At the same time, my family's protective love could feel maddening to me as the youngest. When I was one, the kidnapping of the twenty-month-old son of the famed transatlantic aviator Charles Lindbergh prompted my father to install iron bars on my bedroom windows to deter kidnappers; in my child's imagination, they were prison bars. A few years later, I was hospitalized with pneumonia, a feared killer. This was before antibiotics, and treatment was weeks of quarantine in an oxygen tent. I was too young to read much. TV wasn't really a thing yet. I was not allowed outside contact. Though my family was terrified of losing me, I felt like a hostage, a lonely prisoner in a cellophane tent while my mother monitored every detail from outside. I remember feeling isolated and alone.

The age difference with my brothers—Billy was nine when I was born, Len was five—meant that in many ways I got the attention of an only child. I received a lot of one-on-one time especially with Mother, who was devoted to the baby of the family. When I was eight, in 1939, she took me by boat from Boston to the New York World's Fair. I made her anxious running around on the ship but managed not to fall overboard. At the fair, I got to test out a fancy new Bell telephone. Another favorite memory with Mother is a time we were playing a singing game in the car, seeing who could hold a single note the longest: "Aaaaaaaaaah." When we looked over at the car next to us, the driver was staring at us as if we'd gone mad. We laughed hard.

As I grew up and began to assert myself, Mother's affection began to mutate into something else: control. She rewarded good behavior with gold stars stuck on the fridge, and in classic Jewish mother fashion, she used food as a proxy for love. She was a skillful preparer of matzo ball soup, rice pudding, meat loaf, pot roast, and overcooked vegetables. Cleaning my plate was a requirement. If I didn't like her cooking, obviously I didn't love her. Her love was conditional, and I had to be a good boy to keep it.

My food guilt was compounded when I found out, in elementary school, about her anemia, which was rediagnosed by doctors first as aplastic anemia and, later, as leukemia. When I understood she'd given birth to me against doctors' orders, it seemed to my young mind that she had sacrificed herself for my very existence. To please her, I ate and ate. But I could never please her enough, so I soon grew overweight.

If my mother operated out of a desire to manage and control, my father, by contrast, was motivated by money and status. "Give them hell, George!" I remember Mother telling him in the parlor over some lawsuit. She enjoyed being a conduit to his success. Her family connections, after all, had given him a leg up. She encouraged him to get involved with Jewish charities to elevate their standing in social circles. Dad became president of the temple board.

Soon enough, he didn't need her connections. Dad became good friends with a judge on the Massachusetts Supreme Judicial Court. On weekends, the two liked to go "antiquing" in the New England countryside. (Who knows what they actually did?) The judge awarded Dad the receivership for a big real estate company, Conveyancers Realty. It was a financial plum, and it made Dad rich. He brought in his brother Herbert to help run it, as well as other financially struggling siblings. He even involved me. The Conveyancers Realty office was in the same building as his law practice. Together with my dad's sister Phyllis, I'd help answer the phones.

Then, in 1941, Japan bombed Pearl Harbor, and the United States entered World War II. I was ten. We all pitched in to help with the war effort. Dad became an air raid warden for Newton, making sure that people blacked out their windows at night. Mother and friends in her sewing circle made Bundles for Britain, knitting sweaters and crocheting blankets for war-torn England. My brother Bill, by then a college student at Dartmouth, enlisted in the air force as soon as he graduated; he became a fighter pilot and was stationed in Alabama as a pilot instructor. Leonard enlisted in the navy, going through officer training at College of the Holy Cross in Worcester, Massachusetts.

I, meanwhile, sold war bonds with my Aunt Thelma in the lobby of the biggest movie theater in Boston. In the summers, Mother and I became spotters for the Ground Observer Corps; we took turns sitting from midnight to 4 a.m. in a cabin in New Hampshire, watching for any German planes that might fly in from Canada. The cabin was equipped with binoculars and a direct phone line to a central office. No planes ever came.

After the war ended in 1945, my father's reputation reached new heights, in part because of his talent for raising money. Even before the extent of the Holocaust was known, Dad, at Mother's urging, set about collecting funds for a group called the American Jewish Joint Distribution Committee, to help Jewish refugee children. He became known for his eloquent fundraising speeches. "What would I do if it were my child?" he would say passionately. "Well, I'll tell you what. If it were my child, I'd give every penny that I could beg, borrow, or, yes, even steal!"

Because of his charity and legal work and his growing social connections, Dad was enlisted by Rabbi Israel Goldstein to help found a Jewish secular college near Boston. Jewish students and scholars had long suffered from imposed quotas at Ivy League schools like Harvard and Yale, and Goldstein's goal was to start an entirely new institution, to be named Brandeis University. This would be the Jewish equivalent of Harvard! Donations poured in. In 1946, Dad was named chairman of the university's board, a position he'd retain until 1954.

One early supporter, famously, was Albert Einstein. But he severed his association in 1947, after a falling out with Dad over who should be university president. Einstein wanted Harold Laski, a left-wing scholar, but Dad would not stand for this. Laski was "a man utterly alien to American principles of democracy, tarred with the Communist brush," Dad said in a statement. He would not budge, declaring, "I can compromise on any subject but one: Americanism." (That night Billy,

Leonard, and I satirically poked American flags in the pickles on the dinner table.) Instead, the first president of Brandeis became Abram Sachar, a Jewish scholar. Maybe unsurprisingly, Dad squabbled with him too. Both men were polished public speakers and had their own views on how, and in what venues, to give the Brandeis sales pitch to would-be donors.

Dad and his cohorts raised hundreds of millions of dollars, and he remained a school trustee until his death. The new university, which opened officially in 1948, took over the grounds of a failing medical and veterinary school in Waltham, Massachusetts, and converted the campus. Though I was only a teenager, I helped Dad by overseeing the transformation of a laboratory once used for dissections and cadavers into a dining hall. (I did get a rabbi to bless it.)

As a family, we went for drives in our Packard every Sunday afternoon, us boys horsing around in the back seat while Dad smoked and talked business with Mother up front. Otherwise, though, Dad was never all that present with his children, consumed primarily with his work and moving up in the world. In that stereotypical 1940s way, he was more the cigar-chewing, newspaper-reading authoritarian type, called upon by my mother whenever one of us needed a timely belt lashing. ("Wait until your father gets home!")

He was often not home even at night. As an assistant DA, he needed to bring in extra money, so he worked gigs as the leader of a dance band, playing violin and banjo for parties and weddings. Even as we grew older, he filled his leisure time with other people; a talented violinist, he formed a string quartet with childhood friends, and they'd often meet to play—two violins, a cello, a viola—in our living room. I liked to sneak down and sit on the stairs to listen.

As Dad's public profile increased, his and Mother's original relationship appeared to reverse, at least in terms of who wielded power and influence. Dad was accumulating new friends: CEOs of companies, heads of airlines, fancy surgeons. He became a member of the Presidents Club, and when President Richard Nixon was initiated into the club at a White House dinner, it was Dad—always witty and eloquent—who roasted him, cracking jokes about what a lousy businessman Nixon was.

Mother didn't like this. Though she participated in some of his ventures—she decorated the university president's house at Brandeis— she mostly retreated to her familiar sewing circle of old friends. It didn't help that Dad's high-flying life included extramarital affairs. I was too young to catch on, but my brothers noticed many attractive women come through his law office. (Many years later, when I received a letter from a man who said he thought Dad was his father, Billy and Leonard just shrugged. It was probably true, they said, but who knew? Dad, Uncle Herbert, Aunt Phyllis—all of them had affairs.) I suspect my mother knew too; years later, I caught her staring sadly out the window as my father drove up in his blue Pontiac convertible with his assistant, an attractive female German lawyer, sitting too close to him.

One way to connect with Dad was through his hobbies. An amateur photographer, he had a darkroom in our basement, and sometimes he'd invite me to help develop his photos. These were almost always family pictures. Though he had a mechanized processor to make color prints (an unusual luxury), we more often worked in black and white, and my job was to put the prints through the trays of chemicals: developer, stop bath, fixer. Dad would smoke his cigar, which gave me a headache in those close quarters and probably didn't help the clarity of the photos. I'd stick it out for as long as it took, relishing the opportunity to be with my father.

Music was another way to connect. Both my parents valued music, and there was always music in our home. Dad had his dance band and string quartet. And I still have preteen memories of sitting with Mother in bed under a puffy quilt on Saturday afternoons, listening to the Metropolitan Opera. I learned piano early, and at age nine I started studying cello with an old German teacher who chewed on a cigar and spit over my head. I liked to pretend I was a concert musician, taking bows before an imaginary audience, but I was mediocre at best. People left the room when I practiced. I imagine it was an ordeal for my father to listen, and I happily complied when he insisted I transfer to a new teacher who was the second cellist in the Boston Symphony Orchestra. I harbored hope that I'd get to play with Dad's quartet in the living room one day. That invitation never came.

Dad's brother Milton, who went by Mickey, was also a musician, a well-known orchestra leader who one day brought a friend over, a man named George Gershwin, to play his music for Dad. I'm not sure why; maybe they were hoping Dad would invest in a musical or something. Nothing ever came of it because Dad hated the music.

Mickey gave my family a front seat to a tragedy: the deadliest night-club fire in US history, at Boston's Cocoanut Grove in 1942. On the Saturday after Thanksgiving, Uncle Mickey was leading the orchestra at the club for a huge crowd, raucous after a big football game between Boston College and Holy Cross. As the orchestra played, a fire broke out and spread quickly. People ran for the exits, but the club's owners had locked the emergency doors to prevent patrons from sneaking out without paying, and many got trapped inside. Uncle Mickey was able to escape by climbing out a bathroom window.

No cause for the fire was ever determined. Almost 500 people died, and more than 150 landed in the hospital. Practically everyone in Boston knew a victim. The *Boston Herald* put a photo of Uncle Mickey, standing outside the club in someone's white fur coat, on the front page. Distraught, he took refuge at our house. I can still recall his hysterical sobbing. Many patrons he knew died, as well as several orchestra friends. I had school friends who lost a parent or both parents. Because Uncle Mickey escaped, many of them stopped speaking to me. I was only eleven, and this was my first real experience with death, especially of this magnitude. It was disorienting, particularly because no one close to me seemed to know how to talk about it. The US had entered World War II only a year earlier, and already, it seemed, we were all in denial of death.

My brothers, whom I might have turned to, were not particularly helpful. They were twenty and sixteen years old by then, and they had their sights on a future outside the family orbit. Athletic and good-looking, Billy had inherited Dad's drive. Though he'd had a rebellious phase, climbing out the window at fifteen to run away from home, he eventually channeled his energies, becoming a champion pole vaulter at Dartmouth and never lacking for a girlfriend. Once the war was over, Billy followed in Dad's footsteps and attended Boston University School of Law, then went to work at Dad's law office. He too married an heiress: Helen Mills, a New Yorker whose family ran the sheet-music empire Mills Music Publishing Company.

Leonard, like me, got his looks more from Mother—we had the same round Levin face—and was not athletic in the least. But, like Dad, he had a nose for business, and he showed an interest in money even as a kid, when he printed fake dollar bills on a mimeograph machine so that he and I could play store. His family nickname was Lenny Penny. Appropriately, while stationed with the navy on Okinawa, he was put in charge of exchanging sailors' dollars for the local currency. To please Dad, he too attended Boston University School of Law and worked at the family law office; but after that, he went on to Harvard Business School and started both a record business and a greeting-card business.

Len inherited Dad's musical gift, and he discovered a love for the organ. Unlike our father, though, he had a mystical side, and while in officer training at Holy Cross, he was exposed to church music and fell in love with hymns. We'd sit next to each other at the piano, reading the words of hymns together and discussing the content. Boston had an organ society that arranged for musicians' access to pipe organs at churches and theaters around town, and sometimes Leonard would take me with him. Under the dim lights of a sanctuary, I'd sit in the pews as my brother played Bach, immersing me in glorious music. Len's talent for Bach and Mozart struck a spiritual chord in me. In that music I heard something beautiful, majestic, and bigger than myself.

I was not nearly as athletic as Billy and nowhere near as musical as Leonard. As adolescence set in, I was afflicted by feelings of inadequacy. Some of this was the regular emotional chaos of puberty, but entering Weeks Junior High in Newton certainly didn't help. A big, diverse school with few Jewish students, it harbored a bunch of insecure, aggressive Irish kids who soon figured out how easily they could beat the shit out of a fat, klutzy Jew.

I'd grown conspicuously overweight with my eating for love at home. Thanks in part to Billy, who took to calling me "Satchel Ass," I was deeply self-conscious. Mother, who liked bargains, would take me clothes shopping at Filene's Basement, calling out to the salesman, "Double-Z wide, please!" as she dug through the clearance bins for pants. If I could have disappeared into the floor, I would have.

At school I was called a "fat, dirty Jew," shoved in the hallways, always picked last for soccer. The Irish kids sensed my fear and took advantage. To escape, I clung to a few adults. I stayed after class to clean the blackboard for my eighth-grade homeroom teacher, Miss Donohue, who was wise and kind and took me out for milkshakes. The school-bus driver was also kind, giving me a seat at the front away from my tormentors and letting me operate the bus door as we talked about life. I was miserable, but I was too ashamed to tell my parents or anyone else who might have helped me, like my doctor or the rabbi. My great-uncle Sim was a child psychiatrist, but he'd once told my mother to treat my poison ivy rash with gentian violet, turning my body a ridiculous crimson. There was no way I was telling him anything.

Things were only made worse by my emerging sexual feelings. Though I liked girls—I'd once gleefully kissed Amy, from across the street, and I desperately wanted to impress the pretty girls in eighth grade—I also felt drawn to boys. Sometimes, when Leonard let me sit on his lap to teach me how to drive, I felt a strange excitement, my body vibrating at our proximity as he steered and I pushed the pedals. Other times, I found myself mentally assessing other boys: attractive, unattractive. When I started tenth grade at Newton High School and became an assistant trainer for the football team, I enjoyed being in the locker room, with all those strong, beautiful bodies around me.

I didn't know what to do with these feelings. Sexuality wasn't anything you talked about in the 1940s, certainly not in my family. At thirteen, when my mother caught me masturbating to a book I'd found on Dad's bookshelf (*Let's Make Mary: A Gentleman's Guide to Seduction in 8 Easy Lessons*), she reacted with such horror I didn't know how to behave afterward. When I was sixteen or seventeen, I came home from school and, seeing Mother at the top of the stairs, ran up to hug her. I must have held on for a moment too long, because I began to feel aroused. She pushed me away, blushing and embarrassed, and said, "There are fresh brownies and milk in the kitchen."

As for liking boys? It was a taboo that nobody acknowledged.

Leonard harbored similar inclinations: when he brought friends home from the Navy, they often took more interest in me than a kid brother would merit. But Leonard also dated his share of women, including a girl who wore lipstick, a very racy move for the time, and when the war ended, he married a Wellesley girl from Little Rock, Arkansas, named Sylvia Ehrman. We all went to Little Rock for the wedding. Years later, I would learn that my mother's family tree had sprouted more than one gay offshoot: there were at least three Levin cousins who identified as homosexual, including one flamboyant antiques dealer in Florida. Neither Leonard nor I could acknowledge our true needs or feelings. Caught in a stifling cultural closet, I felt alone in my sexual confusion.

In eleventh grade, my parents enrolled me in Williston Academy, an all-boys prep school in Easthampton, Massachusetts, where Billy and Len had also gone. I finally experienced a reprieve socially. I lost weight, thanks to the unappetizing dining hall food and distance from my mother. I became a trainer for the tennis team and tutored some of the star football players. I even landed a girlfriend from a nearby girls' school.

My interest in boys also grew. This got me in trouble. One time, I was wrestling naked in my room with another kid, and some upperclassmen spied on us through a hole in the wall of my closet. They spread word of their voyeuristic discovery, and for weeks afterward, no one would be seen with me. One guy, a star football player named Bob Dolittle, protected me from the taunting, but I was still ostracized. I'd walk into a room, and everyone would stop speaking. No one would let me in his room.

This went on for months and was profoundly alienating. I had no one to turn to. I couldn't tell my parents. Though it might have made some sense to seek comfort or belonging in my religion, the idea did not occur to me. My family were members of Temple Ohabei Shalom in Brookline. I'd gone to Hebrew school and sung in the temple's Sunday school choir. My first summer job had been plucking chickens for a kosher butcher in Newton. But we were Jews primarily in a cultural and tribal sense.

I felt no connection to my ancestral origins, and Judaism, it seemed to me, was about power: the power of God to unleash plagues, the power of tribes to conquer Canaan, the power to survive amid oppression, the power to make and wield—as Dad and Mother did—socially advantageous connections. It was Dad, in fact, who as president of the temple board hired the rabbi whose job it was to bar mitzvah me. At my bar mitzvah I'd read the Torah but understood none of the Hebrew. All I remembered were the dictionaries, neckties, and fountain pens I received. Many Jews, of course, know and love God. But back then all I saw was empty ritual. I wanted something more, that I could not find.

Lonely at Williston, I compensated by becoming an overachiever. In junior high I'd found solace from bullies by studying, feeling a sense of victory when I made honor roll, so at Williston I cultivated an image of an intellectual: I read Sartre and Camus, became the copy editor for the school paper, played the undertaker in Thornton Wilder's *Our Town*. I wrote an original play about the psychological relationships between students who stayed at school for winter vacation and foreign students who couldn't go home. It was produced in front of the whole school.

Losing weight, I began to enjoy tennis, soccer, and skiing. I also discovered that I took after my father in one positive respect after all: stage presence. On parents' day, when students in my public speaking class were asked to demonstrate their skills, I stood up to deliver Dad's fundraising speech for Jewish orphans verbatim. My parents, whom I'd not told I was doing this, walked in right as I was delivering the punch line—"I would beg, borrow, and, yes, even steal!" I'll never forget the mix of shock and pride on Dad's face.

The truth is, I wasn't an intellectual, at least not in the sense of seeking knowledge for its own sake. My academic pursuits shielded me from others' contempt, from my confusing feelings, from my self-loathing. Posing as an intellectual offered safety. Suffering as an outsider, I withdrew into my mind. My intellectual explorations made me think about who I was. I became an observer of my thoughts, learning to watch how my mind changed. I became curious about the motivations that propelled me and others. Little did I realize that this observer stance would become important.

RICHARD ALPERT
"Dick"

56 Prentice Road   Newton Center 59, Mass.

Entered 1946; Willistonian 3, 4, Copy Editor 4; Log 3, 4; Glee Club 3, 4; Double Quartet 4; Dramatic Club 3, 4; Tennis Manager 4 (W).

Equipped with determination to do right and to establish an honorable record, Dick accomplished a great deal in his two years at Williston. Effective study made him a continual member of the honor list, and his interest in school affairs gave him the incentive to gain distincton in the Glee Club and on the *Willistonian*. Showing a quick mind, Dick could discuss intelligently any type of subject. A good conversationalist, he was pleasant company for any group.

If there was any place where I could breathe free—a place where I felt like myself—it was Willenrica. This was the name for my family's farm in Franklin, New Hampshire, a composite of the Alpert boys' names: William, Leonard, Richard. After my father discovered the property on one of his antiquing excursions, he and Mother bought it as a summer getaway. It was on Webster Lake, with hundreds of acres of woods, and every June, we'd pile into the Packard and flee the strictures of life in Newton.

Summer at the farm was a glorious Eden. To me it meant warmth and connection: the smell of grass, swimming in the lake, rosy dawns. We'd shake off lingering memories of the dreary winter and cold spring—the snow, mittens, rain, galoshes—and reacquaint ourselves with nature and each other. I drove the Farmall tractor mower as soon as I could reach the pedals.

We had a big garden where we grew corn and vegetables and lots of raspberries, which Dad turned into raspberry jam to give away for the holidays. He and I also went fishing, Dad rowing the dory until I was old enough to do it myself. We'd set the anchor where he knew the bass and perch liked to be, then drop a line. Waiting for fish to bite is a kind of meditation, a contemplative state, and we'd sit together, Dad smoking his cigar.

It was also at Willenrica that I bonded most with my brothers, who returned for the summer after being away at prep school or college, later in the air force and navy. Lobbing balls on the tennis court, water-skiing, painting the swimming float before we put it in the water—it was a boys' paradise, with a three-hole golf course and a barn outfitted with pool and Ping-Pong tables and a shuffleboard court.

I especially connected with Leonard, dreaming up enterprises. We started a printing business in the barn with an old-fashioned foot pedal letterpress. We'd set the metal fonts letter by letter, printing stationery, wedding announcements, invitations, posters, and business cards to order. Dad printed gift labels for his jam. Leonard and I also had a fishing worm business, raising them in wooden boxes filled with soil and coffee grounds from the kitchen. We sold worms for ten cents a handful.

Dad happened to mention to his friend Bill Cunningham, a sports columnist at the *Boston Herald*, that he had a son who was interested in playing the pipe organ. Cunningham knew a guy who owned an organ and had tired of it, so he helped arrange for the instrument to be moved to the barn at Willenrica. We all pitched in to help Len put it together, installing the big pipes up in the hay loft. Afterward, we used the barn to host musical evenings that doubled as fundraisers. We invited people from town for soirees of classical music and donated the proceeds to the local hospital. Combining two family passions, music and fundraising, delighted Dad. Mother played piano, Leonard played the organ, Dad played the violin, and I'd play the cello and act as master of ceremonies. I loved the role of emcee, connecting with my family through music, and the happy buzz of people.

Our Willenrica neighbors, the Kerrigans, were also from Newton, where Jim Kerrigan owned a gas station. They were Boston Irish and we were Jewish, but that didn't stop our families from socializing. They had four girls, and our family had three boys. Each young Alpert got involved at some point with his Kerrigan female counterpart (not counting Maureen, the youngest, who was left over). Janet, my age, was my girlfriend. We'd swim out to the wooden lake raft, ducking underneath it to kiss, and ride her horse together.

When we got a new sailboat, I named it after us—*Keraljanard* (for Kerrigan-Alpert-Janet-Richard)—and invited her to join me on its maiden voyage to the middle of Webster Lake. Neither of us knew how to sail. When a puff of wind came, instead of letting out the sail, I pulled it in. Over we went!

When Janet invited me to her high school senior prom, I was elated. Despite my sexual confusion, I cherished our times together, and I thought she was a hot date. After prom, however, I never heard from her. It turned out she'd decided to enter a convent and become a nun—a total shock, seeing as she'd never mentioned anything about it. Later she became a teaching nun at Marymount College, and I would understand that her faith had propelled her. But at the time, it didn't help my self-esteem that my girlfriend chose life in a convent over me.

Still, Willenrica remained a place where I felt safe and free, an oasis from the outside world. At Willenrica, my mother's blood disorder didn't seem as severe, nor my father's preoccupation with work and wandering eye as distracting. My brothers and I did things together; our edges as a family softened. Surrounded by nature, I felt timeless.

It was fleeting—autumn always pushed us back to Newton—but those childhood summers were my first glimpse of inner freedom.

CHAPTER 3

MIND FIELDS

y father wanted me to become a doctor, or at least a lawyer or a businessman. Something that made money. When it came time for college, I applied to Harvard, but despite my father's connections, I didn't get in. Brandeis, where my father's connections *were* ironclad—he was still chairman of the board—had a medical school, of course. But Dad didn't think it fair for me to enroll. Professors would find it too intimidating to grade the chairman's son.

I attended Tufts University, in Medford, Massachusetts, which was known for premed and engineering and also had a medical school. Medford is just ten miles or so from Newton, and for the first two years, I lived at home, commuting to campus in an old Ford truck I brought from Willenrica. Billy and Len were out of the house by then. It was mostly me and Mother. The outsider feelings I'd harbored in prep school didn't change much; as a commuter student, it was easy to feel left out of campus life. I enrolled in premed classes but did poorly, flunking biology and organic chemistry.

On the other hand, my feelings of otherness stirred an interest in something else: psychology. The observer stance I'd developed in prep school—what I'd later call the "witness perspective"—made me naturally curious about the study of the mind and behavior. I was used to looking at myself, noticing my thoughts and motivations and trying to assess those of others. Psychology, it seemed to me, offered a systematic way of understanding my inner life.

This was the late 1940s and early '50s, and psychology was still a relatively new discipline. Though World War II had elevated its status somewhat, as psychology played a part in the war effort, the field was not yet widely appreciated. Psychology itself was dominated either by the ideas of Sigmund Freud, about the compulsions of the unconscious, or by the behaviorist determinism of B. F. Skinner, who studied learning patterns in rats at Harvard with his famous Skinner box, or operant conditioning chamber. Behaviorists focused on observing, measuring, testing, and modifying behavior. The introspective psychology espoused by William James, in which one observed one's internal phenomena, had been largely pushed aside, and Carl Jung's more intuitive and anthropological views had yet to gain traction. Neuroscience and psychopharmacology, which focus on the chemical and functional pathways of the brain, were barely emerging, and there was no real model that explained consciousness.

The psychology department at Tufts was tiny, housed in a small building on campus, and it was not much respected. Its professors focused mostly on experimental psychology, in areas like learning and brain function. But there was also a new field called social psychology, or the study of human relations. Within the hierarchy of the department, which ranked "rat psychologists" at the top, social psychology was considered on the margin of science for its lack of measurability. I was intrigued, and not just for intellectual reasons. Given my own precarious social status, I intuited that understanding how people worked would give me power.

Edward M. Bennett was the lone social psychology professor at Tufts; I think the university hired him as a symbolic nod to the new discipline. Nobody else at Tufts knew much about social psychology, and it fell to Bennett to get the university up to speed on contemporary issues. Since social psychology was not considered scientific, he was on the bottom rung of the faculty ladder, viewed as a real oddball.

But I liked him. He was the first person I met who really thought outside the conceptual box. He was a nonconformist, and I found him inspiring. Bennett believed in me and became my mentor, encouraging me to explore my own mind. I learned about looking at myself objectively. When I delved into my ego self, feelings and thoughts bubbled up, and it was exciting to finally have a framework for them. Unlike in my premed courses, I made good grades. I began to apply personality constructs to people around me, seeing psychodynamics and motivations on a new and intuitive level.

This began to give me a sense of control over my life and relationships, which came in handy my junior year, when I joined the Jewish fraternity Alpha Epsilon Pi and moved on campus. Going from being a mama's boy at home to living with my peers was not an easy transition, and I felt nervous and insecure. The fraternity's president was my roommate. I traded my old truck for a powder-blue Plymouth with a fold-down windshield. Then I applied my charm and psychology insights. In what proved to be an inspired move, I let my new frat brothers borrow an oil immersion microscope I had from one of my biology courses. The guys looked at their moving sperm up close, which was a big hit. In short order, I became an officer in the fraternity.

Even as I found my way, however, I remained self-conscious about my sexuality. One of my frat brothers almost exposed my past. He'd been at Williston, and he threatened to share my reputation for liking boys. I was helped by my brother Leonard, who ran a record store in Harvard Square and knew the guy's father through his business. He talked to the father, who discouraged the guy from outing me. Meanwhile, I did everything to maintain an acceptable facade. I dated girls, went to all the dances, kidded around with the guys.

But I also began cruising the parks at night, picking up men. This was extremely risky, and not just because of social ostracism. Alfred Kinsey had just published his *Sexual Behavior in the Human Male*, and the report, which claimed that some 10 percent of American men were homosexual, caused outrage and panic. Homosexuals were thought of as perverts and a threat to society. If I got caught, I could easily get beaten up, thrown in jail, or, worse, killed. I felt some fear, of course, and guilt. But there was also a thrill to it: the tension of the secrecy, the danger of being found out.

I drove down to Texas with some of my frat brothers for a national Alpha Epsilon Pi meeting. We drove straight through in the Plymouth, pedal to the metal. This was before the interstate highway system, and the towns through the rural South were dusty and poor. At the gas stations, a black man or a white guy in overalls would pump the gas for us. I loved that drive. I don't know how I stayed awake for it. We were running on coffee, cigarettes, whiskey, and adrenaline.

When we got to Dallas, we went to a brothel, or a cat house, as it was called in those days. It wasn't very clean, and it was my first sex with a woman. I was very unsure of myself. She was older, maybe twenty-four, with light hair and skinny legs. She teased me about my inexperience and awkwardness. I just wanted to get it done. Intercourse felt mechanical, but I managed even in my nervousness. When we all got back to the car and the other guys laughed and shared about their conquests, I realized I'd pulled off a rite of passage.

The guys didn't notice I had barely anything to say.

Almost every class I took at Tufts as a junior and senior was in psychology or human relations. I studied the earliest stage of social psychology, child development. As Bennett's protégé, I led the social psych undergrads, a big fish in a small pond.

Choosing social psychology over medicine, over behaviorism, was a big deal. I was putting my chips on people's inner lives, though I didn't yet have even a concept of the soul or the spiritual heart. My approach to the world was through the mind: thinking, verbalizing, seeing interpersonal relationships.

I caught a glimpse of people's deeper selves thanks to a couple of internships that Bennett arranged for me. The summer after my junior year, I worked as a psychological counselor at a camp for diabetic children. Besides counseling the kids, I conducted my first research, measuring the effect of insulin on personality. I felt for these kids, and I discovered that I really enjoyed connecting with them.

After that, I interned at Boston Psychopathic Hospital throughout my senior year and for about six months after graduation. My job was to supervise occupational and recreational therapy for the patients. I was also enlisted to help in a research project, which had me test patients for personality variables and levels of anxiety before and after treatment—how they carried on a conversation, their emotional affect, and so on. Sometimes that treatment was electroshock therapy, and

I was recruited to hold patients down for the procedure. Other times, the doctors prescribed a lobotomy. There were not very many good ways to treat mental illness in those days; morphine helped a little, but widespread use of antipsychotics like Thorazine was still a decade off. Doctors turned to lobotomies when nothing else worked.

I was allowed to observe the lobotomy procedure. So was my roommate, the president of our fraternity, who was also an intern. The patient was anesthetized, and then the doctor, using a hammer, inserted an ice-pick-like instrument through the eye socket. Moving the instrument side to side, like a saw, the doctor severed the frontal lobe—associated with behavior and personality—from the rest of the patient's brain. It was so primitive and medieval that my roommate passed out. Years later, he would become the chief administrator of a big psychiatric hospital, but that day, he nearly upset the whole operation.

After a lobotomy, a patient usually had no personality left. It was as if the personality had died. Because I hung out with patients, helping them with activities before and afterward, I saw this up close. It made me very emotional. I built real relationships and was fond of these people; to see them changed so completely after a lobotomy, basically into vegetables, was deeply distressing. A patient might start out as depressed but heartful, but after a lobotomy, that essence disappeared. He was like a vacant room, zeroed out.

I decided this was barbaric. I did not know much about the soul at that point, and it seemed to me that cutting out a patient's personality in this way left him with absolutely nothing. In befriending patients, I'd feel empathy and compassion for them in their mental anguish. There *had* to be better ways, I thought, to help people who were lost in mental or emotional mazes.

I grew so upset about the procedure that I decided to intervene. This wasn't social psychology theory to me anymore. I took my study results to the head psychiatrist to show how awful and drastic the aftereffects of a lobotomy were. He said he'd look at my notes but insisted that the patients were better off. If I was going to be a good researcher, he admonished, I would need to curb my emotional involvement.

When I tried to speak with the operating doctor, I got the same brush-off. One patient I'd worked with was a construction worker, a nice guy suffering from deep depression. I told the doctor what a good guy he was and pleaded with him not to operate. The doctor told me I didn't have a medical degree and I should mind my own business. This patient, and my data on him, were part of a research project; he was going ahead. After the lobotomy, the guy had a blank look. He didn't recognize me or for that matter, himself.

I did my best to focus on my time with patients, but it was hard. One encouraging light was the director of the hospital's occupational therapy program, a guy named Mac. He was a man full of energy and humor, and he was known around the hospital for how he connected with people. He could cut through a patient's mindset and show her where she was stuck, what she needed to let go of. He kidded people about their mental illness in a lighthearted, kind way. It made everyone relax and feel like they weren't hopeless.

Mac was also flamboyantly, exuberantly gay. He had a broad sense of humor that helped him connect with patients and that even extended to his sexuality. Though I was careful to hide my own sexual proclivities, his example helped alleviate some of my shame. I found Mac's out-front behavior and personal panache admirable. Not only was he not afraid, he used who he was to reach and help other people. I would remember this for a long time.

My father was not pleased by my interest in psychology. He disapproved and tried to think of it as a passing phase. Near the end of my senior year, still hell-bent on my becoming a doctor, he called the president of Tufts, Leonard Carmichael, thinking he could talk some sense into me.

Carmichael summoned me to his office and, without beating around the bush, told me I should go to medical school. In fact, he continued, he was going to make it happen. Looking at me over the stacks of paper on his expansive desk, he picked up the phone and dialed. After a couple of rings, the head of the Tufts University School of Medicine picked up.

"I've got George Alpert's son here," said Carmichael. "Do you have a place for him in the medical school? His organic chemistry grades aren't great. Biology is not too terrific either." He paused, listening and nodding.

Then he hung up.

"Well, that's that," he announced. "You're in."

I took a breath. "Sir, I wouldn't go to med school if you paid me. I'm going to be a psychologist."

Carmichael cocked his head and looked at me carefully. Then, standing up to dismiss me, he said, "You're making a big mistake, Alpert. You'd be a terrible psychologist."

Carmichael was himself a psychologist, so he probably thought he knew what he was talking about. The man had good instincts for bureaucratic politics—he went on to become the head of the Smithsonian Institution—and no doubt he thought me foolish for turning down his gesture.

But he was a behavioral psychologist. He didn't know anything about social psychology. And I resented being "George Alpert's son," as if my interests had no bearing. As if the praiseworthy grades and course work I'd finally achieved amounted to nothing. In the social psychology department, I *was* somebody, and now I was determined to make my own way. I stood up and walked out.

That night, my father and I had a huge blowup. Social psychology was not, he insisted heatedly, a legitimate career. I would not make money, he warned. I would not be successful. I was throwing my future away.

My rebellion felt good. Standing up for myself, against the pressure from my parents and the university president, gave me a sense of confidence and purpose. Dad sent me to Tufts to go to med school, but I was carving out a different path. Psychology was *my* thing.

I was still an achiever: even as I rebelled against my father, I wanted to prove myself by his measures. I needed a plan. Luckily, before I decided what came next, Bennett approached me with an opportunity. A professor of psychology at Wesleyan University in Connecticut was running a program in achievement motivation research, the study of people's need and drive for success. He called Tufts to ask if there might be a talented social psychology student graduating who would become his assistant. The professor's name was David McClelland.

It was the perfect chance to pursue a master's in psychology. That fall, I moved to Middletown, Connecticut. It was the farthest I'd been from home, and I felt like I was reaching escape velocity from my family's orbit. I roomed with a German guy, Hans, also a psychology grad student. World War II was still fresh in everyone's memory, and here I was with a German roommate. I didn't tell my Jewish parents.

The first year at Wesleyan was intense. I studied hard and didn't have much of a social life, but I got so anxious around test taking that I did badly on all my exams. This mediocrity made me deeply insecure. I felt like a phony academic, and I was sure everyone would find out.

McClelland helped give me confidence. As his assistant I participated in his experiments in achievement motivation, and I also ran some of them. He was writing a book about his work, to be called *Studies in Motivation*, which I helped research; it later became widely recognized for championing the psychology of motivation as its own discipline. (Before then psychologists saw motivation as an instinct, like hunger, not an aspect of human behavior worthy of separate study.) McClelland would eventually become well known for his broad body of work on personality and how applying a deeper understanding of it improves both lives and societies. Later in life he'd have a second career as a corporate consultant, applying his theories of human motivation to business.

For all his sharp intellectualism, McClelland—whom I came to know as Dave—was also a patient, tolerant mentor. He cared for me as a person, almost like a father. Away from my family, my adult persona and intellect were just starting to form, and he encouraged me to think and argue for myself. We'd hang out in his living room, discussing his theories on motivation. From my present vantage point, I see human motives as desires and attachments, the seeds of karma that perpetuate the illusion of separation. But back then, we talked about motives as the forces that shape our identity. I was challenged to think about the self in new ways.

This gave me some helpful perspective on my family. Families are such a microcosm for social relations, and I could begin to identify the motivations and needs that drove each of us. My inner work and meditation practice since then have made me even more aware of my drive for power and my need for achievement; this awareness has made it possible to let them go.

My second year, Dave invited me to live with his family. He and his wife, Mary, had a big house in the woods near the university. Foss House, it was called. They had twin boys, Nick and Duncan, and a daughter, Sara. (Another son, Jabez, came later.) The McClellands were generous, relaxed landlords. It was the only family scene I'd been a part of besides my own, and their values were vastly different from those in the Alpert home: less materialistic, more thoughtful.

While Dave introduced me to the rigors of the mind, it was Mary who offered me an inkling of the soul. She was an artist, a painter of animals and mystical, unearthly images—whirling dervishes and the like. She was not a power person. She came from her soul and intuition, a loving presence. She was a different kind of mother, not wrapped up in her children's identity or success. Though physically delicate, she emanated inner strength. She was a contemplative Quaker and deeply reflective. Mary was the first truly spiritual person I ever met. Dave also had a spiritual side; he was a Quaker too, and it seeped around the edges of his intellect. But it was Mary who opened me to the idea of an inner life.

Their spirituality was nothing like the Jewish rites and rituals I grew up with. When the McClellands invited me to a Quaker meeting, I accepted. I'd never been to a Christian service before. Sitting in the silence was my first taste of anything resembling meditation. It opened a door. The Quaker community held a summer retreat at Yelping Hill, a collection of homes near West Cornwall, Connecticut. It was peaceful and simple and intentional. Because of psychology, I'd started to ask fundamental questions about reality. Thanks to the McClellands, I realized that I was also seeking something more profound about my own being.

Besides my work with Dave, I took classes with Michael Wertheimer, an experimental psychologist who taught me statistics and behaviorism. I also studied with an anthropology professor named David P. McAllester, a deep and soft guy with a love of music; he established Wesleyan's ethnomusicology department. McAllester was interested in Native American practices like drumming and rituals, and he had spent time with the Hopi and Navajo tribes in the Southwest. His courses broadened my appreciation for the spiritual ethos of other cultures.

I enjoyed what I was learning, but my test anxiety did not improve. It was so paralyzing, in fact, that when it came time for my final oral exam—the one that would grant me my master's degree—I flunked it. However, Dave McClelland had faith that I understood the material because of all our hours together, and he arranged for me to get my degree anyway. He'd already recommended me as a PhD candidate to a former professor of his, Robert R. Sears, who was the head of the psychology department at Stanford University. I'd gotten my acceptance before I even flunked that final exam.

I drove west to California in the powder-blue Plymouth, from gas station to gas station, on US Route 66. The open skies, the mountains, the towns, the vast landscapes—and the increasing distance from my family—gave me an extraordinary sense of freedom. This was tempered when I arrived at Stanford. With its wide avenues and sprawling buildings, the campus was huge compared to the Little Ivy League of Tufts and Wesleyan. In the psychology hall, I recognized the names on the office doors: these were people whose papers I'd read, giants in the field. I felt like a country boy in the city. This was the big league.

Stanford was a high-level research scene, and in psychology especially, research was the pinnacle of the profession. Bob Sears specialized in the psychology of children, and as his PhD student, I helped both him and his wife, Professor Pauline Sears—or Pat—in their work. Bob was conducting a three-year project to test Freud's theories about child development. There were two parts, one with parents and one with kids. I served as the faculty interface with the nursery school that was collaborating on the children's portion.

The research was to investigate whether certain parent-child patterns engendered guilt, as Freud had hypothesized, and I was tasked with designing the study to test this. We built a box and placed a hamster in it. Then we'd bring a kid into the room and tell her that she was responsible for watching over the hamster and keeping it safe in the box. After some minutes, we'd use a remote control from outside the room to trigger a false bottom in the box, and the hamster would disappear. We'd then observe the kids' reactions through a one-way mirror, noting their distress levels—some of them got very upset—and whether they lied about the hamster's whereabouts afterward.

Those poor kids! We tricked them. I'm so embarrassed when I think about doing this. The experiment appears in *Identification and Child Rearing*, a major psychology text that Sears published about ten years later; he was the primary author, but both I and another faculty member, Lucy Rau, included our research and served as coauthors. I consider the experiment a cruel lapse: abuse in the name of science. Deceiving these children was a breach of ethics. I recently read about a study that tests kids for empathy and compassion; now *that's* a good experiment. It turns out kids have innate compassion to a remarkable degree.

Part of my original attraction to psychology had been to better understand my family, in particular my relationship with Mother. Freudian psychology, of course, focuses a lot on child development and mother-infant relations. Sears knew a Freudian psychoanalyst in Palo Alto and connected us. I decided to undergo Freudian analysis myself.

Freudian psychoanalysis was going mainstream: *Time* magazine put Freud on its cover in the spring of 1956. But I wasn't doing it just for personal insight. Clinical psychology was becoming a vocation, a valid part of social psychology. After my experience at Boston Psychopathic, I believed therapy might spare people from such horrors as lobotomies. I was interested in learning about approaches that restored patients without medical intervention. I marched into Stanford's counseling center and announced that I wanted to study clinical psychology and work as a therapist. I was accepted with the condition that, as part of my training, I undergo psychoanalysis myself, which I already planned to do.

Freudian psychoanalysis was a further education in witnessing—in observing the workings of the mind, as I'd already been practicing—in a profoundly personal way. My ego was observing itself as a thinking mind and seeing my analyst's ego caught up in his role as psychiatrist. Though I couldn't articulate it then, what was missing was the soul.

Years later, having someone see my soul and love me fully would change my life. But then, lying on that analyst's couch, what I was

Richard Alpert Ph.D.
Psychologist

Box 309
Menlo Park, California, U.S.A.

most aware of were undercurrents of manipulation and power. If I made a comment that prompted the therapist to make a note—well, aha! I learned what comments would prompt more scribbling. It was an endless game. I'd challenge the therapist on applying Freudian principles and try to provoke him with statements about, say, his wife. He would just scribble some more. "You hired me so I wouldn't make comments," he told me. "I have nothing to say, and now you're mad at me." I really disliked the guy.

Working as a therapist myself proved much more rewarding. My training at the counseling center was supervised by a woman who let me practice while I was still learning. I'd envisioned therapy as a sideline, but I really got into it. Students came in for help, and it was satisfying to feel like I held a few keys that could unlock answers for people who were suffering. I remained mixed up about power and love—I still yearned for recognition and achievement, still thought of love as something I had to earn and wield—but I recognized something deep in those connections.

My first patient was Victor Lovell, a graduate student in psychology. He also wrote pornographic novels. I was a very spit-and-polish guy then, with papers and plants on my desk. Vic would come in, put his boots up on the desk, and nudge the plants as close to the edge as possible just to provoke me.

Vic introduced me to pot. He also introduced me to his friends, a group of academics, writers, and freewheeling artists who lived just off campus on Perry Avenue. The street was a block long, with several cottages packed in, and everyone called it Perry Lane. Marijuana and all manner of new ideas wafted freely. I got invited to parties and, over time, became a therapist for others on the street: the unofficial shrink of Perry Lane. I met Ken Kesey, a graduate student in creative writing who would, some years later on Vic's suggestion, participate in a series of government-sponsored psychopharmacology experiments and write *One Flew Over the Cuckoo's Nest*.

Psychoanalysis took me inside. On the outside, my academic career was faltering. I wasn't big on research, and research at Stanford was paramount. I was weak in statistics and experimental design, and though I liked working with kids, I felt tests and number crunching offered only a snapshot of reality. The data we worked with was supposed to be statistically significant, but in actuality, we wrote off a big part of it as "error." Anything I'd now consider spiritual fell into this error category. For all the supposedly objective science we were doing, I couldn't shake the feeling that our research was engineered. We were all in a race to find the best data to fit our theories.

What I loved was teaching. As a grad student, I was assigned to grade papers and hold office hours for one of the sections in Psychology 101. It was a seminar of about thirty undergrads, but I developed such good rapport with the students that after several semesters I was put in charge of the other graduate teaching assistants in psychology.

As at Wesleyan, I was terrified people would find out how little I actually knew, but I discovered that connecting with audiences brought out my charismatic, confident self—the self that had once loved being the emcee for music nights at Willenrica and delivering Dad's speech at Williston. I was funny and warm, with a knack for explaining things in accessible ways. I still didn't know much, but I was popular.

CHAPTER 4

WORKING ON
THE RAILROAD

n January 1956, Dad was elected president and chairman of the New York, New Haven and Hartford Railroad. In addition to carrying freight, the railroad served millions of commuters across Connecticut, Massachusetts, Rhode Island, and New York. Dad had been recruited to the board a couple of years earlier, after catching the eye of Patrick B. McGinnis, a flashy Irishman who was then the railroad president. Dad had represented an association of fruit and vegetable shippers in a lawsuit against the railroad and won. McGinnis was impressed.

By that time Dad had also patched things up with Einstein and was fundraising for the new Albert Einstein College of Medicine in New York, becoming an honorary chairman. The railroad's board, a mix of Boston Brahmins from Beacon Hill and Jewish financiers from Connecticut and New York, was looking for someone influential to join them. Dad fit the bill.

Mother was opposed. She didn't trust McGinnis because he was Irish—Jews had their prejudices too. Her fears were confirmed when rumors of financial irregularities and kickbacks began to swirl around McGinnis. Meanwhile, Dad, after doing some real estate research, found an old contract and discovered that the railroad owned part of the land along Park Avenue above the tracks running into Grand Central Station. The land was being used by the New York Central Railroad, cutting the New Haven out of its rightful revenue. The discovery of twenty years of lost income for New Haven led to a big settlement that doubled the railroad's revenue in New York. By the end of 1955 McGinnis resigned abruptly, and the board turned to Dad.

Soon after he was named the new president, Dad called me at Stanford. He was crying. He was leaving his law firm to take the position, and he had no idea what he was doing. "I don't know how to run a railroad," he confessed. "I need somebody here I can trust and confide in." He wanted me to return east and become his assistant. Leonard was busy overseeing the law firm, and Billy was a full-time assistant district attorney in New York.

I had never seen or heard Dad cry before, let alone open up like this. "Why is he calling *me*, for Chrissakes?" I wondered. I didn't know anything about railroads either. But his asking for help—*my* help—was a turning point in our relationship. Our roles reversed, as they would again years later when I helped him die. I felt the weight of love and family obligation. Dad had always looked out for my interests, even if my dreams didn't coincide with his. I had never worked for him as my brothers had. Maybe it was time.

But I didn't want to abandon my studies. So Dad and I came up with an arrangement: I would fly in to help him for part of the week. I started spending four days a week at Stanford and three in New York. I learned a lot in a hurry. One of my projects was to evaluate whether to buy third-rail, overhead electric, or diesel engines. The twilight for railroads in America was approaching—the federal government was building interstate highways, and the country had a new romance with cars—and Dad's mandate was to stay afloat. The New Haven was caught between state regulators, who wouldn't allow a commuter fare increase, and rapidly rising costs. Dad gave news conferences to publicize this; he also testified before Congress to get federal subsidies for commuter rail service.

Working with Dad wasn't always smooth going. Once, for example, when a board member called the office for a financial statement and I agreed to send it along, Dad angrily accused me of usurping his power. But there were fun moments too. I was interviewing some bigwig in Dad's private rail car one evening when I realized I needed to call Mother to tell her I'd be late for supper. The phone on the desk in the railcar had no dial tone, so I asked the office for help. Before I knew it, a switching engine had pulled up, been coupled to the car, and taken us onto another track, where the phone line could be connected for my very important call. Now, *that* was power.

I couldn't tell my professors at Stanford what I was doing because they would have questioned my commitment to the PhD program, so I kept my railroad work a secret. Instead I lived a double life, like a spy. This was before commercial jet travel, and commuting cross-country meant a thirteen-hour propeller-plane flight. Arriving at LaGuardia Airport, I'd be met by a limousine and a secretary; back in San Francisco, I'd traipse through the airport parking lot, searching for my dusty old car. In New York, I was an executive in Grand Central helping the president of the railroad make momentous decisions; at Stanford, I was the graduate student who kept the department lounge stocked with coffee and paper cups.

It wasn't the only double life I was leading. After playing the science-minded academic during the day, at night I'd drive up to North Beach, a dense and diverse neighborhood in San Francisco with a thriving bohemian literary scene. There were bars and cafes and art galleries, and I'd go to City Lights Bookstore to listen to readings by Beat poets and writers like Lawrence Ferlinghetti, Jack Kerouac, Allen Ginsberg, and Gary Snyder.

Ginsberg was unabashedly gay, and Snyder was already becoming a serious scholar of Zen Buddhism. I was especially struck by Ginsberg's openness about both spirituality and homosexuality; his poetry was earthy and spiritual. This world of alternative thinkers was completely out of the box, and it challenged my buttoned-up East Coast perspective. Alan Watts, the Episcopal priest turned Zen philosopher, also hung out in North Beach. He hosted a Sunday morning radio program on Buddhism and spirituality. As he did for so many, Watts introduced me to Eastern philosophy. It was a whole new way of seeing things.

Maybe because San Francisco was more tolerant, I became more sexually active. This too was a double existence: I pursued both male and female lovers, sometimes at the same time. I dated one girl in California named Affie, and together we'd ride on my motorcycle—I bought myself a Triumph, then a Harley—into the hills, to see Affie's family in Santa Cruz. Back on campus, I'd sometimes meet up with a man.

Though I was mostly noncommittal in my relationships, having lovers without a long-term plan, there was one particular fling that would catch up with me. Karen Saum was an attractive undergrad, a history major. We met at a bar, where we chatted about her idols, the political agitators Emma Goldman and Rosa Luxemburg. It turned out we had a friend in common: Karen had lived in the same dorm as Barbara Greer, a psychology undergrad who often helped me organize spaghetti dinners for graduate students at my off-campus cottage on a dirt road called Homer Lane.

Karen rode home with me on my Triumph. We became friends and lovers after that—no strings attached. She was graduating that spring and planned to move to New York. That May, we had not seen each other in several weeks when, the night before graduation, Karen stopped by my cottage to say good-bye. We had one last passionate farewell and didn't see each other again. I didn't know it, but that night would reverberate. More on that later.

True to form, with my test-taking anxiety, I flunked three courses in my first two years at Stanford. The summer after my second year, I received a letter from Bob Sears. My poor performance was a disappointment, he wrote, and if things didn't improve, the university would rescind my scholarship.

I decided I couldn't fail again. The next term I studied for hours, pulling all-nighters, and somehow managed to get As all year. For my doctoral dissertation, I joined forces with a fellow grad student, Ralph Haber, to study the very thing that plagued me: test anxiety. Ralph was quite brilliant and did well on exams, whereas my good grades came from writing term papers. We used each other as subjects to try to figure out what made us different; we also administered tests to undergrads. We did identify an emotional element to achievement: for some people, anxiety led to better performance; for others, it was debilitating.

Despite Sears's disappointed letter, that year I was invited to join the faculty as an assistant professor. This was a huge honor, because it was not Stanford policy to hire graduate students as professors—I was the first. I was offered the position because I'd proven myself to be a good teacher and because there was no one to teach Psych 101.

This meant I also had to decide about the railroad. I could go into business or I could go into academics, but clearly not both. I was interested in the mind more than in trains, and I wanted to teach more than discuss locomotive parts. Dad took it in stride, because Billy agreed to help with the railroad instead.

At my first faculty meeting, the professors who had flunked me in their courses were dumbfounded to see me. I taught about five hundred students in Psych 101, which was a big introductory course. I was entertaining—funny and sparkly—even when I didn't know what I was talking about.

One day, I was visited in my office by Leon Festinger. He was a famous Stanford psychologist who published papers on social comparison and cognitive dissonance. He wanted all the undergrads in my Psych 101 class to be subjects in one of his studies. He asked me to tell my students that the test he was giving them, some kind of personality test that was part of his research, would be used to determine their grade. I said I wouldn't do it; I couldn't lie to my students.

That didn't go over well. The whole department came down on me. My principles were inconvenient. I was called away on some pretext, and Bob Sears came into the class and distributed the test himself. He sandbagged me. There was nothing I could do about it. I could have quit, but that would have been a career ender.

Instead, I got my doctorate. Never mind that I was not the best academic; I was now Richard Alpert, PhD. As my degree ceremony approached, my old mentor from Wesleyan, Dave McClelland, reached out. He had taken a position at Harvard and wanted to know if I'd be interested in joining him. We'd coincided at a conference in Salt Lake City a few months earlier, and afterward he'd sent a letter to Sears. "Dick certainly has charisma," he wrote. "But does he know any psychology?" He was curious whether I could teach. Sears knew I was an excellent teacher—he'd already offered me a teaching contract at Stanford for the following year.

I accepted the Stanford offer. I'd succeeded on the path I'd chosen for myself, and now I was wanted. When the next academic year rolled around, I used my free time to do something that reflected my new-found status: I got a pilot's license. I don't know why I thought I needed to fly. I already had a motorcycle and a sports car.

Once, I rented an ultralight with an open frame and the propeller right behind the seat. To take off, you walked the plane up a sand dune—we were near Santa Cruz—then ran down until you gathered enough speed to get airborne. I'd fly out over the ocean, then circle back with the local farm fields spread beneath. The ultralight was terrifying to land, but there was something in me that loved the risk.

I enjoyed lecturing and teaching that year, but as my contract came up for renewal, I heard from Dave again. He was the director of Harvard's doctoral program in clinical psychology, and he'd just expanded the university's Psychological Clinic into a new research institute called the Center for Research in Personality. He offered me a job as an assistant professor, with a track to tenure.

For a Boston boy, the pull was irresistible. This was Harvard. My family would approve. And I liked the idea of being reunited with my mentor. Dave's lens of motivational psychology offered an understanding of human behavior different from that of my Freudian colleagues.

Professor Alpert had a nice ring.

CHAPTER 5

HARVARD YARD

The Center for Research in Personality fell under the auspices of Harvard's Department of Social Relations. When Dave McClelland engineered my transition to Harvard, his department didn't have enough money in that year's budget. So Dave arranged a joint appointment for me: as an assistant professor in the Department of Social Relations and the Graduate School of Education.

I hit the ground running. The Center for Research in Personality, on 5 Divinity Avenue, was Dave's kingdom. I had a corner office. I helped with research, advised undergrads, and taught psychology courses. I was also the center's administrator, applying for grants and assigning office spaces. We were separate from the psychology department, which at the time was primarily concerned with B. F. Skinner's behavioral research—or, as we called it, rat psychology. Meanwhile, in the education department, I was an assistant to John Whiting, a social anthropologist who was the head of child psychology. Like Sears, who had been his professor, Whiting did cutting-edge research in child development, which was also my focus at Stanford.

Before arriving, I told Harvard that I'd been a psychotherapist at Stanford; as part of my job offer, I was promised a place to continue practicing. I was given an appointment inside Harvard University Health Services, which oversaw Harvard's therapy program. My Stanford therapist, the Freudian psychoanalyst, cautioned me when I left, "You'd better find an analyst to work with when you get to

Harvard; otherwise you're not going to be able to function in the world." Somehow I managed to survive without an analyst.

At Harvard, only psychiatrists with MDs were allowed to be therapists. My colleagues in Health Services looked down on a mere psychologist. They found me a role in a project with students confused about their sexual identity. They had no idea about my sexuality. Harvard was all male then, and these patients shared the same doubts and confusion I did about being closeted. Back then, homosexuality was treated as a psychological disorder. This wasn't freewheeling San Francisco. In straitlaced Boston, it was easy to feel a sense of shame. As I took on the cases, I developed a good track record of connecting with, and helping, these patients. I knew their feelings of ambivalence and inadequacy all too well. Soon my colleagues decided I should be the therapist for all homosexual students and assigned every case to me.

My early days at Harvard involved a lot of academic conceptualizing. These days I would characterize it as the mind thinking about itself. Psychology was a kind of mind trap, a closed system or a self-referential loop. I continued with the child development research I'd begun under Sears and would get in long discussions with Professor Jerome Bruner, a leading Harvard thinker in cognitive psychology, about how we understand children's minds. We talked about how children learn, he from a cognitive perspective and I from a developmental one.

As a teenager, I used to hide on the stairs to listen when Dad led Brandeis board meetings in our living room. I would overhear how they went about hiring and firing professors. I understood then that academia was clearly about who you knew, not what you knew. The power is wielded by money and big names, professors who get grants and have written the most books or papers. I didn't have the books or brilliant research at Harvard, but I did know the power of connections. I was well-spoken and charismatic, and I was good at dropping a Freudian reference or two to impress my colleagues.

I played Harvard's power game. I straddled three departments and had a prodigious workload. I had the big corner office, three secretaries, and a number of research assistants. I was making good money, and I had my own apartment in Cambridge, which my mother filled with professorial-looking antiques. I had a Triumph motorcycle, my pilot's license, and a brand-new, sky-blue Mercedes-Benz imported from Germany. It had red leather seats and a sun roof. I stuck a huge Star of David next to the license plate—a nod to my triumph as a Jewish kid who'd grown up during World War II. At family dinners and reunions, I was now the accomplished professor with opinions that mattered. I enjoyed picking up the folks in my shiny Mercedes. Their youngest son had made it.

With my sense of accomplishment, I also took more risks. I ate more, drank more, collected more possessions and antiques, and sought more sexual escapades. I visited gay bars in Boston and brought lovers to my apartment. I had a girlfriend on one side of Boston and a boyfriend on the other. Despite still playing both sides of the fence, I made my peace with my interest in men. I no longer tried so hard to hide these liaisons; my confidence made me shrug off the dangers of being outed.

Harvard colleagues did not suspect much about this side of my life, until one day, a young man who was staying with me borrowed my Mercedes while I was at work. He and I met through one of my Levin cousins. He tried to pick up a man in Harvard Square who happened to be one of the university psychiatrists. The Mercedes was quite distinctive; everyone knew it was mine. In addition to the Star of David, the car sported a Health Services parking sticker. Word got back to the head of Health Services, Dana Farnsworth, who called me in. "Dick, one of your patients used your car," he said. "You should be more careful."

Perhaps Farnsworth was trying to protect me from the implications. Since I counseled gay students, the idea that one had taken my car for some hijinks was plausible. "Oh, that wasn't a patient," I replied recklessly. "That was a fellow I was sleeping with."

Farnsworth was floored. We never really got along after that moment. It was a mistake, getting in his face. Later he was put in charge of the LSD, psilocybin, and DMT we needed for research. He got back at me then.

Just before the next semester, Dave stopped by my office. "Dick," he said, "we have a new guy coming in. His ideas are interesting, and he seems like a very creative psychologist. Can you find him an office?"

The psychologist's name was Timothy Leary. Dave had met him that summer while on sabbatical in Italy. Leary had a PhD in psychology from the University of California, Berkeley, and he had worked as a clinical psychologist at the Kaiser Foundation Hospital in Oakland, designing tests that mapped interpersonal behavior in new and influential ways. He had made a name for himself in psychology circles with his book *Interpersonal Diagnosis of Personality*, which outlined new methodology for evaluating a patient's behavior and relationships.

Tim was at a low point when Dave met him. A few years earlier, on the eve of his thirty-fifth birthday, his wife had committed suicide. He was trying to sustain his two young kids in Europe. He was on sabbatical to write but suffering from writer's block. He'd run through his grant money and was broke.

A psychologist friend of Tim's from Berkeley, Frank Barron, had gone to visit Tim and arranged for him to meet Dave in Florence. Dave had read *Interpersonal Diagnosis of Personality* and was impressed with Tim's intellect and his unconventional ideas, which challenged behaviorist views. He offered Tim a position at Harvard as a lecturer.

I told Dave that there were no actual office spaces left in the department. But three doors down the hall from my corner office was a mop closet. "Could we put him in there?" he asked. I said, "Sure, I think so."

So Tim got the closet. The hall was the most heavily trafficked area in the department, so this was not a handicap. When Tim arrived, in September 1959, he didn't hesitate to invite anyone passing by into his tiny space for conversation. He was gregarious, a warm and energetic talker with a bright smile and good looks. There was always somebody in his door.

Harvard faculty and students alike quickly realized Tim was unusual. He was a West Point grad and eleven years older than me, but he had a rebellious, independent streak. He wore red socks and white sneakers with his button-down shirt and tweed jacket. Unlike the rest of us, he wasn't impressed by Harvard. We were caught up in our prestige and erudition, while Tim behaved as if he was working an ordinary job. He was the first psychologist I met who thought so openly, and I was interested in his research. Tim was a creative, brilliant whirlwind. I wanted to help him.

Tim and I taught courses together on psychotherapy and game theory. Unlike behaviorists, Tim believed that humans can change how they respond to stimuli. Informed by his own interest in game theory—which studies how competing players relate in a strategic situation—he saw social interaction as a game, which people could be taught how to play. He liked to talk in these terms, how we were each playing "the professor game" or "the Harvard game" or "the student game."

Tim also led a graduate seminar on existential transactionalism. This was a new idea in psychology, and Tim was supposed to be writing a book about it. Existential transaction theory was couched in the language of game theory, but it was a radical rethinking of relationships. In class, Tim talked about how existential transactionalism could transform clinical psychology. The relationships that psychologists usually found themselves in, he said, were asymmetrical power relationships: doctor-patient, experimenter-subject. One person was always superior to the other.

"I don't want that," Tim said. "There are better ways to relate to people." He wanted a model where, instead of detachment, psychologists practiced involvement. When he and our grad students answered patient requests for help, instead of meeting at an office, they went to the person's house. They'd sit at the kitchen table, drink coffee, and ask, "Okay, what is the situation, and how can we help?" The idea was to present themselves as resources, not doctors or authorities. This was revolutionary.

Tim and I began hanging out after hours. He was living with his two kids, Susan and Jack, in a hotel in Cambridge. We were both single, with few other commitments, and we'd spend evenings at the hotel bar, plumbing our life experiences and philosophical views. His game theory ideas resonated with my understanding of motivations and roles. Other evenings, we'd spend time in his hotel apartment with the kids, then ten and twelve years old, or have dinner with the McClellands at their house. Tim was full of stories, and we spent many hours laughing and talking. He had a James Joyce–like literary mind with a wonderfully ironic sense of humor.

Before I transferred to Harvard, I'd been part of a research effort called the School Mathematics Study Group. It originated at Yale University, propelled by the Soviets' launch of *Sputnik 1* and anxiety the US was falling behind technologically. The project was funded by the National Science Foundation and led by Yale professor Edward Begle, who was tasked with improving the math curriculum in American schools. (Eventually, the research led to the short-lived reform effort in the sixties known as New Math.)

One of the professors in Stanford's math department was part of the group, and he needed a research psychologist for a grant he was working on. He'd hired me to assess the effectiveness of the new teaching methodologies that were being designed for math instruction in classrooms. When I left for Harvard, he asked if I could continue helping with the research. It paid well, and I wanted to complete what I'd started, so I agreed to return to California in the summer. I'd also been invited to be a guest lecturer in child development at the University of California, Berkeley, for the following fall semester. Once the visiting professorship was over, I planned to return to Boston and resume my Harvard duties. I was used to bouncing between coasts.

In the spring of 1960, as I was gearing up for this sojourn in California, Tim and I went to a bar one evening in Harvard Square. He was planning to go to Mexico for the summer to work on his book. He was going to take Jackie with him, while Susan spent time with friends in Berkeley. He'd rented a villa in Cuernavaca, he said, where his friend Frank Barron planned to join him. Other academics would also be in the area, including Dave McClelland, who had summer book-writing plans of his own. Dave had rented a house in Tepoztlán, about ten miles from Cuernavaca.

Tim knew I had a pilot's license, and we came up with a plan: Once I finished with my research at Stanford, I would fly down to Mexico to meet him. Then, before returning to our respective posts, we'd fly together on a vacation trip across South America.

I invited seven or eight Harvard students to help me with the research at Stanford. They included Ralph Metzner, a grad student in the existential transaction seminar, and also Jim Fadiman, an undergrad for whom I was academic advisor. I rented a fraternity house for the research assistants and a faculty home, which I shared with Fadiman.

We went into schools around Palo Alto and gathered data, then interviewed the students who were being taught the new ways of doing math. We also met with a lot of junior high school girls to find out whether they liked math; after speaking with them, we interviewed the math teachers they'd had in elementary school. Our research demonstrated that students who'd had female teachers who didn't like math often didn't like math themselves.

That summer in Palo Alto, an entrepreneur named David Padwa came to see me. He had just earned a doctorate at Columbia University and was starting a company called Basic Systems. The business created educational technology and designed curriculum for schools, and Padwa was very interested in our research. He was really smart and an expansive thinker—about law, about politics, about education, about economics. We hit it off well. Our paths would connect again many times.

As the research came to a close, I looked for a plane to rent to fly from California to Mexico City, where I planned to meet Tim. But no one would rent me one, because flying to Mexico was too dangerous. The landing fields were primitive, and the tower flight controllers spoke only Spanish, which I did not understand well. It so happened, though, that my old flight instructor was selling his plane. It was a four-passenger Cessna 172. As soon as I saw the For Sale sign, I told him, "I'll buy it." I did not tell him I was going to Mexico—he might have changed his mind.

The flight was a three-day journey, with stops along the way. When I finally arrived in Mexico City, I went to the operations desk to close out my flight and found Tim there with Jackie. Tim flashed his Irish grin. He had changed his mind about our flying vacation.

"I can't go with you," he informed me. "I've already been on a journey."

The summer before, Frank Barron had told Tim about some "magic" mushrooms he'd eaten in Mexico. Frank talked endlessly about the insights these mushrooms gave. Tim was unpersuaded by his friend's ramblings; as he saw it, drugs were used mostly to manipulate and control patients, and he was against that. Still, Frank was insistent.

Tim was curious despite himself. About a decade earlier, in 1943, the chemist Albert Hofmann had synthesized lysergic acid diethylamide, LSD, in the labs of Sandoz Pharmaceuticals in Switzerland, and popular interest in mind-altering compounds was growing. *Life* magazine had recently published the first-person account of R. Gordon Wasson, a New York banker turned ethnobotanist who consumed fungi called *teonanácatl*, or "flesh of the gods," and experienced visions. Researchers had started examining both the compound in these mushrooms, psilocybin, and LSD for their potential in psychotherapy. At Harvard, a few of our own graduate students had experimented with mescaline, another hallucinogenic compound, found in cacti.

Tim told me he had tried the Mexican mushrooms for himself. A local *curandera* nicknamed Crazy Juana had delivered the dark and wrinkly specimens, and he'd consumed seven of them sitting by the pool at his villa. He was still ecstatic from the magnitude of the experience. "I learned more about my brain and its possibilities and more about psychology in the five hours after taking these mushrooms than in my fifteen years of studying psychology," he later said.

I was impressed. I suggested the experience might be like a marijuana high. Tim said there was no comparison. We drove to Cuernavaca, where I left Tim and Jackie; I'd decided to stay with the McClellands in Tepoztlán.

Tim had told Dave about the mushrooms too, and he was eager to try them. But by the time Dave and I returned to Tim's villa, they were gone. Tim had shared them with other visitors, and he wasn't sure he could get more. No one knew where Crazy Juana was. He promised I'd have my chance as soon as we got back to Harvard. He'd find a way.

I spent the following days giving rides in the Cessna to the kids—Jackie and the McClelland twins, Nicky and Duncan. When it was time to return to the US, I gave Tim and Jackie a ride back to California. I'd scored some marijuana in Mexico, and I filled the wing storage compartments with it. I had a bad case of turista, so I sat on a pile of towels in the pilot seat. Jackie brought back a pet iguana.

In San Diego, there was an international side of the airport, where you went through customs; the other side was the general aviation terminal for small domestic planes. Instead of landing on the international side, I pulled up to the general aviation building. We unloaded the plane and stashed the pot and the iguana in a public locker. Then I went over to the main desk. "Uh, I think I've landed in the wrong place," I said. "Where is customs?"

We taxied back over to customs. The inspector asked Jackie, who was maybe eleven, "Was there anything alive on your plane?" Jackie said, "Oh, I think there were a few flies . . ." Later the iguana got lost somewhere in Berkeley, where I embarked on my visiting professorship.

When Tim arrived back in Cambridge, he ran into one of our graduate students, George Litwin, a Detroit native who'd grown up in a labor union family and who knew something about mescaline. Tim was George's academic advisor, and he'd strongly advised him to stop doing drug research. Tim pulled George aside. "I now understand about these mind-altering drugs," he said. "I have experienced what you were talking about. We need to initiate research in this area immediately. Can you help?"

George told him that synthetic psilocybin was being developed and manufactured by Sandoz Pharmaceuticals, which had a branch in New Jersey. Tim wasted no time. On Harvard stationery, he wrote to Sandoz for a supply. The people at Sandoz did not ask for formal research protocols. They simply sent Tim a bottle of pink research-grade psilocybin pills.

"Good luck in your research," they wrote. "Let us know your findings."

CHAPTER 6

BECOMING NO BODY

O n Saturday night, March 4, 1961, I went to dinner at my parents' house in Newton. I'd just returned to Harvard after my semester at Berkeley. Mother was increasingly frail because of her blood disorder. Dad was struggling with the railroad. A tight-fisted Congress had not approved the federal subsidies he'd lobbied for, and he needed loans and tax relief to stay afloat. In a few short months, the railroad would declare bankruptcy. Dad held on for as long as he could—some said too long.

After dinner, I walked to Tim's house, a three-story mansion perched on a hill only a block away, at 64 Homer Street. He'd rented it from a professor on sabbatical in the Soviet Union and moved in with Susan and Jackie. Newton was just a half-hour drive to Cambridge. The house was grand, with five bedrooms. It had wood-paneled walls, several fireplaces, and bay windows. I was glad it was nearby, because heavy snow had started to fall.

It was my first time seeing Tim since Berkeley, and I was full of anticipation. In the months I'd been gone, Tim had launched a research effort called the Harvard Psilocybin Project with Frank Barron, who was teaching psychology at Harvard that semester. Tim's taste of mushrooms had been so transformative that he'd set out to investigate how psilocybin could be used to broaden human experience. He wanted to find out what kind of people most benefited from it and how its positive effects might be made to last.

Research into hallucinogens was already happening around the country. But many researchers were still using the drugs to mimic psychosis; the CIA-sponsored MK-Ultra project, for example, explored the usefulness of LSD for psychological warfare. Tim was interested in a different line of inquiry. After Mexico, he'd read *The Doors of Perception* and its sequel, *Heaven and Hell*, by Aldous Huxley, about the writer's experiences with mescaline, and he'd recognized his own trip in Huxley's words. He wanted to know how these drugs might enhance creativity and meaning.

Tim had spent the fall involving people in the project. When he heard that Huxley was a visiting lecturer at Massachusetts Institute of Technology, just down the road, Tim asked him to be an advisor. Huxley introduced Tim to Huston Smith, a professor of Asian philosophy at MIT who was interested in mystical experiences; his newly published *Religions of Man* was just becoming popular. Huxley also introduced Tim to Humphry Osmond, a British scientist who was doing research with psychedelics in Canada, using it in promising ways to cure alcoholism. (They met the same night that John F. Kennedy was voted in as president.) Osmond, in turn, connected Tim to Allen Ginsberg, who had participated in government LSD trials in San Francisco—at the same hospital as Ken Kesey. And Ginsberg introduced Tim to such friends as the writers Jack Kerouac and Robert Lowell and the musicians Dizzy Gillespie, Thelonius Monk, and Maynard Ferguson.

Tim was thrilled. He gave psilocybin to anyone who requested it, in exchange for a detailed report on the experience. In keeping with his existential-transaction ideas, he designed the project with an egalitarian, democratic approach. Rather than the usual clinical, detached method, he wanted both subjects and researchers to participate, taking turns ingesting and observing the effects of psilocybin. He wanted not just psychologists but philosophers, religious types, housewives, cabdrivers, students, and all manner of creatives: musicians, painters, poets, novelists. To avoid the impersonal setting of an office, he invited participants to try the drugs in his own home.

I trusted that Tim had undergone something profound in Mexico. I trusted his intellect. He spoke of the mushroom research as following in the introspective psychology tradition of William James, the father of American psychology. Since I was interested in the internal work-ings of the mind, this appealed to me. James, as a Harvard professor in the late 1800s, had studied altered states of consciousness using nitrous oxide. Tim was planning on involving our graduate students in the psilocybin research with a new seminar, Experimental Expansion of Consciousness.

Now it was my turn: tonight, I would journey into the unknown. I galumphed into Tim's house, knocking snow from my galoshes.

Sitting in the kitchen was Allen Ginsberg. He was visiting from New York. Tim had not mentioned he'd be there, so I was surprised. The last time I'd seen him was at a poetry reading at City Lights Bookstore in San Francisco.

Tim generally disliked homosexuals, but he respected Allen's poetry, which had been recently inspired by LSD and mescaline trips. His book *Kaddish and Other Poems* was about to come out. Allen and his lover, Peter Orlovsky, had tried psilocybin for the first time at Tim's house, and Allen had become a great friend and supporter of Tim's. Psilocybin was unlike anything Allen had tried, and he thought Tim could lead the country in a new awakening.

I joined Allen at the kitchen table, and Tim brought out the psilo-cybin pills. We each took one, a relatively small dose of ten milligrams.

At first, the psilocybin felt comparable to a strong pot high, maybe a little more dramatic, a little more intense. But after a while, some-thing else was clearly happening. My consciousness began feeling like it was merging with Allen's and Tim's. Our conversation grew more and more subdued as we relaxed and sank more deeply into a shared nonverbal awareness.

Suddenly, a dog that had been out playing in the snow, belong-ing to Tim's son Jackie, appeared in the kitchen. He was panting from exertion. The three of us watched him, alarmed. The dog's breath was so labored, we were afraid he might be dying. To our by now timeless minds, his mortal struggle to breathe was continuing too long.

The psychodrama of the dog's survival flared. What should we do? It was late Saturday night. We could hardly carry the dog four miles through a blizzard to the vet. We were all high. We couldn't be sure of the dog's state, much less our own. Were we perceiving accurately, or were we projecting from our hallucinatory world? Our collective concern mounted. The dog went into a nearby room and appeared to collapse.

We called Jackie, who was upstairs watching TV. Rather than frighten him with our concerns, we decided to observe his interaction with the dog.

Jackie was not pleased about having his show interrupted. But the crisis resolved instantly when the dog, on hearing the eleven-year-old's voice, leaped back to life, ready to play some more.

Distracted by the melodrama and concerned that I was wasting my trip, I moved to the partially darkened living room to sit alone on the couch. A deep calm pervaded my being. The rug crawled and the pictures smiled, which delighted me.

Then I sensed that there was someone in the corner of the room where, a moment before, there had been no one. Peering into the semi-darkness, I recognized the figure as none other than myself. There I was, a professor in cap and gown. It was as if the Harvard professor part of me had disassociated from the rest of me sitting on the couch. "How interesting! An external hallucination!" I thought. "Well, I worked hard to get that faculty status. But it's just a role. I don't really need it."

I settled back into the cushions, content to be separate from my professorial self. But a moment later, the figure changed. I leaned forward, straining to see. There I was again, this time as a cosmopolitan socialite, my charming and convivial social self. "Okay," I thought, "so that goes too."

Again and again, the figure changed. In one figure after another, I recognized all my social and psychological roles: cellist, pilot, son, lover, and so on. The images were like kitschy caricatures—as a pilot, for example, I wore a World War I leather flying helmet and goggles. It was a cartoon parade of all the ways I habitually thought of myself. "Okay," I mused, "these are all the ways I know myself. But how can I be here on the couch when my roles are over there?"

Now came my Richard Alpert-ness, my basic ego identity. I had always been Richard, going back to childhood, when my parents first called me Richard and I associated the name with who I was. "Richard, you're a bad boy"—so Richard had badness. Or "Oh, Richard, aren't you handsome!"—and Richard felt beautiful. But where was Richard now? Was my Richard-ness just another role? Uh-oh.

Sweat broke out on my forehead. I wasn't at all sure I could do without being Richard Alpert. What if I had amnesia and forgot who I was? Would it be permanent?

"Oh, what the hell," I thought. "So I'll give up being Richard Alpert. I can always get a new social identity. At least I have my body."

But then I looked down—and I couldn't see my body! The couch was there, but there was no one sitting on it. A scream formed in my throat. Adrenaline shot through my bloodstream, and my mouth went dry.

I was about to yell for Tim when a calm, very intimate voice from inside—inside what, I didn't know—quietly asked, rather jocularly considering how distraught I was, "Okay, so who's minding the store?"

It took a moment for me to actually focus on the question. Then it dawned on me: Even though everything I thought of as me, including my body, was gone, I was still fully aware! Not only that, but this aware inner "I" was watching the entire drama, including the panic attack, with quiet compassion and not a little amusement at the fear my ego was experiencing.

I instantly felt a new, profound kind of peace I'd never before experienced. I had just found the "I"—that perceptual point of view, that essence of identity, that scanning device. I'd found that place of awareness beyond form, where "I" exists independent of social and psychological roles. This "I" was beyond time and space.

And this "I" *knew*, it really *knew*. It was wise, rather than just knowledgeable. It was a voice inside that spoke truth. I recognized it and was one with it. I felt as if my entire life of looking to the outside world for affirmation and reassurance was over. Now all I needed was to look within, to that place where I *knew*.

I was just *presence*, unfettered by the usual slipstream of random thoughts, images, and sensations. I nestled into this sense of pure *being*, feeling my way into this timeless, inner self that was independent of outer identity. I felt no need to *do* anything.

Allen was right. This was unlike any experience I'd ever had, because what changed was not any outer sensation or feeling but the experiencer himself—my point of view, my sense of identity. I was home,

home in my spiritual self in a way I'd never before felt or thought possible. It was nonconceptual, indescribable.

Gradually, the sensory world began to reassert itself, and I perceived my body and my senses again. But the Harvard professor and son of George and Gertrude Alpert had undergone a change. Those identities now seemed like familiar costumes, ones I could either assume or slough off. I remained in a quiet, blissful state of clear presence, a joyful, loving awareness. As my mind reengaged and thoughts again began to occupy my consciousness, I felt I would always remember and be able to reenter this state of being, this newly discovered calm center in myself.

It was about three in the morning. It had stopped snowing; the night's storm had turned into a blizzard, dumping the biggest snow of the year over Boston. I decided to venture outside.

The air was breathtakingly cold and crisp. Just beyond the front door, I lay down in the snow and rolled down the hill in front of Tim's house. My ecstatic being was spinning me back into childhood, into a long-forgotten sense of pure joy. I had played on that street as a child. Now that inner child was home, home, home.

No one at all was out on the street. I walked back to my parents' house through the snowdrifts, which came up to my thighs. They were snowed in. My radiant self viewed the house I grew up in with fresh eyes, as if it were a scene from a New England snow globe.

A thought surfaced: "Young tribal buck shovels the walk, wouldn't that be good?" It was a joyful impulse. I was back at my childhood home, and now here I was, home in my heart too. I got the snow shovel from the garage and started digging through the drifts.

After a while, the faces of Mother and Dad appeared at the upstairs window. They looked both alarmed and peeved that I was shoveling the walk. My father opened the window. "Come to bed, you idiot," he called. "Nobody shovels snow at three in the morning!" I looked up and laughed, then did a jig around the snow shovel. They closed the window. When I looked up, they were smiling and laughing. I'd passed along my first contact high.

At that moment, I recalled the work of the sociologist and Harvard professor David Riesman, who in his 1950 book on post–World War II America, *The Lonely Crowd*, had coined the expression "other-directedness," a term for how individuals look to their neighbors and community to define their likes and dislikes. I saw the part in myself that was always tuning to what everybody else wanted. My parents were the voices I'd always listened to. Even when I was rebelling—as when I rejected going to medical school—part of me still wanted their approval.

For the first time, I was listening to a voice inside, and that voice said, "It's okay to shovel snow." Usually, I responded to my parents' judgments and to my professors' and my bosses' expectations. They all held power over me. Now I felt a flow of power, but not from them, from within me. I had an inner impulse that was stronger than my social conditioning. Shoveling the walk was an expression of internal power laughing at external power.

In that moment, I knew I had reoriented. I was reentering my various roles, but from a new place. Under my parents' disapproving glare, I did something joyful for myself, from my inner being, dancing a jig with the snow shovel. It was scary, in a way, to reject those long-inculcated values and trust my heart. But I was asserting myself from my soul. I was free.

We all experience inner and outer conflict. It manifests when aspects of life start to feel unfulfilling and hollow, when work or personal relationships that were once rewarding seem empty. You feel like you're part of some conspiracy of make-believe, where you're supposed to think something's happening but inside everything is desolate. You might be depressed, but it's also the call of the soul. The soul demands that your moment-to-moment experience of living be meaningful and fulfilling. It's not just the ego that needs feeding—so does the spirit. The soul's game is not about reorganizing your external life. It's not about getting a new job, friends, or lifestyle; making more money or getting a new car; finding a new partner or a new therapist. It's about inner reorganization, about reorienting toward your spiritual self.

Psilocybin gave me a first glimpse of that connection. It was the beginning of an awakening to my soul. In that early-morning instant of freedom, a seed was planted, one that would grow into an ability to confront and even disagree with authority, to know and trust the place inside that says, "It's all right."

On the Monday after my psilocybin trip, I showed up on campus to deliver a scheduled lecture for the class Social Relations 143, Human Motivation. As I began, I felt distracted. I wanted to share what had happened on Saturday. The problem was, there was nothing in any psychology textbook that described my experience. I knew my students could benefit, but I had no context—no terminology, no academic explanation—from which to communicate that ineffable new sense of self.

This planted some doubts about psychology. If my psilocybin experience was true, then everything I was teaching about motivational psychology was utterly beside the point. I was teaching stuff, and my students were writing it all down, but the disparity between realities— between my consciousness on Saturday night and my professorial explanations on Monday morning—was disconcerting.

I felt guilty. Was I being a complete hypocrite? Psychologists think that reality is ultimately psychological, and yet the psilocybin trip had shown me that I was more than a psychological entity. Until that moment, the only stirring of my spirit had been in Quaker meetings at Wesleyan. Now, I knew from my own experience there was another plane of consciousness beyond time and space.

After two or three more days, I was talking about the psilocybin trip in the past tense. My personality patterns kept infiltrating my newly liberated mind, old thought habits sneakily reasserting themselves. The material realities of classes and meetings and groceries intruded once again. The pure white of the blizzard melted into piles of dirty snow. Neurotic old Richard was back.

Still, even though I was back in my psychological self, my thinking mind and ego, I was different. The roles—professor, son, pilot, cellist—returned, but I didn't identify with them in the same way. The observer stance I'd long cultivated had new meaning. There was a way to observe life from this quiet center within, from the soul. I'd tasted a reality where I was home in my heart, and even the memory—that lightness of pure being—remained with me.

And yet. I knew I didn't fully *know*, at least not in a way I could explain to my students. I had worked so hard to become a member of the academic community, and now I felt disconnected. Everyone assumed I knew things because I was a Harvard professor. But I didn't know about this, and when I listened to my colleagues, I realized they didn't either. These were lions of academia, at the apex of Western learning. We were all enjoying the world of our own thought forms. We were fascinated by our theories. We were all going on about the workings of the mind.

But we didn't have wisdom. The awareness behind it all, the consciousness that moves it all, was a mystery.

CHAPTER 7

THE HARVARD
PSILOCYBIN PROJECT

By the next week, I was back in Tim's living room, ready for another psilocybin trip. I was no longer sure that my chosen career was on the leading edge of discovery. Psychology studies motivational systems, emotions, personality structure, and social development. I didn't care so much about personality and behavior anymore. I wanted to look into the spirit, to find a way to live at home in the heart.

In his seminal book *Doors of Perception*, Aldous Huxley described a consciousness he called "Mind at Large," a consciousness that gets funneled through "the reducing valve of the brain and nervous system." I realized he was on to something. I'd been studying just one plane of human experience, and it was a limited view. William James himself had noted this in his 1902 classic, *The Varieties of Religious Experience*. "Our normal waking consciousness, rational consciousness as we call it, is but one special type of consciousness," he wrote, "whilst all about it, parted from it by the filmiest of screens, there lie potential forms of consciousness entirely different." Ironically (or maybe appropriately), one of my offices on campus was in William James Hall.

I joined the Harvard Psilocybin Project, becoming a volunteer guide for new participants. Tim and I also put together a team of graduate students to help. These included George Litwin, who had originally tipped Tim off that Sandoz Pharmaceuticals was making research-grade psilocybin; Ralph Metzner, who had helped me with my Stanford research in 1960 and was now an Oxford graduate; and Gunther Weil, a Fulbright scholar who had just spent a year in Europe. Together we ran more sessions—among ourselves, with other graduate students, with friends and family, with volunteers from the community—and collected experience reports from participants. At first, for the grad students, there wasn't quite the sense of going inside and doing explorations; there was a lot of talking and laughing. But as we honed what we eventually called the "set and setting" for the trips, the insights started coming.

Many sessions took place in Tim's living room; others took place in our offices or on the beaches of Cape Cod. Saturday evenings, we'd convene at Tim's house to run sessions for artists, musicians, and other creative types. Many figures in the New York art and literary scene came to us through an art impresario named Van Wolf. Maynard Ferguson came with his wife, Flo. Allen Ginsberg was also a regular. Huston Smith and Aldous Huxley came repeatedly, as did Huxley's friend, the brilliant historian and philosopher Gerald Heard, who saw human progress as the evolution of consciousness. Arthur Koestler, the famous author of *Darkness at Noon*, also participated, though he viewed the experience negatively. Tim always had a girlfriend—some lasted longer than others—whom he'd invite too.

Set and setting was the principle that both mindset and environment were critical to the psychedelic journey. The notion that both participants and guides could collaborate, which came from Tim's work in transactionalism, helped us develop models to maximize insights. To anchor people as they explored the depths of their psyche, we insisted on set and setting factors such as the presence of a guide, soothing music and imagery, and comfortable pillows. This helped lead people into themselves without fear. Intention played a significant role in what came up in sessions, as did an attitude of openness to whatever arose from the depth of the spirit. People worked with trauma or personal imagery, explored mystical experiences, and awakened to creativity and love. The collaborative approach also meant taking our own medicine; I ingested psilocybin along with the participants.

We were practicing what Willam James called "introspectionism," or studying the mind from the inside out. Introspective psychology relies on observation of one's own mental states. Though subjective, it is disciplined. This fit the nature of our psilocybin research: our work was guided by the self-reporting and internal observations of the experimenter. The phenomena we were observing were states of consciousness, thoughts, feelings, and sensory experiences, often about identity and self-awareness.

This is not to say we weren't scientific about it. Introspective psychology is a formal, experimental approach: we kept copious notes, compiled data, compared reports, and designed objective studies, such as on the passage of time. That said, it is hard to quantify or describe certain experiences, and we were also developing new language and categories. Participants reported feeling a sense of unity, and psilocybin softened interpersonal boundaries and opened up communication. We called it the "love drug."

Tim and I brought our individual perspectives to the work. For me, psilocybin offered a doorway into identity and spiritual development. I was interested in its introspective power and possibilities. In guiding trips, I was inspired to bridge the patient-therapist divide, accompanying those ingesting the drug as a fellow soul on a shared journey. This allowed me to let go of whatever my mind was holding on to. I saw my job as helping people release their ego stuff without fear.

Tim, on the other hand, was more focused on the social implications of our research. He didn't disagree with psilocybin's mystical qualities, but he was interested in its potential to solve society's problems. The visionary trips that helped reorder one's self and priorities—these could be harnessed and applied, he thought, toward behavioral and social transformation. His utopian vision was that psychedelics could educate, illuminate, and rehabilitate people's otherwise insoluble problems.

Later Tim gained notoriety for confronting institutions to provoke this social awakening. As an iconoclast, he gleefully undermined the Establishment. But in those early days, he was very empathetic and supportive. I knew and respected Tim's creative intellect, and from being drinking buddies, I knew he was not destructive on an interpersonal level. More than anything, he was deeply curious and exuberantly optimistic.

In March 1961, Tim got a chance to test his utopian vision when he received a letter from Harvard's Department of Legal Medicine.

Two officials in the department were looking for help in the psychological rehabilitation of prisoners. At the time, prison work was considered a dead end for psychology research, because criminals never changed and the environment was so grim.

But Tim saw opportunity. We'd overseen more than a hundred psilocybin sessions by this point, and for all the reports of ecstatic insights, we were missing hard data that could show what good the drug was doing. Our psychology colleagues, including Dave McClelland, were asking questions about our lack of long-term studies and quantifiable measurements. With its constrained population, prison offered just the environment for us to collect data in. And unlike our studies on creativity, it offered a direct statistic with which to measure the effect of psychedelics: the recidivism rate.

Tim invited the prison officials for lunch at Harvard, and they were duly impressed. Then he had to charm the warden and the prison psychiatrist at the Massachusetts Correctional Institute at Concord. This took some doing. Everyone agreed that trying to reduce the recidivism rate was a worthwhile endeavor, but the idea of using drugs to do it raised some eyebrows. So Tim invited the prison psychiatrist, W. Madison Presnell, to his house to try psilocybin for himself.

Presnell was the first black psychiatrist we had ever met. He was a very insightful therapist; he saw through personality and into people's deeper being, which helped him in his work with prisoners. He was also a bit of a rascal. He was impressed that Harvard researchers were coming to his domain, and he was glad for the prestige we were lending his position. After his trip, he agreed to enlist volunteers for our study. He was supportive, but he also made it clear he wasn't going down with the ship if anything went south. This was risky business.

In the Concord Prison Experiment the idea was to use psilocybin to stimulate insight and behavioral changes in convicts and to see whether over the long term the intervention reduced the recidivism rate, which in the state prison system was around 70 percent. If it worked, it would be a great boon to society.

Convicts often get offered shorter parole terms in exchange for volunteering for a study by some drug company. Tim didn't want to do that. It was inappropriate for what we were trying to accomplish.

His attitude was, "We have found these experiences very interesting. We want to share them with you. In fact, we're going to experience them along with you." That way, there could be trust right from the beginning.

It was a six-week program, with two psychedelic sessions—one at the start and one near the end. Most of the inmates were nearing release. The sessions took a group therapy format, with four or five inmates. The guides for the sessions were our graduate students from the Department of Social Relations, including Ralph Metzner, who signed up immediately, and Gunther Weil. Sometimes the inmates took the drugs under the supervision of the grad students; sometimes the grad students took the drugs too. Sometimes they exchanged roles, and the prisoners acted as guides. This reinforced trust. We administered psychological tests before and after.

These grad students had never been inside a prison. Sharing an extreme psychological intimacy with hardened criminals was a dramatic change from academia. A Harvard student might be guiding a murderer. But it was such a leveling experience that real bonding occurred despite the differences.

The project continued for two years, until mid-1963. In subsequent lectures and papers, Tim would claim that the recidivism rate declined dramatically and that the experiment was proof that psychedelics could engineer the kind of social change that fit his visionary ideals. "The main conclusion can be stated as follows," he wrote at one point. "One and one half years after termination of the program, the rate of new crimes has been reduced." In later years, these claims proved to be exaggerated. Years later a long-term review by researchers Rick Doblin and Michael Forcier found Tim's claims did not withstand more rigorous analysis. Recidivism did go down with intentional, personal contact—both Tim and our grad students invested a great deal in their relationships with the inmates—but it was unclear whether psilocybin had much to do with this.

I worked mostly in a supervisory and administrative role, negotiating with prison officials and setting up the protocols. What was radical to me about the experiment was the attempt to develop valid therapeutic models with psychedelics. It was similar to the studies going on with alcoholism and depression. The main problem was little follow-up was done after the prisoners' release. We had no budget for halfway houses or to continue the study over an extended long term. Ultimately, the project would prove that, while psychedelic insights can serve as a catalyst for behavioral change, transformation requires sustained attention and work. I would learn this in my own life soon enough.

In May 1961, President John F. Kennedy appeared before Congress to call for an ambitious space exploration program. He wanted to put Americans on the moon before the decade was out. "Space is open to us now," he declared, "and our eagerness to share its meaning is not governed by the efforts of others. We go into space because whatever mankind must undertake, free men must fully share."

Chasing the moon was not what Tim and I were doing, but in many ways the president's words captured how we saw our own scientific efforts. We too wanted to conquer space—inner, not outer, space. We were intranauts, not astronauts, at the cutting edge of human consciousness.

We had some support at Harvard, most notably from Henry Murray, the former director of the Harvard Psychological Clinic, who volunteered to try psilocybin. Many of our other departmental colleagues, however, were starting to harbor doubts about our research. Stories were flying around campus about our sessions with artists and flamboyant musicians and about graduate students taking drugs. Though our methodology involved reporting on internal states and subjective experiences, Tim and I believed we could show demonstrable effects on creativity, as well as therapeutic benefits and religious or mystical experiences.

Dave McClelland and other faculty members didn't buy it. In their view, scientific data had to be objectively verifiable, which is hard when you are talking about highly subjective internal experiences. Objective knowledge must be repeatable, so that it can be studied by more than one person; what we were doing, said our colleagues, was self-validating our work. Behaviorism was still paramount for many of the psychologists at Harvard. A good scientist observed measurable changes in behavior, designing rigorous protocols, testing rats in labyrinths, and collecting data.

But you couldn't use rats to explore awareness. Our research wasn't about measuring every little behavior—it was about life-altering *experience*. Our colleagues didn't accept this paradigm. The psilocybin project staff would gather at lunchtime in the library of the Center for Research in Personality and discuss our trips, trying to develop language for them. Lunchtime began to be noticeably divided between those who were in the psilocybin project and those who were not.

This only exacerbated the growing rift between us and the other faculty. It wasn't just about scientific methodology. Our research was attracting more graduate students, leaving other professors with fewer assistants to run surveys and experiments. The psilocybin project was the most exciting thing happening.

The crack within our department widened further that August, when Tim, Frank Barron, and I traveled to Copenhagen for the Fourteenth International Congress of Applied Psychology. We were scheduled to speak at one of the opening sessions, as was Aldous Huxley, before a gathering of professionals from all over the world. Before our lecture, I caused an inadvertent stir by attending a party with some Danish journalists and sharing some psilocybin so they could understand the research I was describing. My photo appeared in the newspaper with a headline about the crazy Harvard professor who was distributing poisonous drugs.

This caused consternation among psychologists at the convention. Their shock only grew when Tim lectured about the potential of psychedelics to cut through the "game" of Western life and change human behavior and consciousness. I spoke about the value of the inner journey—how psychedelics were worth investigating for their visionary qualities alone. Their mystical insights, I said, could produce love and peace.

Love and peace and personal growth are not the stuff of conventional scientific inquiry. Some attendees told Tim we'd set Danish psychology back twenty years. People wondered what on earth was going on at Harvard.

The conference was our first public declaration of the promise we saw in psychedelics for real change. On the one hand, it brought us attention. On a stop in London after the conference, for example, we tripped with the novelist William Burroughs, who enjoyed the experience so much that he flew to the US and moved into Tim's house temporarily to participate in our research. Burroughs had famously killed his wife in an accident trying to shoot an apple off her head like William Tell, and he was an acerbic character. He'd tried all sorts of drugs; if there was ever someone who knew about pharmacology from the inside, it was him.

Our stance made people in the Harvard scientific community nervous. When we returned, Dave distributed a memo at one of our faculty meetings in which he outlined his growing concern. "Many reports are given of deep mystical experiences," he wrote, "but their chief characteristic is the wonder at one's own profundity." He wanted fewer subjective reports and more control and hard data.

In response, I set to work crafting a memo of our own, making sure our research was collected in one place, writing out our findings thus far for the benefit of our colleagues. One day in October, as I was still putting these files together, Tim received a visitor at our Harvard offices. Michael Hollingshead was a tall, eccentric Englishman who was broke and depressed after experimenting with LSD in New York. After inviting him to lunch, Tim sent Michael on his way, but a few days later, he received a letter. In messy, feverish handwriting, Michael explained that he was so freaked out he could not leave his apartment. He was thinking of killing himself.

Neither Tim nor I had tried LSD. We knew Huxley had, as had Allen Ginsberg and Alan Watts. A few months earlier, we'd received a letter from Bill Wilson, the founder of Alcoholics Anonymous, who credited LSD with alleviating his alcoholism.

Tim wanted to help Michael. He let him crash at his house and thought Michael might help him lead discussions about consciousness with our students. Michael claimed to have worked at Oxford, but it wasn't clear if that was true. Many of his statements seemed unreliable.

What we did know was that he and John Beresford, a doctor in New York, had obtained a large supply of LSD from Sandoz in Switzerland, ostensibly for bone-marrow experiments. The two had slipped into taking it themselves, mixing the LSD with water and confectioners' sugar to make a syrupy paste. The paste filled a huge mayonnaise jar, which Michael now carried with him. At Tim's house, he encouraged Tim to taste it, saying it was far more revelatory than mushrooms.

Tim shrugged it off, until one afternoon in December. Maynard Ferguson and his wife, Flo, were visiting, as was George Litwin. Michael offered them all a taste from the mayonnaise jar with a spoon. After watching the Fergusons trip for a few minutes, Tim decided to finally try LSD for himself.

He would eventually describe the experience as the most shattering of his life, writing that his first spoonful of LSD had "flipped consciousness out beyond life into the whirling dance of pure energy." But in the immediate aftermath, as the drug's effects wore off, he sobbed uncontrollably, overcome by the feeling that he had died and been reborn. After that, he did not speak for days.

Compared to his usual talkative self, he was muted and dull—so much so that I grew alarmed. George was also distant. Something profound had happened, and I wasn't sure what it was. I warned whoever asked not to take the drug.

"We've lost Timothy," I went around saying. "We've lost Timothy!"

CHAPTER 8

ACIDIFICATION

L ike a high-voltage jolt, LSD changed the nature of the Psilocybin Project at Harvard. Psilocybin, as we'd experienced it, was a relational and unifying drug. The doses we administered were relatively small, six to eight milligrams, and the trips we guided lasted just three or four hours. Participants remembered their names and situations even as they reported feelings of oneness. Boundaries melted with a sense of warmth and understanding. Psilocybin softened the ego and opened the heart.

LSD blew all that away. It caused, not a softening of the ego, but its death. You might not remember your name or where you were or how you got there, floating out in the free space of consciousness. Michael Hollingshead's sugary white paste offered no real way of determining dosage—a spoonful might have contained up to 250 micrograms—and a trip could last for an entire day or even longer. A few high-dose psilocybin trips had already taken us to the existential edge, so to speak, but LSD went beyond that. LSD was transcendent.

Coming down from an acid trip, it was hard to communicate what had happened, because the drug took you to a plane that was so different from normal waking consciousness that words were useless. Sometimes you couldn't even remember the trip because the memory was specific to that other state. Sometimes your experience went so far beyond the discursive thought process that you saw people around you almost as artificial, mechanical figures caught in a dream world.

This was Tim's experience. When he finally spoke after his first trip, he kept describing the puppet world we were living in. LSD had shown him how human conditioning was all mechanical, how we were all like plastic dolls. At home, he saw his daughter, Susan, as playing the perfect teenager-puppet game. His trip had taken him to that causal plane where free will and fate are paradoxically simultaneous, so when he came down to the physical reality of everyday life, everything seemed robotic in comparison. As if to confirm what we knew about set and setting, Tim's taste of LSD seemed to authenticate what he already felt about life: that it was all a game, in which human interaction is defined by our assigned roles and rituals and strategies.

Looking back, I see that when awareness gets disconnected from compassion and interrelatedness, it can feel robotic or puppet-like. Tim's observations also foreshadowed the fundamental realization we'd have a few years later about psychedelics in general: that a trip is just that—a trip—and you have to come back. At the end of the day, for all your new insight, you still have to take out the garbage.

Hearing Tim talk like that scared me. It was so lacking in the heart space I'd discovered with psilocybin. I could sense that LSD might shift the paradigm of our research away from what I felt was the most important aspect of our work: psychedelics as a vehicle for internal education and spiritual growth.

I resisted the mayonnaise jar at first. Several weeks after Tim's LSD initiation, his trusted collaborator Frank Barron, who had helped guide the research for the Psilocybin Project, returned to San Francisco to get married. Michael became a kind of all-around assistant to Tim, and it was hard to know what to make of this. Tim was well aware that there was something unscrupulous about Michael, but he was his conduit to LSD, and Tim revered him as a "wise alien trickster." Tim had jokingly developed a scale of moral reprehension—he'd rate you as a rascal, rogue, scoundrel, and so on—and the two of them often joked about where Hollingshead fell on this scale.

Michael was funny and good-natured and a storyteller, like Tim. But he also had a dark and untrustworthy side. There was no way to gauge the veracity of his stories, and when it came to psychedelics, he completely sidestepped our efforts to develop a thoughtful framework.

Every day at Tim's house, he took a dose of LSD, spooning it out of his jar like peanut butter. He'd pour himself a scotch and plant himself in front of the TV, tripping to whatever images were on the screen. In group sessions, he disregarded the sense of safety and comfort we tried to create, playing instead with how suggestible participants were. Rather than follow our code of openness, he liked to confuse and manipulate you. His approach to psychedelics was not about growth or insight. It was to freak out, to go as far as possible.

Eventually, I decided to lick the spoon myself. When I finally did, I realized that all this time in previous psychedelic sessions, I had been screwing around in the astral plane. LSD went beyond the astral, beyond form. It took you deeper, stripping away more of the layers of mind, and it lasted much longer. The peak of a trip carried you into a nova of consciousness and pure energy. Psilocybin had opened my spiritual heart. Now LSD opened the recesses of my mind and connected me to the very source of cosmic energy. No wonder Tim hadn't been able to speak.

After his initial trip, Tim couldn't tolerate large doses of LSD. He took smaller doses. I, on the other hand, embraced it with gusto, experimenting with the highest doses I could tolerate. Tim and I agreed to expand our approach, incorporating LSD and another psychedelic, dimethyltryptamine (DMT), into our research. The Harvard Psilocybin Project became the Harvard Psychedelic Project. We held more sessions and even introduced LSD to the inmates at the Concord state prison.

I did an LSD trip with the prison psychiatrist, W. Madison Presnell. That day still stands out in my memory: tripping on acid, I saw him as a brilliant light inside a coating of skin. The civil rights movement was just beginning to really swell—the Freedom Riders had made news headlines a year earlier—and I'd not yet fully examined any residual racial prejudices left from my Jewish upbringing. Seeing that light radiating from Dr. Presnell, I was struck by how the skin that coated each of us was just that: a coating. Inside both of us was light. This upended my thinking about any supposed differences. We were the same essence, connected.

As with psilocybin, an LSD trip was contingent on the set and setting paradigm we were developing. A successful death-and-rebirth journey depended on the intentions, experiences, and fears you brought to the session. LSD was also so much more intense than psilocybin that it was imperative to have a supportive environment and a guide, especially if you were new to the drug. It was such a powerful psychedelic that without these things to ground you, you could be terrorized by your fears and easily get lost in a bad trip.

What was most striking about acid, though, was that it made mysticism and spirituality practically inescapable. You'd come out of a session reeling with awe, your ego having been dissolved into colors and sensations. You were shaken to your core by the awareness of a divine life energy. Even the criminals at the Concord prison used religious imagery to describe their LSD trips.

As scientists, Tim and I didn't have the tools to really explain this. We didn't know of any published research that tracked with our experiences. Since we'd had a few religious thinkers already participate in our research, like Huston Smith and Alan Watts, we turned to them to help us explore this mystical quality. Tim also made several visits to the Harvard Divinity School to enlist faculty and students who might want to try psychedelics. Smith began hosting a Sunday gathering at his house for us to run sessions. People who stopped by included Walter Houston Clark, a professor of psychology of religion at Newton Theological School, and Walter Pahnke, a medical doctor who was pursuing a PhD at Harvard in philosophy and religion.

We saw a lot of Alan Watts, author of books on Buddhism and psychology, who was at Harvard as a visiting professor. Alan was also a wonderful cook, and he became a good friend. As I knew from my Stanford days of listening to his Sunday morning radio show, he could put Eastern philosophy into everyday language and make it accessible. He tripped with Tim over at his house, and we often compared notes with him on the beauty and visions wrought by psychedelics, which he saw as sacraments. In early 1962, when he was writing *The Joyous Cosmology*, a vivid account of his psychedelic experiences, he asked me and Tim to pen the foreword. "We must provide more and more people with these experiences and have them tell us, as Alan Watts does here, what they experienced," we wrote.

Thanks in part to Alan and Huston, who shared their knowledge of Asian philosophy, Tim and I grew more and more curious about how other cultures thought of consciousness. Tim started collecting books on Buddhism, yoga, and tantra. He also met a former air force major who had become a Hindu monk. The monk was a follower of a woman named Gayatri Devi, who ran the Ramakrishna Vedanta Society, an ashram outside Boston. An acid trip with everyone at the ashram convinced Tim of Hinduism's insights into ultimate reality. In February 1962, Allen Ginsberg and Peter Orlovsky left for India for a year and a half. Allen came back chanting "Hare Krishna" with a squeezebox harmonium.

One Tuesday in early 1962, Tim and I sensed we were finally circling around some answers. The Saturday before, I'd had an LSD trip that was completely ineffable. I'd traveled through planes of consciousness that left me utterly mystified. I was still searching for a way to understand it when Aldous Huxley stopped by for a visit. Aldous, who often described his own first psychedelic trip as a religious event—he called it a "gratuitous grace"—brought a copy of the *Tibetan Book of the Dead*, the Walter Evans-Wentz translation, under his arm.

This classic Buddhist text, otherwise known as the *Bardo Thodol*, outlines the conscious experience of death and the interval before the next rebirth. It is used by Tibetans as a guide for dying. It was as if I was reading a travelogue of the worlds I'd just passed through. The process of dying described in the book was eerily identical to the dissolution of the ego on psychedelics. Here we had reference points for our acid trips, though from a very different cultural perspective.

As Western psychologists, Tim and I had thought we were delving into unknown territory, making up theories as we went along to explain our experiences. But this ancient book from the East offered a detailed understanding of this very terrain. Other beings had traveled before us, charting how to navigate the inner planes. The maps we'd been searching for already existed.

Our faculty colleagues were less than enthused by our discoveries. In February 1962, I distributed my memo describing the effects of psychedelics we were tracking with prisoners, theologians, and therapy patients. This seemed to quell the skepticism within the psychology department, though not for long. A week or two later, Andrew Weil reported in the *Harvard Crimson* about our plans to lead a "mushroom seminar" for graduate students in theology, behavioral science, and philosophy. The notion that drugs were on Harvard's syllabus—even in a controlled setting and with no undergrads—put other faculty members on high alert.

My boss at Health Services, Dana Farnsworth, wrote a letter to the *Crimson* about the dangers of mescaline. Dave McClelland asked us, again, to collect more observational data. Two other professors, Herb Kelman and Brendan Maher, maintained that certain graduate students were feeling pressured to take psychedelics against their better judgment. We were abusing our power as educators, they said, and behaving irresponsibly by not recognizing the potential ill effects of psychedelics. When Maher saw a letter on one of the secretary's desks that Tim had written to Sandoz requesting more psilocybin supplies, he tore it up.

Kelman asked Dave to call a meeting with clinical students and faculty to address concerns about our project. In mid-March, Tim and I showed up at 5 Divinity Avenue to find a packed room.

Things got heated as soon as Kelman took the floor. Kelman had been one of the government-sponsored research scientists who participated in the surreptitious CIA mind-control experiments at Harvard a decade earlier. If he'd taken LSD himself back then maybe he would have been more favorably disposed toward our work. He accused us of being anti-intellectual and creating a cult-like atmosphere around our research. He said our project should be restructured or terminated. Maher brought up psilocybin's medical risks and accused us of carelessness.

Tim, though surprised by our colleagues' vehemence, shrugged off the anger coming in our direction. We *were* cognizant of the risks, and there was no evidence the amount of psilocybin we were administering in our sessions was dangerous. I said our research followed on that of William James. It was innovative and showed evidence of positive behavioral change. Harvard was known for supporting exploration and discovery. Wasn't that what we were doing?

News of our department's tense clash appeared the next day in the *Crimson*. The story was picked up by Boston newspapers and the newswires. "Hallucination Drug Fought at Harvard—350 Students Take Pills" read the headline in the *Boston Herald*. The headlines were annoyingly sensational. We'd given psilocybin to many subjects, yes, but they weren't all students, and now suddenly the story was two Harvard professors running a wild drug ring.

This was not exactly good press for Harvard. The story caught the attention of the FBI, the Food and Drug Administration, and the Federal Bureau of Narcotics. The Massachusetts Department of Public Health opened an investigation. The inquiry led only to a requirement that a licensed physician be present whenever we administered psyche-delics; otherwise, the state allowed, our research could continue. Tim and I took this as a good sign: the state considered our work safe. But Harvard administrators were not happy with the scrutiny from gov-ernment agents. Soon afterward, Tim and I were ordered to turn over all of our psilocybin to Farnsworth at Health Services—our research *and* personal stashes—for him to keep under lock and key.

I refused to hand over my personal supply, invoking my rights as a citizen. I suspected, too, that because of the incident in which I flaunted my bravado over my sexuality, Farnsworth was going to make my life even more difficult. Tim, on the other hand, agreed to hand over everything. As far as he was concerned, we had plenty of LSD to keep us busy.

During a gathering at Huston Smith's house, Walter Pahnke, proposed an idea for his thesis dissertation. He wanted to create a careful study in experimental mysticism to establish whether psychedelics could induce a genuine religious experience. He proposed giving a group of divinity students psilocybin during a church service on Good Friday.

Tim and I helped Pahnke maximize every factor of the set and set-ting to produce a religious experience. Thanks to Walter Houston Clark, we found twenty volunteer subjects at Newton Theological School, whom we pretested and screened with psychiatric interviews. Huston Smith was among the volunteers. Half the group would receive psilo-cybin, while a control group received a placebo. There would be trained graduate-student guides to work with the students, and afterward,

Pahnke would chart participants' reactions with a questionnaire he devised about the mystical experience, based in part on the work of the Princeton-based philosopher W. T. Stace.

If what our Harvard colleagues wanted was systematic research with controls, this was it, the gold standard, a double-blind, medically supervised experiment. The only problem was that our psilocybin was under tight control, and Farnsworth and a newly formed supervisory committee were dragging their feet on approving the study.

Tim tracked down the psilocybin we needed by contacting a psychiatrist in Worcester. On April 20, 1962, we convened at Boston University's Marsh Chapel. No one could predict what would happen, so we agreed to isolate the participants in the basement. Half the group received an envelope with a pill of psilocybin; the other half received an envelope with a pill of nicotinic acid, which mimicked the onset of a psychedelic trip by producing a mild niacin flush. The inspiring sermon by the chapel's charismatic preacher, Dean Howard Thurman, a mentor of Martin Luther King Jr., was piped into the basement from above. As hymns began to play, the students settled in on the basement's benches. None of them were told what to expect.

Neither the students nor the observers knew who got the psychedelic and who got the placebo, but it was soon obvious. The nicotinic acid wore off, and students who had taken it sat listening attentively, whereas those on psilocybin lay down or wandered around the room, fixated on their visions. They recorded their experiences in Pahnke's extensive questionnaire immediately afterward, as well as a few days later and again six months after that. The psilocybin subjects, it turned out, experienced states and levels of consciousness that were indistinguishable from classic mystical experiences. The control group by and large did not.

As far as we were concerned, the experiment was a complete success. It laid to rest doubts about psychedelics as a vehicle for mystical insight. Although for us it was one experiment among many, it quickly became famous in psychological and religious circles. It was eventually even written up in the mainstream press—*Time* magazine ran a story called "Mysticism in the Lab"—and it stirred a public debate about whether a religious experience was valid if induced by chemical means as opposed to spiritual practice. The Good Friday Experiment, also known as the Miracle at Marsh Chapel, would turn out to be our most public project at Harvard, a landmark event of the Harvard Psychedelic Project that left a lasting perception of our work.

This isn't to say there wasn't pushback. Dave told our graduate students Ralph, Gunther, and George that they were not allowed to do their thesis research with psilocybin, and after the experiment, there were rumors that Walter Houston Clark would get fired from his seminary. Walter Pahnke got his PhD, but a few follow-up studies he had planned were canceled.

Still, to most of us in the Harvard Psychedelic Project, the conflicts over our drug supplies and methodology were mostly an annoyance. This was the dawn of the sixties, and we saw ourselves as part of the growing cultural push to move beyond the political status quo, sexual mores, social institutions, racial barriers, old concepts and limits. We took note of Harvard's strictures, but they didn't seem terribly consequential. We were inner explorers and revolutionaries. I was sure Harvard would catch up.

CHAPTER 9

HOTEL NIRVANA

With the spring semester drawing to a close, those of us in the Psychedelic Project pondered ways we might continue our research without so many administrative hurdles—if not with psilocybin, then at least with LSD. Tim and I came up with the idea of a summer session, but there was no way we could do that on campus. We remembered a little fishing village on the Pacific Ocean that we'd seen from my plane on our trip back from Mexico, a place called Zihuatanejo. It was lush, with gorgeous beaches. It could make the perfect set and setting.

Tim and I took a quick scouting trip in my airplane. We brought along Peggy Hitchcock, a young woman whom Tim had recently met in New York City. Peggy was a trust fund baby—her mother was an heir to the Mellon fortune—and she was excited to be a part of cutting-edge research by two Harvard professors. She was already familiar with mescaline, and we introduced her to psilocybin and LSD. I ran her first psilocybin session at my Harvard office. Peggy had an apartment on Park Avenue, which she allowed us to use for meetings and to run sessions for people in the city, including her ex-boyfriend, the saxophonist and heroin junkie Allen Eager. Just as often, she'd come to Cambridge to participate in our research sessions.

In Zihuatanejo, we found lush jungle and beautiful sunsets, as well as the eighteen-room Hotel Catalina, which was run by a grumpy Swiss man. Since the summer was rainy season and few people visited, he happily agreed to rent out the entire hotel to us. The brochure called the hotel a romantic hidden treasure in the sun. Tim would eventually call it Hotel Nirvana, the ultimate destination resort.

Soon, about thirty-five of us from the Psychedelic Project—professors, graduate students, friends, spouses—showed up to continue with our experimentation uninhibited. For six weeks, we set about our quest, which took on new depth in the warm tropic surf and the supportive embrace of fellow explorers. Group LSD sessions began in the morning, with a dose of 100 to 500 micrograms ingested by participating individuals; others agreed to serve as guides or ground control. The trips would usually last until late afternoon, and afterward we'd share observations and notes. Then we'd exchange roles as explorers or support team members.

Next to the ocean, surrounded by exotic flora, the hotel was a peaceful, sensual setting. We bonded together inside and on the grounds. It was like a psychedelic ashram. We were a tribe of adventurers, each pursuing his or her personal enlightenment but united in our search. We were explorers of the inner frontiers, the planes of consciousness. We were seekers of Truth.

Tim's kids, Susan and Jack, arrived as soon as school let out. I found myself taking care of the kids a lot, which I enjoyed. It was a peaceful summer, and the kids were happy. I was also sort of the operations guy, managing relations with Harvard from a distance and running our group's budget. I'd make bread in the hotel kitchen and keep a tab on supplies. This could lead to its own kind of adventures. One day, when we were running low on milk for the children, Tim and I decided to fly to Acapulco in the Cessna to stock up. Zihuatanejo had a small airstrip, and a certain Captain Gustos was in charge. He also ran the fuel concession. You had to buy your gas from him at whatever price he felt like charging.

Since Captain Gustos was so stingy, Tim took a giant jerrican with us in the back seat, so we could bring back some fuel along with the milk. We got down to Acapulco and loaded up; as we started to take off, the control tower radioed that our front wheel wasn't on the ground, because we had too much weight in the back. We took off anyway, and I started to light a joint. Tim glanced back at the full fuel tank in the seat behind us and said, "Maybe that's not such a good idea."

It was near sundown. At the time, you were not supposed to fly in the dark in Mexico, but we'd decided to anyway because we were smuggling in the gas and wanted to avoid Captain Gustos. Coming into Zihuatanejo, you had to land between two mountain ranges. We could not see them, and there were no lights at the Zihuatanejo airstrip, so I was pretty anxious. But I knew that there was kind of a V between the two lines of mountains, and if I could fly right between this V, we'd be fine. Somehow we managed it, and as soon as Gustos heard our plane land, he and his men came looking to see who the culprits were. I parked as quickly as I could, and Tim and I got out and hid. They didn't catch us. We got our gas and milk to the car. The kids were happy, and so were we.

I was too busy running operations to really help with one of the summer's other projects: an effort by Ralph and Tim to rewrite the *Tibetan Book of the Dead* into a psychedelic manual. Like me, Ralph had initially been so alarmed by Tim's reaction to LSD that he refused to try it. But in the relaxed atmosphere of Zihuatanejo, he asked Tim to guide him in a session. Ralph had been studying the Tibetan Buddhist model, and the two agreed to test the *Tibetan Book of the Dead* as the map we thought it might be. As Ralph began to hallucinate, he found himself alternating between beautiful, radiant experiences and fearful, ugly ones. He felt trapped by the scary imagery until he remembered the words in the book, which admonish the traveler to see both good and terrifying images for what they are, images in one's mind, and to let them pass by. Ralph came down from his trip buoyant. He said he felt freer than he ever had before.

I didn't do much of the writing, but I did supply data—descriptions of my trips that ran practically parallel to parts of the book—and lots of conversation. Even as we continued to collect reports and discuss ideas and theories late into the night, I was longing to return to home base. That home in the spiritual heart was still the only place where I felt completely at one. Eventually I would come to know it as the Atman.

My most meaningful trips happened when I took psychedelics on my own. So one night, I ingested LSD and went out in the ocean surf. The stars were all out, and the ocean was filled with phosphorescent sparks. I couldn't tell the stars from the phosphorescence or differentiate up from down.

As the waves washed over me, I became disoriented. The waves just kept coming in. I started to be afraid of dying. I was convinced I was going to drown in the ocean, and the repercussions of my death filled the whole universe. I would cease to exist. A vision came to me of a little girl, down the road in time, holding a picture of me up to her mother. She was asking, "Mommy, who is this man?" and her mother said, "I forget." Nobody would know. I would fall, disregarded, into the sea of time. I felt an abject sense of terror.

Luckily, I remembered to come up for air. When you took a trip on your own, you were supposed to have a ground-control person watching out for you. Emerging from the surf, though, I realized I could no longer see my person. My scout had gone off somewhere else and forgotten all about me.

I thrashed toward the shore and pulled myself onto the beach. I was lying there, panting, when two people found me and picked me up from the flotsam and the seaweed. Still in the intense grip of my near-death experience, I was babbling about how bad and how irresponsible we were, fooling around with this stuff. Tim came along, and I ran up to him, white-faced. I shook him and said, "This is dangerous. We've got to do something!" Nobody was taking me seriously, which made me furious. Tim said, "Calm down, you're just paranoid." He got me a cup of tea.

It was true. I was paranoid. Then I became afraid I was an embarrassment to the psychedelic movement. I'd almost gone too far. Tripping alone in the ocean at night was probably not the best strategy. I was always the one trying to keep it together, and my brush with annihilation had evoked my primal fear of death. It was a classic bad trip. Fear keeps you alive, but it also keeps you from letting go into your soul, your true inner self.

When the six weeks of our Zihuatanejo stay drew to an end, Tim organized a farewell baseball game with the locals. Timothy was a great fan of baseball, which was also the most popular sport in Zihuatanejo. Unbeknown to us, word in the village was that we were the Harvard University varsity squad. This brought out a big audience of villagers and farmers who wanted to see the athletes in action.

The Harvard team all took LSD before the game. I played the outfield, very far out. We had only a handful of good players, really. But owing to the temporal distortion of the acid, our team's sense of timing was greatly enhanced, and we started scoring run after run. The first baseman later described how the ball floated toward him in space, leaving plenty of time to swing the bat or get under it for a catch. He said the ball came to him in slow motion.

We did not intend to win. The whole idea of the baseball game was to generate a feeling of goodwill with the town, to end the summer on a high note (so to speak). Tim began switching out our average players for our mediocre ones, so that we lost our advantage. Finally, the Mexican team tied up the score, much to everyone's delight. Afterward we all celebrated in town together, partying into the night.

It was a wonderful ending to our psychedelic family vacation. The jungle, the ocean, and the bottle of LSD had all worked to unite us. Much like my experience as a boy at Willenrica, the proximity to nature and its beauty made me feel more comfortable in the universe. My terrifying near-death trip aside, I felt I'd advanced my spiritual journey. And through our group bonding, I'd felt my identity open more deeply to meeting others as souls.

We'd entered a timeless state together, an endless summer.

CHAPTER 10

NEWTON COMMUNE

hen we returned to Cambridge, wanting our endless summer to continue, we decided that we should all—professors, students, friends, family—move into one place together. We could live inexpensively and better as a group than as individuals. We were spending almost all of our time together anyway; moving into one house would allow us to concentrate on the explorations about ourselves and the values we shared. It only made sense.

Tim and I found a big green house at 23 Kenwood Avenue, in Newton Center. I signed the lease. I moved out of my antiques-filled apartment and joined Tim and Jack and Susan. We were followed by Ralph and his girlfriend, Susan Homer, whom he would marry that fall. Ralph was doing postdoctoral work on psychopharmacology at Harvard. The other house members included a young guy named Foster Dunlap, his wife, Barbara, and their son, Alexander, who was three or four at the time; Buster, a musician and street dealer; Michael Hollingshead and later his girlfriend; and a Wesleyan grad named Frank Ferguson, who was Tim's assistant. Peggy Hitchcock had a room in the house, and she would commute back and forth from New York City. There was also a guy who slept next to the furnace, whose mother was a sugar heiress. He was one of those people we collected who wanted to try psychedelics.

A few months later, Gunther Weil and George Litwin rented another home in Newton Center and set up a second household, along with their wives and a few others. Between the two houses, most of the Harvard

Psychedelic Project team lived together. Tim and I resumed teaching on campus and keeping tabs on the Concord Prison Experiment. We continued our research into LSD and DMT, running experiments at the house on language learning and problem solving. We also set about creating an "experiential typewriter," a contraption meant to help someone on a trip record his or her experiences in real time.

When I moved in, I brought along my antiques, but communal life proved pretty hard on them. When one got trashed, which happened frequently, it felt like a friend had died. Despite that, I discovered I liked group living. I helped take care of Tim's kids and made sure the cars ran. I took care of the finances and paid the bills. We were responsible Harvard professors, after all. I baked bread, as I had in Zihuatanejo, and everybody pitched in on maintenance and dishes and cutting the grass. We all cleaned.

Although it was a rented house, Tim decided we should make some changes. He wanted to enlarge the kitchen, so we started to take down a wall. Once we started knocking it down, we discovered it was load bearing and had some vital plumbing. So we had to leave it. The kitchen remained partially demolished thereafter. Demolition was easier than reconstruction for Tim—in retrospect, a side of his personality to which I should have paid more attention.

We also built an inner meditation room for psychedelic sessions that could only be accessed via a ladder from the basement, which meant visitors had no idea it was even there. The notion of the room was inspired in part by the writings of Hermann Hesse, which Tim and Ralph were reading and interpreting as coded accounts of psyche-delic explorations. The room had mattresses and pillows and Indian bedspreads. It was very quiet and peaceful, a place where you could shed the layers of outer activity and relax into the silence, entering the emptiness that Buddhists describe as *sunyata*. Someone was usu-ally tripping or meditating there, which made the room the center of consciousness of the house. It was the heart cave of the Newton commune. It was in that room that I had one of my first experiences in solo meditation.

One time I emerged from the basement still tripping on acid after a session in the room. Our musician friend Maynard Ferguson, who came by the house frequently, had hired a housekeeper for us. She was about fifty years old, and she'd come up from the South the day before by bus. She was sitting in the kitchen, drinking a cup of coffee, when I appeared from out of the basement. Taking one look at me, she screamed, threw her coffee cup aside, and came running to fall at my feet, yelling that she'd seen Christ. Seeing this solid, conservative-looking woman kneeling at my feet completely freaked me out; it quickly brought me down, and I fled into the next room. She told me later that when she'd seen me coming up the stairs, all she saw was radiant, golden light. I can't explain her experience, because she wasn't on any drug. I don't think her cooking was ever the same after that.

We continued to hold our Saturday sessions, as we'd done at Tim's old house. We had many visitors, familiar faces like Alan Watts, Aldous Huxley, Maynard and Flo Ferguson. There were new faces too: Robert Thurman, a Harvard grad who had recently been to India; the psychologist and dream researcher Stanley Krippner; anthropologist Jean Houston; Martin Orne, a hypnosis researcher; Paul Desmond, the saxophonist in the Dave Brubeck Quartet; visual artist Bruce Conner; and jazz pianist Charles Mingus.

For me, communal life made up for what I lacked not having my own nuclear family. In particular, it satisfied my craving for love. For all my cruising of parks and men's rooms, my desire was often more for intimacy than sex. I craved affection, and intercourse with lovers was in some ways an afterthought. What I wanted *more* was the interpersonal depth. Lust was a force, certainly, but what I was really seeking was love. My Newton family offered the kind of soul sharing and communion I was seeking. Later I came to call that level of sharing *satsang*, a community of seekers after truth.

My enjoyment of communal living lasted many years to come. At the time, I was particularly drawn to Foster, who was one of the smartest people any of us had ever met. He had been a psychiatric patient and struggled with schizophrenia, which none of us knew at the time. What we did know was that he was a hippie leader, which was rare at Harvard, and an independent, unusual thinker. Tim didn't like him, but I felt an attraction toward him and hired him as an assistant. At one point Foster threatened to burn the house, and we had to talk him down. He ultimately ended up in a mental hospital. Though we conceived of our living arrangement as a collaborative effort by a group of spiritual explorers, there were times when it also felt like a therapeutic community. In any case, the bonds were strong.

Psychedelics, especially psilocybin, brought a new depth to my sexual life. Because it opened up the soul level, I could connect with women and men alike in ways that went beyond the body, beyond physical drive. In particular, I could experience my bodily attraction to men as secondary. The side of me that cruised parks and impulsively outed myself to Farnsworth was converted to the intuitive, bonding nature these drugs brought forth.

I found the experience so profound that I wanted others to know it too. When I connected with young men, on campus or elsewhere, I'd offer to turn them on. We'd trip at the house, sometimes writing up reports as part of the research, sometimes just enjoying the social occasion. Because of the intimacy of the experience, I became less guarded. That got me into trouble.

The ties and connections we were forging in Newton stood in stark contrast to the ever-increasing suspicion and distrust we were experiencing from Harvard, even with our research psilocybin under tight control. Dave McClelland, for example, got into an angry argument in the fall of 1962 with Ralph, George, and Gunther about scientific methodology. They were trying to persuade him that one could be scientific about inner states. He got so frustrated that he told Ralph, "If you're thinking like that, we shouldn't have given you the PhD degree." Ralph said it was too late, they already had.

Meanwhile, the department committee that was to oversee our work decided that, because of the personal stash of psilocybin I'd refused to give up, it was impossible for them to establish proper control of the drugs. They decided there could be no more university support for our work unless we turned over everything. In response, Tim and I declared in October 1962 that we would separate our psychedelic research from Harvard. We agreed to return our university funds to the Department of Social Relations and announced that we were creating a nonprofit, the International Federation for Internal Freedom, to support psyche-delic work. Our board included Ralph, Gunther, George, Huston Smith, Rolf von Eckartsberg, Walter Houston Clark, Alan Watts, and Paul Lee, a student of Paul Tillich. We named Dr. W. Madison Presnell our medical director.

The Cuban missile crisis, which brought Americans and the Soviets to the brink of nuclear war, happened that same month. To us, our standoff with the Harvard administration felt equally charged. We had one final, symbolic confrontation with the university one Saturday night, when a last shipment of psilocybin was delivered to the Center for Research in Personality. Ralph was supposed to pick it up, and he was waiting in the office. Somehow, Brendan Maher, a professor who'd been openly hostile to us, had found out that we were getting this last shipment, and he sent an assistant to confiscate it from us. When the package arrived, Ralph and the assistant both lunged for it. They tussled, but Ralph was determined. He forced the assistant to let go, saying that the administration had no right to the package because it was addressed to us. He came back to Newton with a case of twenty bottles of psilocybin.

Our formal dissociation from Harvard did little to appease university officials, though. There were more and more reports around campus about students experimenting with consciousness-expanding drugs. Typically this had nothing to do with us; psychedelics had entered youth culture. Students could easily score mescaline or LSD on their own. Farnsworth and the university dean, John Monro, issued a statement warning undergraduates about the drugs' mind-distorting hazards. This caught the attention of the papers again, and before we knew it, our work was being called out on the front page of the *New York Times*. In the article, published in December 1962, Monro blamed "over-enthusiastic scientific experimenters" for promoting drugs on campus. He mentioned rumors of "private psilocybin parties" with students and "mail delivery of drugs" from Mexico.

Tim and I responded in the *Crimson*, decrying Harvard administrators for being hysterical and inaccurate. But the damage was done. The FDA declared that it was opening an investigation of illegal drug sales in Cambridge. Tim and I forged ahead, issuing a statement of purpose for the International Federation for Internal Freedom. Our idea was to create small research groups around the country with volunteers who wanted to explore consciousness. The research drugs would be supplied by IFIF ("If-if," as we called it), along with manuals on how to handle them. "We are fully aware that institutions, however libertarian their purpose, tend to restrict and inhibit the development of spiritual freedom," we declared in our statement. "They often end in external control of internal freedom. This danger we seek to avoid."

Our first attempt at procuring the drugs was unsuccessful. Maybe foolishly, we used Harvard letterhead to request psilocybin and a hundred grams of LSD from Sandoz, enough for one million doses. The lab checked with university officials, who blocked the order. So that was that. But we did open an office, publicize our mission, and announce plans to start a research magazine, the *Psychedelic Review. Life* magazine sent reporters and photographers to spend a few days with us and published a positive story titled "The Chemical Mind Changers." Tim wrote to Albert Hofmann, the developer of LSD, directly for supplies; he also made plans to hire our own chemists. I actively fundraised among our New York and Boston circles. One of our goals was to return to Zihuatanejo, replicating our experience there for a wider public. We announced that the IFIF summer training program would begin May 1.

Before long, we'd received hundreds of letters from people around the country asking for information—including my old acquaintances from Stanford, Vic Lovell and Ken Kesey, who by this time were hosting their own LSD parties in California. We organized maybe fifty research groups. Applications for the summer program rolled in, this time by the thousands. We could only accept a few hundred, so I got busy screening applicants.

We were charting an exciting course, succeeding despite our critics. This became all the more clear to us in February 1963, after our neighbors in Newton complained to the city council about our commune. They were upset by all the carrying on in the house, what with so many people and cars coming and going. Ours was a single-family residence, they said, in a neighborhood zoned for single-family homes, and our large group was in violation of code. This was well before communes had become widespread. The neighbors were also uptight because we had a black person, Buster, living with us, though that was never said publicly.

The Council of Aldermen of Newton held a public hearing on whether to evict us for violating the single-family residence rule. My father, who had returned to his law practice after the railroad's bankruptcy, came to our defense. Tim and I attended the hearing. Dad came out like Clarence Darrow, thumbs in the vest of his three-piece suit, gold watch chain swinging, former district attorney that he was. He argued that, even though we weren't all related, we still met the criteria of a single family, because we ate together, shared our finances, and cooked in the same kitchen. We were part of "the family of man." The aldermen couldn't argue with this definition. Dad won, and we stayed.

As the negative press, consternation from the administration and other faculty, and my amicable folly with Ronnie Winston moved inexorably to a crescendo, we remained wrapped in our work, largely oblivious. Tim continued planning for the next phase. I was shepherding students toward the semester's end.

I was unaware of the impending conclusion to my Harvard career right up to my confrontation with Nathan Pusey. Then, of course, it all shifted.

In retrospect it was inevitable. The protective reflex of the institution against radical change and the circling of academic wagons opposing the perceived subversion of the Harvard psychology establishment should have been apparent.

CHAPTER 11

THE CENTER
DOES NOT HOLD

ince leaving Harvard, Tim had been busy. Our idea for
Mexico was to create an international research center
where IFIF members could have psychedelic experiences,
continue with experiments, and train other guides. We
dubbed it the Psychedelic Training Center. Tim signed a
two-year lease on the Hotel Catalina and struck up relationships with various psychiatrists and chemists in California and
Mexico to involve them in our effort. Joseph J. Downing, a psychiatrist who was the director of the San Mateo County Mental Health
Department, agreed to attend the 1963 summer training program to
observe our sessions and make notes.

To my alarm, Tim also promoted our project to the media, reaching
out to reporters at CBS, *Time*, *Life*, *Newsweek*, and the *Saturday Evening
Post*. As it was, we were already attracting enough attention, not just
from federal agents but also from other national media outlets. The
press painted us as a drug cult. But as far as we were concerned, this
wasn't about getting high on some Mexican beach. We were serious
about the training, about creating the conditions for change and insight.

To transfer our work to Zihuatanejo permanently, the summer
program had to be a success. Ralph and Susan Metzner flew down to
Mexico to serve as guides during the first few weeks, followed by a few
others, like Gunther Weil and Frank Barron. I was to join them as soon
as I finished up our first issue of the *Psychedelic Review*, set to publish in
June. In Boston, I took care of Tim's kids, Susan and Jack, and managed

administrative details, screening and handling applicants who wanted to join our utopian experiment.

In Zihuatanejo, Ralph and Susan converted one of the hotel cabins into a dedicated session room. They decorated it with drapes and pillows and brought in candles and incense. There were about forty or so guests at the outset, which put Susan and Ralph on a very busy schedule. They led sessions with groups of three or four people every morning and evening. After a session, participants were required to wait three or four days before doing another, to prevent building a tolerance to the drugs. This meant that there were groups of people at the hotel all along the spectrum: orienting beforehand, in a session, or reintegrating afterward. For several days and nights, Ralph and Susan served as guides without interruption, catching naps when they could.

Tim guided some of the sessions as well, though a lot of his time was spent in Mexico City trying to make political connections to ensure the center's success. He and Ralph continued to collect notes for our psychedelic adaptation of the *Tibetan Book of the Dead*, and at one point, Tim came up with an idea. On the beach there was a beach hut on stilts, which served as a lifeguard tower. He proposed that every day, one member of the group would be tripping up in the tower, as a representative for everyone. The tower was visible from anywhere on the property, so they were always aware that there was someone in that high state. This gave every person a constant reference point for his or her own consciousness. Every day thereafter, we had a ceremony to install a person in the tower; the group later gathered to hear about the person's trip. It was a creative way of bringing together group consciousness.

The beach in general was a good backdrop for sessions. Ralph and Susan reported that the ocean served as an excellent tool for bringing someone through a difficult phase of an acid trip. If a person was struggling with fear or suspicion or frustration, they would help him or her to the water's edge, rolling their body in the sand and allowing the waves to wash over them. The experience of nature—the air, the surf, the sun, the sand—washed away the bad feelings.

The participants were happy, and Dr. Downing wrote up positive reports. He would later become one of the psychiatrists who pioneered the therapeutic use of the drug MDMA. Attendees were having such a productive time, in fact, that many of them wanted to extend their stay.

But this would soon prove impossible, and not for logistical reasons. Thanks to our notoriety in the papers, a few days after the retreat opened, a number of uninvited Americans began to show up in Zihuatanejo to get their own taste of consciousness. They camped outside the grounds of the Hotel Catalina and smoked marijuana, which, unlike psychedelics, was illegal. They had nothing to do with us, but rumors started flying. Shortly before IFIF's arrival, there was a murder in the area, and a local police chief told the Mexican newspapers that the gringos and their crazy drugs were responsible.

Tim's efforts in Mexico City did not go well. The previous summer, he had delivered a paper on our work to a meeting of psychiatrists, in which he mentioned opening our institute for psychedelic exploration. This was not well received, and a certain Dr. Dionisio Nieto from the National Autonomous University of Mexico began a campaign to have our work stopped. He'd had a bad mescaline trip, and he was critical of our quest. In retrospect, we should have involved Mexican psychiatrists in the project much earlier and hired Nieto as the resident psychiatrist.

Someone notified the health ministry of Mexico. American government agents were also keeping tabs on our activities. Although we were outside the jurisdiction of the US government, the CIA, the Justice Department, and the US ambassador to Mexico began pressuring local authorities, and finally the Mexican government decided to kick us out.

A couple of federales showed up at Zihuatanejo to explain to Tim that they were shutting down the program. Their stated reason was that we weren't allowed to run a business on tourist visas. Tim, Ralph, and the others packed up, buried their supply of psychedelics on the grounds of the hotel to avoid being stopped and searched, and headed to Mexico City to regroup.

The program had lasted for all of six weeks. I was in Boston the whole time. As I tried to make sense of these events from a distance, I received a call. On the line was a political friend of Peggy Hitchcock's, a man in Boston who was in the waste-handling business. The unceremonious end to our program had already made the news. "I think it's terrible what they're doing to Tim," the man told me. I said I was planning to go to Mexico to help salvage the situation. "If I put up money for your plane ticket," he replied, "can I go too?"

So he and I traveled together, flying first to Miami, on Eastern Air Lines. I'd packed a glass bottle of liquid LSD in my suitcase, but with the others all being watched as suspects, I didn't want to let on to my companion. Besides, this man and I didn't really know each other. In Miami, the two of us were sitting on the airplane, looking out the window, when the bags began to be unloaded. The baggage handler was violently throwing the luggage around. Suddenly, I noticed that the next bag down the ramp was mine. My heart sank. The bottle of LSD! But what was I going to say?

Of course, the bottle broke, and I discovered when we arrived in Mexico and I opened my suitcase that the LSD had been absorbed into my white silk suit. Later, we cut up the suit into little pieces and ate them to save the doses.

In Mexico City, we had a long discussion about our situation. The group was tired and feeling battered from all the harassment, but we also had the program to think of. Several hundred people had signed up for the summer training and had already sent in deposits. Given the positive results so far, we wanted to continue. We agreed to try to relocate. Tim had received an invitation from an American on the island of Dominica in the Caribbean. Tim and a few of the others went off to Dominica while Ralph and I stayed behind to organize logistics. For our new base of operations, I shipped a Land Rover, food, and other supplies to Dominica. We also shipped a hundred-pound bag of Heavenly Blue morning glory seeds, which were to be our LSD substitute for the summer program.

When I bought the bag from the seed wholesaler, he reported it to the government. An FBI agent came to visit us. I said, "I just love morning glories." They weren't illegal, so there wasn't much he could do. One seed was about the equivalent of one microgram of LSD, so a threshold dose was anywhere between sixty and one hundred seeds. They never really worked all that well for an acid trip. They tasted terrible, and the alkaloids in the seed coat made you thoroughly sick before you got high.

Ralph and I took a plane to join the others. To get to Dominica, you have to fly to Antigua first. On our layover, I went to the beach for a swim. To my surprise, I saw Tim and the others walking toward me on the beach. The group had been thrown out of Dominica the day before. The island politicians had assured Tim that IFIF was welcome—they wanted the tourism—but they failed to mention that political infighting was roiling their government. Their opponents, under pressure from American authorities, accused Tim of heroin trafficking. He'd had to flee under imminent threat of arrest. It was a mess.

I was shocked—and angry. I'd already shipped everything to Dominica. I'd spent months fundraising, even selling some antiques and my motorcycle to help. I'd given Tim money to use with government officials, to grease the wheels. But in Mexico he'd spent that money on a speedboat. Now here he was, getting us kicked out of another country. We got into a big fight on the beach. At the time, I felt like he was the irresponsible one. But in retrospect, I was too.

As long as we were in Antigua, we thought we might as well stay. I arranged for all our stuff to be redirected, and we looked for a place to set up operations. There weren't any big houses we could afford, so we ended up renting an abandoned nightclub called the Bucket of Blood, near the beach. We knew we had to win over Antigua's government officials and its medical establishment, so we hosted cocktail parties every day. The island's psychiatrists all came to check us out. The head doctor was an expert in lobotomies, which of course I knew something about.

We ran some LSD sessions among ourselves and continued rewriting parts of the *Tibetan Book of the Dead*, but the questions over our future were making us all feel anxious and listless. One day Frank Ferguson, high on LSD, decided the only way out of the uncertainty was to sacrifice himself for our cause. He walked to the office of the lobotomy doctor and, standing there in his bathing suit, demanded a lobotomy.

In Frank's mind, he was offering himself as the bridge between our group and Antigua's authorities. The doctor threw him out of the office and reported the incident to the island's medical board, whose approval we were waiting on. Needless to say, the board gave us a thumbs-down, and we were asked to leave Antigua.

We were back to square one.

We were now about $50,000 in debt. Back in Newton, we glumly discussed what to do next. Our psychedelic training center seemed permanently doomed.

Then Peggy had an idea. Her twin brothers, Tommy and Billy Hitchcock, had just turned twenty-one and come into their inheritances. They'd bought a big estate in Dutchess County, New York, as a tax shelter. The property—twenty-five hundred acres outside the town of Millbrook—had a huge mansion on it that her brothers weren't going to use. Maybe, she suggested, they'd let us move there.

Peggy and I were good friends by this point. I'd taken her in the Cessna to visit my folks at Willenrica, where we landed on Dad's three-hole golf course. We'd also flown to visit her family on Long Island, where they held polo matches on the Mellon estate. Peggy and I had also flown to her mother's island in Canada, where a chauffeur took us to a private lake to fish. Peggy sometimes brought her little white dog in the back seat of the Cessna, and every time we hit an air pocket, the dog would go airborne.

So we had some shared history, and I immediately understood the potential of what Peggy was proposing. She and I got in the car and drove up to Millbrook to take a look at the mansion, which everyone called the Castle. It was a big, ornate manor house that a gas-lamp magnate had built in the late 1800s. It had four stories, with towers and turrets on the outside and a wraparound porch. By the time Peggy and I got there, it was evening. We explored the old mansion by candlelight. Going from room to room, we saw fireplaces, intricate woodwork, tapestries on the walls. We decided the house was perfect.

Peggy suggested that I guide a psychedelic session for each of her brothers, and then they'd agree to let us move in. Billy was a stockbroker. He was on vacation in Acapulco at the time, so I flew to see him. I gave psilocybin to him and his South American girlfriend in a swimming pool. Tommy, a race car driver, had visited us in Zihuatanejo, so he already knew what we were about. He and I had had a deep trip there. The Hitchcock twins agreed to rent the mansion to us for a dollar a year.

We packed up our shared house and took off for Millbrook. Most of us making the move were part of the Newton commune: me and Tim, his kids, Ralph and Susan, Foster and Barbara Dunlap and their son. Frank Ferguson and his wife, Lora, came for a short while; Michael Hollingshead also joined us. There was a clinical psychologist who'd attended the training in Zihuatanejo, Gary Fisher, who came with his wife and children too, but they left after a month or so. He was interested in the therapeutic effects of psychedelics on schizophrenia and autism. Peggy moved in as well, though she also kept her apartment in New York. By this time, she and Tim had become on-again, off-again lovers.

The estate wasn't a tropical utopia, but it was a nature paradise. There were vast meadows, lush pine forests, and fields of corn and sunflowers. There was a lake for swimming, a waterfall, and a creek with beautiful stone bridges. There were apple orchards, and paths through the woods, and some livestock, and horse stables. The property also featured several other residences, like a two-story chalet that contained a bowling alley and a house we called the Cottage, which featured lots of marble and a swimming pool. The Hitchcock brothers used the Cottage as their getaway, throwing parties there for their rich friends from New York. They loved having us around, their strange and unusual friends, and would show us off as their pet project.

The Castle, which we began to call the Big House, had ten bathrooms, and its sixty-plus rooms included a kitchen, a dining room, several living rooms, and a library. About ten of us were in residence most of the time; on weekends we'd host half a dozen guests. There was another residence, called the Gate House, that Maynard and Flo Ferguson moved into with their four children later that fall. Flo became a central player in the Millbrook scene; she was sort of a mother to many of us. She was a strong woman—classy, adventurous, social— and was often sarcastic in our communal meetings. Flo was the one behind Maynard's music career; she held together their circle of musician and artist friends.

In contrast to the hangers-on we'd attracted in Zihuatanejo, we were back to being an intimate circle, glad to finally continue our research. As in Newton, we continued our family sessions, sometimes taking LSD together by the fireplace while we played music recordings. Mostly, though, we did individual sessions, taking turns as guides.

It was sedate and introspective, with careful dosages. We were often joined by other friends and colleagues from the Harvard Psychedelic Project, who drove up from Cambridge to participate in discussions and reports. Aldous Huxley came for a visit too, though briefly; by this time he had returned to California, and he was weak from cancer. He liked what he saw at Millbrook, though.

We designed experiments in living and came up with different frameworks to test our interpersonal dynamics. We liked going outside for sessions—we had a couple of favorite hills—but we also made use of the other buildings. One experiment involved two people sequestered for a week in the bowling alley house, to see how tripping together affected them and the rest of the community. Another effort put different couples on the third floor of the Big House, to see how they negotiated their sexual jealousy. Yet another experiment was a variation on the lifeguard tower in Zihuatanejo: every week, we designated one person to trip for all of us in a building we called the Meditation House. Unlike the other experiments, this one was more about inner spiritual growth. When the week was over, we would parade over together from the Big House to hear what insights the person had returned with.

Tim insisted on keeping notes and records of all the sessions. We designed forms to record a person's journey, trying to develop specific metrics for bliss and other moods. As we continued rewriting the *Tibetan Book of the Dead*, we wanted as much data to work with as possible, to see how closely a psychedelic trip matched the soul's journey through the bardo, in between death and rebirth. Tim, Ralph, and I continued to write and edit the *Psychedelic Review*, which Ralph largely oversaw, going to Cambridge to get it printed.

Our reputation and the attention of the press was such that our doings at Millbrook attracted the curious. Ralph and Tim and I often found ourselves giving talks on consciousness to visitors. If someone really wanted, we guided a trip, but we did not administer psychedelics to outsiders except occasionally. When we did, we interviewed the person first, with a questionnaire designed to cement a loving relationship with the guide. We were committed to creating a supportive set and setting. Sometimes I'd make a participant wait a few days, to get him or her into a more conducive mindset for a trip. Afterward, we did postsession debriefings.

Allen Atwell, a painter who taught art at Cornell University and had studied Indian tantric traditions, was one visitor who came for a session. His guide was Ralph. He spent almost his entire trip laughing. Allen later painted the famous mural of the Nepali eyes on the outside of the Big House. Other visitors included a mix of psychology, literary, and arts people, such as the psychiatrist R. D. Laing, the futurist author Robert Anton Wilson, and the arts publisher Felix Morrow.

Peggy invited the famous jazz bassist Charlie Mingus, who came up from New York in his sports car and played out in the orchard, because he didn't want to perform with all the white folks around. He ended up staying for a while and helped prune the fruit trees. He and I bonded over the social ostracism we'd both faced—he because of the color of his skin, me because of my sexuality.

About an hour from Millbrook, there was an experimental art collective called USCO, cofounded by poet Gerd Stern, artist Steve Durkee, and audio technician Michael Callahan. Stewart Brand, a Stanford biologist who would later go on to start the *Whole Earth Catalog*, was also friends with the USCO crew. We met Stern while still at Harvard; he was friends with Allen Ginsberg. But in an even more curious connection, Steve Durkee had married my old friend and Stanford student Barbara Greer.

Barbara arranged for us all to meet, and the USCO artists often came to Millbrook. We'd sit around and dream up ways of translating the psychedelic experience into sounds and images. Steve Durkee helped us turn the maids' quarters in a wing of the Big House into meditation rooms, painting beautiful, bright spiritual murals in each room.

On the freezing-cold night of November 22, 1963, we got word that President John F. Kennedy had been assassinated. There was snow on the ground, and all of us stopped what we were doing, caught in the silence of the night. We turned on the TV and watched the newscasts over and over. Soon afterward, we learned that Aldous Huxley had died on the same night. The loss of our great friend and mentor at the same time as our president felt like a profound synchronicity. I took comfort that Aldous's wife, Laura, with whom I'd grown close, had been at his bedside. At his request, she administered LSD as he drew his last breaths.

"Concentrate on the light," she instructed. Knowing Aldous, he had.

———————

We felt as though we could transform society. We were an eclectic group of people with a higher vision for living, interacting, and problem solving with the help of a greater consciousness. Intuitively we were communal. We cultivated vegetable and flower gardens; we shared chores and babysitting. We were kind of hard on the Castle—we played football inside and kept cats and dogs and a monkey—but for the most part, communal life went pretty smoothly. I had an aardvark named Arty, who used to nestle into me, his snout in my armpit. I baked bread as usual, maintained an eye on Jack and Susan, kept the cars running, and helped manage the bills.

There wasn't a lot of money coming in. Tim and I gave some college lectures and presented at a couple of conferences, but we needed to generate more income. We decided to rebrand our efforts, abandoning the name IFIF to create the Castalia Foundation, a new organization by which we could support ourselves. The name came from Hermann Hesse's book *The Glass Bead Game*, which features a community of seekers in a fictional place called Castalia.

We decided to turn our informal talks for visitors into weekend workshops. These Castalia Foundation seminars launched at a fee of seventy-five dollars per participant. The seminars didn't include psychedelics; the idea was to equip attendees with the tools for an acid trip without being suppliers. We didn't have enough LSD to share with the public, and anyway, we didn't want the kind of sensationalism that had plagued us in Zihuatanejo.

We'd show workshop attendees how to run a session and how to create a good set and setting. We used slides, music, candles, incense. Our aim was to teach about the spiritual journey, so we covered other areas of interest too: meditation, Gestalt therapy, Sufism, exercises in self-awareness inspired by the mystic G. I. Gurdjieff, hatha yoga, tantra, and even karate. Sometimes we'd color the food in the dining room—the butter green, the milk blue—or play auditory tricks, with a microphone or a gong, to challenge people's expectations. One of our workshop participants, I remember, was Khigh Dhiegh, an American TV and movie actor who introduced us to the *I Ching*, the ancient Chinese divination text.

The seminars helped structure our weekends and gave us a way to handle visitors, who were now coming by the droves, particularly from New York. Van Wolf, the art impresario and talent agent we'd met through Peggy, was always bringing guests from the fashion world: models, photographers, other agents. Word was out that Millbrook was a good place to party on the weekends, and it didn't matter that we didn't share our drugs; visitors brought their own.

As the months went by, we continued guiding sessions for individuals, especially for people who could help us financially. Saul Steinberg, the beloved *New Yorker* cartoonist, came at one point, as did trumpeter Miles Davis, then at the forefront of innovations in jazz. Even Ralph's mother came to visit us; he guided her on a trip that she really enjoyed.

Some friends from my California days also paid us a visit. Ken Kesey, after participating in the government-sponsored drug tests while a student at Stanford, had published his novel about psychiatric patients, *One Flew Over the Cuckoo's Nest*, to widespread acclaim. He'd also been cultivating fame of another kind, forming a commune of his own with former Stanford colleagues, bohemians, and literary figures. Together they'd been freely experimenting with drugs, throwing parties and sharing LSD with anyone interested. In June 1964, after the publication of his second novel, *Sometimes a Great Notion*, Kesey and his Merry Pranksters decided to take a cross-country trip in their rainbow-colored bus, which they christened *Further*. They decided to stop in at Millbrook.

They arrived in July, with the expectation of a grand meeting: East Coast and West Coast, a convergence of our experimental communities. But they didn't tell us they were coming, and when their bus pulled up on a Sunday, honking and blaring music, we were not ready for a raucous party. We had just finished a family psychedelic session the night before, and we were all very tired. Tim wouldn't come down from his room—he said later he had the flu—so it was up to me, Ralph, and Susan to serve as the welcoming committee.

Allen Ginsberg, back from India, was also on the bus; he'd boarded in New York to help lead the Pranksters to Millbrook. It seemed to us that the Pranksters were on speed. They were all jumpy, especially the driver, Neal Cassady, the model for the Dean Moriarty character in Jack Kerouac's *On the Road*. There was also a young Stanford philosophy professor on board, Jane Burton, who happened to be pregnant. A former girlfriend of Kesey's named Dorothy, who would go on to marry my student Jim Fadiman and become an award-winning filmmaker, had arrived at Millbrook a few weeks earlier, and she was as surprised to see them as we were.

Kesey and his Merry Pranksters thought we were inhospitable and arrogant, but it was just bad timing: the Millbrook crew wanted to go to bed. It's true we had philosophical and stylistic differences. The Prankster approach was to get as high as possible and see what happened; we were committed to inquiry, inner exploration, and set and setting. They were the wild, let-everything-fly, party-down division of the psychedelic movement; we were the buttoned-up researchers. Tim would famously change course, becoming the psychedelic Pied Piper. But at the time, he felt strongly about limiting LSD, considering it a sacrament not to be sullied by indiscriminate use.

Tim, Ralph, and I threw our energies into putting the finishing touches on our psychedelic manual. We asked Alan Watts, who by this time was living on a houseboat in Sausalito, California, to read the proofs. He declared it to be a rare psychiatry book that attempted to classify the states of consciousness. That August, our guide for how to use mind-expanding drugs was published as *The Psychedelic Experience: A Manual Based on the Tibetan Book of the Dead*. We dedicated it to Aldous Huxley. The first printing sold out so quickly, the publisher had to print several more runs. We had a best seller.

The broad reach of the book made us realize that even though we no longer occupied an intellectual perch at the apex of academia, we were at the cutting edge of a much greater paradigm shift. Psychedelics were expanding the consciousness of not just a few researchers and their subjects, but a great swath of American culture.

CHAPTER 12

MILLBROOK MORPHS

W hen we first moved to Millbrook, I towed a U-Haul full of furniture, rugs, and all kinds of household stuff from Newton. Foster Dunlap, our resident Harvard hippie student leader, came with me, because he wanted a ride to Freewood Acres, New Jersey, where he planned to visit Geshe Wangyal.

Geshe Wangyal was a Mongolian Buddhist priest and teacher who had arrived in the US in the mid-1950s after fleeing Tibet; afterward he also helped bring over the Dalai Lama. One of the first Tibetan lamas in America, Geshe Wangyal had founded a monastery in Freewood Acres. Bob Thurman, then a Harvard PhD student who dropped in on our house in Newton from time to time, had become his student. He convinced Foster, with whom he was good friends, that studying with Geshe Wangyal would further his spiritual work. I decided I'd visit too.

Geshe Wangyal was the first Tibetan Buddhist I'd ever encountered. A diminutive older man, he lived in a small community of Mongolians in the neighborhood, and he served as their lama. In years to come, he would develop a reputation for being wild and temperamental, but I found him sweet and peaceful. We sat and had tea. Later, I would have called our visit a darshan, a spiritual encounter. Wangyal made such a deep impression on me that I wanted to give him things. I told him he could have anything in our U-Haul. One of his students chose a blue rug that had been in my bedroom in Newton to put in their chapel. If they'd known the things I had done on that rug!

The lama gave me a beautiful silk robe he wore when he fled from Tibet. I kept the robe for a long time afterward, wrapping myself in it to meditate. I wore the robe in the meditation tower at Millbrook, a cupola we painted gold inside. I'd sit in my Tibetan robe, surrounded by golden light, and think I was getting messages.

I was taken with Geshe Wangyal in part because, as psychedelic explorers, Tim and I and the others were increasingly convinced that the answers to our quest lay somewhere in the East. The *Tibetan Book of the Dead* had offered us an initial map, but many of the other works we were reading—Hermann Hesse's books, the Tao Te Ching, the Bhagavad Gita, *In Search of the Miraculous*, P. D. Ouspensky's exposition of Gurdjieff's teaching—also prompted the notion of a journey to the East. While Tim and I were busy getting kicked out of Harvard, Allen Ginsberg, on his trip to India, had met the Dalai Lama and discussed consciousness with various swamis and gurus, including Dudjom Rinpoche and Swami Sivananda. He'd returned with a new sense of creative and spiritual energy, which we saw when he came to Millbrook afterward.

At Millbrook, we were dabbling in yoga and chanting, and sometimes I'd even do readings from the writings of Meher Baba, an Indian spiritual teacher who had visited the US. But we didn't fully understand these things. So when Ralph was invited to go to India with Gayatri Devi, the leader of two Ramakrishna ashrams, in the fall of 1964, we all agreed he should accept. Devi was going to India to set up an ashram in Bengal for her thousands of followers, and this would give Ralph a front-row view into Indian religious culture. He would study yoga and consult with Hindu and Buddhist teachers about psychedelics as aids to meditation. We thought of it as research for the Castalia Foundation.

Tim wanted to go to India too, but he and I had a busy lecture schedule. Thanks to our seminars and *The Psychedelic Experience*, we were becoming popular speakers, which was a good way to raise money for Castalia. That fall, as Ralph wrote us letters about his adventures and insights (after his time with Devi, he went to the village of Almora to learn from the Buddhist scholar Lama Anagarika Govinda), Tim and I spent a lot of time traveling, lecturing to standing-room-only crowds in San Francisco, Big Sur, Monterey, Palo Alto, New York, and even Minnesota.

Tim had another interest too: Nena von Schlebrugge, a beautiful fashion model who grew up in Sweden and with whom he'd fallen passionately in love. The daughter of a German baron, she'd arrived at Millbrook for a Fourth of July party. At the time, she was the face of Winston cigarettes, and her picture was on all the New York City buses. After taking LSD with Tim, they quickly got engaged. In a way, this was in keeping with how we did life at Millbrook. Relationships were constantly being dissolved and reforged: Peggy Hitchcock had moved on from Tim; and Ralph and Susan's marriage had also come apart. Susan took up with a photographer in New York; Ralph fell in love with a friend of Nena's. The only relationship that didn't seem to change was Maynard and Flo Ferguson's.

Nena traveled with Tim to California, and the two of them decided to get married at Millbrook that winter. In December, at their wedding, I served as Tim's best man. It was a fairy-tale affair, with lots of big-name guests from New York, like the photographer Diane Arbus and Monti Rock III, a celebrity hairdresser. Charlie Mingus played the music. There was a huge feast—roasted pig, salmon, ham, salads—and champagne. The reception punch was spiked with LSD.

For their honeymoon, they decided to combine their interest in each other and the East, settling on a monthslong tour of India. Leaving Jack and Susan to my care, they made plans to meet up with Ralph and explore both consciousness and love.

Tim and Ralph had been committed to our scientific research, convinced as ever that psychedelics could be used for social science and to advance creativity in the culture. All the data was especially important to Tim; even the musicians he invited to Millbrook had to write reports on their reactions and how their art changed. Ralph, too, was constantly making notes about what was going on with our subjects.

I wanted to let participants be creative in whatever form they wanted. I cared less about the power of psychedelics to transform the intellect and more about their ability to transform relationships. I was still filled with longing, still on the search to return to that home in the heart I'd discovered—the Atman—and social psychology was not taking me deep enough. Each time I guided a session, taking a psychedelic with participants, I didn't want to just collect an interesting report. I wanted to connect at the spiritual level. I wanted to guide people toward that soul place in themselves.

That's what psychedelics had done for me. They'd helped me understand love and compassion in ways I never had before. They also helped me explore my sexuality, my *human-ness*. In a way, psilocybin and LSD gave me license to be who I was. With psychedelics, I could look at myself honestly, inside and out, and accept what I saw. I could say, "What you are is okay." I didn't have to hide.

Millbrook had a live-and-let-live atmosphere, but my interest in men could make people I cared about uncomfortable, like Tim. I'd wondered sometimes if psychedelics might be a tool that could help me make sense of my attractions, taking me deep enough to uncover their roots. Psychedelics did give me primal insights into my sexuality, but my innate bisexual orientation remained, and my sense of shame, ambivalence, and inadequacy around sex stubbornly returned each time I came down from a trip and reentered my personality.

Eventually, I realized that what I *really* wanted was to go beyond myself. I wanted to reach a place of ever-higher consciousness more often and more deeply—that place where definitions and differences didn't matter, because I was connecting with others as souls. I aspired to the expansion of the heart, not just the mind. I wanted to get to the source of enduring love.

That's what I was looking for when I devised a new research project, an effort we eventually called the "Bowling Alley experiment." Together with Michael Hollingshead and a sharp, offbeat photographer named Arnie Hendin, who was always coming up with ways to shatter people's expectations, I came up with an idea: what would happen if we stayed high for an extended time? It was my own version of social science. I wanted to see whether, if we took LSD continuously over a given period, we could come as a group to a place of lasting unity and harmony.

Six of us, men and women, agreed to give it a try. We all moved into the house with the bowling alley, and for two weeks straight, we each took a large dose of LSD, 400 micrograms, every four hours. I was the guide, and I kept notes on how people were relating to one another. My goal was to observe what social dynamics developed. I hoped to see our competing egos dissolve into a state of shared consciousness. Maybe a group creativity would emerge.

As it turned out, I had a very optimistic view. At first, we were happy to be together. It was fun. We all felt we had entered into a joyful state together. But after a week, the stress of living in a confined space began to dominate. We all developed a tolerance to the LSD and stopped reaching a higher consciousness. We began to fall back into our egos—and all of us had strong egos to begin with. Our edges began to fray, and we fought like hell. Love was the goal, but interpersonal friction and ragged egos won.

The more trips I guided, following a person's consciousness into other realms, the more the progression became familiar: going beyond personality and into other states, then reintegrating back into form. I kept looking for ways to maintain and stabilize the insights of those other planes and to go ever deeper.

Besides yoga, we experimented with other practices. At one point, I traveled to Boston to study with Michio Kushi, the Japanese teacher of macrobiotics. About half of us at Millbrook radically changed our diet for a month or two. Macrobiotics were a good balance to psychedelics. In macrobiotic terms, the drugs are very yin (very spacey), and the whole grains and veggies of the macro diet are yang (solid and grounding). The diet helped balance our forays into other worlds.

In general, though, my answer to everything—including a serious bout with the flu—was to take LSD. I wanted to stay high, to get through my ego. To help fill Millbook's coffers, I continued turning on rich people. I also did fundraising gigs at artistic venues in New York. Some were in partnership with our USCO friends; I would lecture, and they would accompany with a psychedelic light show. In the spring of 1965, we put together one really big show, with slides and multimedia, at the Village Vanguard jazz club in Greenwich Village. Alan Watts, Charlie Mingus, and Michael Hollingshead participated. I was the master of ceremonies. I sat on a stool and told funny stories about growing up and being at Harvard. People found me so entertaining, and the show was such a success, that the owner invited me to come back as a performer.

The club had local talent perform onstage one night a week. I did a few appearances as a stand-up comic, wearing a fedora. One night, I even opened for Miles Davis, talking to the audience about the new psychedelic era as a strobe light flashed in the background.

My sense of ease onstage went back to the family music evenings we hosted for charity in our barn at Willenrica, when I was emcee. As a teaching assistant and a professor, I'd learned the value of humor. It was one reason I was popular as a teacher. Even now, in my spiritual talks, I rely on humor, because it brings lightness to the journey. Humor illuminates the paradox of the infinite Spirit fitting into this all-too-human form.

I enjoyed running Millbrook in Tim and Ralph's absence. I was surrounded by a cast of imaginative, experimental, and artistic friends. But there was trouble brewing. Certain personalities, like Michael Hollingshead and Arnie Hendon, were manipulative and disruptive, and within our commune, not everyone agreed with my insatiable quest to stay high for greater understanding. Divisions started to erupt: about who was maintaining order, who was doing the dishes, who was advancing our understanding of consciousness. Our sense of shared exploration and openness, once easy, became elusive.

As my world at Millbrook was starting to show fissures, my brother Leonard's was collapsing entirely. Struggling with emotional stability, he entered a delusionary world that eventually landed him in a mental hospital.

After his marriage to Sylvia Ehrman and the birth of their three daughters—Kathy, Liz, and Cindy—Leonard had enjoyed family life and creativity. He'd bought a house in the suburbs outside Boston and embraced both domesticity and work. He ran the law office when Dad took over the railroad, and cultivated orchids in a little greenhouse off the living room. He constructed a light organ that, when he played music, lit up a waterfall in the backyard with colors corresponding to the notes.

Len cared deeply about his wife and daughters, but he was unhappy. At the law office, he hired an Irish guy who became his lover. Len justified his hire to Dad—the guy was politically connected—but they were actually making it on the conference table. He and Sylvia remained friendly, but the marriage crumbled. He wanted the freedom to have gay relationships. Sylvia was understanding but insisted he move out. They divorced in November 1963, and he moved to a hotel on Harvard Square, where he knew he could pick up guys.

Leonard's emotional stability deteriorated. He began to act out. He got a big house, then rented a truck and removed Dad's choice antiques that had come from our grandfather into his own house. Len had a lot of suppressed anger toward Dad, and he did this to get back at him. Knowing Leonard had the antiques goaded Dad to go to Leonard's house. He found Leonard sitting naked in the middle of a circle of women, burning money.

A high being like Leonard can use the power of his will to go deeper into his soul, or he can lose himself in delusions of power and paranoia, as Leonard did. The combination of his anger at Dad, his secret homo-sexuality, and his desire for money and power sent him off the rails. He was searching for love, but he came at it from his ego, and his life, much like Dad's and mine, revolved around power.

Drugs, first psychedelics and later heroin, aggravated his delusions. Before Tim left for India, Leonard came to visit Millbrook. He was so unstable that he demanded Tim touch his feet. He'd listened to me talk about my exploration of the heart, and in his delusion would mimic me, trying to appropriate a sense of spiritual power for himself. Some of my Millbrook friends went to his house and gave him psychedelics. They thought they were doing me a favor! But the drugs just trapped him more in astral planes, the imaginary worlds of ego fantasies.

Eventually, Len was arrested for stealing a car. He thought he was Christ, and, well, Christ needed the car. Dad still had an inside track with the authorities from being an assistant district attorney, and he bailed Leonard out. He cut a deal so that Leonard would go to a mental hospital instead of prison. Committing his son was really hard for Dad, but it was the only way to keep him out of jail. First he had him sent to a country club hospital outside Boston. Later he was transferred to Boston Psychopathic Hospital, where I had interned years before.

I visited the hospital with friends from Millbrook, thinking to spring Leonard, but the authorities wouldn't let him go. For a long time, I felt responsible for my brother. Because of his instability and underlying mental illness, Len imitated what I was doing and took it to extremes: he emulated my psychedelic explorations, then developed a heroin addiction. I felt guilty that I had influenced his drug taking and maybe even his homosexuality. It took me a long time to comprehend that Leonard had influenced me too. Close as we were, these issues remained unspoken and unresolved for the rest of our lives.

When Ralph came back from India in the spring of 1965, followed several weeks later by Tim, both were dismayed by the scene at Millbrook. The new residents I had invited rubbed them the wrong way. They viewed the discord and disorganization within the group as a result of my irresponsibility. They thought I had allowed our research community to stray from its mission and felt I'd created a drug commune with all kinds of hangers-on. It wasn't how I saw it, but I didn't disagree.

They did like the idea of the psychedelic theater performances we'd been putting on with USCO, and in June, we set up a regular Monday-night multimedia series called *Psychedelic Explorations* at the New Theatre, on East 54th Street in Manhattan. The shows included lectures, improvisations, discussions, performances by the Castalia Foundation and USCO, and an informal question-and-answer time at the end. Tim found my nightclub comic routine ridiculous. After coming to see me one night, he declared, "This is absurd!" I didn't perform again after that.

Things grew increasingly strained. Millbrook divided loosely into two camps: those who wanted to stay high and those who wanted a sense of working order. We in the first camp moved into the Bowling Alley, where we could maintain a high state of consciousness as a closed experiment, while the others remained at the Big House. To help heal the rifts and rebuild the community, Tim and Ralph declared they were limiting the number of people who could now join Millbrook.

Meanwhile, in India, Tim and Nena, the newlyweds, were having their own troubles. They'd joined Ralph in Almora and visited the Taj Mahal, tripping on the grounds under the moonlight, deeply moved by the monument built by an emperor to remember his beloved wife. But things grew edgy between them, and when they returned to Millbrook, they were fighting. Peggy Hitchcock married a doctor soon after their return, and we all attended the wedding. That hardly helped.

Tim confided his problems to me, and I proposed the perfect solution: a joint LSD session with the three of us. It was a really bad idea. In our heightened state, we turned on one another, and the rifts grew deeper. Tim's relationship with Nena didn't survive. They divorced that same year.

Tim went on to meet Rosemary Woodruff, a model and actress who moved into the Big House and became his partner. Nena, for her part, got together with Bob Thurman, who by this time was an advanced student of Geshe Wangyal and had been ordained as the first American Tibetan Buddhist monk. He'd taken on the name Tenzing. The two met the same week Tim and Nena were signing their divorce papers. They married in 1967 and pulled away from Millbrook. Bob gave up his monastic status, attended graduate school at Harvard, and eventually became a professor of Asian studies at Columbia University. He is now a noted scholar of Tibetan Buddhism. Bob and Nena have four children, one of whom is the actress Uma Thurman. Nena became the founding administrator for Tibet House in New York, which their son Ganden now runs, and she and Bob run the Menla Buddhist retreat in upstate New York.

In June 1965, I took a vacation from the chaos at Millbrook to the south of France, where I'd been invited to run some sessions. Afterward, I took a side trip to Switzerland, where I had lunch with Albert Hofmann, the revered Sandoz Pharmaceuticals chemist who synthesized LSD and psilocybin. We talked about Tim's love of provocation and the public eye, and LSD as a sacrament. Hofmann had an exalted view of LSD— he'd taken a sublime trip with his wife among the flowers of an alpine meadow. I felt he understood my desire to journey to the edge. This was helpful once I returned to the US in the fall.

The division between the two camps at Millbrook was untenable in the long term. Tim and Ralph continued the psychedelic shows while I was in Europe. When I returned, they asked me to meet them at a coffee shop in Poughkeepsie, New York, where they said they didn't think I should return to Millbrook.

To be honest, I understood. It was true that Millbrook had changed— I couldn't deny it. And in the wake of the disastrous LSD session with

Tim and Nena, more distance felt called for. There was a destructive side to Tim's personality, and since my return from Europe, Tim had also been trying to turn Susan and Jack against me. I needed space too.

Besides, I was starting to feel a deep spiritual dissatisfaction. Sometimes, when people asked whether they should keep doing psychedelics, I responded with a phrase I'd learned from Alan Watts: "When you get the message, hang up the phone." But I hadn't taken this advice myself, and constantly getting high and coming down was becoming its own kind of despair. I could touch those other planes of consciousness and love, but I couldn't stay there.

Both Ralph and Tim were intellectuals who dealt in conceptual realities. But we kept getting stuck in our intellects, and our concepts kept bringing us down. We'd ascend into sublime spiritual states and then come right back into our personalities.

I was not as much of an intellectual. I was more empathic and relational, and now I was feeling an existential frustration. I knew I was on to something, and I wanted to figure it out. In a way, getting kicked out of Millbrook was just the escape hatch I needed. In fact, there was a perfect metaphor in my experience as a pilot. While Tim and Nena were in India, I'd borrowed Billy Hitchcock's plane to fly to Millbrook. I had three other passengers and a dog on board. It was a twin-engine, underwing plane that had retractable landing gear, something I wasn't used to because my Cessna had fixed landing gear.

On the approach to the grass strip outside Millbrook that we used for landing, I forgot to put down the landing gear. I also failed to check the wind sock. I landed the plane on its belly on the grass, with the wind behind me, rather than, as required, pointing into it.

The plane landed too fast—and kept going and going. At the end of the landing strip, there was a stone wall with a wooden rail, and beyond that there was a street. We took down the rail and somehow must have bounced and barely cleared the wall. We also crossed the street. Finally, we stopped in a field. Miraculously, none of us, dog included, were hurt. I looked out from the cockpit to see an abstract sculpture of crumpled metal. The twin propellers of the plane were dug into the meadow.

I managed to shut down the electrical system to prevent us catching fire. I had to call Billy to give him the bad news: "Uh, Billy, it's about your plane. . ." I must say he was very good about it. "I'll call the insurance company," he replied. But another pilot saw what happened and reported me to the Federal Aviation Administration. They ordered me to get recertified.

My leadership at Millbrook had been like my flying. I'd been reckless or ill-prepared—or maybe both—and I'd kept going and going and going, breaking through our arrangements and structures. Though ultimately nobody had been hurt, my decisions had not come without a cost. I'd been impulsive, and my judgment was in question. In my wake, Tim and Ralph saw a crumpled mess.

By leaving, I could try again. Somehow, I was going to find the door to my freedom. Tim and Ralph were already making their own plans to raise money for Castalia. They decided to tour several cities that fall and winter with a new, nondrug, theater-based multimedia show, which they called *Psychedelic Sessions*. I was still interested in the inner journey. I'd already intended to do some lecturing, and I figured I could raise more money than either of them. I set out for new territories.

CHAPTER 13

EAST VERSUS WEST

The winter of 1965–1966, I went back to France to run a psychedelic session for a painter I'd met in New York. Although he was French, he lived in a big Park Avenue apartment with his wife and kids. "Look," he said, "why don't we fly over to my chateau at Deauville in France, where it's quiet, and we'll do the trip there?" That sounded fine to me: "chateau" conjured a country palace with vineyards, gardens, and a butler. We agreed on a fee and expenses, and he flew ahead to Paris. I soon followed.

He picked me up at Orly Airport in a big Oldsmobile convertible. Most cars in France then were quite small, Citroën 2CVs and the like. "I have to stop and see my mother for a minute," he told me. "It won't take long. You stay in the car." We drove to a house in the middle of Paris that took up almost an entire block. My eyes grew big. I could only imagine what the chateau might be like.

Deauville is a prestigious old resort on the coast of Normandy. Along the way, we stopped at a little grocery. My host emerged with bread and cheese, which was wonderful, because I was starving. As we drove into town, we passed hotels, fancy seaside villas, a horse racing track, and a casino. Then we pulled up to our destination. It was a rustic, two-story country house, quite small and modest. *This* was the chateau?

There was no butler. And no heat. But I did have the LSD, so we got started on our trip. We were beginning to take off when suddenly the painter left the room. I wondered where he was going until some minutes later he reappeared, dressed in a leather suit. He was really into the leather scene, it turned out. He ordered me to pee inside the suit so that it would be more slippery. "I don't think that's in our contract," I replied. I was starting to dislike this guy. I told him to use his own pee.

In response, he got angry. We were tripping more and more intensely, and he began shouting at me. After a few minutes, he left the room in a huff. "I'm going upstairs to paint in my studio," he announced.

A bit later, he returned. He was even more angry and upset. The LSD was affecting his creativity. "My painting is ruined!" he yelled. "I can't paint anymore!"

He was pretty flipped out. Things were not looking good. I'd been planning to travel to England next, but with the way things were going, I was not going to have the money to get there. I'd been counting on what this guy was going to pay me, and now there was no mention of my fee. I had to figure something out.

He went back upstairs to paint some more. "Okay, you paint," I said. "I'm going to go gamble at the casino."

I put on my white shirt and sunglasses and walked to the casino, where I found my way to a roulette table. Roulette was the only thing I knew how to play. Still high on acid, I could see my chances in slow motion. As I looked at the wheel, I'd see a black number light up, so I would put money on the black—and win. Then I'd see another black number light up, and so on. I cruised from one roulette wheel to another until I saw a particular number light up. I kept winning, not a whole lot, but enough to get me to England. There, I looked up Tommy Hitchcock, who had a house outside London where he lived when he was doing his race car driving, and stayed with him.

Eight months later, I got a plain envelope in the mail with no return address. Inside was a clipping about a big juried art show. I recognized this guy's painting as the one he had done when we were at the chateau. It won first prize. His painting wasn't ruined after all.

―――――――――

I had other enlightening moments in Europe. When I got to England, I met up in London with R. D. Laing, the psychiatrist who had spent time with us at Millbrook. We decided to take LSD together. He convinced me that he knew less about psychedelics than I did and that I needed to be the guide. This bugged me—why did I have to be the protector on a trip?—but I agreed. I put on some Miles Davis records and tried to make the environment comfortable.

Once the acid started to take hold, I realized Laing had taken off everything but his shorts and was standing on his head. At the time I didn't know much about yoga, so this struck me as absurd. Then Laing walked over to me and looked into my eyes. He was big into nonverbal communication, and as I looked at him, I could see in his face that he was defenseless, like a child. I suddenly felt very nurturing and protective. No sooner did I have that thought than his face changed, ever so subtly. Now he looked paternal, like *my* protector.

Within seconds, his face changed again. Now he was a student, asking questions of his teacher. Then he was a teacher, and I was the student. This was all happening in silence, all in the body language. For the next six hours, Laing and I went through about eighty different social roles, taking turns in each role. Therapist and patient, patient and therapist. Executioner and prisoner, prisoner and executioner. And so on. Some of it was quite scary. But we were establishing contact in the place where we were behind all these roles, beyond all social games. We were sharing knowledge as equals.

When I returned I had some lecturing scheduled in California, and I decided to just move there. My work with the School Mathematics Study Group was, curiously, still happening, and my USCO friends— Stewart Brand, Steve and Barbara Durkee, Gerd Stern—had left New York and were producing psychedelic light shows out in Berkeley. I was eager to check out the psychedelic scene on the West Coast. By then it was pretty wild. Ken Kesey and his Merry Pranksters, after their cross-country tour, were hosting delirious parties at Ken's farm at La Honda in the Santa Cruz Mountains. They included fluorescent paint, music, sex, and members of the Hells Angels.

Kesey went public with the revelry soon after I arrived, when he launched his infamous Acid Tests, a series of LSD-fueled rock parties with visual displays. Of course, I attended. He and his Pranksters would set up a big bowl of Kool-Aid spiked with acid made by the underground chemist Augustus Owsley Stanley III. Everyone at the party could take as much of the Kool-Aid as they wanted. Naturally, things often got out of hand, with loud confrontations and sexual escapades. The Grateful Dead became the house band, with Owsley as their sound engineer. They would play for hours with Jerry Garcia's wandering guitar solos as people in colorful costumes danced to the light shows.

It was all beautiful and chaotic, truly the wild west. By comparison, our scene on the East Coast, with its homegrown light shows and lectures and stand-up routines, felt pedestrian and academic. In California, no one wore suits or sat at desks or droned on about mind expansion; they just got caught up in the ecstasy. Unlike Tim and me, with our attention to detailed reports *about* the psychedelic experience, Kesey and Owsley simply shared the experience with everyone. Owsley's mission was to get the purest acid to as many people as possible. He was the alchemist of consciousness.

I moved back into my old place from Stanford days, the little cabin on Homer Lane. It was convenient for my School Mathematics Study Group research. Then Steve and Barbara Durkee came to visit, and we agreed to move in together. We all missed communal living. We found a place in Los Altos, the same neighborhood where Steve Jobs and Steve Wozniak later started Apple in their garage. The property had a main house, with another house and an apricot orchard out back.

By this time I'd also reconnected with Jane Burton, the lovely philosophy professor who visited Millbrook with the Pranksters. Jane agreed to move into the back house with me and her baby daughter, Emily. The Durkees had a baby girl too, Dakota. Stewart Brand set up a tent in the orchard, where he sometimes came and stayed. We took mushrooms there. He began a campaign aimed at NASA the following year, calling for the release of the agency's rumored first satellite photo of the whole Earth. He believed the photo would change how we all saw the planet. He was right—and when he got access to the now-famous photograph, he used it on the cover of the *Whole Earth Catalog*, a master compendium of resources for the New Age, which he launched in 1968.

My relationship with Jane did not last long; she left me for Gerd Stern. But for the most part, our little community lived happily. There was a eucalyptus grove where Steve and I tripped together and felt the trees breathe. We would laugh and laugh. Every Saturday we held a family session, and during the week Steve and I would travel around California together, lecturing about psychedelics. He was a good speaker, very confident. Often, people who took acid for the first time would write to us to share their experiences and questions. There were so many letters that Barbara helped with the correspondence.

In the evenings, around the dinner table, we brainstormed ways to transform society: with psychedelic light shows, centers to help the dying, intentional communities for collective awakening. Eventually we gravitated toward creating an eclectic spiritual commune. At Steve's prompting, we decided on a framework for how it would work and even drew up a charter. Within a year or two, the dream would take form.

Along with many other creative people, the Durkees had become devotees of Meher Baba, an Indian spiritual teacher. Meher Baba was known for keeping silence—he communicated in writing—as well as his books *God Speaks* and *Discourses*. Little cards with his picture that said, "Don't worry, be happy" were ubiquitous. He famously traveled through India in a blue bus. One day, Steve and I saw an ad for a blue school bus. Steve was struck by the Meher Baba connection. It was in decent shape, so we bought it and turned the back of it into sleeping quarters.

Meher Baba was growing alarmed by the use of psychedelics in the West. One day, a letter came to Los Altos with a message to Meher Baba's followers. Drugs were spiritually damaging, he declared. His followers were not to take LSD or have anything to do with those who did.

His pronouncement put us in an uncomfortable situation. Steve and Barbara wanted to follow Baba's teachings, and I wanted to keep lecturing on psychedelics. We could have put curtains across the room, or one of us could have moved out. I felt like Meher Baba was breaking up our little commune.

I was also confused. In my experience, drugs had opened me to my spiritual heart, not damaged me. I decided to write to Meher Baba asking for clarification, telling him what I'd learned as a researcher. "These chemicals, if wisely employed," I wrote, "seem to provide a key to unlock the door allowing the sunlight of Reality to shine for a moment." For many people, I continued, the experience helped them "consider their spiritual work seriously rather than get lost in atheistic intellectualism." Perhaps, I wrote, he did not understand how LSD was different from other drugs, though I suspected he did. "Can you help me?" I asked.

Meher Baba wrote back. "Your letter made me happy," he replied. "I know you are a sincere seeker of Truth." Perhaps LSD could arouse spiritual longing in some, he acknowledged. But LSD could not sustain that longing. The experiences I described, he said, were "as far removed from Reality" as a mirage from water. "No matter how much you pursue the mirage, you will never reach water, and the search for God through drugs must end in disillusionment." I could take LSD three more times, he told me. Then I should stop completely.

I loved Meher Baba, but back then I wasn't that kind of a follower. I had years of research behind me. I thought, "What does he know? Nice old man in India, never took acid."

I kept on going. In January 1966, Kesey and other friends—Stewart Brand, Allen Ginsberg, Neal Cassady, the Grateful Dead, the Hells Angels—put together a three-day Acid Test in San Francisco known as the Trips Festival. Thousands of people showed up. Something was happening, and I was in the middle of it. The counterculture was underway.

Meanwhile, Millbrook was undergoing its own changes. Michael Hollingshead left to share the gospel of LSD in London. After touring with their *Psychedelic Sessions*, Ralph and Tim made new plans. Ralph followed a new girlfriend to New York and was working on a book and more issues of the *Psychedelic Review*. Tim received an advance on an autobiography. He decided to close Millbrook and go to Mexico so he could write.

But at the Mexican border, in December 1965, Tim and his family were busted for possession of pot. It was a miniscule amount; still, the US authorities in Laredo, Texas, threw the book at him. Rather than plead guilty, Tim insisted on a trial. Though our friendship was still strained, I flew down to the court in Brownsville to support him, and I raised funds for his legal fees.

The Texas jury convicted him in forty-five minutes, and the judge gave him thirty years. Tim appealed, and the sentence was later thrown out by the US Supreme Court. His writing plans foiled, Tim returned to Millbrook and reopened it, bringing in a whole new cast of characters: more artists and musicians, some teachers and lawyers, journalists, publicists. He wrote prolifically. Ralph visited from New York, and they continued with weekend seminars, group psychedelic sessions, and light shows—in part to pay Tim's legal fees.

Still, his troubles grew. In April 1966, Millbrook was raided by G. Gordon Liddy, then assistant district attorney of Dutchess County. Liddy, a former FBI agent, later became notorious as one of President Richard Nixon's White House "plumbers" in the Watergate scandal. Liddy didn't find much at Millbrook, but the raid was the first of more to come. Then, in May, Tim was called to testify before a congressional subcommittee inquiring into LSD use. It brought Tim so much negative attention he decided to dissolve the Castalia Foundation. Public anxiety about psychedelics was growing. The press ran lurid stories about people going crazy on LSD and jumping out of windows.

In part to cut through the growing controversy, that June, the University of California, Berkeley, sponsored a six-day LSD Conference, the first of its kind on the West Coast. The idea was to counter the hysteria by presenting serious research on all aspects of psychedelics: religious, legal, philosophical, artistic, scientific, therapeutic.

I was on the advisory committee. The organizer was Dick Baker, a one-time Harvard undergrad, now a student of Suzuki Roshi at the San Francisco Zen Center. He invited many of the old Harvard-Millbrook circle to speak: Tim, Huston Smith, Allen Ginsberg, Frank Barron. Baker had planned for the conference to be held at UC Berkeley, where he taught, but when university officials realized how controversial the event had become, they got cold feet. They struck Ginsberg from the program because his gay political poetry was too radical and moved the conference off campus, to a venue in San Francisco.

Allen came anyway and stayed the whole week. The evening before the conference started, there was a kickoff party at a mansion in Marin County. About two hundred of us went. Owsley was passing out acid. We were all milling around the pool, waiting for the Grateful Dead to start playing, when one of the hosts announced that everyone needed to move their cars, because the neighbors were complaining about blocked driveways. This made us all anxious. Raids were starting to happen—the police had already shown up at my house in Los Altos—and if the neighbors called the authorities on two hundred people who were high around a swimming pool, the conference would be doomed.

Fortunately, we all managed to move our cars, high as we were. Owsley and I met for the first time at the party. He was into the politics of psychedelics, using them for social change. He was a kind of visionary in that way. I was still on my search: I wanted to experience more of those astral planes, planes of consciousness, and mythical archetypes. My own experiences so far had been about identity, oneness, and love. I wanted to continue my quest, and Owsley's White Lightning—pure 300-microgram tablets—was my ticket. Owsley was like a magician, or a sorcerer's apprentice. He loved to couch everything in mystery. We soon became close friends.

The conference the next day was picketed by Meher Baba followers. His pronouncements against drugs had circulated, and I was one of the bad boys.

When it was my turn to speak onstage, I told the audience about my correspondence with Meher Baba. I explained Baba said I could take LSD three more times but then had to stop. I had taken my three hits, I continued. Then, in a show of happy defiance, I consumed a fourth dose of acid then and there.

I later understood that Meher Baba was a spiritual authority in my life. He was an *upaguru*, a "guru along the way"—something Maharaj-ji later alluded to cryptically. ("You have another guru," he said. But he was also teasing, because we both knew he was my guru.) If I knew then what I know now, I might have heeded Meher Baba. But I didn't want to be told what to do.

Caroline Winter was a Brit, a beautiful and intelligent woman almost as tripped out as I was. She and I met at the Fillmore Auditorium in San Francisco in mid-July 1966 at a concert featuring the Grateful Dead and the Jefferson Airplane. Owsley introduced us. He was busy working as the sound engineer, so he put a tab of acid on each of our tongues and nudged us out onto the dance floor.

Allen Ginsberg was there, too, and the three of us got in my '38 Buick and drove to the Playboy Club where Maynard Ferguson was playing. We were stoned and wild-eyed and they didn't want to let us in until Allen produced a yellow plastic Playboy key, which was something they sent to celebrities to get them to come to their clubs.

Afterward we went back to the Fillmore, where we danced the night away in ecstatic union, swirling in the colors of the light show, dancing soul to soul. About 3:30 in the morning, Joan Baez jumped onstage and sang the closing number, "In the Midnight Hour," with Mimi Farina, Marty Balin from the Airplane, and Pigpen from the Dead. It was supposed to be the closing number, but the show went on for hours. Caroline and I both held the memory of that incredible night for many years afterward.

Caroline had come to the US from London and traveled around the country on a Greyhound bus until she got to California. She was working as a secretary at a real estate office when she met Owsley, who was looking for a place to rent. He invited her to the Grateful Dead's very first performance. She'd been to every concert since.

At the end of July, Caroline left for London to attend her brother's wedding. In August I traveled to go see her, along with Owsley, who hoped to find chemical suppliers for his acid manufacturing. By this time, I'd become an LSD distributor. On my lecture tours, people would come up after a talk and ask, "Do you know where I can get some?" And I would say, "Well, I just happen to have some . . ." Because it was on small squares of paper we called it "blotter acid."

The Hells Angels were distributors too. One of them lent me a motorcycle, and I drove it down to Stanford. I wanted to see the place after my time away. I went to the counseling center, where I'd trained as a psychotherapist, and looked in on my old office. There was Vic Lovell, now a therapist himself. He was wearing a tie and jacket. I was dressed in motorcycle clothes. I sat down and put my dirty boots up on the desk. We had a laugh. Then we went out and smoked a joint together.

I persuaded Caroline to return to the US to be with me, and she flew back to join me at the end of September. In early October, we decided to head east. We drove cross-country in the old Buick with my white cat, Namla, and after stopping at Millbrook, we found an apartment on East 59th Street in New York.

Caroline was my longest, closest female relationship—we had a deep connection. I considered her my soul partner, though that didn't stop me from sneaking out at night occasionally to pick up young men. With the loosening sexual mores of the sixties, my double life felt like less of a burden.

I continued to lecture, and we had all sorts of visitors. People would stop by to discuss psychedelic insights and politics at all hours. On weekends, Caroline and I would drive to Millbrook to visit. Tim had invited some thirty extra people to come live there who had been kicked out of the Ananda ashram upstate for taking psychedelics. Tim took them in at Millbrook as refugees, but there was friction between the old and new Millbrook residents, who disagreed about how to run the place.

Millbrook was also stressful because the authorities were increasingly after Tim. After dissolving Castalia, he founded the League for Spiritual Discovery (acronym: LSD), a quasi-religious organization that offered First Amendment cover for his use of psychedelics. But Liddy's raids continued; Tim, Billy Hitchcock, and even teenage Jack all faced charges at one point. The local police used any pretense to stop cars going to and from Millbrook. I told Caroline to dress plainly, in a turtleneck and jeans, whenever we went there. We didn't want to attract attention by looking like hippies.

One of our visitors in New York in the fall of 1966 was David Padwa. We'd first met during my summer research at Stanford, then reconnected at Harvard and tripped together at Millbrook. He'd sold his company, Basic Systems, to Xerox and received Xerox stock, which he had to hold for a year, during which he'd also worked for Xerox as a consultant. The stock doubled in value, and now David had time on his hands and money to burn. Earlier in the year, he'd gone to a work conference in Tokyo and decided to stop in India for a vacation. An acquaintance in Bombay introduced him to Harish Johari, a poet, musician, sculptor, and yogi. David hired a car and a Sikh driver, and for five or six weeks, he and Harish toured northern India.

When David rang the bell, I was sitting in the bathtub, as I loved to do. He came in, and as I soaked, we started schmoozing about India. He had felt at home and connected in India, he told me. He wanted to go back.

I was feeling the pull of India too. Caroline and I had been talking about going. Clearly there were people in the East who knew more about the maps of consciousness than we did. I felt an affinity for Buddhism; the *Tibetan Book of the Dead* was important to me, and by this time I'd met several Buddhists, like Geshe Wangyal, whom I admired. I thought of myself as a Jew-Bu. (Eventually I became a Hind-Jew.)

David told me his plan for an overland adventure to India. At the start of the new year, he would leave for Europe, where he planned to buy a Land Rover, outfit it, and have it shipped east. The improved Land Rover could accommodate two people. David had taken some Buddhist initiations and done some Buddhist training in India, so I liked the idea of traveling with him. I have a penchant for hanging on to somebody who *knows*, as I did with Tim and, eventually, my guru.

"Listen," I replied. "I want to show you something." I pointed to a valise and told David to open it up. It was full of money. I was traveling around to university campuses, I explained, lecturing on Psychedelics 101. "Every time I give my talk, I get a round of applause, and then everybody leaves. But there are always four or five guys that hang out after who want to go have a beer, and then they want to know where they can get acid."

Me, a nice Jewish boy from Newton, Massachusetts, had become a drug dealer. I was Owsley's main distributor. The other was the Hells Angels. But with the raids on Millbrook, I was starting to feel some paranoia. And in California, as LSD was outlawed, Kesey held one last Acid Test "graduation" at the Winterland Ballroom in San Francisco, and about five hundred of us gathered for a last hurrah at what we named the Love Pageant Rally.

Authorities everywhere were suspicious. I was growing uncomfortable and a little frightened. For all my awe at the power of LSD, I was starting to think I'd gone as far as I could with psychedelics. Although I was one of the quintessential spokesmen for acid, the trips I was taking myself were no longer special. I wasn't getting new insights. All the theoretical underpinnings I'd developed as a researcher and for my many lectures felt inadequate. My trips felt *too* astral, too full of mental imagery. I was also bored and disillusioned with all the egos in the psychedelic scene. There were so many nutty and neurotic people. The personal and lasting transformation we all sought was elusive.

After my discovery of the *Tibetan Book of the Dead* and other spiritual writings, I'd become convinced that people in the East had been engaged with the mysteries of consciousness for centuries. At first, I'd thought people in India must know all about these planes of awareness. But many of my friends had gone to India—Tim, Ralph, Allen Ginsberg—and by now, I wasn't so sure. They had all met good pundits, learned religious people, but they hadn't met anyone who really seemed to *know* from the inside.

What if we were the ones who knew the most about these inner planes? That was a frightening thought, because we didn't know much. Tim liked to say, "Trust your mind," but that was just a slogan. We were groping our way in the dark, wandering without a map in these unknown territories of the mind and spirit. Our bottle of LSD came without instructions.

Maybe trying to find someone who knew was a wild goose chase. Was looking for a wise man a kind of quixotic parental quest? Was it wishful thinking, wanting a sage who could teach me? But I wanted—I *needed*—to understand transcendence. I'd blown through the psychology profession and burned my bridges to academia. I'd explored all the chemical possibilities I could find. If I headed east, maybe I could find someone who could read the maps of consciousness. There had to be people who did know.

It was worth a try. At the very least, it would be an adventure. I told David I would go.

CHAPTER 14

MOTHER

y mother fought leukemia for years, but in 1966, as I was gallivanting between the coasts, her bone marrow stopped producing blood. She'd always been the strong one in the family, the real power in the home. Now she couldn't keep up with Dad or run the household. This was especially devastating to her because, as a firstborn matrilineal Jewish daughter, Mother always anticipated being the caretaker for her mother, who was herself frail. Now her sister Edna assumed the family mantle while Mother spent months in and out of the hospital.

Mother saw her doctor as a medical deity. The atom had been split in the 1930s. Science seemed omnipotent. In reality, the cancer treatments of the time had little to offer. To the doctor, Mother was an experimental patient. He kept promising her that new treatments would work, but none did. I've often wondered why she never lost faith in the doctors. Maybe it was all she had.

Dad's life was the most affected. At least outwardly, he maintained the role of devoted husband. My brother Bill was busy with his job and family in New York; in addition to being a lawyer, he was a stockbroker now, and he and Helen had kids. Leonard wasn't in any sort of mental shape to be a caretaker. I tried to visit Mother as often as possible, making trips from California and New York whenever I could.

The visit I remember most took place in July 1966, when Maynard Ferguson and I drove back to Boston from the Newport Jazz Festival in Rhode Island. I was tripping on mescaline when I came into Mother's hospital room. She was on morphine for the pain. Her spleen was enlarged, which made her belly look pregnant. This embarrassed her terribly.

I sat in a corner of her room. From time to time, other relatives, friends, nurses, doctors, and Dad would stop in. "Gertrude, you're looking wonderful," they'd each say. "You'll be out of here in no time." Everyone was cheery and upbeat. Then they'd go into the hall, shake their heads, and whisper, "She won't last a week." It was all lies. Everyone was in denial, masking their own fear of death with false joviality. In that denial, they were trapping Mother by seeing her as who she had been, not as she was in this moment: a dying person.

When everyone was gone, I sat and held her hand, not saying much. Then we started talking about death, from a really calm place. We'd never done that before. "You know, I'm going to die," she said. "What do you think death is?"

"I don't know," I replied. "But looking at you, it's like I see you inside a burning house. The house is being destroyed, just as your body is being consumed. But you and I are still here. The body will go, and you'll still be there. It seems to me, the way you and I are connected isn't really defined by this disintegrating body. You sound just like you've always sounded. I feel like I've always felt. Your body is decaying before us, but the way you and I love each other, I just believe that love transcends death."

It was the first time I really experienced Mother as a soul. We were truly communicating as souls. Before I left home, her dominating love had created such a deep attachment that I'd been bound to her for approval. Sitting with her now, I remembered a time when we'd been up in New Hampshire and Mother was playing with her grandchildren. They were down by the beach at the lake, happily pushing one another around. She'd grabbed my young nieces and nephew, forcibly trying to rein them in, to control them. Mother loved her grandchildren—until they began to act out.

It was heartachingly familiar. The scene had taken me back to my own childhood. I saw those same patterns of anxiety and control. But it dawned on me that this was something in her, not in the grandchildren or in me. For so many years, the dynamic had affected my image of her, fueling a latent resentment. But this hang-up with control—it was about *her*, not about me. Her restraining my childish behavior came from her own insecurity.

It was not my fault, I realized now. I knew she loved me a lot. Sitting by her bedside, recognizing her as a soul, I was finally able to acknowledge the purity of her love. I could begin to let go of my anger.

That encounter in the hospital began a restoration of our relationship. So when I met Caroline a week or two later and we began going together, I decided I would introduce her to Mother. We stopped in Newton during our move to New York. Mother was home from a hospital stay, and I wanted her to meet my new girlfriend. I'd already described Caroline to Mother as coming from an English blue blood family, including the fact that she was Charles Darwin's great-granddaughter.

When we arrived, Mother was sitting in her Queen Anne chair in the bedroom, a blanket around her. She looked regal, an upstanding Jewish matriarch. Caroline had just bought a new miniskirt in London, where everybody had been wearing miniskirts for years. She was young and fresh faced and exuded a lovely warmth.

Mother's gaze at Caroline was a withering inspection of her son's prospective mate. Her eyes lingered on the miniskirt. It was clear my new girlfriend did not pass muster. I was thirty-five, and it was time I got serious about someone. Mother wanted to see me with a partner before she died. But this young woman wasn't Jewish, nor did she seem like much of a blue blood. "She's much too young for you," said Mother when she thought Caroline was out of earshot. "There she is, in her English miniskirt."

Poor Caroline didn't handle it very well. It was important to my family that I marry someone Jewish, and she couldn't help but make the wrong impression just by dint of who she was. I honestly didn't care that she wasn't Jewish, though I felt the burden of pleasing my parents.

That winter, Mother went back into the hospital. Caroline and I talked about going to India, but then David came by, and I hatched my plans with him instead. He was off to buy the Land Rover in England, at the Solihull plant near Birmingham. This was like going to Detroit to customize a car. First, though, he would stop in the US Virgin Islands, where he had set up residence for tax purposes, to do some necessary paperwork. He promised to send word as soon as everything was ready.

In January 1967, David made it to Europe. But then he got side-tracked by a great romance and ended up in Spain. This delayed our departure a couple of months, so while I was waiting, I joined Tim on a speaking tour. With Millbrook under constant surveillance, Tim had announced that he would not be there as much. He felt called to go public with his advocacy of psychedelics. He was lecturing throughout the US and staying in California for long stretches, staging press conferences and psychedelic gatherings around San Francisco.

Tim's public renegade profile was growing. He'd given up thinking that LSD should be administered only as a carefully controlled sacrament, and because of all the harassment from authorities, he was growing more strident in his beliefs. Now he championed the idea of sharing psychedelics with as many people as possible. He embraced his role of counterculture provocateur.

On January 15, we appeared together at the Human Be-In, a gathering of some twenty thousand people in San Francisco's Golden Gate Park. I helped inspire the name for the event, when I suggested to the main organizer, visionary artist Michael Bowen, that I liked the idea of all of us just *being*. We were being-in. A be-in. The Hells Angels ran security, and Owsley distributed his newly illegal White Lightning LSD. We shared the stage with Allen Ginsberg and others, like political activist Jerry Rubin; poets Lawrence Ferlinghetti and Gary Snyder; and Dick Baker, organizer of the LSD Conference the previous year.

When it was his turn, Tim, high on acid and wearing an Indian-style white tunic and flowers in his hair, urged the audience to "turn on, tune in, drop out." It was not the first time he'd used the phrase, but the setting was his most public venue yet, and the proclamation turned Tim into a psychedelic prophet. Those of us who were close to Tim knew what he meant: he was telling people to drop out of their ideologies and tune in to a deeper reality. But the phrase got interpreted differently. People thought Tim was saying that you should drop out of society and take drugs all the time. He didn't disavow that idea. He was becoming more sophisticated about his social game playing, and he wanted to see how far he could push things.

In retrospect, for such an astute follower of game theory as Tim to get sucked into the charged polarities of that cultural moment revealed his tragic flaw. Whether it was ego, rebellion against authority, or becoming a legend in his own mind, Tim allowed himself to become the adman for the hippie drug menace. I was a passenger on that train, too, as were Allen and the others. The Human Be-In at Golden Gate Park was a milestone for a movement. Whether because of karma, the grace of God, or the subtle dance of the universe, we all got off at different destinations.

After the Be-In, Tim and I had no shortage of appearances. But more and more, it seemed Tim was in it for the public show and personal gain. He didn't care about the social science research part anymore or even about the mystical insights. He liked being at the center of a new hippie movement, liked provoking the authorities who didn't understand his work anyway. He sought advice from Marshall McLuhan, the media expert, who told him that he would maintain an image of strength if he was always positive and smiled in public. Tim did this for years, even when he was sentenced to prison again. In newspaper photos, he almost always appeared grinning.

A week after the Be-In, in the middle of all this activity, I received word that Mother had died. She'd wanted to stay at home, in her own bedroom, as she deteriorated, but both the doctor and Dad prevailed on her to return to the hospital. My aunt Edna had lamented, "Gertrude is dying by herself in a hospital room." The doctors decided to remove her spleen, and she did not survive the surgery. She died at Peter Bent Brigham Hospital. She was sixty-four.

Feeling guilty about being far away, I hurried back to Boston for her funeral at our temple in Brookline. I desperately wanted to see her body in the casket, but Dad wouldn't allow it. I think he felt she was too disfigured by the illness. I kept my emotions walled off and decided to take some LSD for the service.

I sat in the front row with Dad, Billy, and Len, as well as my sisters-in-law, Helen and Sylvia. Before us Mother's coffin was covered in roses. For the length of their forty-four-year marriage, Dad and Mother had exchanged one red rose on every anniversary, a symbol of their love for each other. When the ceremony was over and the rabbi was done speaking, we remained seated in our pew while the casket was wheeled out. As the casket passed my father, one rose from the blanket of flowers fell off and landed at my father's feet. We all noticed but didn't say anything. When we left, Dad reached down and clutched the rose.

I'd spent considerable time with Mother in the hospital, far more than anyone else in the family. The cloud of denial around her death stayed with me. Even the rabbi had been of no use when he visited her. I realized how death, the greatest transition in life, was unacknowledged in our culture. My new perspective was influenced by the *Tibetan Book of the Dead* and by friends like Aldous Huxley, who had approached his death so differently. We need to see death as the rite of passage that it is. It can't be celebrated if the setting is one of fear and dishonesty.

The rose was a clear signal of that transition. Mother was still here, even if her body wasn't. As our family got in the limousine to head to the cemetery, Leonard, seeing the rose in Dad's hands, said what we were all thinking. "She sent you a last message," he told Dad. "Yes!" all of us in the car agreed. It was an acknowledgment of a reality that none of us had ever discussed.

At the cemetery, the family sat in front of Mother's coffin, with the guests across from us. We were on one side, and some three hundred people were on the other side, looking at us. I sat at the end of our row. It was a sunny day, and as I sat there, high on acid, I saw a golden light emanating from the casket. Suddenly, I sensed Mother's presence. It felt like a bird had landed on my shoulder. Her spirit was close. We watched the burial together.

She didn't seem particularly upset. In fact, I felt her commenting rather humorously on the proceedings. I wanted to smile or laugh or at least talk to her, but I was afraid of what people might think. "Oh, he's the one that takes drugs," they'd say. "He smiles at his mother's funeral." I was already the "druggie son"; I didn't want to make things worse.

"Your mother's a real saint," Mother's oldest friend, Rose Aronson, said to me that day. "You created a real heartache for her." She was referring to my notoriety with psychedelics and my having been fired from Harvard. But sitting there with Mother's spirit, I didn't feel disapproval. I felt peace. Together, Mother and I marveled at her burial. There was so much love.

———————

Curiously, I didn't feel much loss after Mother died, at least not in the immediate moment. As a psychologist, I knew to be wary. "No grief reaction," I told myself. "Watch out." As people do, I avoided painful emotions by staying busy. I distracted myself with work—more lectures, more fundraising—and time with Caroline.

Tim returned to Millbrook and was doing some lecturing too, though the heat from government agents continued, with more raids at the estate. That April, Owsley decided to visit New York City with a cohort of friends. I'd stopped distributing drugs for him, but we remained deep friends, and I was delighted to see him. Though he and Tim had crossed paths in California, they'd not spent any time together, so Caroline and I arranged for Owsley to visit Millbrook. I'd already introduced Owsley to Nick Sands, the underground chemist for the League for Spiritual Discovery, and they'd hit it off. (Owsley encouraged Nick to move out to California, offering him the services of his lab partner, Tim Scully. Sands and Scully together created Orange Sunshine acid in doses by the millions.) Owsley and Tim had both been so instrumental in my life and Caroline's. Two central figures in the psychedelic movement, about to become friends. Or so I hoped.

I should have remembered the Merry Pranksters and how *that* meeting of the minds went. True to form, Tim gave Owsley the cold shoulder, sequestering himself with Rosemary upstairs. He was not all that interested in Owsley—he already had his own chemist—and made himself out to be the leader of the psychedelic movement, which Owsley found extremely irritating. Bad chemistry for the chemist mage. It was a short visit.

Caroline and I were disappointed. To make matters worse, as Owsley and his friends were leaving Millbrook, they got stopped by the cops. I suppose they looked like troublesome hippies. Owsley was jailed for a night; we got him out the next day. With typical largesse he had given away all his drugs at Millbrook and had none on him. The cops had nothing to hold him on.

That same spring, Caroline and I decided to take a break from New York. Steve and Barbara Durkee had left Los Altos, California, and were moving north of Taos, New Mexico, where they had purchased land for the commune we'd all dreamed of. It was called the Lama Foundation, after the cluster of homes down the mountain. (In Spanish *lama* is "mud" or "slime," after the spring mud season and the thick mix used to make the adobes for the buildings.) The Durkees invited us to visit. Caroline and I flew to California to pick up the blue bus, and together we drove through Arizona and New Mexico. We camped and stopped at various festivals, and as soon as people heard I was there, they'd line up to speak with me about psychedelics. It was a fun odyssey.

After meeting the Durkees in Santa Fe, we went up the Sangre de Cristo Mountains to see the property, north of Taos at 8,600 feet. Herman Rednick, a mystic painter who became a spiritual mentor for the Lama Foundation, had helped find the land. A friend, Jonathan Altman, a Zen and tai chi practitioner who lived near us in Los Altos, assisted in buying it. The land, outside the hamlet of Questa, was sacred to the Taos Pueblo Indians. We met with them, everyone sitting outdoors in chairs, dressed in our Sunday best. Lama would be a self-sustaining intentional community and a spiritual school. All spiritual traditions would be honored. The Taos Pueblo and Native American Church elders also became mentors.

Since there were no buildings on the property yet, Caroline and I lived in the bus. We had some beautiful moments, watching sunsets together over the sweep of the mesas below the mountains. But as a couple, something wasn't working, and we both knew it. At some point, Caroline realized I was bisexual. We had a soulful intimacy, and there was no question we were in love, but we also had plenty of friction and felt physically incompatible. We adored each other, but we couldn't cohabit long term.

When David Padwa wrote that his India preparations were finally together, our separation felt timely and natural. Caroline had a moment of recognition from when she was a teenager and her father had left her mother for a male lover. She remembered the same ambiguous feelings coming up between her parents. It was a karmic coda: that memory allowed her to see the reality of our relationship and, perhaps, to let go.

David had gotten the Land Rover outfitted for our trip, creating a consummate overland chariot: pop-up roof, beds that flipped down, refrigerator, toilet, sound system. In June 1967, the Six-Day War between Israel and its Arab neighbors had just taken place—not the most auspicious time for two Jewish guys to drive through the Middle East—so David arranged to have the Land Rover shipped to Tehran, where we would pick it up and start driving. Meanwhile, I received a grant from New Mexico's Museum of International Folk Art to collect traditional musical instruments from India. In July 1967, I flew to Paris to meet David.

That same summer, the Durkees began building Lama Foundation. Caroline stayed to help, digging trenches for the first water pipes and making adobe bricks. As the buildings came together, she let the Durkees take her place on the bus. Steve and Barbara had two daughters by then and later would have two more. Many of us have come and gone at the Lama Foundation over the intervening years, but the bus remains there as a dwelling.

Meanwhile, after yet another police raid that culminated in the arrests of forty people, Tim closed the Big House at Millbrook, retreating with Rosemary into a tent in the woods. But I was buoyant. I was ready. *Sgt. Pepper's Lonely Hearts Club Band* had just been released. From all across America, one hundred and fifty thousand young people were about to descend on San Francisco for the Summer of Love.

This would be the summer of love for me too—in an entirely different way.

PART II

PILGRIM OF THE HEART

The heart is
one in all of us.

MAHARAJ-JI

TOP, LEFT TO RIGHT The family mascot; Bar Mitzvah, 1944; Richard Alpert as a young man
MIDDLE, LEFT TO RIGHT Captain of the Intranauts; Tripping, 1962; About to become Ram Dass
BOTTOM, LEFT TO RIGHT NYC, 1975; On the road for Seva, 1992; On Maui, 2014

10

11

TOP At Willenrica, Franklin, New Hampshire
ABOVE Worms for sale! With Leonard at Willenrica

TOP With Leonard, Bill, and Dad
ABOVE Dad with Albert Einstein

ABOVE With Janet Kerrigan in New Hampshire
OPPOSITE Dancing with Mother at a family wedding

16

17

18

TOP Whirling Dervish, painting by Mary McLelland
ABOVE LEFT David McClelland
ABOVE RIGHT Mary McClelland

19

20

TOP On a cruise ship to Hawaii

ABOVE Dad was appointed president of the New Haven Railroad in 1956

Teaching a seminar at Stanford

22

23

TOP The Doctor is in. Timothy Leary at Harvard
ABOVE Timothy Leary

24

25

TOP Ralph Metzner with Timothy Leary
ABOVE Monitoring Ralph Metzner with the Experiential Typewriter

TOP LEFT From an interview in a German magazine
TOP RIGHT With Leary at the Bucket of Blood in Antigua
ABOVE With Peggy Hitchcock and Tim Leary in Mexico

Harvard Fires 2 in Drug Row

By HERBERT BLACK

Two Harvard psychologists who for months have been the center of controversy over experiments with hallucinatory drugs, with some of the tests involving Harvard students, have been dropped by the university.

They are Richard Alpert, professor of clinical psychology, and Timothy F. Leary, lecturer on clinical psychology.

Alpert's parting with Harvard is an out-and-out dismissal, the first under the regime of Pres. Nathan M. Pusey.

The reason for his dismissal, according to Dr. Pusey, is that Alpert violated a promise not to give consciousness-expanding drugs to Harvard students without permission of the university and prior clearance by the college medical department.

Leary, on the other hand, has been "relieved" of his post for "failure to keep classroom appointments." The Corporation voted to relieve him of his pay as of Apr. 30. He went to California without notifying officials and skipped

DROPPED by Harvard. Richard Alpert, clinical psychology pro-fessor (left), and Timothy F. Leary, lecturer on same subject.

OPPOSITE Timothy Leary and Professor Richard Alpert
ABOVE From the Lowell, Massachusetts, *Sun*, May 29th, 1963

TOP LEFT Peggy Hitchcock
TOP RIGHT With Peggy in Mexico, 1962
ABOVE With Susan Homer, Timothy Leary, and Peggy Hitchcock in the kitchen at Newton

34

35

36

37

TOP Tim Leary riding bareback at Millbrook
ABOVE Millbrook, circa 1965, face by Allen Atwell

CHAPTER 15

JOURNEY TO
THE EAST

After meeting in Paris, David and I flew nonstop to Tehran. We arrived to discover the Land Rover ensnared in a Kafka-like hell of Iranian bureaucracy. We required just the right piece of paper to liberate it from customs, a matter of significant diplomatic negotiation and a glittering opportunity for local graft. While we waited for the paperwork to clear, we decided to fly to Isfahan, a city known for its stunning architecture.

Isfahan was a capital of ancient Persia, and its Imam Square is one of the largest public squares in the world. The Shah Mosque, with its hand-painted tiles and geometric art, was breathtaking. Because of the Six-Day War, there were no tourists, and as we wandered the city— its palaces, mosques, minarets, bridges, and a huge bazaar—David and I had it all to ourselves. Our guide was Ferydoon Agahi, a Sufi fellow with family in Tehran. When he heard us discuss India and learned that we planned to drive through the city of Mashhad, home to Iran's largest religious shrine, he asked if he could hitch a ride.

Since he could translate Farsi for us, we agreed. We set out in the reclaimed Land Rover, heading east across the Alborz Range and down along the Caspian Sea. There were no road maps, so we used old aviation maps. As we drove, Ferydoon narrated the history and culture of Iran. David and I were both interested in Sufism and the different schools of Islam, and as we listened—stopping to see exquisite art and architecture all along the way—we developed a deep appreciation for the great beauty of Islam.

We remained insulated in the Land Rover. We listened to Vivaldi tapes and ate peanut butter while observing the life and culture outside. The Land Rover was crammed with so much stuff that we couldn't move around, so at some point we began to off-load. We gave a steel trunk to a young woman along the road who was getting married. We found we didn't need the refrigerator, so we gave that away too. Finally we got the car stripped down enough for easy traveling. But it was still a Western bubble we sat comfortably inside.

David has an encyclopedic mind, and we enjoyed connecting intellectually, though we had different perspectives on just about everything. We discussed psychology—me from an academic standpoint, him on its real-world application—and also environmental issues, which David knew a lot about. I had parted company with Tim, and he had parted with his company, Basic Systems, parallel experiences we bonded over and teased each other about.

David kept a faithful travel journal (many of these details are thanks to him). He also read and memorized Persian poetry, which he recited as we drove. One of these works, *The Conference of the Birds*, was written by the great Sufi poet Farid ud-Din Attar, from Nishapur. When we passed the town on the way to Mashhad, we stopped to visit his tomb. We also visited the white-marble mausoleum of Omar Khayyam, another of Nishapur's famous poets.

Then we got to Mashhad, which is called "the holy city of Iran" because it is home to the tomb of Imam Reza, Islam's eighth Shi'a imam. The shrine around the tomb is immense, with a golden dome and minarets and many surrounding courtyards. The blue tile work and calligraphy are intricate and beautiful.

Ferydoon was going to visit the tomb, and we told him we wanted to see it too. "No, no," he said, "you are not Muslim. You can't go in." Non-Muslims can visit the courtyards but not the tomb. "Oh, come on!" we protested. David said he would disguise himself in a hijab, as a woman.

"You are insane," replied Ferydoon. "They will kill you. They will really kill you. Don't do that." So we hung around outside. There were almost no Western tourists, but people were very friendly. We got to observe such Shi'a devotional practices as chanting, crying, and recitation.

After leaving Ferydoon, we went on toward Afghanistan, another 150 miles to the border. The dividing line between the two countries was a simple barbed-wire fence, stretching into the distance. Across the road, a long red and white pole on a hinge, with a padlock on it, served as an entry gate. That was the border crossing. We stopped at the gate, not knowing what to do.

There was a shack up on the hillside, and we watched as a guy came down to meet us. We handed him our passports. He looked at my passport and turned some of the pages, holding it upside down. He had no idea what he was looking at.

The man's features were Mongolian or Chinese, totally unlike those of the Persians and Afghans we had seen. We learned later the Afghan government had a practice of assigning men from the eastern part of the country to the western border. The border agent lifted the gate, and we drove another few miles, to a town with an administrative center where they would mark our passports with an entry stamp. The official took out a stamp, but instead of inking it on a pad he licked the stamp with his tongue. Then he stamped the passports. He was reusing the ink already on the stamp.

Outside on the porch, we found a dozen Afghan men sitting on benches, talking and drinking tea. They all had rifles and wore bandoliers of bullets. They looked rugged and dangerous, like extras out of a Khyber Pass B movie. As we walked out, they went quiet. They watched intently as we strode toward the parked Land Rover.

On our drive through Iran, David and I had been smoking a lot of dope. I'd brought along a big bag of Owsley's White Lightning, but we'd limited ourselves to one small LSD session by ourselves at the hotel in Tehran. Now, feeling the stares of these hardened fighters, I rummaged through the car for our hash pipe. It was an awkward-looking thing, with a big wooden bowl, a brass stem, and a mouthpiece.

I filled it with dope and lit up, then passed it to David. The gunmen watched. David smoked a bit. Then he gave it to one of the guys, who had a smoke and passed the pipe. Everyone had a toke. In a few minutes, the atmosphere changed from tense to relaxed and contemplative.

We continued peacefully on our way. Entering Afghanistan was like turning the clock back centuries. Now it's a war zone, but back then it was pastoral, with sheep and herdsmen, subsistence farms, and mountainous landscapes. Occasionally we'd have to stop and wait for flocks of sheep to clear the road.

It was very hot and dry. In Herat, we spent a couple of days in a hotel and went swimming in the pool. It was wonderful, the first swim we'd had. From there, we planned to drive to Kabul on a northern route, through Mazar-i-Sharif, but the road was so bad we were forced to turn around. Instead, we went south through Kandahar, later the power seat of the Taliban.

This road was a brand-new highway, built by the Soviets. It had no road signs, but it was a perfect two-lane ribbon of asphalt—not a crack in it, soft shoulders on either side. We passed a drinking well, also built by the Soviets, and met a couple of French kids who were hitchhiking to India. In Ghazni, just south of Kabul, we stopped at the Museum of Islamic Art, one of the most beautiful museums I have ever seen. It had just opened its galleries a year earlier. Years of conflict have since damaged some of the collections, but at the time, I was struck by the splendor of both the artifacts and the building, which was the mausoleum of the Persian scholar Abd al-Razzaq. The mausoleum's architecture is thought to have inspired the design of the Taj Mahal.

Finally, we got to Kabul, a third-world city that, like many others, was modernizing. Of what was to come from Communists or jihadists there was no sign; instead, the streets were filled with young people who worked for United Nations agencies, the women walking around in short skirts. It felt like Bangkok or Manila. The king was still on the throne, although he lived mostly in Italy.

For the equivalent of two dollars we scored a kilo of hash—"Take all you want!"—and then headed north, to see the giant Buddhas at Bamiyan. We took the Salang Pass, a very high and dangerous road through the mountains. The two sixth-century statues, carved out of sandstone cliffs in the Bamiyan Valley, were famous for their beauty and craftsmanship, as well as their imposing size. The taller of the two was more than 170 feet tall. At Bamiyan, we climbed up a hidden stairway and sat on top of the great Buddha's head. The head alone was gigantic, some fifteen or twenty feet high.

I was still so much the psychologist that any spiritual significance of the Buddhas was lost on me—I thought of them simply as artifacts—but David, who understood Buddhist history and philosophy, was moved. In March 2001, the Buddhas were blown up by the Taliban, an act of destruction that prefigured the attacks of 9/11.

Back in Kabul, we met up with a friend of David's, a Pakistani Sufi named Tariq Hamid, who served as a translator. Tariq had been part of the psychedelic scene in New York and was sort of an intellectual type. The plan was for us to travel over the Khyber Pass, into and across Pakistan, then through Amritsar, Jammu, and on to Srinagar, in Kashmir. I don't know why, but I didn't want to do that. Maybe I was fed up with the driving and the endless scenery or with needing Tariq as a translator.

In any case, I decided to fly ahead to India. I wanted to see the Taj Mahal and Fatehpur Sikri and all the things I'd heard about from Tim and Ralph and Allen Ginsberg. Since David had already seen all these tourist places, he was fine with me taking off. We agreed to rendezvous in a couple of weeks in Srinagar.

───────

For the two weeks I traveled on my own, I played at being a tourist, staying at fancy hotels. It was the luxury side of India, though wealth and poverty are never that far apart there. Then I headed up to Srinagar, where David and I had agreed to meet on a houseboat called the *New Ruby*, on Dal Lake. Srinagar is in the Kashmir Valley, next to a couple of lakes, and it's known for its incredible water and mountain vistas.

When I got there, I met two American girls, Beth and Jacqui, who were going around the world. It was a serendipitous encounter—they were just wandering—and I invited them to join David and me on the house-boat. We boarded a water taxi, called a *shikar*, to cross Dal Lake. Halfway across, we spied another shikar, and who should be on it but David?

We all stayed together on the *New Ruby*—David slept with one of the girls—and for the next several days we relaxed and got high. We had some celestial LSD parties on the houseboat, awed by our surroundings. After some days, we decided to trek to Amarnath cave, a Hindu shrine farther up in the twenty-thousand-foot Himalaya peaks, about forty miles from Srinagar. David loves mountains. Amarnath is a deeply sacred pilgrimage site because of its ice stalagmite, formed from the meltwater that drips from the ceiling of the cave and believed to be one of the Jyotirlingams, a phallic representation of Shiva. The pillar of ice changes in height and size with the season and temperature, and it is called a "lingam of light" for how it catches sunlight. The cave is surrounded by snow most of the year, and every summer, thousands of devotees make a pilgrimage.

The owner of our houseboat and his father had led expeditions for foreigners during the British Raj, and they had equipment and tents. It was before the pilgrimage season, and they told us it would be cold. We hired ponies. When the ponies could go no farther, we walked. We had saddle sores and blisters. It was a two-day trek from base camp. The cold and snow and miniscule mountain trails were more than we'd bargained for. David wrote in his diary: "Unbelievable ascent up the side of the river chasm. Terrifying ice crossings, two thousand foot drops, three-foot wide path on slippery soft shale. Hair-raising quality for several hours—'How did I get myself into this?' thoughts. Turning the corner into Amarnath Gorge, with a meadow on the shoulder with a million colored flowers—for only two weeks a year." Finally, we made it to the cave. Even though I had no inkling of its meaning, I was impressed. (Later, Maharaj-ji said to me, "You went to Amarnath. But you didn't know what it was.")

After Amarnath, the girls went their own way. David and I continued on to Dharamsala, a city on the edge of the Himalayas where the Dalai Lama has taken refuge since fleeing Tibet in 1959. There, we met with Keith Dowman, a great student of esoteric Buddhism who is fluent in Tibetan and has studied with Tibetan yogis. We also tried to get an audience with the Dalai Lama, who was then about thirty years old. With no advance notice, we went up to the gate at Swarg Ashram, his headquarters. "No, he's in meditation today," we were told. "Maybe tomorrow."

We decided to wait. Anyway, we couldn't really leave: the Land Rover needed repairs. Climbing an immensely steep hill near Dharamsala, we'd heard a cracking sound from one of the front hubs. Then the Land Rover had given a great shudder and ground to a halt. We managed to back down the hill to a repair shop in McLeod Ganj, a little suburb of Dharamsala. The mechanic fished around under the car and in the rear differential box and then stood up. His hands, full of black grease, held thirty or forty fragments of metal. The front hubs of the Land Rover had slipped, and with all of the torque suddenly being applied to the rear axle, the gears had stripped.

We didn't know what to do. There was no hope of finding replacement parts in Dharamsala. India had plenty of Jeeps but no Land Rovers. The only answer seemed to be to contact the British Consulate in New Delhi for help getting parts.

Fortunately, the Dalai Lama was now ready to see us. We went to the audience with His Holiness. He was open and engaging. He was curious about my psychedelic work, and we talked about consciousness and LSD. He was fascinated by Western technology, and these drugs were a Western phenomenon. He was a fellow explorer of consciousness within his Tibetan framework—which I wasn't entirely ignorant of, thanks to the *Tibetan Book of the Dead*. He urged David to read Nagarjuna, one of Buddhism's most important philosophers, perfect for David. Afterward, we visited the Dalai Lama's mother and his sister, who ran a children's charity. We stayed in the guesthouse run by his brother, which is still the in place to stay.

I was impressed. The Dalai Lama was close to us in age, practically our peer, and he had all these monks around him, treating him with deep deference and respect. I gave His Holiness a diffraction grating bindi and showed him how you could put it on your forehead, where it made rainbows. I was so naïve. I wonder how he saw us? Probably as babes in the woods.

We tried to locate a truck to take the crippled Land Rover to Delhi, to no avail. Eventually we figured out that even though the rear wheels were gone, if we put it in four-wheel drive, the front wheels still had traction. It was a precarious scheme, but it worked. Occasionally the front wheels would also lose traction and the engine would rev pointlessly. I discovered that if we packed the front hubs with gravel and pounded it in with a hammer, they would hold together for a while.

We left Dharamsala for New Delhi, passing through Kurukshetra, where the epic battle of Mahabharata is said to have taken place, the scene of the Bhagavad Gita. After several hundred miles, we got to India's capital and made our way to the British Consulate. Officials there said we could get a new axle assembly from Calcutta, which we proceeded to order. While we waited, we spent time looking around the city and visiting Tibet House, a new five-story outpost of Tibetan art and culture. The Land Rover was becoming a saga unto itself.

Harish Johari, the poet-musician-sculptor-yogi whom David had met on his previous sojourn in India, came to meet us in New Delhi. One of his first commissions as a sculptor was a statue of Hanuman, the Hindu monkey god, for a temple in his hometown of Bareilly. He made other temple statues and was also known for his painted frescoes. He was an Indian renaissance man; he eventually was recognized for his writings and lectures on everything from astrology to chakras.

Once the Land Rover got its new rear axle, we drove with Harish to Bareilly, to visit his family's home. Then we went on to Varanasi, or Benares, the holy city on the banks of the River Ganges and one of the most intensely religious places on the planet, a major pilgrimage site. Many Hindus come there to die and be cremated along the banks of the river, which is considered holy.

We stayed in a small hotel near the Ganga, close to Manikarnika Ghat, one of the holiest of the cremation grounds. I was overwhelmed by the number of people wandering the streets, waiting to die. There were lepers and people with obvious deformities and visible cancers. Each person carried just enough money to pay for the firewood needed for their cremation. I could barely look at them. I felt waves of horror. I thought they should all be in the hospital. I couldn't connect with or even confront them as human beings.

I remained a tourist, caught up in my bubble—exuding Western pity. The sights and ideas I'd encountered in India were churning inside me, but I was viewing the culture through the windshield of the Land Rover. From my correspondence with Meher Baba, I had some sense of India, but it was still a mystery. Temples and pilgrimage places gave me a strong hit. The mystery was in the people. The culture was pulling me in, but I didn't understand it.

Benares was a forced immersion, my first encounter with the reality of India. No more tourism: we sat by the burning ghats and watched families bring bodies for cremation. As the body burned, the oldest son or another family representative would crack the skull with a stick to liberate the dead person's soul. The ashes were taken to the river's edge and dumped in the sacred waters of the Ganga.

David, Harish, and I went out on a boat on the Ganga and took LSD. It was Harish's first trip. David took a lower dose so he could hold the ground. The corpse of a young girl, maybe four years old, bumped gently into our boat, bloated and discolored. Young children are sometimes just put in the river, as are saints and yogis.

Seeing the body really did something to me. It was a true initiation into impermanence. That and god intoxication filled Benares. I was so freaked out I went back to the hotel and hid under the bed.

From Benares, we drove to Kathmandu, in Nepal. We stayed at the Soaltee Hotel, a five-star luxury hotel that had been built by the prince of Nepal and inaugurated a year earlier by King Mahendra. Hungry, we went into town and ended up at a restaurant called the Blue Tibetan, a popular hangout for foreigners.

Somehow people knew who I was and that I was presumably a source for LSD. In my quest for people in the East who knew about planes of consciousness, David and I had freely given of my supply to any holy man who wanted to try it. I'd hoped these men could offer the understanding I sought, but no one had offered me any fresh insight. One guy said, "It gave me a headache." An old Theravada Buddhist monk said, "It's good, but not as good as meditation." Another man asked, "Where can I get more?"

The scenery and our adventures had been breathtaking, but so far no map reader had emerged. I was starting to feel depressed. We'd seen the Dalai Lama, been to Amarnath and Benares, now Kathmandu—yet I wasn't any closer to the answers I was looking for. Our trip was winding down, and David was talking about flying to Calcutta, then stopping in Japan on our way back to the US. In Kyoto we planned to meet up with Alan Watts, Gary Snyder, and the poet Philip Whalen, who were all there visiting Japanese temples and studying Zen Buddhism. It wasn't a bad plan, but what was I going to do when I got back?

We met some French hippies at the Blue Tibetan and got to talking. As we sat there, a tall, arresting figure walked up to our table. He was a westerner, about six foot seven, with a blond beard. His hair was coiled in blond dreadlocks, sadhu style, and he was wearing *malas* and a dhoti. He'd heard about ex–Harvard Professor Richard Alpert and his supply of LSD. We invited him to join us.

Originally Michael Riggs, a twenty-three-year-old surfer from Laguna Beach, he had been living in India for several years and was now named Bhagavan Das. He seemed to know his way around. He looked the perfect yogi; at the same time, he could lapse into California surfer slang. I liked him.

We invited him over to the Soaltee and took LSD together. We hung out for several days, discussing Hindu and Buddhist philosophy and smoking hash. When we went down to the hotel swimming pool, he started performing puja, offering water in the pool. People began to pull their kids from the pool because this holy man was using it. His emanation was very strong.

There was something about him; I could feel Bhagavan Das knew something I needed to know. When he said he was going on a pilgrimage to several Buddhist temples, I asked to go with him. The reason I'd come to India was consciousness, not religion, but I knew I had hardly plumbed the country's spiritual depth. I didn't want to go to Japan—not yet. I felt, in a visceral way, that I was incomplete with India. I needed to go deeper.

I was also attracted to Bhagavan Das. He picked up on this, and he figured that was why I wanted to travel with him. But that wasn't my main motivation: I truly felt pulled by something inside. In any case, he was attracted to me too—though in his case it was about the LSD. Richard Alpert, of "Leary and Alpert," was well known, and he knew wherever I went, psychedelics went too.

David still intended to go to Japan. He decided to leave the Land Rover in Harish's care, with instructions to give it to me if I wanted to use it. So as David took off for Calcutta to catch a flight farther east, the rest of us drove back to Harish's home in Bareilly. There, Bhagavan

Das and I left Harish, the Land Rover, and my Western baggage—literally and figuratively.

We set out barefoot. Bhagavan Das taught me to beg for food to turn me into a bhikkhu, a Buddhist monk. I'd find myself squatting on the street, begging with my *kamandal*, or sadhu pot. People would drop in a coin or two for the holy man. Meanwhile, in my *jhola* shoulder bag were my passport and my American Express Travelers Cheques, as well as my bottle of LSD.

We stayed in pilgrim rest houses called dharmsalas, some put up by the government, with concrete rooms and wooden beds. At first it was an adventure, and the spartan conditions didn't bother me. But it was very hot, and as the days went by, I needed to distract myself from the blisters and bad food. I tried to entertain myself narrating my past exploits to Bhagavan Das. I thought he would be amused, but he was completely uninterested. When I told stories, he replied, "Just be here now." I was thrown back into myself. Just be. Here. Now.

After two months of arduous travel, Bhagavan Das said he needed to visit his guru. He'd gotten a notice from the Indian government that his visa had expired, and he knew his guru could fix the paperwork. He asked if we could drive the Land Rover up to the Himalayan foothills, where his guru was. I had no interest in gurus or the garish trappings of Hinduism, but I grudgingly agreed.

We returned to Bareilly for the Land Rover, then began driving up to the hills. When nightfall came, we stayed with a family that Bhagavan Das knew. Like Harish, they were devotees of the monkey god, Hanuman. They welcomed us into their modest home and fed us a simple meal. Exhausted from our travels, Bhagavan Das and I found places to bed down on the floor.

My Western stomach hadn't taken well to our many days of begging for Indian leftovers, however, and my innards were rumbling. Suddenly, I felt the urgent need for the toilet. There was no indoor plumbing in the house, so I felt around for the door to the outside. Stumbling, I headed for the outhouse. With no electric lights, the night was pitch black. I slowly groped my way along the short distance to the privy. Overhead the shimmering stars seemed so close they appeared as hanging lights. It was like a hallucinatory van Gogh painting.

There's something profound about staring into the cosmos, and in that moment, I suddenly felt Mother with me. Not since I was on LSD at her funeral had I been with her as a soul, and in the months since, I'd not made time to mourn or acknowledge my sadness—what with the family commotion, the upheaval at Millbrook, my relationship with Caroline, my travels with David and Bhagavan Das. My emotions were still mixed and raw. Now in her presence again, I felt joy. It was as if she'd come in spirit to give me her love.

I had to laugh. Here I was, a Freudian-trained psychologist who'd endured years of psychoanalysis, on my way to the outdoor toilet, thinking about—of course!—my mother. My professional self loved the incongruity. Even in this tender moment, I was retreating into humor and irony to sidestep the gaping emptiness of Mother's death. The thought passed.

I continued under the stars to the outhouse, emptied my innards, and stumbled back to the silent house. I fell into a dreamless sleep.

CHAPTER 16

THE MAPMAKER

The next morning, we commence a hair-raising ride up into the hills. The road switchbacks up from the terraced farmlands in the plains, twisting back and forth as we climb thousands of feet over stream-scored hills covered in mist. We traverse ridges with sheer drop-offs and past remnants of landslides. Anywhere else, these hills would be mountains, but we're in the twenty-five-thousand-foot upthrust of the Himalaya range.

As we snake upward through one spectacular panorama after another, I sit in the passenger seat, sulking. Bhagavan Das is driving. He's taken charge of our deluxe camper, and he won't let me take the wheel. But I want to be the one driving. I've spent weeks in this customized Land Rover, and David left it for me. It is my right and responsibility.

Besides, I'm not sure about this guru thing. Bhagavan Das seems deeply affected at the prospect of seeing this guy. He's alternately singing and crying as we climb higher and higher on the precarious mountain roads. I hope he's watching where he's driving.

I'm not into gurus. I consider myself a Buddhist, and I thought Bhagavan Das was a Buddhist too. Gurus are a hustle. Hinduism is a chaotic vortex of calendar art and a garish, endless pantheon of neon-lit gods and goddesses. It's a cacophony of unintelligible Sanskrit blaring over distorted speakers. In my bag, next to my passport and traveler's checks, I have a return plane ticket to the US. I plan to use it soon.

After hours of tortuous driving, we pull off the road, stopping by a small temple perched by the curb on a steep hillside. The vista of green hills receding into the crystal-blue Himalayan sky is breathtaking. Or it would be if I weren't feeling so uptight.

A small crowd gathers around the Land Rover, seemingly out of nowhere. We're still in the car, and I can't really read the mood of these people, but Bhagavan Das starts talking to them. They all seem glad to see him, jabbering in Hindi. I have no idea what they are saying. He asks one of them something, and the guy points up the hill. Bhagavan Das asks if I want to come see his guru. He gets out and lopes up a narrow path.

My first impulse is to stay with the car to protect it. People are milling around it. They're in a celebratory mood, but after Bhagavan Das leaves, they seem agitated. They're trying to make me understand something. Finally, I understand that they're urging me to follow Bhagavan Das. I think, "Do they want me out of the way so they can trash the car? Or steal it?"

They keep yammering at me and pointing up the hill. Their insistence propels me out of the car, and my curiosity overcomes my paranoia. I follow the path Bhagavan Das took, glancing back at the Land Rover as it disappears from view.

The path levels out into a small terraced field. People are sitting around an old man seated on a low plank bed under a tree, wrapped in a plaid blanket. There are about twenty people, many in white. It looks like some kind of cult. Or a picnic at a mental hospital. I'm not going near it.

I hang back at the edge of the scene. I see Bhagavan Das lying flat on the ground, his hands extended and touching the old man's feet. He calls him Maharaj-ji, which in Hindi means "great king." He's weeping ecstatically. I think this must be some bizarre ritual that's part of the cult. Fragrant incense rises into the air, mixing with the smell of pine needles. Other people come up and touch the old man's feet with their hands or bow their foreheads to his toe, which is sticking out from under the blanket.

I'm not touching anyone's feet. I was a Harvard professor! I remain at a distance, slouching with my hands in the pockets of my jeans, trying to be invisible. I am not part of this scene. The old man is talking to people, and they all seem very happy.

He turns toward me and points. He says something in Hindi. "Abba gabba gabba" is all that comes through. "You came in a big car?" someone translates in English. Everyone in the group turns toward me. I feel even more uncomfortable. I say, "Yeah." The old man says, "Will you give it to me?"

Before I can respond, Bhagavan Das jumps up. "Maharaj-ji, if you want it, it's yours!"

I freak out. Everybody in the group looks at me and laughs delight-edly. They all know Maharaj-ji never asks for anything except maybe an apple. But I don't know that. I splutter, "You can't give him that car! That's not our car to give away. It's David's."

No one pays any attention. They're laughing and smiling and talk-ing among themselves and sharing lighthearted conversation with Maharaj-ji. Only the translator continues to watch me.

Maharaj-ji turns to me again. "Do you make much money in America?" he asks. I figure he must think all Americans are rich, so I play along. "Yeah," I say, "at one time I made a lot of money in America."

"How much did you make?"

"Well, one year I made $35,000. Some of it in cash."

They calculate the exchange rate of dollars into rupees. It's a siz-able amount. Maharaj-ji speaks again. "Will you buy a car like that for me?" he asks.

This is the fastest hustle I've ever seen. My father is good at shak-ing the tree—that's how he raised funds for Brandeis University and Albert Einstein College of Medicine, after all—but he's not this good. I'm clearly not in Boston. I've barely even met this guy in the blanket, and he's already asking me for a $7,000 car ($55,000 today).

I say, "Well . . . maybe."

This whole time, he's been smiling at me. My head is spinning. What has Bhagavan Das gotten me into? Everyone else is laughing. They're not being malicious, they're just enjoying hanging out with the old man in the blanket. Everyone knows he's putting me on. Except, of course, me.

Maharaj-ji sends us to eat, to have some *prasad*, blessed food. We follow a couple of people down the hill to where the little temple is. The temple has a large statue of a monkey enshrined in it. The Land

Rover is still parked next to it. I am reassured: that's my world, and it is secure. This new scene makes no sense at all.

Bhagavan Das and I sit on a veranda that looks out over the mountains. They feed us a mound of vegetables and spicy potatoes and pooris. It's delicious food. After we eat, they give us straw mats and blankets to rest on. We are way up in the mountains—no telephones, no lights, no nothing—and even though they are very hospitable, it's an uncomfortable bed, and my stomach is still unsettled. Bhagavan Das is chatting animatedly with the Indian devotees. I still feel disoriented.

After a brief rest, they bring us sweet chai tea. Maharaj-ji calls for us. We climb back up to the terrace where he's sitting. He motions for me to sit on the grass in front of him. I feel more uneasy. What's going to happen? The translator sits down next to me.

Maharaj-ji looks at me. "You were out under the stars last night," he says.

"Yeah, I was," I reply. Inside, I'm thinking, "We're making conversation. Anybody could have been under the stars last night."

"You were thinking about your mother," he says.

This shocks me. Where is this going?

"Yeah, I was," I reply. How does he know about my mother? I haven't mentioned anything about her to anyone, not even to Bhagavan Das.

"She died in the last year," continues Maharaj-ji.

"Yes."

"She got very big in the stomach before she died."

"Yes, that's right."

"Spleen, she died of spleen." Up to this point, he's been speaking in Hindi, and the whole conversation has been through the translator. Now he looks directly at me and says "spleen" in plain English. I feel shock and confusion.

How does an old man wrapped in a blanket in the Himalayas know intimate details about my mother? Mother was so embarrassed by her swollen belly. Suddenly, the spirit of my mother floods back over me.

Inside, my rational mind, like a computer in overdrive, tries desperately to figure out how he knows all this. I start running through every possible paranoid scenario. "Okay, they brought me here, and this is part of some CIA thing," I think. I recall the raids on Millbrook. "He's got this dossier on me. Wow, they're pretty good!"

But how could he know about my mother? I didn't tell anyone about last night. My mind keeps running in circles, getting nowhere. No matter how fantastic my story lines get, none of them make sense. My mind can't handle it. This is beyond my wildest fantasy. It's definitely not in the cognitive psychology textbook.

As a Harvard scientist, I have an intellectual position on anything psychic or supernatural. If I hear about it secondhand, I say, "Well, that *is* fascinating. We certainly must keep an open mind about these things. There's some interesting research being done in this field. We'll look into it."

If I were high on LSD, the observer in me would say, "Well, how do I know I'm not just projecting and creating this out of whole cloth anyway?" But right now I'm not under any chemical influence. And I'm certainly not at Harvard. He just said "spleen" in plain English. How can he *know* that?

My mind goes faster and faster, trying to figure out how Maharaj-ji knows this. Finally, like a cartoon computer stuck in an insoluble loop, the bell rings, and the red light flashes. My mind just stops. I'm stuck. My rational mind gives up. It just goes, *Pouf!*

At that same moment, there's a violent wrenching in my chest, a very painful pull, and I start to cry. Later, I realize it was my spiritual heart opening. How fitting that when he says "spleen" and my mind blows and my heart opens, the organ that killed my mother becomes the key for my awakening.

I've been looking for someone who can show me more about planes of consciousness, but in the intensity of this opening, I forget all about maps or mapmakers. Concepts from my past are not even remotely relevant. After weeks of pilgrimage, being here now with blisters and bad food, I realize Maharaj-ji is orchestrating my awakening. The people around him know what is happening. This is what a guru does.

Suddenly, sitting there, it occurs to me that if Maharaj-ji knows my thoughts about my mother, then he knows all my other thoughts too— including all the things I'm most ashamed of. My bisexual double life.

My intellectual pretense. My anger at my mother. I can't bear that he knows all this. These are things I keep carefully hidden. I'm convinced that if people were to know them, they wouldn't love me.

I'm sitting on the grass looking down, thinking about all these things I'm so ashamed of that I don't want anyone to know. He's sitting just above me, on his plank bed. I know he knows every one of these thoughts. He's talking to other people as if nothing out of the ordinary is going on.

Finally, I summon the courage to look up at him. He's looking back down at me from only a few inches away—and all I see in his face is total love. I know he knows all these things I'm so ashamed of. He knows, but instead of criticism, all I feel is great love coming from him. He's not judging me or mocking me or laughing at me. He's just talking to people. I look up at him, and he looks down at me, and I realize he's just loving me with pure unconditional love.

The flood of emotion dammed up from not having mourned my mother collides with the impossible fact that this old baba in the Himalayas knows every detail about me, everything in my mind—and loves me anyway. Something inside me shatters. Or melts. Or dissolves. My spiritual heart cracks open, and something deep within, the part of me that has been hidden, releases in my chest, the heart chakra. I am pulled into my soul.

I start to sob. I am overcome with the immensity of this journey, halfway around the world, to find this loving old man who knows such intimate details about my life and who loves me in a way I have never been loved.

I cry and I cry and I cry. I'm not sad, and I'm not happy. The nearest I can come to describing it is that I'm crying because I have come home. I keep saying to myself, "I'm home, I'm home, I'm home." I've carried this load of secrets and shame all my life, and now the journey is finally over. Such a relief. I've arrived at the place I've been looking for, at home in my soul. I feel a sense of completion, of integration. And this deep, deep love.

The shame of all my hidden stuff washes out of me, all the thoughts and judgments. The paranoia about the car, about the guru, is all gone. I am left with a feeling of release, of all-pervading love and peace.

I am living in the presence of Maharaj-ji's unconditional love. I have never been loved so completely. My parents loved me because I was a good boy, my lovers because I loved them back. There were always conditions on love. Now there are no conditions; there is only pure love. I, who never felt worthy of love, am dissolving into it.

That one look, seeing Maharaj-ji's view of me, changes everything. Who he sees is a different self than the one I know. He sees me as a soul, and now I can see myself as a soul. He is the loving witness to my life, not just this life, but all my incarnations and reincarnations. He sees me from beyond time—from infinite time, because the soul is infinite. He sees the past and the present, and since he knows everything about me, he knows my future too.

In that moment, Maharaj-ji breaks me out of my self-contained universe, my egocentric world. Instead of seeing my life as a personal history or career, I see myself as a pilgrim on a spiritual journey. I am no longer an isolated ego narrating my own story line; I am a soul, evolving toward oneness. I am a pinprick of awareness in the star field of the cosmos. I am part of it all.

Maharaj-ji looking down at me with such love is indelible. It's not a memory. His love is always with me. It reverberates through everything in my life.

CHAPTER 17

INSTANT YOGI

Maharaj-ji sent me to stay overnight at the home of my translator, Krishna Kumar (K. K.) Sah, in the nearby town of Nainital. I learned that Maharaj-ji moved about constantly and had many temples, including the one where we'd met, in Bhumiadhar. The statue of the god I'd seen was of Hanuman, the Hindu monkey god who embodies selfless service and devotion. Maharaj-ji's temples were all centered around Hanuman.

Nainital is a hill station founded in the nineteenth century by the British colonizers. Set around an eye-shaped lake, the town was a popular resort and summer capital under the Raj. K. K. and his family took me into their home, a three-story building in the bazaar, with easy grace. Dazed and wiped out from my crying and my heart opening, I was a basket case. They treated me with generosity and caring, as if I was a familiar relative who had been away and just arrived back home.

All around the house were pictures of family saints and gurus, some living, some revered for generations. K. K. put me in a bed where a great saint once slept. This was an intimate world, a household filled with a spiritual vibration, and I felt myself resonating with it. Maharaj-ji told K. K. to feed me double roti, or toast. He knew the condition of my stomach too. I *was* toast.

I continued weeping in bursts through the night. A new perception of myself—of my spiritual self—was taking birth amid this simple Himalayan family. That heavy load of grief, guilt, regrets, and insecurity that made up my mental burden was lifting, leaving me lighter, more joyous. I was floating on the ocean of Maharaj-ji's unconditional love. It felt like a carrier wave through everything, an atmospheric undercurrent.

As I got ready for bed, I went looking for something in my shoulder bag. Rummaging around inside, I came across my bottle of White Lightning LSD. I thought of the holy men with whom David and I had shared pills on our road trip and how none of them had shed light on my questions. I stared at the bottle.

"I've finally met someone who knows!" I thought to myself. "Maharaj-ji will know what LSD is. I'll ask him." Then I fell asleep and forgot all about it.

The next morning, around ten o'clock, a sadhu named Hari Dass arrived. Hari Dass kept mouna, or silence. He wrote on a chalkboard to communicate. He lived at Hanuman Garh, one of Maharaj-ji's temples outside Nainital, whose construction he'd overseen. He had also supervised the construction of the Bhumiadhar Temple. Hari Dass had stomach problems, maybe from living on two glasses of milk a day or from doing the dhauti kriya, a traditional yoga purification in which you cleanse the digestive system by swallowing a long strip of cloth. Hari Dass took out his slate and wrote in English, "Maharaj-ji instructed me to teach you yoga."

Without thinking, I agreed. There were many things I didn't understand, but I did know that something within me had shifted. I wanted to stay. My initial fear of Maharaj-ji wanting the Land Rover or taking advantage of me was now completely absent. A seed of something new had taken root in me.

Hari Dass took me to another of Maharaj-ji's temples, called Kainchi, where I was to stay and learn yoga. Kainchi is about nine miles by road from Nainital. The word kainchi means "scissors" in the Pahari hill dialect, so named because it is near the confluence of two rivers. The area has since become a stopover for vacationers in the Himalayas, especially after India's middle class burgeoned and cars grew ubiquitous. These days it's also known as a pilgrimage destination for entrepreneurs, from both India and Silicon Valley; Steve Jobs and Mark Zuckerberg have visited.

In 1967 it was a secluded place removed from the world. Hari Dass had also overseen construction projects there, including a bridge over the river. We traveled on a State Roadways bus packed with locals, chickens, and parcels from the bazaar. The mountain road wound around countless switchbacks until, far below, we caught sight of the Kainchi ashram, a small collection of whitewashed buildings nestled in the valley floor.

Hari Dass led me to the temple, which featured representations of Shiva, Vishnu, Lakshmi, and Hanuman. It was built around the cave of another old saint and great Siddha, a perfected soul named Sombari Baba. Kainchi was considered a gateway to *siddha bhumi*, the inner plane where those beings live.

I was given a simple room with walls of whitewashed cement. I was happy to have a quiet place. I needed to get my bearings. I was still reeling from the events of the previous day. Before leaving, Hari Dass wrote on his chalkboard that he would come back soon.

The next day, Bhagavan Das drove up in the Land Rover. I had almost forgotten about the car, that precious vehicle I'd been so uptight about. He reported that Maharaj-ji was still at Bhumiadhar and that we could go see him the following day.

Bhagavan Das drove us the five or six miles to Bhumiadhar. We found Maharaj-ji inside the ashram, in a small room crowded with people. He was sitting on the *tukhat*, his wooden platform bed. The other devotees made way for us, until I was sitting right next to the tukhat. Next to me, the principal of the local school was rubbing Maharaj-ji's feet.

Two days earlier, I'd been appalled by these customs. Now I, too, yearned to rub Maharaj-ji's feet. Maharaj-ji was talking to different people. When the principal got up to leave, I edged up to Maharaj-ji, excited and nervous, and gingerly began to rub his feet.

After a few moments, Maharaj-ji withdrew his feet under the blanket. Immediately, I felt chastened. I saw that my efforts at devotion had come from my ego. I'd brought my achievement-motivated *doing* mind to something that was just pure *being*. My ego was up to its usual strategy of trying to achieve something or get some reward, and that was blocking the flow of love and energy from Maharaj-ji. This was a first taste of Maharaj-ji's subtle way of teaching. Later I learned that touching the feet is more than just a cultural custom. Spiritual energy from a saint or yogi flows through the feet.

Maharaj-ji went outside and sat on the stone parapet by the road. He motioned me to come closer and asked, through K. K., my interpreter, "Do you know Lincoln?"

"Lincoln was president," I replied. "He lived before my time."

"Lincoln knew God was the real president," he said. Then he asked, "Do you know Gandhi?"

"No, but I've heard of him," I said.

"Be like Gandhi," said Maharaj-ji.

"I'd like to be," I replied. He paid no attention to my response.

I had no idea what to make of this exchange. He was not talking about Lincoln or Gandhi as historical figures. They were present for him in a way I could not grasp.

Days later, in the bazaar, I bought small round spectacles like those Gandhi wore. Maybe I would see things the way he did. But I wasn't about to live on goat's milk and almonds, or travel around in a loincloth, or spin the thread for my clothes, as Gandhi had. Sometime afterward, I heard a story about Gandhi. He was on a train, about to depart from an Indian railroad station, when a reporter outside called out, "Give me a message for your people!" As the train began to move, Gandhi hastily scribbled on a piece of paper bag. "My life is my message," he wrote.

I think that's what Maharaj-ji was trying to tell me. His directive had to do with participating in the human condition. Our relations with one another are ultimately rooted in who we are—what all our experiences, education, and karma have made us. Life is the message.

I returned to Kainchi, and a few days later, a messenger arrived. "Maharaj-ji wants to see you right away," he said.

Bhagavan Das and I drove back to Bhumiadhar. As soon as we arrived, Maharaj-ji called out, "You have a question?"

I couldn't think what he meant. Maharaj-ji seemed impatient. "Where's the medicine?" he asked. He touched his head and said, "You have medicine for the head? Get the medicine."

Maybe he had a headache. "I'm sorry," I said. "I don't have any aspirin. I'll look and see if I have something else."

I went to the car and got my shoulder bag. When I returned, Maharaj-ji spoke again. "Medicine for my head," he said.

I poked around in the bag and pulled out my traveling pharmacy.

"What's that?" Maharaj-ji asked.

I poured pills out in my hand to show him. I had more than one psychotropic drug in my stash. There was a little of everything.

"That's STP . . .," I said. "That's Librium, and that's . . ."

"Does it give you *siddhis*?"

"What is *siddhis*?" I asked for a translation. Someone said, "*Siddhi* means 'power.'"

I figured he was talking about strength. "Maybe he's losing his vitality," I thought, "and wants some vitamin B12?" He was an old man, after all.

Vitamin B12 was one thing I didn't have. I felt bad that I didn't have what he needed. By this time I would have given him anything. If he wanted the Land Rover, he could have it. I apologized, putting all the pills back in the bag.

Bhagavan Das whispered to me. "Maybe he's talking about the LSD," he said.

"You mean LSD?" I asked Maharaj-ji.

"*Ah-cha*, yes!" he replied. "The yogi medicine, LSD."

I thought Bhagavan Das must have told Maharaj-ji about the Western "yogi medicine," though later he said he didn't. It hadn't occurred to me that Maharaj-ji meant LSD. I didn't think of LSD as medicine!

I dug back into my bag and pulled out the bottle. I had five pills left. I poured them into my hand to show Maharaj-ji. Owsley had made this particular batch specially for my travels, and it was very pure acid. Each pill contained 305 micrograms, a substantial dose that I knew would give me a powerful trip. And by this time I had a high tolerance.

Maharaj-ji extended his hand. I put one pill in his palm. I was concerned. This was too big a dose for an older man. For someone over sixty, you start gently, with maybe 50 or 75 micrograms. More than 300 micrograms of pure LSD is pretty well guaranteed to dissolve anyone's ego. Some of the people I'd given acid to in India had experienced a bad trip, and I'd had to guide them through it. I was worried he'd get disoriented or upset. Any overwhelming fear might be too much for his nervous system.

Maharaj-ji looked at the pill. He motioned with his chin and put out his hand again. I put a second pill in his palm. Now he was going to take 610 micrograms. He motioned again, and I put a third pill—a total of 915 micrograms—in his hand. That is a huge dose of LSD, for anyone!

He took one pill. I was sitting to his right, and I watched as he took the second, and then the third. He tossed them deliberately, one at a time, into his mouth. He drank a little water.

The scientist in me thought, "Well, this is going to be interesting!" The veteran psychedelic explorer part of me thought, "He's an old man, and I'm responsible." I began watching for signs of distress.

I sat at his feet all day. I was watching carefully, ready to take notes or respond if help was needed. I knew this psychedelic territory well. I had a lot of experience guiding people through LSD sessions, and I'd taken well over three hundred psychedelic trips myself. This was truly the acid test.

But nothing happened, nothing at all. Maharaj-ji went on talking with other people as usual, addressing their personal issues, jobs, marriages, children. Every now and then, he would look at me and twinkle. From time to time, he would close his eyes and go within for a few moments, as he often did. Then he'd be back chatting animatedly and moving about on the tukhat.

Absolutely nothing happened! Whatever Maharaj-ji's sadhana, or spiritual path, had been, it had taken him way beyond LSD. It was as if Maharaj-ji's consciousness encompassed LSD and everything else too. Sitting there before him, I experienced something like a contact high. But there was also another kind of high, a space I was not used to. It was a boundless feeling of pure presence. There were no edges, no boundaries, no concepts to hold on to. I wasn't looking for love, but I felt that too.

From my Western standpoint, LSD was the strongest tool I had, the most powerful drug I knew for accessing other states of consciousness. Yet it had no effect on Maharaj-ji. My first reaction was disappointment. Part of me was hoping he would be impressed and tell me something profound about psychedelics.

On the other hand, the fact that nothing happened told me that he is beyond the body, beyond physical form. He is just being love. On some level, even after my heart opening, I still thought of psychedelics as a path for the West, instant chemical enlightenment. I had been using acid to shift my plane of consciousness, but now I realized that Maharaj-ji *is* all the planes of consciousness. I had to go from one plane to another, but he is already in all of them.

With his demonstration, Maharaj-ji had taken on my psychedelic karma so I could get my ship on course. It was a momentous change in how I viewed the meaning of my psychedelic experiences. At that point those experiences were a significant part of my identity, but Maharaj-ji was showing me I could let go of psychedelics, with all the ups and downs, and come into true oneness. Maharaj-ji stands in two planes of consciousness at once, one foot in form as an individual soul and one foot in the vast formless ocean of love, in undifferentiated oneness. He is a living paradox of form and formless.

Maharaj-ji was showing me the Atman, the One. Gradually, I began to see my spiritual being less in terms of planes of consciousness and more as a continuum, a unity of being, all One. For Maharaj-ji there is no discontinuity. His state didn't change. That was the teaching.

Maharaj-ji had answered my question. I'd found not only the maps but the mapmaker himself.

With the Himalayan winter approaching, the Kainchi ashram closed down for the season. Only a skeleton staff kept me company: a cook and a *pujari*, or temple priest, and a sweeper to keep the temple clean. My solitude was magnified by the language barrier. The cook and the pujari spoke only Hindi or Pahari, the hill dialect. The sweeper, who was clearly crazy, barely spoke at all, and when he did, it was often an incomprehensible yell.

But they absorbed me into their routine, and gradually I began to feel as if I belonged. At the end of the day, we would all sit together by the fire in the kitchen and talk, even though we didn't understand much of what the other said. The sweeper was what in India is called a *mast*, a "God intoxicant," someone who is functioning only partly on this plane. He would cry. He was sweet, but sometimes he was not all there. I think Maharaj-ji kept people like that around to care for them. I came to love him.

I would take my food and go back to my room. I had a kerosene burner with which I would make tea. Sometimes I would cook for myself in the room, oatmeal or kitchari, one pot on the one-burner kerosene stove.

Every day, at about eleven in the morning, Hari Dass would arrive, and he would write on his chalkboard, "Maharaj-ji says . . ." There were detailed instructions for everything about my care, right down to my clothes, which included a warm white woolen robe called an *ulfi*. Hari Dass taught me about the eight limbs of yoga and other spiritual practices for my daily routine. Since he didn't talk, he was unlike any teacher I'd ever had. Our exchanges were brief and cryptic. He wrote things like "If a pickpocket comes to see a saint, all he sees are his pockets."

Before becoming a yogi, Hari Dass had worked as a clerk in the Indian Forest Service and had been a member of the RSS, the Rashtriya Swayamsevak Sangh, a fundamentalist organization known for social service. RSS members believe that India should be a Hindu nation rather than a secular democracy. (The assassin who shot Gandhi was a former RSS member. The current prime minister of India, Narendra Modi, was also in the RSS.) When he wasn't teaching me, Hari Dass was at Maharaj-ji's temples in Nainital, doing maintenance and construction work. He also had devotees of his own who visited him at Hanuman Garh, the temple outside Nainital.

I later learned from Tim Leary that he'd met Hari Dass while in India on his honeymoon. He took a bus from Almora to New Delhi and was intrigued by a sadhu on the bus. Tim spoke to him. Hari Dass wrote on his chalkboard. After their exchange, Hari Dass got off the bus at Kainchi. Tim almost got off to follow him but couldn't quite bring himself to divert from his Delhi journey. Tim just missed meeting Maharaj-ji. That near miss is a mystery.

My exchanges with Hari Dass were poignant and direct. I'd ponder his pithy teachings for days. The silence made me feel as if I was being initiated into an esoteric society, getting secret inner teachings. I tried imitating him and keeping silence and writing on a chalkboard too. I was mostly silent anyway, since so few people around me spoke English.

I was a good student, but my eagerness to learn was rooted in my desire for power. I was fascinated by Maharaj-ji's ability to read my mind, and I wanted to know how to access those siddhis, or psychic powers, in myself. Maharaj-ji said things like "I hold the keys to the mind" and "All the money in the world is mine."

I heard stories about him appearing in two places at once and bringing dead people back to life. Indian politicians would come for his blessing before national elections. When the Chinese almost invaded after an incident on the Himalayan border, Indian army generals pulled up at the ashram gate to ask Maharaj-ji for help. He said the Chinese would stop at the border, and they did. This was power! At the same time, Maharaj-ji utterly shunned publicity and kept this all "under the blanket."

The scientist in me wanted to know how this all worked. Though Maharaj-ji's love was the greatest power I had ever encountered, I thought it was Maharaj-ji's psychic power that had opened me. When I met him I was still in the grip of my Western mind and my psychology training. I couldn't fully take in the depth of that love. Maharaj-ji bathed me in unconditional love, but unconditional love doesn't have a place in psychology. Psychology is about understanding the mind and relationships with the mind.

Soul wisdom comes from God. It was years before I fully recognized that what had really opened me was Maharaj-ji's love. Since then I've learned love is the true expression of a realized being. Power comes from love, not the other way around. Over the years, that love has become the dominant theme of my inner journey. My path has become a pilgrimage of the heart, a journey from the mind to the heart.

It took my gradual immersion into yoga at Kainchi, that quiet, austere place, for me to begin to understand. I had my simple whitewashed room, a charcoal brazier for occasional warmth, and a reed sleeping mat, which was the only thing between me and the concrete floor. In the predawn hours, I'd wake up, read holy books, meditate, and do yoga asanas and *pranayama*, breathing practice. Once the sun was up, I'd take a frigid bath in the stream flowing by the temple. That woke me up! Hari Dass told me a good yogi bathes before doing any puja or yoga, but I wasn't ready for that icy river at 4 a.m. in the dark.

After bathing, I would sit out on a flat rock and listen to the river in the sun.

The diet was monotonous: rice and dal and a few chapatis, day after day. Maybe some squash or greens. I made milky tea in my room on the kerosene burner. None of it was designed for taste, although the cook, like most Indians, put chilis in everything. Food changed from a source of delight, a way to satisfy desire, to simple sustenance that maintained the temple of the body. I ate a lot and still lost weight.

Winter descended. Down in the valley, we had sun from about ten until two. Sometimes it snowed. With charcoal braziers, the actual heat radius extends about a foot, and you have to keep a window open to vent the deadly carbon monoxide. I was given a shawl, but I don't remember being cold. The atmosphere I was learning in was thick and rich. In my bare room, I felt warmed by Maharaj-ji's love.

Sometimes his presence was so strong that I would look around to see if there was someone else in the room with me. I was experiencing joy. I didn't understand why. It was just arising in me, and the room was filled with it—pure soul joy, the living spirit.

Practicing yoga daily for months, I began to feel internal changes. I was doing asanas, the physical poses of hatha yoga, slowly, not strenuously, and practicing pranayama breathing exercises morning and evening. I felt lighter and lighter. At times it felt like being on LSD, but from within my own body, my own being, not mediated by an external chemical. My mind grew quieter and quieter.

Hari Dass braided a special nine-stranded rope belt that I was to wear under the ulfi, holding up a simple loincloth. It felt like a kind of initiation into the yogi renunciate club. He also made a waxed string to pass through my nostrils for the *neti kriya*, to clear my nasal passages for pranayama.

Maharaj-ji would list the very human qualities of lust, anger, delusion, and greed (in Hindi, *kama*, *krodh*, *moha*, and *lobh*), with the admonition that you have to deal with your obstacles before you can really enter onto the spiritual path (sadhana). Just because you decide you're on a spiritual path doesn't mean habitual patterns vanish.

The word *yoga*, in its original sense, comes from the same root as *yoke*, because it harnesses the sometimes contradictory input of body, mind, emotions, and spirit into the One.

In a very real sense, yoga is about evolving from being somebody to being nobody. That was hard to get my mind around, because I was brought up to be a somebody. This was a far-reaching and subtle shift in how I defined myself. Who I thought I was, the old role models, even my identification with my mind itself, were changing. I still had lots of stuff to let go of, but I was starting to identify less with who I *thought* I was and more with who I *actually* am. Maharaj-ji's grace was to clear out the old models, allowing me to see myself as a spiritual being. It continues to this moment.

At Hari Dass's direction, I fasted and drank only water every Tuesday, which was Hanuman's day. As time passed, my body started feeling lighter—not physically so much as metaphysically, less dense and less attached to the material plane. I slept very lightly on the straw mat on the hard floor. Dreaming and waking began to converge.

In the afternoon, I would be half meditating, half daydreaming in my room . . . and then, suddenly, the bus to New Delhi would honk loudly as it rumbled down the road to stop across from the temple. The horn would bring me back. Sometimes, hearing the bus, I would get out my airline ticket. I'd hold the ticket and go out and watch the bus leave, imagining myself aboard. I'd imagine my excitement landing in New York or remember moments from the past, like dancing at the Fillmore with Caroline.

Some residual part of Richard still longed for the comforts of home, paying homage to my old life. But I didn't really want to be anywhere else. I'd surrendered to being at Kainchi, in this timeless space. I was a being in transition. I still had a healthy ego, but the temple, the yoga, and the meditation were literally changing my mind and body and ushering me into my spirit.

The ashram had a little library, and I read spiritual poetry and stories of saints: Kabir, Ramana Maharshi, Tulsidas's Ramayana, the Bhagavad Gita, Tibetans like Tilopa and Milarepa, and T'seng T'san, the Third Chinese Patriarch of Zen. I was gleaning concepts and mulling over new constructs. Ramana Maharshi's "Who am I?" practice of self-inquiry, for example, was inspirational. At seventeen, he had lain down on the floor of his uncle's study and pretended he was dying, becoming the "I" beyond the body. I, too, was changing, but it was subtle. I didn't understand everything in the books, but between Buddhist paradoxes and bhakti devotional poetry, I was uncovering a path within.

Bhagavan Das came and went. He arranged with Harish Johari to use the Land Rover, but I didn't know what he was doing or where he went; I didn't care about the Land Rover anymore. He had a separate room next to mine, on the upper floor at the back of the ashram, and during his intermittent visits, sometimes he'd practice playing a sitar I had bought for him. I'd hear the penetrating notes and progressions of the ragas through the wall and feel an appreciation for this otherworldly culture I'd found. He was a heartful presence, bringing me Buddhist texts to study from the library.

Bhagavan Das was spiritually gifted. Maharaj-ji gave him a lot, initiating him as a disciple, which he did very rarely. Years later, my path with Bhagavan Das diverged; he ended up leaving people feeling betrayed and strewn by the wayside: a wife, a daughter, a son, friends. For me then, he was a true *guru bhai*, a spiritual brother.

Another part of the renunciate package included being celibate, or brahmacharya. Maharaj-ji wove my sexual energy into my sadhana, my spiritual practice. Part of becoming a yogi is learning to channel innate sexual energy, or *bindu*, into spiritual energy, or *ojas*. The cosmic energy, what the Hindus call *shakti*, manifests internally as the so-called serpent power, or kundalini. It was not such a big leap from the suppressed sexual energy of my closeted urges to brahmacharya, which actually means "on the path to Brahman," or God. The yoga concept is that if you intentionally restrain the sensual energy and bring it back inside, you can transform it for consciousness. Hari Dass once wrote on his chalkboard, "If you dam a river it builds up force."

Maharaj-ji's unconditional love loosened the shame I had around my sexuality. The moment I realized he knew everything in my mind, it began to release the burden I felt about my dual life, as well as other negative self-images. I began to actually love myself. Because Maharaj-ji loved me as a soul, he reflected my soul back to me. Souls don't have gender; they aren't hetero- or homosexual.

One day, Hari Dass wrote on his chalkboard, "Maharaj-ji sent Bhagavan Das to pick you up." Hari Dass meant it on the spiritual plane, but it was still a wonderful double entendre, a hint of Maharaj-ji's cosmic humor. Whether Bhagavan Das picked me up or I picked him up remains an open question.

The only other regular visitor I had at Kainchi was K. K. Sah, the interpreter. Dressed in an Almora tweed sports jacket, a wool scarf, and a jaunty beret, K. K. would walk several hours over the hills from Nainital to bring me a mango, biscuits, sweets, or special things his sister, Bina, had cooked for me. He also brought me a wool scarf and other winter clothes. I couldn't fathom a friend like that, who would walk half a day through the cold and sometimes snow just to visit.

While Hari Dass taught me yoga, K. K. gently immersed me in the profound traditions of the yogi saints and the devotional poets of North India. He was following Maharaj-ji's instructions to care for me. He understood the transformation I was undergoing. K. K. had been with Maharaj-ji since childhood. His own parents had died when he was young, and Maharaj-ji was like a father to him. K. K. worked as a municipal clerk in Nainital, attending to local government, but he could be very childlike and innocent. Maharaj-ji had blessed him to "be always like a child." K. K. used this as a license to take "liberties" with Maharaj-ji, work, and social conventions. He never married.

K. K. was steeped in the traditions of the saints and the spirit. He was a patient and erudite guide to the Ramayana, the inner mystical stories about Ram and Sita and Hanuman. He'd write out mantras and texts in my notebook, especially from the Ramayana, taking me into the book's deeper levels of meaning. K. K. was quiet and unassuming—shy, even—but his love and spiritual depth began to soak into my heart, just as with Hari Dass and yoga. I still can't label the depth of this man's love for God and for Maharaj-ji. K. K.'s bhakti, or devotion, was a key to my opening to Maharaj-ji's unconditional love.

Through K. K., I began to understand the tradition of saints and Siddhas. K. K.'s brother-in-law, a lawyer named Indra Lal Sah, came to visit too. I remember sitting on the ground at Kainchi with him as he shared his experiences of the Indian saints Papa Ramdas, Anandamayi Ma, and Sombari Baba. Listening, I realized there was a spiritual context, a tradition of saints and yogis, that Maharaj-ji fit into. Later, in my room, I erected a puja table, an altar, full of pictures of these saints. The books and pictures of Indian saints that K. K. and Bhagavan Das gave me came alive. I would be sitting in the corner and I would turn, feeling someone present in the room. As my mind emptied of thoughts, I would be filled with Maharaj-ji's presence.

At first I thought of the Ramayana stories as myths. But as I meditated, settling into the rich silence and otherworldly atmosphere of the temple, the saints in my pictures, as well as the temple deities—some of whom were also in the stories—became living presences. On the inner plane, the Ramayana characters are not just symbolic or allegorical. It is a many-leveled drama that is always going on, even now in this moment, albeit on another plane of reality. That inner world became as real as my concrete room. Those luminous beings became family.

Several times, K. K. invited me to his home for meals. K. K. is a wonderful singer and musician, and sometimes the evenings included *kirtan* and *bhajan*, with K. K. chanting names of God in Sanskrit or singing songs from the great devotional poets. Others would join in. I remember one young guy whose singing was so melodious and skilled that I was convinced he must be a professional. Then two old guys sang who were out of tune and their voices cracked, but their devotion was so incredible they blew me away.

I'd sit on the dirt floor in front of the wood fire in the kitchen of K.K.'s sister Bina, and she and K. K. would stuff me with the most amazing Indian food. K. K. would distract me with some question, and when I'd look down at my plate, Bina would have put more food on it. It was a playful and loving dynamic, unlike any in my own family.

In later years, when Westerners came to see Maharaj-ji, he'd tell his devotees, "Feed them, feed them." The Indian devotees would feed copious amounts of *pooris* and *aloo*, spicy potatoes and flat bread cooked in ghee—true comfort food. Coming from Maharaj-ji, this was prasad, food blessed with unconditional love.

Maharaj-ji saw that in childhood, many Westerners hadn't been fed with real love. This was certainly true for me: for years, I'd fed my emotional emptiness with Mother's chocolate cake and home-cooked brisket, things she pushed on me as a Jewish mother's expression of love. But that kind of love had not fed my soul. Maharaj-ji gave us the opportunity to taste unconditional love in the extended family of Indian devotees, who so freely and graciously fed and took care of us.

Though I was under Maharaj-ji's tutelage through Hari Dass and K. K., I did not spend that many hours in his physical presence. He was often traveling. When I did see him, he sometimes gave me clues that only made sense afterward. Once, we were talking, and out of the blue he said, "There's a woman in India looking for you." I couldn't think what he was talking about. Later, after I returned to the US, I learned that my ex, Caroline Winter, had visited India while I was there. She was touring architectural and historic sites at the same time that I was in the Himalayas.

Maharaj-ji's body was strangely double- or triple-jointed. Once, a famous surgeon came to see him. Maharaj-ji showed him his arm, which could bend backward at the elbow. The doctor said, "You must have had a childhood injury." Maharaj-ji showed him the other one, which did the same thing. "And what about this one?" he said. He used to go to the children's ward at the local hospital and perform yogic tricks for the kids. He would place his forearms flat on the floor and, thanks to his double-jointed elbows, do a complete somersault without taking them off the floor.

Most of my own interactions with Maharaj-ji, by contrast, were from the inside. Whether I saw him or not, I felt his presence. For a being like him, there is no discontinuity or distinction between the physical and pure consciousness. You could sometimes tell this from his eyes, which had long lashes and were often half-closed. They were rarely fully visible. Sometimes one eye was focused and the other was out of focus, off somewhere else. It was like he had one foot in the world and one in the formless.

Maharaj-ji showed me there are many paths up the mountain but the peak is one. About different religions, he often said simply, "*Sub ek,*" "All one." He said, "Hanuman and Christ are the same. They both serve

God." And he said, "Christ gave up even his body for the truth [dharma]. But he never died. He lives as the Atman in everyone." Buddha, Christ, Moses, Mohammed, Krishna—all aspects of the same being.

We all have our path to discover. Maharaj-ji said, "Don't see differences." When his children encountered the caste system, he said to his son, "If you cut your finger, what color is the blood? If an untouchable child cuts their finger, what color is the blood? Blood is the same, people are the same." My path of the heart comes from Maharaj-ji. It's called *guru kripa*, the guru's grace. I ended up in India, but the trip is not Eastern or Western, it's inner. I can't do it the way other people have done it, and you can't do it as I have, although sometimes we find ourselves traveling together.

I kept a diary at Kainchi, but it was not a diary in the classic sense—I didn't record my activities or what I was doing with my time. I filled the pages mostly with spiritual quotes. It wasn't that I thought the details of life were unimportant. I just had no sense of creating a record for the future, because I wasn't thinking about the future. It was literally immaterial. Everything is here and now, just immanent *being*.

Maharaj-ji also kept a diary, which I saw years later. All he wrote in its pages was "Ram Ram Ram Ram," the name of God. Every day, he wrote a page or two of "Ram Ram." That was it. We think of a diary as personal history, but there was no self-consciousness, no ego, no personal narrative. When Maharaj-ji left Kainchi for the last time, he gave his diary to Siddhi Ma, the close devotee who would take over running the ashram, and said, "Now you write it."

I don't understand why he wrote pages of "Ram Ram" every day or why he wanted Siddhi Ma to continue it after he left. I don't know if there is anything to understand. It's just the name of God. Maybe he was just keeping close to Ram, or maybe that was all that was going through his mind. "Ram Ram Ram Ram . . ."

One day at Kainchi, after the morning puja, the pujari came up to me and managed to communicate that there was a guy at the temple who was troubled and needed guidance. They brought him to see me, which was bizarre in itself. Not only did I not speak his language, I still didn't know much about the culture. The man gushed a stream of rapid Hindi. He ended on the rising intonation of a question.

I could tell it was a question from his body language. The guy waited. I had no idea how to respond. Because I was learning to surrender, I decided to ask Maharaj-ji. "This is really your business," I said inside.

I looked at the man. "Yes," I replied.

I was winging it, and I had no idea whether my yes meant he should leave his wife or do some dastardly deed. But I felt the yes come through me, so that's what I said. I could see the man was overjoyed to get an answer. I was learning to trust Maharaj-ji—trust that I could leave it to him, trust that he wouldn't allow me to harm another being. This was a whole new level of psychotherapy practice.

From this opening space of awareness, I began reperceiving the events in my life from a new, spiritual point of view. My old self-judgments and regrets, my wants and desires and noisy obsessions, were dissolving in the silence. I began seeing myself as if from the outside, from a quiet, calm place of detachment and love. How did I get to this little temple in the Himalayas, where my life looked so radically different? I was thirty-six years old, and I was seeing my life as if for the first time. It was similar to the outsider view I'd practiced as a child, but I was reimagining myself through Maharaj-ji's eyes, as someone worthy of receiving unconditional love.

I started participating in the daily puja rituals at Kainchi. On visits to Nainital, I'd visit the *murti*, or image, of Hanuman, at the Hanuman Garh temple. Hanuman is a multifaceted character from the Ramayana, itself a multilevel saga of divinity, humanity, power, and love. Both god and monkey, Hanuman is so powerful that, as a youngster, he inadvertently grabs the sun, darkening the day. To keep him in check, the other gods curse him to forget his powers unless someone reminds him. Hanuman eventually meets Ram, who is Love incarnated as a warrior prince. Hanuman becomes his most devoted servant.

When Ram's wife, Sita, the mother of the universe, is kidnapped by Ravana, the king of the demons—the sense pleasures run amok— Hanuman is reminded of his power and flies across the ocean from India to Sri Lanka to locate her. Hanuman is renowned for his exploits, but his greatness derives from the depth of his love for Ram, for God. The temples Maharaj-ji built feature Hanuman as the main deity. Many devotees were convinced that Maharaj-ji was himself Hanuman.

The Hanuman Garh murti was a bright-orange cement figure, ten or twelve feet tall. My Jewish bones protested, and I imagined what my former Harvard colleagues would say if they saw me prostrate myself before a giant cement monkey. I knelt anyway. I was learning to express devotion, just as Hanuman embodies pure devotion to God.

That's how much my consciousness had shifted. Back in my room at Kainchi, I remembered all the lectures I'd given about the mind and motivational systems. Western psychology had cut me off from my home in the heart. I'd been arrogant, thinking I knew something. Maharaj-ji's consciousness felt so vast by comparison.

As the weeks passed, I pulled out my airplane ticket less and less. When I did, all those memories seemed farther and farther away, until finally they seemed as if they belonged to someone else.

CHAPTER 18

QUICK,
GET IN THE CAR

O ne day, after I'd been at Kainchi about six months, Hari Dass said, "Maharaj-ji gave you a name: Ram Dass."

I asked, "Is that good?"

He said, "Yes." Ram is an incarnation of God in form, and *dass* means "servant." I was being named after Hanuman, servant of Ram.

Then Hari Dass said, "Maharaj-ji gives you his *ashirvad* for your book."

I said, "What's ashirvad and what book?"

Ashirvad means "blessing." This blessing for a book was quite unusual. Maharaj-ji was notorious for not allowing anyone to write about or publicize him. People who did so often ended up being "transferred"—never seen again in the circle of devotees—or they couldn't get darshan, couldn't get to see him. What was this book I was supposed to write?

Soon after that, in late February 1968, Maharaj-ji told me to go back to the West. He said I would come back in two years. He promised he would meet me when I returned. He didn't say where or when. He said not to tell anyone about him.

Two years seemed like a long exile from what I had come to feel was a heaven world. He didn't tell me what to do in the West. The only specific teaching he'd really given me was to be like Gandhi, and he hadn't even explained what he meant by that. I was a teacher—a professor!—but Maharaj-ji didn't say anything to me about teaching.

Anyway, it's not like I really had a curriculum to take back. Under Maharaj-ji's blanket, I'd experienced a complete shift in my persona, from former Harvard professor to a yogi. I was like a leaf being carried on a stream to the ocean. I'd been launched on a lifelong evolution from ego to soul, from neurotic separateness to my deeper being. I'd gone from running my own show to turning my life over to the guru. I was beginning to see myself as part of the *lila*, the cosmic dance—a soul in a divine play led and orchestrated by God within.

I told Maharaj-ji I didn't feel pure enough to go back. My insecurity was magnified because I knew I'd barely scratched the surface of what Maharaj-ji had to give.

He had me stand up and turn around several times, looked me up and down, and said, "I don't see any impurities."

And that's how Maharaj-ji sent me back into the lion's den, into the maelstrom of karma, family and social drama, the seductions of senses, and ingrained habits I had temporarily been isolated from.

I took the bus down from the Himalayas, through the bustling bazaar of New Delhi, and to the airport, bracing for the long flight and customs. Because I was flying across the Pacific, I decided to stop off first in Japan, as David had done, and connect with Alan Watts and Gary Snyder, who were both still there. I meditated with Gary at a tiny house he had in the mountains, and Alan took me around Kyoto. Seeing Zen temples through his eyes was amazing. After all, he'd been my first opening to Eastern philosophy, when I'd listened to his radio program at Stanford and tried to meditate as he instructed over the airwaves. After my six months of silence in the Himalayas, it seemed like Alan talked a lot.

From Japan, I flew to San Francisco, where I met Suzuki Roshi on the recommendation of Alan and Gary. Suzuki Roshi, who came to the United States from Japan in 1959, was a founding father of Zen in America. He had attended the Human Be-In in 1967, but we'd not met then. I sat zazen with him at the San Francisco Zen Center. He was old and fragile, but he sparkled. When he laughed, he really lit up. Zen practice resonated with me because it was clean and unadorned. It also worked with the mind, what I would call the jnana-yoga part of me. Soon after Suzuki Roshi published his now-beloved modern Zen classic *Zen Mind, Beginner's Mind*.

It was as if I was reentering my old life gradually and in reverse. When I finally flew to Boston, Dad picked me up at Logan Airport. He had his gray Cadillac and was chewing a cigar. I was wearing the white ulfi robe and carrying a tamboura, with my mala and puja stuff in a cloth shoulder bag, a jhola. I had a bushy beard, and I was wearing sandals from the Gandhi handloom store made from cows that had died naturally.

My mother had wanted a girl, but it wasn't until I started wearing a white robe at the ashram in India that I actually got a dress. Dad, wearing his cashmere overcoat and fedora, took one look at me and said, "Quick, get in the car before someone sees you."

As we drove to Newton, Dad talked about making that year's batch of raspberry jam. Spring was around the corner, and he was thinking about Willenrica. He asked if I wanted to help make the jam. It was a gesture, his way of trying to connect his son Richard with this strange being who'd gotten off the plane.

Dad had a new woman on the scene. That afternoon, he told me about Phyllis Hersey, a secretary at an organization where young entrepreneurs were mentored by experienced businesspeople, of whom Dad was one. She was twenty years younger than Dad. I liked her almost immediately. She was both grounded and fun, argumentative and willful. She smoked and played poker and was a good match for Dad.

Dad was surprised I was so accepting, and it made him happy. Our family cook, Mary, who kept house for us in Newton, had a harder time adjusting. Mary anchored the household, especially after Mother's passing. I think she wanted to take care of Dad by herself. Now here was Phyllis, and Mary couldn't be the mother of the house she'd hoped to be. Phyllis was so warm, though, they soon made peace.

I stayed in my childhood bedroom. I'd left Kainchi, a spiritual womb, and returned home to a flashback of an entirely different stage of my life, when the hooks of the parent-child relationships seemed real. Those attachments were now faded shadows. Maharaj-ji was with me, was part of me. I was less in my ego. I was witnessing the changes from a clear, calm place in the heart. Maharaj-ji's cosmic humor at inserting me into this regression was inescapable.

In Kainchi, I had read the story of Krishna, the blue-skinned avatar of God in his form as a rakish young cowherd. One of the most beloved aspects of Krishna is when he dances and sports with the cowherd girls, the *gopis*, in a cosmic love play called the *Ras Lila*. At one point, in order to keep them all satisfied and to reassure each one that she alone is the sole object of his amorous glance, Krishna takes ten thousand forms so that he can sport with all the gopis at once.

Krishna's lila of cosmic love play is a metaphor for God's play with each of us in our inner being. Returning to the West, then, was not a reason for culture shock, just a change of scene in Maharaj-ji's lila, the play. The backdrop had changed, but it was still his melo-dharma.

I used to tell people, "If you want to see how you are doing with your spiritual work, go spend a week with your family." That was from my own experience. When it came to communicating about my time with Maharaj-ji, only Phyllis and my brother Leonard seemed to understand. Still, something of Maharaj-ji's unconditional love came across even to Dad and Billy. I was different. My new being was lifting the burden of guilt and shame from my childhood and adolescence, focusing in on my heart. Maharaj-ji's love was coming through me.

From this compassionate and detached place, I bonded again with Leonard, who was still in the mental hospital. He was always spiritually inclined, and because he had also passed through different realities, we could connect as souls. When I talked about witness consciousness, Len knew what I meant.

One day we sat together in one of the visitors' rooms. Len was wearing a blue suit. I had on my white robe and prayer beads. After a while, a bell rang, letting us know that it was time for visitors to leave. Of course, the inmates had to stay behind. Pointing to the absurdity of our respective garb, Leonard said, "I don't know why you should leave and I have to stay." Then he said, "I want to tell you a secret."

He leaned over conspiratorially. "You know, Richard, I'm Christ."

"I am too," I replied.

"No, you don't understand," he said.

"The reason you're in this hospital," I said, "is that you think you're Christ, but you don't see that everybody else is Christ too."

Although Len became crazier and I became more of a yogi, we still came together in the heart. I saw his mental problems from a spiritual perspective: he was having astral visions and experiencing other planes, but he was still caught up in the power and greed fantasies that had weighed on him since childhood.

Billy and his wife, Helen, by this time had raised two children, Peter and Trish. Bill set up his own private law practice in New York with Peter. Helen was an active fundraiser for breast cancer research at the Albert Einstein College of Medicine. They ran in wealthy, influential circles. After I'd left my job as Dad's assistant at the railroad, Bill had helped Dad by handling the real estate for the New Haven, much of it in the heart of Manhattan, which was a big deal. He and Helen lived on Long Island. Like Dad, he became president of their temple. He hired the rabbi and often sat onstage.

Bill didn't know what to make of my transformation. At first, I was still Richard with my family. Dad would call me "Rum Dum." Billy, more cutting, called me "Rammed Ass." Since he'd called me "Satchel Ass" as an adolescent, I suppose this was an evolution.

In the past, I would have reacted with hurt and anger. Before I left for India, when Bill was still helping Dad engineer real estate settlements for the railroad, we ran into each other at the airport in New Haven. We were both going to Boston, but I was flying in my Cessna, and Billy was waiting for the commercial flight, which was late. I offered him a ride. As soon as we got into the air, he began criticizing my flying. I wasn't up to his military flight instructor standard. True, I was a little haphazard about maintaining precise altitude, and the altimeter needle moved up and down. Billy kept on me so pointedly that I gave up. "Fine," I said, "you fly the plane." He flew the rest of the way.

That captures the essence of our relationship: rivalry and competition. But now I saw Billy from a soul perspective. My brother's karma was to go through life as a materialist: a star athlete identified with his body, socially connected, married to a wealthy woman. Even his religious life was institutional and consumerist. We were on different journeys. I didn't have to react to his sarcasm and power plays with resentment. I could choose compassion and let go of the rest.

While at Kainchi, I received letters from Allen Ginsberg, telling me how he'd been arrested in New York protesting the Vietnam War, and one from former students of mine at Wesleyan University, Sarah and David Winter, who were now married and teaching psychology at Wesleyan themselves. They invited me to speak on campus. I also received an invitation from Bucks County Seminar House, a small conference center in rural Pennsylvania that organized encounter groups and psychological seminars.

Except for Allen, none of them knew I was in India, and I postponed responding to them. Now, tentatively, I began to reach out. In March 1968, I drove down to Wesleyan from New Hampshire, tooling down Interstate 91 to Connecticut in my old '38 Buick, which I'd taken out of storage. My appearance, sponsored by the psychology department, was arranged as an informal talk in a big, modern, living-room-like space with couches and bookshelves.

No doubt everyone expected me to talk about psychedelics and psychology. Though LSD was banned in California, it wasn't illegal throughout the US until that October, and interest in the drugs still ran high (pun intended). Tom Wolfe's *Electric Kool-Aid Acid Test*, about Ken Kesey's escapades with the Merry Pranksters, was about to hit bookstores, as was *The Teachings of Don Juan*, Carlos Castaneda's hallucinogenic spiritual journey with a Yaqui shaman. Thanks to the media coverage over the years, plenty of students knew about Leary and Alpert.

I walked in, barefoot, dressed in my ashram whites and prayer beads and a bushy beard. Faces reacted in shock. This wasn't Professor Richard Alpert prepared to deliver a lecture on psychedelics. I sat cross-legged and began to talk about my experiences, from psychedelics to traveling to India, from meeting the guru to living at the ashram and learning yoga. I reflected on where all this was taking me in my consciousness.

I was feeling Maharaj-ji's presence deeply. As instructed, I was careful not to mention his name or the location of the ashram. But everything came back to him. I was carrying this jewel of Maharaj-ji's presence, and however much I honored his dictum, he was the fulcrum for my transformation. He'd named me Ram Dass, a servant of God. I figured the best way to serve was to do what I'd always done, help others understand their situation and find their own way home.

My talent is the gift of gab, and Maharaj-ji put it to work. I said I'd met someone whose consciousness was beyond all the states that LSD opened up. When a being like Maharaj-ji takes acid, nothing happens because he already *is* in that state of unified consciousness. He is already there. Already *here*.

Many of the students had tried psychedelics, but it was the first time they'd heard anyone connect their experience with the deeper meaning they were seeking. I said that watching Maharaj-ji take LSD taught me that the source of consciousness was not linear, rational, or conceptual. There was no way I could rationalize the place he was coming from. Maharaj-ji demonstrated that his consciousness was not changeable by chemicals. His medicine was more powerful than mine: his medicine was love. His taking LSD brought the two together for me, consciousness and love. And love was clearly winning. In a hallowed temple of the mind on a cold New England night, this was a radical shift.

In the West the idea of surrendering to a guru carries negative connotations. It implies giving up power to another human being. But that internal surrender is really about letting go of the things that keep you separate, your own fetters. You surrender to something greater than yourself, to a love beyond form. The word *guru* literally means "remover of darkness," or one who can enlighten you. A guru is different from a teacher. If you think of the spiritual path as the road to your true self, a teacher is someone who stands next to you, giving directions. A guru, on the other hand, is up ahead, beckoning you from the destination. The guru knows the journey is an illusion; his job is to get you to see that there is nowhere to go, that you are part of the One.

Leading the audience into imagining Maharaj-ji's state, I slipped into another state of consciousness myself, speaking from the soul viewpoint, from within. Maharaj-ji's soul mirrors my soul, and I found myself reflecting him too, through some sympathetic vibrational connection.

My judging mind, my scientific logical thinking, had turned off, I told my listeners. I could feel intuitively that Maharaj-ji transcended any mental concept I had. Yet I was caught in a bind, because part of me was still clinging to knowing through my mind. I was preoccupied with Maharaj-ji's power, the power of this new consciousness as I understood it.

Curiously, though, what my listeners felt and saw coming from me was love. I thought I was in my lecturer role, offering thoughts about consciousness, but I exuded love. My audience recognized this, though I didn't experience it myself.

It got later and later, but barely anyone rose to leave. After a while, someone turned out the lights. Questions came out of the darkness. The talk had started at 7 p.m. and it continued past three in the morning. That night, I stayed over with the Winters at their house. The next day, students began dropping by, wanting to hear more.

Whether I knew it or not, I was beginning to inhabit this new being, the devotee, the yogi in training. It was Maharaj-ji's stealth takeover of my ego. It was about love, not power. I was becoming Maharaj-ji's mouthpiece.

In early spring, I drove with Dad, Phyllis, and Phyllis's mother, Angela, to our family farm in Franklin, New Hampshire. With the nearby lake, its meadows and trees, Willenrica felt restorative and familiar. Here I could be a yogi again.

I moved into the maid's room above the kitchen, which had wood paneling that reminded me of Kainchi. Since I was now a servant of God, it felt right I should occupy the servant's quarters. It was also the warmest room in the house. I hung Indian bedspreads on the walls and slept on a mattress on the floor. There was space to do yoga and set up my puja table altar. I had a new ashram.

I spent my time in solitude, renewing my meditation practice. I also spent time with the family. Phyllis commented on my loving demeanor. Dad, Phyllis, Angela, and I went out to dinner a couple of times a week. In the warm weather, Dad and I went fishing on the lake. We didn't care if we caught anything. Sitting around the fireplace, playing cards with the folks, washing dishes, going for walks in the woods, taking boat rides around the lake on Dad's floating cocktail lounge: it was all a seamless fabric of being. As at Kainchi, I was living in the present moment and witnessing it all from my soul.

It was Phyllis who broke the ice and started calling me Ram Dass. The others slowly got used to it. I began to use both names in public. Soon after we got to Franklin, I went to the grocery store for supplies.

When I came out, three teenagers were lounging by the car. They'd seen my Buick, black with a big spare tire on the side, and were expecting to find their old drug connection from Boston. They hoped to score some acid. "I'm not that kind of connection," I said. Instead, I told them I knew what could take them higher than any drugs. I invited them to come by the farm later.

They did, and after a long discussion about consciousness and love, they asked if they could bring their mothers, as well as the minister from the local church, to hear me. Some weeks later, Dad invited his pals from the Presidents Club to visit the farm, and I got the opportunity to speak to them too. These guys were all heads of corporations and airlines and such, and as they sat by the fire, nursing their drinks, one of the presidents asked me what kind of work I did. I think Dad wanted me to tell exotic stories of the East to amuse them, but instead I told the story of my journey, talking about Maharaj-ji and spiritual India for a good hour or two. It was dark in the firelit room, and my listeners were quiet and attentive. They were thinking about it all. Dad seemed proud, happy that the evening was going so well. He had no idea what I was talking about, but that was okay. Seeing these powerful men fascinated by my stories got his attention. Maharaj-ji's hand was stirring the pot.

Mostly I kept a low profile, focusing primarily on my practice, but that September, I took up the invitation I'd received to speak at Bucks County Seminar House. My talks, for a weekend workshop of about twenty people, made such an impression I was invited back the next month. The lectures were recorded and soon got picked up by the New York radio station WBAI-FM.

In 1968, FM radio was our social media. Listener-supported WBAI was at the heart of the counterculture. It was known for fighting censorship, protesting the Vietnam War, and championing gay rights and other social justice issues. Between two hundred thousand and six hundred thousand people tuned in daily. One popular show was *Lunch Pail*, hosted at noon by Paul Gorman, a former speechwriter for the liberal Senator Eugene McCarthy. He interrupted his usual broadcast to feature my talks, broadcasting them as a series called *Transformation of a Man*.

Before I knew it, people were wanting to know more. Students from Wesleyan—like twenty-year-old Jim Lytton, who eventually became Rameshwar Das, my coauthor on this book—were coming up to the farm because they felt pulled inwardly. Others heard me on the radio or came to other talks, such as one I gave at the Universalist Church in New York. Steve and Leslie (later Mohan and Radha) Baum heard me speak at the Universalist Church and wrote to me about how to maintain a spiritual high. I said they could come see me. They arrived at the farm after a snowstorm, in a big yellow Cadillac convertible.

I taught the basics of meditation and yoga, gave out malas made with New Hampshire pinewood. Purely from word of mouth, there was soon a steady stream of curious callers at Willenrica. One was Jeff Kagel, a student from Long Island who had recently quit a rock band. Eventually he became Krishna Das, a beloved leader of Indian devotional chanting, or kirtan. Another was Dan Goleman, a graduate student in psychology at Harvard. Danny would eventually go to India himself, become a *New York Times* columnist, and write a psychology best seller, *Emotional Intelligence*.

At Harvard Danny was a member of the graduate school program committee. He arranged for me to give a talk at Harvard, where I'd already reconnected with a few of my old friends. It was the first time I'd returned to campus. I showed up in my white robe and beads and talked for five or six hours—plenty of interest from students, though no doubt some professors thought I was nuts.

My old boss David McClelland had by this time traveled to India himself. After publication of his book *The Achieving Society*, he developed training courses in India to help spur entrepreneurs and became a successful business consultant. When I returned from India, he and Mary invited me to dinner at their rambling Victorian home in Cambridge. Mary was teaching art at Cambridge Friends School, which she'd helped found. She listened enthusiastically to my account. Dave and I had been in completely different worlds in India; I think he was jealous of my experience.

He and Mary were still Quakers, but they sought out other traditions as a way of deepening their spiritual path. During their travels, they met a German homeopathic doctor, Hugo Maier, a disciple of the late Indian sage Sri Ramana Maharshi. Hugo became one of Mary's deep spiritual mentors. Dave also liked to spend time with a mystical car mechanic named Karmu.

Dave really wanted to know about the spiritual side of India, which was so different from his time working with entrepreneurs. We'd known each other through many changes, and he wanted to understand this transformation of my identity to Ram Dass. Back in my Wesleyan days, under his tutelage, I had come to understand who I was in terms of my motivations and achievements. Now Maharaj-ji was my motivational model.

Of course, the state in which Maharaj-ji lives isn't "achievable"— you can't *achieve* your way to God. You can only surrender. You make the effort to purify and clear your mind, and then you have to let it all go: desires, attachments, ego, mind, conceptual thoughts. It was the polar opposite of achievement motivation, this cultivation of desirelessness. Maharaj-ji used to quote a line from the poet Kabir that went, "I walk through the market, and I am neither a buyer nor a seller." Besides their affectionate welcome, Mary and David were very open to hearing about Maharaj-ji. A couple of years later they went to India to see him for themselves, and Mary made one of her inimitable sketches of Maharaj-ji.

Reorienting with Dave was similar to the adjustment with Dad. After his initial shock over my transformation, Dad proved surprisingly accepting. The next summer, when I asked to set up an ashram in the woods at the farm, up the hill from the main house, as a place for spiritual practice, he was fine with it. Oh, he still called me "Rum Dum," but it was with affection. Sometimes he and Phyllis would take me and whoever was around to a little Italian restaurant called Angelo's and treat everyone.

I was gradually winnowing out the elements of my old life from my new Ram Dass identity. My old Cessna was still at Hanscom Field. I had no desire to fly it. After meeting Maharaj-ji, I didn't feel the need. Leonard, once out of the mental hospital, flew it around instead. Against the backdrop of the material culture I grew up in, I was deepening the place I'd begun to live in at Kainchi. That's not to say I did it perfectly. If sending me back to the West was Maharaj-ji's test, it was a test I failed, over and over.

In the rarefied atmosphere of the temple in the Himalayas, maintaining celibacy, or brahmacharya, helped me concentrate on God. This didn't work so well for me back in the West. All my old sexual desires arose, and I was often distracted. At some point I gave up on celibacy. And though I continued to wear my sadhu clothes, the ulfi and so on, I began to evolve adaptations, like just wearing white.

I still felt Maharaj-ji strongly. I could feel his compassion (and sometimes humor) for my predicament in the West. So I picked myself up each time, and gradually my practice and stability grew firmer.

I thought I should work on the book he'd given his blessing for, so I put together a proposal for a travelogue about India. I envisioned a "visiting the mysterious East" account, replete with my adventures across Asia and culminating with meeting the guru. I gave it to an agent to shop around. Nine publishers turned it down. Whatever book Maharaj-ji's blessing was for, this wasn't it.

In early March 1969, Phyllis and Dad were married at the temple in Brookline where he was chairman. The cantor, who instructed Phyllis in Jewish religious customs so she could convert, married them. I walked Phyllis down the aisle and was the one to give away the bride. She wore white.

Others in my family worried Phyllis was a gold digger and they'd lose their inheritance. Dad's siblings came to the wedding, but Mother's relatives didn't come, out of loyalty to Mother. Bill and Len and their families attended, with muted enthusiasm.

I was just a loving presence, maybe the only family member who was not uptight about it all. Because Maharaj-ji had helped me find peace with my feelings about Mother, I was happy for Dad to find a new wife.

In addition, Maharaj-ji told me not to accept my father's inheritance. Because I no longer had any claim on Dad's money, any thoughts I might have had about Phyllis's intentions toward Dad's wealth just dissolved. After the ceremony, there was a reception back at the house in Newton. A few months later, Dad and Phyllis sold the Newton house and moved into a red-brick townhouse on Beacon Street in Boston.

Later in March , I was invited to speak at the Sculpture Studio, owned by an artist, William Bowie, on East 77th Street in Manhattan. I sat in front of one of his pieces, a metalwork sunburst. I gave a series of lectures over sixteen consecutive nights, and as word got out, the audience kept growing. Forty people showed up the first night, then fifty, then seventy.

I didn't plan what I would say. At the start of each evening, I meditated with earplugs that Hari Dass had made for me. I cleared my mind and opened myself to Maharaj-ji, using his mantra: "Ram, Ram, Ram, Ram, Ram." Then I picked up my tamboura and started chanting to the droning overtones, mantras I'd learned from K. K. or Bhagavan Das, at times to melodies I made up. Sometimes I sang in English or organized rounds with Kyrie Eleison. Often we chanted "Sri Ram Jai Ram Jai Jai Ram," the mantra Hanuman is said to always be singing.

I shared what I'd learned in the months at the ashram, using the diary I kept in Kainchi and quotes I collected from holy books as jumping-off points. These quotes were from Buddhist and Hindu and Sufi and Christian esoterica, like the Philokalia from the Greek Orthodox tradition or the teachings of the Essene Desert Fathers. I talked about being present in each moment of life.

I did my best to answer audience questions. I talked about how the going up and coming down of psychedelics had ultimately been dissatisfying for me. To stay in my heart, I needed a strong, consistent spiritual love. The discontinuity between states I'd experienced on LSD was only resolved when I met Maharaj-ji. For a being in that state, *sahaja sthiti samadhi* in yogic terms, there is no discontinuity. As Maharaj-ji often said, "Sub ek," it's all One.

Some people got high as I talked. I got high too, but not from psychedelics. I was stoned—with love. Maharaj-ji was coming through me. I loved my audience, and they reciprocated. It was a shared consciousness, intimate and powerful at the same time.

Near the end of the series, a woman named Lillian North came up and handed me a thick stack of transcripts from the talks. She was a court stenographer and had transcribed them all! I was about to set out for the West Coast, where I'd been invited to teach a meditation workshop at the Esalen Institute in Big Sur. I put the pile of transcripts in the trunk of my trusty Buick.

Esalen, which was founded in 1962 as a retreat center where people could explore personal transformation, was already a hub for the human potential movement. Friends like Aldous Huxley and Alan Watts had lectured there, and its seminars—designed for learning and insight—were in some ways like the workshops I once helped organize for the Castalia Foundation. I'd first been invited with Tim Leary in 1964, after Esalen's cofounders, Michael Murphy and Dick Price, attended one of our lectures in San Francisco. We ran an LSD session for them. Now I was returning to run a spiritual retreat as Ram Dass.

I stopped in San Francisco, where I saw Owsley, the Grateful Dead, and Stewart Brand. Alan Watts was back from Japan, staying on his houseboat in Sausalito, and I stopped by to see him too. When I finally got to Esalen, they told me I was staying with a writer, John Bleibtreu, and his wife, Catty, down the road. John was a former stockbroker whose book about environmental issues, *Parable of the Beast*, had just come out and was getting good reviews.

As he was pulling my suitcase out of the car, John noticed the stack of transcripts in my trunk. He said, "What's that?" I told him, and he asked if he could take a look. After reading through them all, he said he thought there were some good stories. He marked the passages he liked best. Curiously, the sections he picked turned out to be moments when I'd completely disappeared into the collective awareness at the Sculpture Studio.

"You know, there's a hell of a book here," he said.

CHAPTER 19

FROM BINDU TO OJAS

By the late 1960s, more and more people were enmeshed with anti–Vietnam War efforts, as well as with civil rights and feminism. The military draft hung like a sword over young men. Martin Luther King Jr., the civil rights leader who vocally opposed the war, was assassinated in April 1968; two months later, Senator Bobby Kennedy, headed toward the Democratic presidential nomination, was gunned down too. The Black Panthers and the militant Weathermen responded with violence. Yippies and other protesters battled police outside the 1968 Democratic National Convention that summer in Chicago. The Stonewall Riots erupted a year later, in June 1969. Despite glimpses of promise—the US put the first man on the moon—President Richard Nixon's administration was not trusted. He vowed to end the conflict in Southeast Asia, yet we were mired in it. American atrocities like the My Lai Massacre and US bombing in Laos and Cambodia dominated headlines. For many young people, the expectations of college, a good job, raising a family were off the table.

Across America, young people were rebelling against institutions and materialism. The positive flip side of rebellion was a spiritual renaissance, the New Age, that was as far-reaching as the psychedelic upheaval I'd been a part of. But it was deeper and in some ways braver, because it asked people to reassess and actually live with the existential moment. Having the courage to look at your culture and demand that it be living spirit was a big shift. It's like a kid who's been playing with toys and grows up. The things you accepted and held dear now seem like children's playthings. You needed new ways of thinking and seeing.

Despite good intentions of families, churches, and synagogues, religion hadn't answered the hearts of its youth. Interest in Eastern thought was continuing to grow. New teachers made their way to the US, like the Buddhist scholar Lama Govinda, who settled in San Francisco, and A. C. Bhaktivedanta Prabhupada, the founder of the Hare Krishna movement, whose orange-robed followers were chanting in airports. Other Americans, seeking authentic wisdom of these ancient cultures, made pilgrimages to the East and returned as teachers themselves.

As I'd been a pioneer on the frontiers of the mind, now I was an agent of change in this emerging spiritual landscape. My talks and interactions certainly came from a different place than when I was a rabble-rousing psychonaut. What I offered now came from Maharaj-ji within me, a kind of being that was not polarizing or divisive. All I had to do was get out of the way and let Maharaj-ji come through.

In late spring of 1969, as the weather warmed, I moved from the maid's quarters at Willenrica to a one-room summer cabin behind the main house. As I cooked my Ayurvedic kitchari of rice and dal on a Coleman camp stove, I could smell Dad's steaks from the kitchen. I still had to go to the main house to use the bathroom, because the cabin had no plumbing. But the separation made me feel more like a yogi. I put up my Indian bedspreads and puja photos, creating a new spiritual womb.

That summer, some of the young people who had been visiting and writing me letters at Willenrica came to stay. Something had awakened in them. They were being pulled to integrate their inner and outer being, perhaps in response to the explosive cultural fragmentation taking place. Jeff Kagel, now Krishna Das, was the first to move to the farm; Dad hired him as a handyman. He was followed by others, including Danny Goleman, Jim Lytton, and Steve and Leslie Baum. These students were already practicing the yoga and meditations I'd taught them; now, we practiced together.

About twenty people set up tents in the woods around the three-hole golf course and brought supplies: rice, lentils, and flour for making chapatis. Every morning, I gave talks in the barn. We'd all sit on the floor together, and I'd share words from the Bhagavad Gita and other Eastern texts.

More people arrived as the summer progressed, mostly for the day, especially on weekends. Cars would be parked on both sides of the driveway and out on the road by the lake. Many of my young visitors had been searching for meaningful spiritual practices, and I would sit under a tree, talking about getting high—and staying high—without drugs. Those on the farm would prepare prasad, blessed food that was offered to Maharaj-ji and shared with whoever came.

Willenrica became yogi summer camp. We held meditation sessions before dawn and did yoga on the lawn. Campers practiced fasting and keeping mouna, silence. They went around barefoot. We chanted and sang kirtan, Jeff playing on his guitar. Peter Kahn, later called Shabda, led Sufi dances on the golf course. Shabda now heads a branch of the Western Sufi order.

It was a spontaneous community, united in discovery and generosity, centered on a commitment to awakening. It was not just spiritual work. We built a darshan house in the woods, constructed tent platforms, and dug latrines. Everyone helped around the farm. When Dad wanted a tree moved, the whole gang pitched in to move it. We mowed the lawn and the golf course on Dad's Farmall tractor and picked raspberries for his holiday jam. By then I was receiving so many letters with questions that I desperately needed help replying to them all. One young woman, Barbara (later Parvati) Markus, who eventually became a book editor, typed my responses.

Even when young people started coming up the driveway by the hundreds, Dad and Phyllis received everyone graciously. My brother Bill got uptight. "Get those people the hell off the golf course!" he said once. But Dad shrugged it off. He consulted on the building of the darshan house. I think he even paid for the lumber. Our camp was attracting outside attention, but Dad was cheerful about it, even after some church people from Franklin were publicly scandalized when they came upon a camper taking an open-air shower in the woods. When filmmakers Elda and Irving Hartley, who had made a movie with

Alan Watts, showed up at Willenrica, they interviewed Dad for their documentary. You can see him in *Evolution of a Yogi* standing by the golf course and smiling. "I think this is all great," he says, beaming.

I, meanwhile, felt more and more like the ventriloquist's dummy. A growing community of people—a satsang—were finding Maharaj-ji, even though they'd never met him. I was using every skill I'd acquired as a teacher, therapist, and psychedelic guide. But really I was just the worm on the hook and Maharaj-ji, the fisherman. As a kid at Willenrica, Leonard and I sold fishing worms. Now I was the lure.

That August, the Woodstock music festival took place in upstate New York, four hours away. Some yogis defected from summer camp for rock 'n' roll anthems, but not many. Woodstock's declaration of interdependence, with its potent mix of hedonism and activism, framed the need to find a place of inner calm from which to view society's chaos. The woods at Willenrica were a refuge from the vortex.

I often wondered why Maharaj-ji gave me my new name through Hari Dass, why he hadn't given me the name himself. Finally I realized it didn't matter. He had planted the seed of love that would turn Richard Alpert into Ram Dass, a servant of God. I had embarked on a pilgrimage that would last my entire lifetime, a pilgrimage to that place of love in myself, to become, as Maharaj-ji is, One.

I saw Maharaj-ji's monkey hand in the karmic stew at every turn. His trademark was the constant parade of coincidences and synchronicities lubricating everything. This became especially evident that winter, when I drove to the Lama Foundation, the Durkees' new community in the mountains of New Mexico.

By this time, Lama was an impressive work in progress. The residents had built a geodesic dome complex, along with a kiva-like prayer room. There was also an octagonal kitchen building with an upstairs dining area. They had incorporated the Lama Foundation with the stated purpose of serving "as an instrument for the awakening of consciousness," and they welcomed spiritual seekers. The residents—self-styled "Lama Beans"—lived on the grounds and pitched in with construction, gardening, and cooking.

I ran Lama's first spiritual retreat and my first as Ram Dass. It was a seven-week winter retreat for Lama residents and a few of my students. We were up at 8,600 feet in the cold, crystalline air of New Mexico. Looking west over the ancient seabed of the Rio Grande basin, we saw breathtaking sunsets. Each participant lived in seclusion for a week, in an individual cabin. Every day, I'd go around in the snow and visit each soloist. The cabin became the mind world of the person inhabiting it. Together we worked on individual practice.

I also delivered food, which I loved doing, because it reminded me of Maharaj-ji, who was always giving out prasad. (After the retreat, a big picture of Maharaj-ji went up in the kitchen, where he became a presence in the lives of Lama Beans from then on.) Participants also came to my cabin to check in and talk. There was a bell at the bottom of my cabin's stairs. The person leaving would ring the bell at the end of the interview so the next person could come. It was like a Zen *dokusan*.

Some of the Native American elders who'd helped with the community's development came up to visit, including Little Joe Gomez, of the Taos Pueblo. He was an early mentor for Lama. After Steve had designed the dome complex, Little Joe had directed its construction. Because the land was a sacred site, a part of the heritage of Native Americans, it was important to all of us that we receive their spiritual input on how the land should be used. Later we attended peyote ceremonies at the Native American Church, down the mountain. We were forming a bond that remained an important current in the stream of spiritual teaching flowing through Lama.

Another person who came to Lama was Caroline Winter, my ex. After her architectural tour of India, she'd gone to London to take care of her mother, who was sick with cancer, and then returned to the US. We'd reconnected briefly in Big Sur when I was teaching at Esalen and realized we both planned to be at Lama at the same time—a sweet coincidence. I saw it all as Maharaj-ji's doing. There was a poignant feeling between us. Caroline eventually went to see Maharaj-ji herself, and he named her Rukmini, after Krishna's spouse. She married someone else and has a daughter. We retain great affection for each other.

When I first arrived at Lama, Steve took my bags out of my car and noticed the transcripts of the Sculpture Studio talks, still sitting in my trunk. As John Bleibtreu had, he asked, "What's that?" Steve read them with care, paying attention to the passages that John had marked. He was also inspired. Like Steve, several of the Lama Beans were artists: Tenney Kimmel (later Sarada Singer), Jody (Dwarka) Bonner, Hans (Siddiq) von Briesen and his then-wife, Frances (Noura). Over dinner, we began to brainstorm ways that the passages could be illustrated and turned into a book.

We decided to create a twelve-by-twelve-inch corrugated box, like a pizza box, containing a book, photos of Indian saints, a reading list, and an LP vinyl record of kirtan chanting. A do-it-yourself kit for awakening. The book was titled *From Bindu to Ojas*, meaning "from material to spiritual energy." The book would tell the story of my journey to Maharaj-ji and include a how-to for yoga and spiritual practices called "A Spiritual Cookbook." I worked on the text for each page, and when I was done, Steve would take it to the artists. "I'd like to work on that one," one would say and get to illustrating. Steve coordinated the design and production. The pages were printed on brown paper and hand bound with twine.

I went out touring and lecturing to raise the money to produce the *From Bindu to Ojas* boxes. Over the next several months, I spoke in California, Maine, New Hampshire, Massachusetts, New York, Connecticut. I spoke on college campuses and at churches. I was invited to speak at the Menninger Foundation, the famed psychiatric clinic in Topeka, Kansas. I also lectured at the Alternative Media Conference at Goddard College in Vermont, a gathering of underground reporters, radio DJs, record company promoters, cartoonists, musicians, and poets. The Hog Farm, the hippie commune that had helped run Woodstock a year earlier—led by the peace activist and clown Wavy Gravy—ran a campsite for the conference. One participant, the program director of a progressive FM station in Montreal, had been playing my talks on the air practically nonstop for months. His name was Mitchell Markus, now Raghu Markus, who heads our Love Serve Remember Foundation. Around us, the country was being whipsawed: the first Earth Day was held in April 1970, inaugurating a new love for the environment, only to be followed a month later by the devastating National Guard shootings of unarmed student protestors at Kent State University in Ohio. The search for meaning and answers felt more pressing than ever. At each talk, I told people about *From Bindu to Ojas* and handed out postcards they could send in to Lama to secure a free copy.

The money from my lectures covered printing and production costs, and that spring, we mailed out about a thousand boxes. But so many people were sending in requests that we quickly ran out. We did another printing, but demand was still outpacing what we could produce. So Steve reached out to a guy in New York who had attended one of my talks at the Universalist Church, a sales manager for Crown Publishing named Bruce Harris. After the talk, Bruce had asked if I'd thought about writing a book and given me his card. Now I actually had a book.

Bruce flew to Albuquerque and met us at a Ramada Inn. Steve and I spread out the artwork for the core book on the two double beds. Bruce loved it so much he took one of the boxes back to New York to show his boss at Crown. His boss, also his publishing mentor, said, "Well, okay, let's show it to the editor in chief and see what he says." The editor said, "There's no way you should publish all this drug stuff. This guy is notorious. It will blacken our name as publishers."

Bruce went home, and the next day he went into his boss's office. He said, "Look, there are three ways we can do this. We can publish the book. Or we can do a distribution deal. Or I'm gonna quit." His mentor looked up in surprise and saw that Bruce was serious. He replied, "Okay, we'll work something out."

Crown distributed the book. Bruce didn't think *From Bindu to Ojas* would fly as a title, and he suggested the simpler *Be Here Now*. We agreed. The first printing of 7,500 copies sold out quickly. When Bruce saw a young man reading it on the subway, he knew it would do well. Little did we know that *Be Here Now* would become a catalyst for an entire generation. It went on to sell more than two million copies. It was carried in the backpacks of thousands of people on their spiritual journeys. It would be called the "counterculture bible" and influence seekers as varied as Steve Jobs, George Harrison, and Michael Crichton.

Be Here Now is the book Maharaj-ji gave his blessing for.

That summer I returned to New Hampshire, where for a few weeks we held a second yogi camp. Many people wanted to know about India, and students wanted to meet Maharaj-ji for themselves. I wasn't supposed to tell anyone where to find him, but I gave three of them permission to write to K. K. He took the letters to Maharaj-ji, who at first refused any involvement. But K. K. persisted, and Maharaj-ji eventually relented. In August 1970, three New Hampshire yogis—Dan Goleman, Jeff Kagel, and Jim Lytton—started out for India.

I was anxious to get back to India too. My two-year exile to the West was up, and I wanted to return to Maharaj-ji. I was tired of talking, and I felt distracted. I was getting lots of questions from young people about psychedelics and their role in the spiritual path. I would never deny, not then or now, the great awakening that Albert Hofmann's sacraments catalyzed for me. They brought me to my guru's feet. But doubts and questions were now percolating in me too. What exactly had happened with Maharaj-ji when he took all that LSD I gave him? How had there been no effect?

I couldn't shake the thought that maybe he hadn't really taken all the acid. When he'd tossed the three pills into his mouth, I'd been sitting off to his side. I thought I saw the pills go into his mouth. But maybe he threw the acid over his shoulder and just pretended to swallow. It had all happened so fast. Had I actually seen the pills go down? Could Maharaj-ji possibly have conned me? Could anyone take that much LSD with no effect?

Were these niggling thoughts just the fading traces of my scientific training and my judging rational mind, the old psychologist? I felt embarrassed to have doubts, but there they were.

I tried thinking of Maharaj-ji as a research subject. From everything I knew, what he had done was well beyond the boundary of the possible. I took only one of those White Lightning tabs at a time, and I was an experienced user. He had taken three. One of Maharaj-ji's senior devotees, Gurudatt Sharma, had told me that Maharaj-ji's digestive chemistry kept the LSD from entering his bloodstream; Maharaj-ji was using a yogic power to prevent poisons from entering his system. As a physical explanation it still made no sense in terms of consciousness. After all was said and done, Maharaj-ji was a *siddha purusha*, a great yogi beyond form, and he kept stretching my model of what a human being could be. Was this just another demonstration of his power?

"My medicine is love," Maharaj-ji said, the clear implication being that his medicine was stronger than my "medicine." In my heart, I felt the truth of Maharaj-ji's unconditional love. I knew I had changed. But my mind was in that uncertain territory between knowing and not-knowing, between my head and my heart. The rational part of me wanted to understand how he was beyond LSD.

My heart was at his feet, but my mind still wanted to know.

CHAPTER 20

A WORLD TOUR

I know you're going back to India," Hilda Charlton said on the phone. "I think it would be advantageous to you to spend time with Swami Muktananda before you go." It was September 1970. Hilda, an increasingly popular spiritual teacher in New York, and I had become friends. Her guru, Nityananda, was a great Siddha like Maharaj-ji, legendary for his powers. Maharaj-ji had called Nityananda "a good sadhu," which from him was the highest praise. As a young woman, Hilda was a dancer in the style of Isadora Duncan. She traveled colonial India supporting herself doing dances in the maharajas' courts. She was a wonderfully astral teacher, leading a weekly group in New York in which she invoked saints she'd met in India, astral beings like the ascended masters of Theosophy, Native American chiefs, and her guru. Her séance-like meetings and chanting generated strong shakti, spiritual energy. Through Hilda many young people maintained their spiritual path, right in the middle of Manhattan.

I respected Hilda, so I went to meet Swami Muktananda. The swami was a Saivite, a worshiper of Shiva. Like his guru, Nityananda, Muktananda was said to have impressive siddhis, or powers. New York was the second stop on an initial world tour. He was staying in upstate New York at Big Indian, the ashram of Rudi, Albert Rudoph, an Asian-antiques dealer who was also a direct follower of Nityananda. Muktananda planned to travel around the US, then back to India by way of Australia and Singapore.

I arrived at the ashram around noon and quietly joined the lunch line. As I waited, someone came up and said the swami wanted to see me. I was surprised. I hadn't announced myself in any way. When I entered Muktananda's room, he was wearing a red-orange wool hat, orange robes, orange socks, and dark sunglasses. He looked like a jazz musician. He took some ash in his hands, came over, and painted three horizontal stripes on my forehead, the ceremonial mark of a Saivite. I said, "But Baba, I'm a Vaishnava"—followers of Vishnu like Hanuman use a vertical mark. "That is for your guru," replied Muktananda. I thought, "Well, okay, Maharaj-ji is Shiva too."

Muktananda was not yet known in the United States. Two of his top Indian devotees, a sister and brother named Amma and Papa Trivedi, came to find me. "Baba is on a world tour," they said. "Maybe you could introduce him? You could sing and dance at the beginning of the programs." I was better known than Muktananda was, so they wanted me as a warm-up act to attract bigger audiences.

They told me the dates of the tour. The first event coincided with the exact date I'd chosen to fly back to India. I didn't want to be touring when I was supposed to be back with my guru. "I'm well known," I thought to myself, "but I'm going to see Maharaj-ji."

Before the afternoon music program started, an announcer asked if anyone played the tamboura. I raised my hand. I joined the six or so musicians on stage, who sat in a circle. There were about two hundred people in the audience. Muktananda led everyone in the chanting, singing and playing his *dotara*, a two-stringed gourd instrument. He was an impressive musician.

During the chanting, I had a waking vision of Maharaj-ji dancing in the middle of the stage. He danced over to me, pointed to Muktananda, and said, "Help the man." I had never had a vision of Maharaj-ji like this before. I was so excited that when the music ended, I told Muktananda I would help him. Looking back, I wonder if that vision actually came from Maharaj-ji. It was not beyond Hilda, who was also present, to do something like that. After all, Nityananda was known for his powers, so his followers probably had some siddhis up their sleeves too.

I helped plan the tour with Sridhar Silberfein, a friend with a health-food business in Topanga, California. We made arrangements for the

38

39

40

41

TOP LEFT   Relaxing by the pool
TOP RIGHT   Tim and Nena on their honeymoon in India
ABOVE LEFT   Caroline Winter, later Rukmini, circa 1966
ABOVE RIGHT   Smoking in bed

Mother at her birthday party

43

44

TOP Allen Ginsberg and Timothy Leary at the Human Be-In
ABOVE Human Be-In poster

TOP LEFT With David Padwa in the Himalayas | **TOP RIGHT** Bhagavan Das
ABOVE LEFT Climbing Khyber Pass | **ABOVE RIGHT** Amarnath cave, Kashmir
OPPOSITE Neem Karoli Baba in Nainital

50

51

TOP Maharaj-ji's gaze
ABOVE With Maharaj-ji, 1971

52

53

TOP Visiting K. K. Sah, circa 1967
ABOVE Maharaj-ji, Kainchi, 1971

Kainchi Ashram

TOP A page from Maharaj-ji's "RamRamRam" diary
MIDDLE K. K. Sah's brother and sister at their home in Nainital
BOTTOM My room at Kainchi

58

59

TOP Learning from Hari Dass Baba, Kainchi Ashram, 1967

ABOVE Meditating in the snow, Kainchi, 1967

TOP My coauthor and compatriot, Rameshwar Das, in India, 1970
ABOVE Bhagavan Das, 1967

TOP At Hanuman Garh temple, Nainital, 1967
ABOVE Phyllis and Dad at their wedding

64

65

TOP Meditating at Willenrica, circa 1968
ABOVE Sculpture Studio talks, Manhattan, 1966

TOP LEFT With David McClelland, Cambridge, Massachusetts, circa 1973
TOP RIGHT Meditating in the family cabin at Willenrica, 1969
ABOVE Speaking to a weekend group at Willenrica, 1969

Raja Yoga

1. Yama — ^{Panch Shila (Buddha)} ¹Non-killing, truthfulness,
   ⁽³⁾non-stealing, ⁽⁴⁾continence, ⁽⁵⁾non-receiving.
   ⁽¹⁾Ahimsa, ^{Satya}⁽³⁾Asteya, ⁽⁴⁾Brahmacharya, ⁽⁵⁾Aparigraha
2. Niyama — (habits & observances) (Restraints)
   Tapas - austerity   e.g. fasting
   Svādhyāya - study   mantras
   Santosha — contentment
   Shuucha - purity (cleanliness)
   Ischvarapranidhana - self-surrender to God.

3. Āsana - posture

4. Pranāyāma - controlling the vital forces of
   one's body

5. Pratyāhāra — restraint of the senses from
   their objects.
6. Dhāranā - confining Chitta (mind-stuff) to a
   certain place.
7. Dhyāna — meditation or concentration - mind flows in
   unbroken current toward the one point.
8. Samādhi - when the external part of perception (e.g. Shabda/sound)
   is rejected & one meditates only on the internal part (meaning)
   6, 7 & 8 are called Samyama. (inner yoga)

69

My Kainchi yoga diary

70

71

The Dome at Lama Foundation, 1974

twelve people in the group. It was like a royal tour. Sridhar was good at this stuff. He is still an inveterate spiritual impresario.

We launched the tour on the East Coast. In Boston, I was doing my song-and-dance routine, warming up the audience for the swami, when I spotted my brother Leonard sitting in the front row. During the intermission, he went out and bought orange slacks and an orange turtleneck, just like Muktananda's swami clothes. At first I found it disrespectful, then funny, then sad.

Len was mocking my reverence for Muktananda. He still believed he was Christ, and he wanted me to worship him. His Christ complex was an example of how attraction to spiritual power can lead one astray. The nineteenth-century Bengali saint Ramakrishna said, if you get siddhis, psychic powers, on the spiritual path, don't use them. They get you in trouble. He meant that if you identify with being powerful, you can get caught up in a spiritual ego and forget surrendering and merging into God.

In psychology, this is "delusions of grandeur." Leonard's encounter with Christ, which he first experienced at Holy Cross, was inside him, but he would never discuss it with me. He was committed to *his* self-image—which meant *other* people were the ones with delusions—and to his sensual cravings for power and money and sex. The drugs didn't help, either. I was sad to see his creative and spiritual side so confused. Inside, he was having a spiritual experience, but it was so mixed up with his ego that he couldn't distinguish between them.

I would soon learn about the distracting nature of spiritual and material power myself. After traveling across the US with Muktananda, we got to Australia. Muktananda was playing the dotara and singing in a private home before about sixty well-to-do people. As he sang, everyone began experiencing *shaktipat*, spontaneous manifestations of shakti. I remember the look of total disbelief on the face of one guy, with a vest and a gold watch chain, as he performed mudras, intricate yogic gestures with his hands. It was obviously something completely foreign to him. The guy's secretary was bouncing around the room in the lotus pose. I felt nothing. I thought, "Well, Maharaj-ji's sparing me from this one."

Afterward, back at our hotel, those of us on the tour were chatting in one of the central hallways, waiting for Muktananda. When he finally came out of his room, he walked up to me. Muktananda was a short man. He reached up, pulled me down, and kissed me on the lips. It was completely unexpected. It was not an intimate kiss, it was just hard.

It briefly engaged my sexual desires, though, and I wondered, "What did he do that for?"

In retrospect, it was kind of a seduction of power, a way to cement his link to me physically. He was pulling me into his orbit. That October, when we arrived in India, there was a big welcome-home rally for Muktananda at a soccer stadium in Bombay. Thousands of devotees attended the return of the swami. On the dais, there were three chairs: one for Muktananda, one for me, and one for the chief justice of the Maharashtra Supreme Court. The judge and I gave the warm-up speeches; the judge delivered his in Marathi. I was introduced as the "Harvard professor," a very good credential in India. Bringing back a Harvard professor was a coup for Muktananda. No one mentioned I'd been fired.

The next day, we drove to Muktananda's ashram in Ganeshpuri, a few hours north of Bombay. There were fireworks, and hundreds of devotees lined up to greet the guru. They all brought offerings. The audiences went on for two days. Muktananda sat on a big throne, and he sat me on a lower throne next to his. In India, traditional offerings to holy men are flowers and money. Muktananda would take the rupee notes and put them under his cloth. The flower malas, chains of marigolds, he hung around my neck. I sat under a mountain of marigolds. Muktananda took in a lot of money.

While we were at the ashram, there was a dedication ceremony for a full-body black marble murti of Nityananda. The dedication was a big event, a ritual to bring shakti, or sacred energy, into the murti so it could be worshipped. Devotees of Nityananda came from all over India and across the world.

One of them was Rudi, who flew in from New York as a VIP devotee of Nityananda. Our rooms were next to each other. The day of the ceremony, one of Muktananda's devotees came to get me. But no one told Rudi the puja was happening, and he was left out. It was a major slight, especially since Rudi had traveled halfway around the world to be there. I felt embarrassed. I wasn't even a Nityananda devotee, and here I was, seated next to Muktananda.

It was a competition for Nityananda's mantle, and it went back to Muktananda's first visit to the ashram in Big Indian. Rudi, who craved legitimacy in Nityananda's lineage, had wanted Muktananda to anoint him as a swami, but Muktananda never did so. Rudi finally anointed himself Swami Rudrananda. A few years later he died when his small plane crashed flying up to his Big Indian ashram.

Muktananda was deeply devoted to his guru, there's no question. But Muktananda was caught up in power. Even I got distracted by the trappings of his scene and the spiritual politics he liked to play.

One night, Muktananda told me to stop meditating in the satsang hall at the ashram where everybody sat and invited me to meditate in his "cave," a personal room in the basement where he did his own meditation. At 3 a.m., I went down to the cave. A sadhu with a large key opened the iron gate for me. The cave room was very dark and hot. I took my clothes off and began to meditate.

Immediately, I began to experience shakti. My kundalini (the "serpent power" latent in the spine) began to rise. I entered into a visionary state of pure energy, in which I was flying. In the vision, I was kneeling in the air before Muktananda. He was sitting at a desk, and I was floating in front of him. Then I proceeded to shoot over his head, still flying. When I came out of the vision, I was so energized, I couldn't sit anymore, and I decided to leave the cave. I rattled the gate until the sadhu with the key came. It was about 4 a.m. I raced for the outside courtyard to get some air. In the distance, I saw Muktananda and Papa Trivedi walking together at the end of the courtyard. I ran over to them, barely touching the ground. Before I could speak, Muktananda said, "Ram Dass, did you like flying?"

I was blown away by the whole thing. Flying is considered one of the yogic siddhis, and Muktananda was manifesting his powers, perhaps to seduce me into becoming part of his entourage. That astral flight was a dramatic display of siddhis, more than I'd experienced with Maharaj-ji. Unlike Muktananda, Maharaj-ji kept everything "under the blanket." He used his powers without seeming to do anything.

Muktananda's powers were impressive, but they didn't touch my heart. Later, I remembered when I'd first met Maharaj-ji, he'd said, "You want to fly? You'll fly." I told him that I had a pilot's license and a Cessna. But he wasn't talking about flying an airplane.

All the special treatment from Muktananda—the places of honor, the access to his cave, the show of powers—was a kind of lure to see if I might become his lineage holder, or heir. His devotees could see my potential from how I attracted audiences on the tour. Papa Trivedi, the president of the ashram board of trustees, invited me over to his home one evening. Before dinner, he told me, "The doctor said that I have to take a little scotch every night for my heart." I nodded, expecting him to bring out a medicine glass.

Out came an ice bucket and two glasses. I didn't really drink, but I remembered the days when I loved scotch and soda. As he poured himself a glass, Papa Trivedi said, "Would you like some plain soda?" I said, "No, I'll keep you company." On one drink, I could barely find the table. We staggered through dinner. The next evening we started a little earlier. Liquor is one of the stimulants used in tantric practice to rouse the shakti—I figured tantra was for me!

Papa Trivedi wanted me to stay on and become part of the scene, because Muktananda was taking an unusual interest in me. Amma Trivedi, Muktananda's secretary, told me, "We've never seen Baba react to anybody the way he does to you." Then she continued, "Maharaj-ji was your first guru. Now you've met your real guru."

I wasn't convinced. I already had a guru—and I wanted to see him again. By mid-November, I took leave of Muktananda. He was making plans to travel around India at the start of the new year on a *yatra*, or spiritual pilgrimage; I promised I'd rejoin him then. I headed for Nainital. I couldn't wait to see Maharaj-ji.

By the time I finally got to K. K.'s house, the weather had turned cold. Maharaj-ji was no longer in the hills—not at Kainchi or any of the other temples. He was nowhere to be found.

Years before, Hari Dass had written on his slate, "Desire is the creator, desire is the sustainer, desire is the destroyer. Desire is the universe."

Just as I'd originally been fascinated with Maharaj-ji's mind reading, I was nearly seduced by Muktananda's siddhis. Now I saw how this preoccupation with power had gotten me sidetracked. If I hadn't gone on the grandiose world tour, I would have found myself at Maharaj-ji's feet a month earlier.

I was disappointed. Maharaj-ji hadn't met me in India as he'd promised he would. In my fantasy, we would meet at Kainchi, and I would bathe in his unconditional love again. Unlike Muktananda, Maharaj-ji didn't want anything from me. I only wanted to bask in his love again.

In Nainital, I met up with the handful of young westerners who had arrived in India ahead of me, Jim Lytton (soon to be renamed Rameshwar Das), Jeff Kagel (who would become Krishna Das), Dan Goleman, and a few others who had found their way on their own. They were staying at the Hotel Evelyn, owned by K. K.'s cousins. They had all been with Maharaj-ji since mid-September, but then he had sent them off to see some other baba in Mussoorie with instructions to come back on a certain date. When they returned, he was gone, leaving no forwarding address. Typical Maharaj-ji lila . . . the local devotees and the staff at Kainchi didn't know, or wouldn't give out, his whereabouts either.

Bhagavan Das, who was still in India, had once again overstayed his visa, and Danny and Jeff had gone with him on a fruitless search for a way to extend it. En route they stayed at the Burmese Vihara in Bodh Gaya, where the resident teacher, Anagarika Munindra, had invited his friend S. N. Goenka to give Vipassana meditation courses. The word was Goenka was a good teacher. Since we couldn't locate Maharaj-ji, we decided to attend the course in Bodh Gaya.

Bodh Gaya is where Buddha sat under the bodhi tree and became the Enlightened One, meditating until he conquered maya, illusion. It is a pilgrimage destination for Buddhists from all over the world, a UNESCO World Heritage site. It is located in the eastern state of Gaya, one of the poorest in India. There's an ancient stupa, the Mahabodhi Temple, and Tibetans give teachings, or *wangs*, under a descendant of the original bodhi tree. The Burmese Vihara, where Goenka was teaching, is a nearby monastery with barebones accommodations for pilgrims and a rich Buddhist library. Goenka was a former businessman trained in Vipassana, or insight, meditation by a great Burmese master, Sayagyi U Ba Khin. He was giving ten-day courses on Vipassana assisted by Munindra, an erudite Buddhist and former Krishna devotee.

Goenka's courses in Bodh Gaya proved to be a nexus for spiritual seekers. Word spread by the social media of the time, that is, word of mouth, one westerner to another. A group of us arrived from Nainital and, over the next month and a half, we took three or four of Goenka's courses. There were about ninety westerners in each course, including people like Linda and John (soon to be Mirabai and Krishna) Bush, who had just arrived in India. Mirabai later collaborated with me on Seva Foundation and two of my books. They were English teachers at the University of Buffalo in New York. I remember we talked about how everything in our lives happened for our awakening. Now, here we were, in these strenuous meditation marathons, and liberation was really hard work.

Other students included Sharon Salzberg and Joseph Goldstein, now well-known Buddhist teachers, who became lifelong dharma friends. Joseph had been in the Peace Corps and had been studying with Munindra for some months before we got there. Vipassana is the practice of moment-to-moment mindfulness, and both Joseph and Sharon went on to help spark the mindfulness movement in the West.

Goenka's courses started with three days of *anapana*, simply observing the breath, usually at the tip of the nose, until you can maintain concentration on the breath moving through the nostrils. After that, we began what Goenka called "sweeping," a systematic scan of body sensations and thoughts using the heightened focus from the breath. As we did our sweeping, we were to bring to bear the three central insights of Buddhism: *dukha*, *anicca*, and *anatta*, or suffering, impermanence, and nonself.

Goenka was a hefty guy with a deep voice that reverberated through the meditation hall without a microphone. Every morning, he chanted from the Pali Canon or in English, and at the end of each dharma talk, he repeated the same admonitions three times: "Be happy. Be happy. Be happy. Be peaceful. Be peaceful. Be peaceful. Be enlightened. Be enlightened. Be enlightened." He and Munindra made an interesting teaching pair. Munindra, who wore a white robe, was almost ethereal. Goenka, by contrast, was more earthy. Sometimes, after his morning dharma teaching, he'd leave us in the meditation hall and go to his nearby bedroom, where he'd munch on breakfast radishes. Sitting at the front of the sitting room, I could hear the crunching, sometimes followed by loud belches. In the silence of meditation, the burps were stentorian.

The long days of sitting in meditation proved rife with distractions, from the buzzing flies to excursions of mental fantasy, long trains of thought that could carry me away for entire meditation periods. The last one-hour sitting of the evening was supposed to be done without moving. The pain in my knees was sometimes excruciating.

As the weeks went by, I started experiencing pressure in my head and feeling a lot of shakti. I felt the kundalini rise into my *ajna*, my third eye. After all my experiencess with Muktananda, I thought, "This is great! My third eye is opening. Maybe I'll finally get some siddhis."

Every few days, we'd have personal check-ins with Goenka. I told him I was experiencing kundalini up my spine. I expected him to congratulate me on this sign of spiritual advancement. Instead, he told me not to get distracted. From the Vipassana standpoint, a chakra opening was just another sensation to be observed and let go of. "Go out to the garden," said Goenka, "run the energy down your arm, and get rid of it."

In the garden, I focused on letting go of the energy, visualizing myself sending it into the ground. I saw a blue light coming from my hand and into the soil. "This energy is important," I thought to myself. "Goenka is a Buddhist, and kundalini doesn't fit into his world view." After that, I went back to the Vipassana and didn't experience any further kundalini. When I felt pressure again in my forehead, I didn't say anything to Goenka. The shakti and the Vipassana sensation were the same energy, but they represented two different paths up the mountain.

The food at the vihara was sparse and uninteresting, with the last meal at midday. An occasional round of tea in the back courtyard, when we could break our silence, became a major event. I had a *kuti*, or hut, next to Joseph's, by the tea stall in the courtyard. In the evenings, all the bhakti refugees would come to my hut to gossip a bit and share contraband cookies or *momo* dumplings we'd smuggled in from the bazaar. We'd also do bhakti stuff like chanting. By Buddhist retreat standards, we raised hell. Joseph complained about all the noise.

In between Goenka courses, we'd go out for more dumplings or visit the Tibetan noodle stalls. A couple of people took psychedelics, just to break the monotony of watching the breath and "sweeping" eighteen hours a day.

Bodh Gaya was a spiritual jamboree, with pilgrims from all over. There were Japanese, Thai, and Tibetan teachers and monks, in yellow and maroon robes. We'd go to the bodhi tree and listen to the lamas give teachings. At one point, we visited a Tibetan monastery to meet the Dalai Lama's teacher, Khunu Lama. He was old and fragile but very welcoming. We also met Kalu Rinpoche, who had been a teacher for His Holiness and would soon begin teaching in the West. At one momo shop, I met a Western Tibetan nun we called *ani-la*, which means "nun." She eventually became Lama Tsultrim Allione, a teacher of Tibetan Buddhism and the founder of the Tara Mandala center in Colorado.

By the end of the Goenka courses, I was quiet inside. The hectic travel of the Muktananda tour had receded into the rising and falling waves of the breath. Nevertheless, I was still preoccupied with finding Maharaj-ji. The principal object of Vipassana meditation is the breath, but I was thinking about him all the time.

I loved "sweeping, sweeping, sweeping," cleaning out the mind. But the meditation was bringing my mind more and more to one point, to a concentrated state—which is the same place where I meet Maharaj-ji in my consciousness.

But I couldn't figure out how to find him in India. Where was he? One day in the middle of our last course, I happened to sit next to one of my artist friends from the Lama Foundation, Tenney Kimmel (later Sarada Singer). After helping on the manuscript for *Be Here Now*, she'd come with fellow Lama artist Jody (Dwarka) Bonner to India too, traveling by bus from England. During our tea break, I told her I was thinking about Maharaj-ji instead of following the breath. I wasn't sure I could do any more Vipassana. "I think I'll go and look for Maharaj-ji," I said.

Tenney said she'd like to go too. She had an idea. She and Jody were friendly with the owner of the bus that carried them across Asia, a guy named Gino. It was a Mercedes bus, fancy and comfortable. (The bus had compartments under the floorboards which Gino used to smuggle hash to England.) Maybe Gino would agree to take us on the bus in search of Maharaj-ji. By the end of the course, word had spread over the coconut wireless to the other meditators. Many others wanted to come too, including Danny, Ramesh, and Krishna Das.

When Gino showed up with his bus, twenty-four of us were ready to leave Bodh Gaya.

We decided to look for Maharaj-ji in New Delhi. I was supposed to meet up with Muktananda there, so it was as good a place to start as any. But as we approached the turnoff for Allahabad, a city that plays a central role in Hindu scriptures, Danny said he wanted to visit the mela, or festival, ground. Allahabad is where three sacred rivers—the Ganges, the Yamuna, and the Saraswati—converge. Every twelve years, the city hosts an important festival known as the Prayag Kumbh Mela. I was worried this was too much of a detour, but after a lot of reflection, I decided to tell the bus driver to turn off toward Allahabad.

As we approached the place from which one can take a boat out to where the rivers meet, we saw an unusual Hanuman temple by the roadside. It was unusual because it is underground, and the Hanuman murti is lying down. We were looking out the bus windows when suddenly Ramesh yelled, "There's Maharaj-ji! Stop the bus!"

Our driver screeched to a halt in the middle of the road, and all of us poured out of the bus. We fell at Maharaj-ji's feet, semihysterical with joy.

Maharaj-ji had been walking along the road with his devotee Sudhir Mukerjee, a professor in Allahabad known as Dada, meaning "older brother." Dada told us later that Maharaj-ji had turned to him suddenly and said simply, "They've come."

Maharaj-ji had known. In case I'd forgotten, this miraculous being was reminding me he knows everything and is with me every moment. My anxious decision making and weighing of alternatives were seen in advance by Maharaj-ji. What did that say about my supposed free will?

Maharaj-ji and Dada took a cycle rickshaw through the dusty streets to Dada's house, and we followed in the Mercedes bus. I can still picture the sleek Mercedes bus trailing the funky rickshaw through the dusty lanes of Allahabad. As we got to know him, we realized Dada was an extraordinary devotee. He was like an extension of Maharaj-ji's hand, so deeply anchored in his surrender to Maharaj-ji that we once observed him turn and respond to Maharaj-ji's call a fraction of a second before Maharaj-ji's voice actually summoned him. When Dada was a teenager he met Maharaj-ji at Calcutta's Dakshineswar Kali Temple. Maharaj-ji offered him a mantra, which Dada initially refused, although he then began to use it. He didn't see Maharaj-ji again for thirty years, until they met in Allahabad. By then Dada was an economics professor at the university. He was a socialist and maybe a Communist, and he was not interested in holy men. But when his wife, Didi, heard that Maharaj-ji was at a neighbor's house, she talked Dada into going. As soon as he walked in the door, Maharaj-ji said to him, "Don't you have a mantra?"

In the summer, when the university was out of session, Dada and Didi would journey up the hills to Kainchi, but Dada's house in Allahabad had become Maharaj-ji's regular winter camp. It would fill with devotees whenever Maharaj-ji showed up. When our bus pulled up to the house, at 4 Church Lane, we found that Didi, together with Dada's mother and auntie, had been busy preparing food since early morning. They were following Maharaj-ji's instructions to prepare lunch for twenty-four people—our exact number.

After we'd spent about five days in Allahabad, Maharaj-ji sent us to New Delhi to meet up with Muktananda. I didn't want to go, but Maharaj-ji insisted. "You promised him," he said. "You promised him you would go."

When we got to the capital, I stopped by the American Express office to pick up mail. There, I saw another bus full of westerners. This one was carrying members of the Hog Farm, the hippie commune led by Wavy Gravy. They had traveled overland from Europe, through Kashmir, and were on their way to Kathmandu. After crossing paths with him in Vermont, I knew and liked Wavy.

Maharaj-ji devotees and Hog Farmers agreed to meet at the Kumar Gallery, one of New Delhi's art galleries. There was going to be dinner and dancing, and I was also supposed to give a talk. But things did not go exactly as planned. One Hog Farm member was Brook Beecher, a big guy who was Wavy's brother-in-law. He was also hearing impaired and mentally disturbed. As I began to deliver my talk, Brook decided I was stealing attention from his friend who was still dancing. He bashed me on the head with a rock he was carrying from Mount Ararat in Turkey, the resting place of Noah's ark.

As people pulled Brook off me, he yelled, "Holy men are full of holes!" My weeks of meditation in Bodh Gaya must have been effective: my head was bleeding, but I felt nothing but compassion for him.

It was an otherwise convivial gathering, and afterward, the Hog Farmers continued on to Kathmandu. Some trekked in the Himalayas. Later we learned that while they were in Nepal, they were recruited as extras in the Bollywood movie *Hare Rama Hare Krishna*, about decadent hippie culture. The movie came out in June 1971 and included a couple of songs titled "Hare Rama Hare Krishna" and "Dum Maro Dum" (Puff After Puff). The producers provided the Hog Farmers with all the hash they could smoke while just being themselves on-screen.

"Hare Krishna" is known as the Maha Mantra, the great prayer, to Krishna. It was always chanted at Maharaj-ji's temples. In the movie, however, it was used to mock the stoned-out, ignorant hippies. It was a blockbuster success throughout India, and for months we were trailed by Indian kids howling, "Hare Rama Hare Krishna" and "Heepee, heepee, heepee!" with consummate glee. We had unkind thoughts of the Hog Farmers for provoking such unwanted attention.

It was an early taste of how increasing numbers of westerners would change the experience of India and, for that matter, would change India too. On the one hand, I was happy to meet other seekers. Larry and Elaine Brilliant, two of the Hog Farmers, for example, would soon end up with Maharaj-ji. Larry was the commune doctor, an MD with radical politics. His and Elaine's paths would comingle with mine in ways we could not foresee. On the other hand, the influx made things unpredictable. Westerner enclaves formed in places like Goa, which turned into an international party scene. Other waves of westerners converged on holy places like Benares and Rishikesh, drifting on the river of the spirit, a circuit connected by seeming serendipity to teachers and gurus of all stripes.

Meanwhile our yatra with Muktananda was departing New Delhi for South India, and we needed wheels. I bought a used VW van from an American couple, Rajendra and Jai Shri, who were students of Hari Dass. They were going back to the US. Our yatra caravan, following in the dust of Muktananda's pearl-blue Mercedes, included two VW vans: mine, in which I rode with five others, and another with several European devotees.

At one point, the Europeans decided to go ahead of the group to visit Ramana Maharshi's ashram at Arunachala. They were driving at night and, in the pitch dark, they crashed into an unlit barrier at a road construction site. Two or three people died, others were injured. I was deeply upset by what seemed like the sad and senseless death of young people I'd come to know and like. Muktananda said that because they had been going there on pilgrimage, they would reincarnate at Arunachala, a powerful holy place. That was a new thought for me, and I held to it in the midst of grief.

CHAPTER 21

POWER PLAYS

One morning, in a small temple town, Muktananda woke me up at 4 a.m. It was just him. He led me down an alley, then up a long flight of stairs. We entered a small room above a temple, where he had me sit on the floor across from him. He gave me a mantra, which I went on repeating. Afterward, I must have fallen asleep. When I woke up, I was alone. It was about 9 a.m.

Someone came from the group and said, "Baba wants to see you." I followed the messenger to Muktananda, who was sitting in a big room with other people. He motioned me over.

"What was that mantra about?" I asked.

"It will give you great wealth and powers."

"Unless it gives me compassion," I replied, "I don't want power. I don't want power without compassion."

Muktananda looked at me disdainfully and walked away. That moment illuminated the contrast between Maharaj-ji's path of the heart and Muktananda's predilection for power and wealth. Of course, both those qualities resonated in me, which was why I was attracted to Muktananda in the first place. I realized at that moment that my focus had shifted, from my head to my heart.

Later in the trip, Muktananda sent me to the ashram of Sathya Sai Baba, at Whitefield near Bangalore. He wanted me to arrange a meeting with Sai Baba, who was a well-known guru with many followers. Muktananda thought Sai Baba was a fake.

When I got to the ashram, I stood in the men's line for an audience. "Ah, Ram Dass!" said Sai Baba when he saw me. He took me to a small room, where he materialized a medal out of thin air and gave it to me. It was a silver coin with a gold-colored rim. I was impressed, although it didn't look like real gold. When I left the darshan hall, I showed it to an old sadhu outside. "That's not a siddhi," he said. "He has a ghost who transfers these things from a warehouse." Maharaj-ji subsequently said something similar about Sai Baba, "He brings Dharma [Truth] down to the level of magic."

This was all spiritual politics. And I was in the middle. The next day, when our group arrived at the ashram, devotees were lined up on both sides of a driveway where Sai Baba was greeting people. Muktananda had his driver go straight up the middle of the driveway. When Sai Baba ignored the car, Muktananda got out and grabbed Sai Baba from behind in a kind of bear hug, supposedly to suppress his powers. (Later, Muktananda told me that Sai Baba had no power.) Then Muktananda got back in the car.

Sai Baba went inside, and a devotee told us we could wait in the darshan hall. There was a throne at one end and a stack of folding chairs at the other. Muktananda got himself a folding chair and sat down to wait. Sai Baba didn't show for a long while. I went to his devotee and said, "You better get your man here." He said, "He's giving an interview for the newspaper." I said, "You can't let Muktananda wait." Leaving Muktananda cooling his heels was not what I'd arranged.

Their meeting was a kind of interguru Olympics of yogic powers, a clash between two spiritual lineages. Muktananda was a Shaivite from the line of Nityananda, a great *avadhoot*, beyond everything. Sai Baba was said to be an incarnation of an earlier saint, Shirdi Sai Baba. When Sai Baba entered the room, the two met in the middle. Muktananda recited to him the story of Narcissus, the Greek myth about the supremely vain character who looks into a pool to admire his own beauty. I felt like I was with two adolescents. I was disappointed in both of them.

The yatra concluded with our return to Ganeshpuri. Though we settled easily into the ashram routine, those of us who knew Maharaj-ji wanted to get back to him. Ramesh flew to New Delhi, then went directly up to the hills to do a retreat at the kuti in K. K.'s family orchard, where several saints had stayed.

I went to meditate in some caves at Surat that I had heard about, where you just sit and they bring you food and water. Like a meditation hotel. It was very hot, and I took off my clothes. There was a comfortable swinging chair in my cell, like a hammock chair. The food was good.

When I meditated, the mantra Muktananda gave me for wealth and power kept coming into my mind. I was still attracted to power. I wasn't going deeply into the mantra, though. I was just using it to examine my attachments to power and wealth. I could see how really using it would increase my affinity for them.

I didn't see Muktananda again for several years, back in the US. He was on another world tour by then and still sore that I'd rejected the opportunity to be his heir. When he died, his legacy was marred by the machinations of his devotees. Given his history of power games, it was ironic and maybe fitting. When I told Maharaj-ji about Muktananda's private dining room with gold plates and his pearl-blue Mercedes, he said simply, "He holds on too much." That was long before rumors of Swiss bank accounts and allegations of sexual misconduct.

I think Maharaj-ji put me with Muktananda to work through my desire for power. I fantasized about inheriting his scene, but Maharaj-ji was just running me through my power trips. The balloon of my ego would inflate, then Maharaj-ji would let the air out, sometimes gently, sometimes just, *Pop!* Once, an old lady came by and took out three *paisa*, or pennies, she had tied up in her sari. She offered them to Maharaj-ji. He pointed at me and said, "No, give it to him. He needs it."

Maharaj-ji kept giving me these experiences with power until I saw it was love, not power, that matters.

In Allahabad Maharaj-ji said to meet him at his ashram in Vrindavan, an ancient temple town near Agra, in northern India. Vrindavan is where the god Krishna spent his childhood, and it is a center of Krishna devotion. Danny Goleman, Jody (Dwarka) Bonner, and Krishna Das picked me up in our VW van, and together we drove the twenty or so hours.

When we got to Vrindavan, Krishna Das, whom Maharaj-ji also called "Driver," missed the turn to the ashram, and we had to go the slow way through the bazaar. When we got to the ashram, there was no sign of Maharaj-ji. The priest said he was probably up in the mountains.

Crestfallen, we got back in the van to leave. Just as Krishna Das was putting the key in the ignition, a small Fiat sedan pulled up and skidded to a halt in a cloud of dust and gravel. Maharaj-ji got out with Gurudatt Sharma, a longtime devotee from Kanpur. Without even glancing at us, Maharaj-ji strode into the ashram. No greeting, no word of acknowledgment, nothing. We sat there stunned.

Years later, Gurudatt told us that Maharaj-ji awakened them at two in the morning and said he had to get to Vrindavan right away. As they approached Vrindavan, Maharaj-ji abruptly told the driver to stop. They waited for ten minutes, a pause that coincided with our detour through the bazaar, perfectly timing his arrival to our moment of greatest despair.

We followed Maharaj-ji into the ashram, and he asked us about Muktananda. I told him about the yatra, and before I could mention my visit to Surat, he said to me, "It's good to meditate without clothes." I'd thought I was alone in that cave. Apparently not.

Unbeknownst to Danny and Krishna Das, on the long drive from Surat, I'd made out with Dwarka in the back of the van while the other two drove or slept. Dwarka and I had been lovers when we had privacy during the whole yatra. Now that we were sitting in Maharaj-ji's office, he pointed at Dwarka. "You gave him your best teachings," he told me.

No one else got the joke besides me and Dwarka. Maharaj-ji had a hilarious sense of humor, but understood only by those he intended it for. I'd been feeling guilty about fooling around, but the lightness with which he treated my lust freed me from taking myself so seriously. He was saying, "You want to keep getting lost in that? Okay, but don't get lost in shame and guilt too. It's just a desire." He saw everything. Those hidden feelings weren't hidden from him.

Maharaj-ji's teaching was intimate, funny, straight to the heart, and not heavy-handed, though he could be very fierce too. I associate that cosmic humor with the feeling of his grace. Being able to laugh at oneself *is* grace.

Sitting with Maharaj-ji in the temple courtyard one beautiful evening, Maharaj-ji asked me a question. It was near dusk in Vrindavan, where Krishna performs his love dance with ten thousand cowherd girls, the gopis. Indians refer to this time of day as "cow dust" with romantic precision.

"Did you give me some medicine last time you were in India?"

"Yes, Maharaj-ji."

"Did I take it?"

"I think so."

"Do you have any more?"

My doubts about whether Maharaj-ji had consumed the LSD I'd given him on my first trip to India had carved a well-worn rut in my mind. In the US, I'd reverted to my psychologist role, thinking of him as a subject in an experiment. It was my rational mind trying to explain what I'd seen. There was also a vestige of my cynical professorial self that didn't believe. Once back in India, though, my concerns seemed unimportant. In his presence, my doubts receded until he reminded me.

I went to my room and got my medicine bag. I had five White Lightning LSD pills, but one was broken. He took the four whole ones out of my hand, one at a time. Then, one at a time, so I could see, he carefully placed them in his mouth, making an *ahhh* sound, as if he really enjoyed them. He was hamming it up for dramatic effect.

He asked for water and said, "Will it make me insane?"

"Probably," I said.

He pulled the blanket up over his head and, after disappearing for a minute, peeked out. His eyes were rolling around in his head and his tongue was hanging out the side of his mouth. His face had an expression of shock. He looked completely psychotic.

"Oh, God, what have I done?" I thought in a panic. I had gauged his weight, but I didn't know his age, and there was no telling what such a heavy dose would do to him this time. "He was such a sweet old man!"

Maharaj-ji laughed delightedly. It was a total put-on. He stopped playacting and said, "Got anything stronger?" He was beaming. He was just playing with my mind, like a kid with a toy. He went back to talking with people, completely ordinary conversations, at least for Maharaj-ji. I was watching like a hawk. Nothing happened. Nothing at all.

So Maharaj-ji delivered the coup de grace to my doubts. Not only did he validate the first experience; he again showed he could read my mind, with all my uncertainty. I'd known inside that I had come to the end of my psychedelic path. He confirmed that assessment. Actually, he rubbed my nose in it thoroughly.

Chagrined, I began to see the humor in the whole thing. In both LSD incidents, Maharaj-ji was laughing at my Western reliance on externals and stretching my conception of his consciousness. I had thought of psychedelics as a spiritual path, and now he was pulling that conceptual rug out from under me. From the place of oneness where Maharaj-ji sits, psychedelics are just a fragmentary shard of a vastly deeper reality. He showed me they are a limited window, all the while reflecting back to me the deeper place of love within myself.

The question arose repeatedly with other westerners. Many had reached Maharaj-ji thanks to life-changing experiences with psychedelics. They wanted to know if they were real. "These medicines were known in the Kulu Valley long ago," he said, "but yogis have forgotten about them." He said psychedelics could be useful if you took them in a quiet, cold place and your soul was turned toward God. "They allow you to come into the presence of Christ, to have darshan, but you can only stay for two hours."

It was good to visit Christ, Maharaj-ji said, but it was better to be Christ. "This medicine won't do that," he continued. "It's not the true samadhi, absorption in God. Love is a much stronger medicine."

That statement lowered the curtain on my psychedelic life. After my first encounter with Maharaj-ji, I continued to talk about psychedelics in a positive way; I was still grateful for them, but now they became less important. I focused on stabilizing my experiences through yoga and meditation. Oh, I continued to take trips now and again. But drugs were no longer a mainstay in my spiritual toolbox. As Alan Watts said, I got the message and I was hanging up the phone. I was becoming comfortable in my own awareness, my true being.

I always honor what psychedelics have done for me. They are an entry point, a path through colorful astral planes and exquisite experiences. I touched my soul on psilocybin. The problem is, you have to come down. Now when I hear about people tripping, I think of it as letting children play. Let them enjoy the colors and patterns and sounds. I am being pulled more deeply into my heart, into the witness, into the One with Maharaj-ji. He is the gravitational pull of the sun in the heart, Ram.

I kept in contact with Anagarika Munindra, the Vipassana teacher from Bodh Gaya who hosted Goenka. When I learned he spent summers in the Himalayas, meditating in the village of Kausani, I asked to join him. I felt pulled to deepen my meditation practice. Munindra agreed to lead a retreat for a few of us during the monsoon. I arranged for housing near a school called the Lakshmi Ashram and paid to have a new cistern installed, so we'd have water. When I told Maharaj-ji of our plans, he said, "As you like." Not exactly an enthusiastic endorsement.

There were five of us, ensconsed in our retreat house, when Munindra pulled out. His mother was ill, and he couldn't come. Monsoon season in Kausani was filled with leeches and rain, rain, rain. Once in a great while, the Himalayas peeked out to remind us of the towering peaks shrouded by the clouds.

From our hill aerie we could see the bus stop at the bottom of the hill. One day, we noticed some westerners get off the bus. They trudged up the hill to the house. Maharaj-ji had sent them to our retreat. The next day, a few more came, and the day after, even more. Every day, more people arrived on the bus. Maharaj-ji told them to study meditation with Ram Dass.

I had planned to be a humble student for the summer and become an ace meditator. But Maharaj-ji set me up. Now I was the de facto teacher. Remember the old saying? "Those who can, do. Those who can't, teach." My meditation vacation was short-lived. Teaching was how I was really going to learn. There was no escaping Maharaj-ji.

There were now about twenty of us, so we moved to a larger space at the Gandhi Ashram, on the ridge below. Gandhi was once interned there by the British Raj, to remove him from the political scene. It didn't work any better than my retreat plan. Maharaj-ji's pressure cooker had not been turned down, just moved to a different burner on the stove.

We practiced a mixture of bhakti devotion and meditation. We'd start the morning chanting Ram's name or singing kirtan, then we'd meditate. The program emerged from who we were. We all knew we'd been put there by Maharaj-ji to work on ourselves—or, rather, for him to work on us together.

As I quieted down, Maharaj-ji was a constant presence. My recent teaching experiences—at Wesleyan, Bucks County Seminar House, the Sculpture Studio, Lama Foundation—had all seemingly come about through my initiative. Kausani was all Maharaj-ji's doing. It had that flavor of everything coming together perfectly, the availability of the Gandhi Ashram, the monsoon weather. It was too wet to be outside.

My role as teacher included guidance counselor and therapist: my old roles with new tricks. All the training I had in psychology, psychedelics, and spiritual practices was called upon. When I sat with people individually, we would look into each other's eyes, going deeper and deeper through layers of personality into our souls. I would say, "If there's anything you feel you can't tell me, tell me." Deep feelings, spiritual aspirations, and decades of neuroses bubbled up. Maharaj-ji's compassionate presence allowed a lot of internal work to be done.

It was intimate, it was truthful, it was sometimes painful and sometimes beautiful. We all made great effort to go within. I was helping the participants witness their psychological games. We were dismantling the ego, thought by thought. Spiritually, we saw ourselves as *sadhaks*, seekers on the path, instead of in interpersonal relationships. When I sat with someone, we would start with those interpersonal and personality layers, spiritual and psychological stuff mixed together. After a while, we'd get into this place where we were just hanging out together as spiritual friends, witnessing the mind river flowing by.

The teacher role fanned my ego, except that Maharaj-ji kept undercutting it. For example, the most intimate conversations from our one-on-one sessions were overheard from the room above mine through a hole in the ceiling. Intimate confessions strangely became common knowledge.

I was contending with monstrous egos, and not just my own. Maharaj-ji attracted strong personalities, smart and neurotic individuals, some borderline psychotic. Just to get to India in those days, you had to have an incredibly strong drive and sense of purpose and in normative terms be beyond the pale. Picture this crew of characters cooped up together in this tiny Himalayan village for a month in the pouring rain with nothing to do but meditate. It was like a Thomas Mann novel. We would call it *The Last Resort*. Maharaj-ji had sent them all to my doorstep to study with me. An exquisite structure for ego deconstruction, including mine!

The incessant rains made everyone stir crazy. Other forms of exploration surfaced besides devotion and meditation. Ed Randel, a psychedelic artist who Maharaj-ji named Harinam Das, had some PCP mailed to him from the US. PCP is an anesthetic that is used as an animal tranquilizer and also has mind-altering effects. Old patterns die hard. The risk-taking psychedelic explorer still lived in me, and I decided to take PCP with Ed. I got very high and partially paralyzed from the anesthetic side effects. It took me a while to come down and reintegrate. I was still attached to ecstatic experience, to my greed for bliss.

Over that month of July 1971 that we spent together at Kausani, a feeling of warmth and unity emerged, despite the gossip and backbiting and our being cooped up. The pervasive feeling was love, a foundation that cemented our ties to one another. When we finally got permission to return to Kainchi, we were eager to get to Maharaj-ji. He gleefully teased me, "Ram Dass's meditation teacher didn't come. Ram Dass is the teacher!"

We reinstalled ourselves in the Hotel Evelyn in Nainital. As often as Maharaj-ji allowed, we went to Kainchi. We loaded into the VW van, some of us, including me, perched on the rooftop luggage rack. After a couple of weeks as our trusty chariot straining up the Himalayan hills, the chronically overloaded and underpowered VW engine broke down.

We tried to get it repaired in Haldwani, a nearby town at the foot of the hills, but the mechanic there had never seen an air-cooled rear-engine VW. He got nowhere. Maharaj-ji kept repeating, "Take it to Delhi, take it to Delhi!" Finally, we hired a flatbed truck to transport it and found a mechanic in Ghaziabad, on the outskirts of Delhi, who knew foreign cars. He opened the engine compartment, listened, and with a flick of his hand fixed the engine right away. The van ran fine for a while after that.

When we were with Maharaj-ji, time and space didn't exist. His presence seemed vast and eternal. He would say things about the future that we couldn't understand. At times you couldn't tell whether he was talking about the past, the present, or the future. He used to quote the fifteenth-century poet-saint Kabir as if he knew him. Other times, Maharaj-ji would give one of his close devotees, like Gurudatt Sharma or the schoolmaster K. C. Tewari, a whack on the head, and they would go into samadhi. Gurudatt or K. C. would be gone, his body would turn stiff, he'd stop breathing. On one of those occasions, Maharaj-ji said, "I can do that to him because we've been together for many births."

Kabir, Lincoln, Christ—Maharaj-ji spoke of them as if they were present for him. It's as if Maharaj-ji's eternal present intersects our timeline at a perpendicular from another dimension. Like the story of two-dimensional Flatland seen from our three dimensions, Maharaj-ji sees time from outside our reality. When he spoke of Christ, tears rolled down his face. It was as if he was witnessing the crucifixion. Later he told us to meditate the way Christ meditated. When asked how Christ meditated, he said, "He lost himself in love."

After hearing Maharaj-ji talk about Christ, reading the Bible became an oracular experience. To our new ears, it grew into a living book, which is what the Bible is actually supposed to be. If the weather was fair, we sat on the veranda of the Hotel Evelyn and read from important spiritual texts. On Sundays, I'd read from the Gospel of John or other parts of the New Testament. I hearkened back to early Quaker meetings with my friends, the McClellands. Several of us wore crosses around our necks. On Tuesdays, we'd read the Ramayana chapters about Hanuman, the monkey god. Maharaj-ji likened Christ and Hanuman through their selfless service to God.

K. K. Sah came to the hotel to teach us the *arti* ritual, the "waving of the lights," an offering to the guru, to God. It took us a while to learn the Hindi. In great triumph, we were brought forth from the back of the ashram to perform for Maharaj-ji and the Indian devotees. I'm not sure whether he was showing us off or having a good time at our expense. It was probably some of both. Everyone enjoyed it. We didn't care as long as we got to hang out more with Maharaj-ji.

At Kainchi, they gave out small booklets with a picture of a flying monkey. Krishna Das asked what it was. That was our introduction to the Hanuman Chalisa, forty Hindi verses in praise of Hanuman by the sixteenth-century saint and poet Tulsidas. At first, we massacred the Hindi pronunciation, but gradually many of us memorized it.

The tradition is to sing it 108 times in a day. Each recitation takes ten to fifteen minutes, which means most of a day. Thanks to Krishna Das, who has recorded it many times, these days you can hear the chalisa online or on satellite radio wherever you are. I thought it would be too hard to learn in the West, but it's amazing how it has gained a foothold. Many people learn the chalisa as their main spiritual practice.

Dada Mukerjee often served as our translator, which we loved because he and Maharaj-ji had a very playful relationship. Dada was always blissed out when he was with Maharaj-ji. Being with the two of them was ecstatic and often funny. Because Dada was an economics professor, his English was perfect. He was sometimes embarrassed about translating Maharaj-ji's colorful language. We delighted in their interaction. Dada would give assent to anything Maharaj-ji said: "Hahn, Baba, hahn, Baba. Tikh hai, Baba." (Yes, Baba, yes, Baba. Okay, Baba.)

Witnessing Dada at Kainchi was seeing someone in heaven. There was a streak of deep compassion in his nature. He and his wife had no children, although his wife, whom we called Didi (sister), was the headmistress of a school. They took great care of animals, feeding their leftovers to neighborhood dogs and cows. At Kainchi, the otherwise fierce temple watchdogs cried and moaned when Dada left. Maharaj-ji was ever affectionate and tolerant of Dada's habits. Dada had a dispensation to take smoking breaks, even though smoking around a holy man was considered disrespectful. Maharaj-ji would hold up two fingers and pantomime smoking, motioning Dada to go around the corner. When Maharaj-ji died, Dada stopped smoking.

Dada told us that one time he and Maharaj-ji were sitting quietly. Dada looked over, and in place of Maharaj-ji, he saw a large golden monkey, Hanuman. Another time, Maharaj-ji took Dada's hand at Kainchi, and they walked off together. They disappeared from view. Maharaj-ji returned, but Dada was nowhere to be found.

Other devotees grew concerned and searched for him. Dada was found up the road, wandering in a daze. He was flushed and in an ecstatic state. He had no recollection of what had happened.

My mother always fed everybody who came to our house. Maharaj-ji did the same at his temples. When we asked Maharaj-ji how to raise kundalini, the spiritual energy, he said simply, "Feed everyone and love everyone. Remember God."

Food was a way Maharaj-ji distributed blessings. The Hindu custom is that once a high being touches the food or it is offered to a deity it takes on that vibration and is blessed food, or prasad. Devotees brought bags and baskets of fruit and sweets to the ashram. Maharaj-ji would distribute his blessings with dead aim. Someone would be deep in meditation in the back row and be startled by a sudden apple or banana going *thump!* in the middle of their chest (or occasionally in the testicles).

Maharaj-ji was said to have Annapurna siddhi, the power of the goddess of abundance. When he was around, there were always heaps of pooris and potato *subji* beautifully prepared in vast quantities. Besides potatoes, the diet consisted of wheat, butter, and sugar— basically carbs and fat. By conventional standards, not healthy—but prasad is metaphysical food. Prasad transmits blessings. If you can receive it as such, it's holy communion. Satsang members who got hepatitis and were forbidden by the doctor from eating anything with oil or spice ate deep-fried pooris and spicy potatoes at the ashram and recovered.

Maharaj-ji saw that we hungered, and not just for food. One time, Krishna Das was visiting Kainchi with a wedding party from his adoptive Indian family, the Tewaris. He was overwhelmed to see the affection between all the cousins of the various generations. It was so different from what he'd experienced growing up on Long Island. He asked Siddhi Ma, the Mother of the ashram, about it, and she said, "This love is what you missed growing up. When you were a child, love was used to control you." That was true for me too.

K. K. says that love in traditional Indian families is the founda-tion of bhakti, or devotion. In their multigenerational households, grandmothers often perform daily puja, or worship, and they pass that love for God on to the little ones. Kids grow up in that devotional atmosphere, sharing love with siblings and cousins in the close proximity of extended family.

Ideally, an Indian family is also satsang, spiritual family. The first time I was in India, I experienced that devotional bond with K. K., his relatives, and other Indian devotees. Now I was back, this time with a gaggle of westerners. This circle became the core of a Western satsang. Living with satsang changed my kindred identification from my blood family to my spiritual family. Satsang is loving and supportive, and it doesn't have so much of the element of power that had consumed my birth family.

This is not to say our satsang was one big, lovey-dovey, happy hippie family. The westerners around Maharaj-ji sometimes competed for his attention, which we facetiously called the Grace Race. Everyone was going through intense personal transformations. Kainchi was a pressure cooker.

The Hotel Evelyn became part ashram, part hangout, and part therapy office. We came to call our main practices the "five-limbed yoga": eating, sleeping, drinking tea, gossiping, and walking about. Even though I'd given few clues to Maharaj-ji's whereabouts, I was now surrounded by westerners, many of whom I'd inspired to come.

It was different from being a solo yogi in the Himalayas. Like everyone else, I had karmic stuff to work through: anger, lust, power. Maharaj-ji confronted me with my attachments, sometimes with gentle humor and sometimes with situations from which I had no escape. He gave me the title commander in chief of the westerners, then promptly undermined my authority and attempts at order at every turn.

Meanwhile, we were joined by new devotees, like Elaine and Larry Brilliant. After Wavy Gravy and the Hog Farmers left India, Elaine had stayed on to attend one of Goenka's Vipassana courses. She met Mirabai Bush, who encouraged her to join us at Kainchi. She was quickly absorbed into Maharaj-ji's love field. He named her Girija, "mountain daughter," after the consort of Shiva.

Girija wrote to her husband, Larry, asking him to come back to India to see Maharaj-ji. When Larry, who was a trained doctor, finally came,

Maharaj-ji told him that he would work for the United Nations and help eradicate smallpox. As a hippie doctor Larry had no experience in public health. He couldn't imagine how Maharaj-ji's prediction would be fulfilled.

Remarkably, Larry eventually became second in command of the World Health Organization's smallpox eradication program in India and Bangladesh, where the last cases on earth were seen. Maharaj-ji said, "This is God's gift to humanity, because of the dedicated health workers. God will help lift the burden of this terrible disease from humanity." It was one of the only times in history that a major disease has been wiped from the Earth.

Although the Indian devotees were enormously welcoming and tolerant of us crazy *videshis* (foreigners), we missed some colorful details by not speaking the language. One day a woman who had rented a cowshed from a farmer in the valley reported her place had been broken into and some of her things stolen. An intense and rapid exchange ensued between Maharaj-ji and the young interpreter, which was translated as, "Maharaj-ji says you should lock your door."

Later that day, after lunch, the westerners were sitting around when the translator, Ravi, a young Indian guy, came by, laughing to himself. He said, "What Maharaj-ji really said was, 'These stupid sisterfuckers don't even know enough to lock their doors! What do they expect?'"

I was watching Maharaj-ji from my old room at Kainchi, on the second floor. I was kind of spying on him. Earlier that morning, he'd again told us to love everybody. I saw Maharaj-ji call up one of the Indian devotees who worked at the temple and start berating the guy, who cowered in front of him.

I was shocked. Now I thought Maharaj-ji was a hypocrite, that he would tell us to love everybody, and there he was, tearing into this fellow. He was a fraud. And I had brought all these westerners to see him. I felt betrayed.

Dada Mukerjee came to find me. Maharaj-ji told him, "Ram Dass saw me get angry" and sent him to talk to me. Dada explained that Sharma, the helper, had let a whole storage room of potatoes rot. Food that could have fed a lot of people had been wasted through his negligence. Still, I couldn't face Maharaj-ji. Sharma came by, asking for people to intercede for him with Maharaj-ji. I walked out to the bus with him.

When I came back into the temple at the front gate, Maharaj-ji was standing up near the tukhat. I felt like I had to confront him about telling everyone not to get angry while he was blowing his top at this guy for letting a few potatoes spoil.

What I had missed was that Maharaj-ji had not said, "Don't get angry." He'd said, "Love everybody." Although Maharaj-ji had apparently lost it with Sharma, he hadn't been attached to the anger. It had been necessary. Dada had already tried to tell me this. "Maharaj-ji loves Sharma," he said.

Later that day, at our afternoon darshan, Maharaj-ji spoke to a couple who were having relationship issues. I'd been counseling them about anger in their relationship. He said to them, "No matter what someone else does to you, never put anyone out of your heart."

It was a teaching I needed. I was frustrated with all the other westerners hanging around Maharaj-ji, and anger toward my satsang sisters and brothers was building up. I'd hoped my time in India would renew and replenish me after all the teaching I had done in the US. But every time I tried to be alone, Maharaj-ji sent me more students. Over the year I'd been in India, I'd had exactly eleven days when I was not surrounded by westerners.

At the hotel, I'd been meeting with couples and individuals to help them iron out their relationship issues. There were a number of westerners who arrived at Kainchi as friends or casual lovers, and when they came to Maharaj-ji, he declared them married.

These couples had no particular idea what this spiritual marriage meant. I was left to help pick up the pieces and sort out the mysteries of their relations. They would come to my room for advice. It was both spiritual counsel and talk therapy.

I felt like none of the westerners had any understanding of dharma. I was mad and feeling very righteous about it. So I put a note on my door that read, Do Not Enter. For two weeks, I refused to see anyone. The others told Maharaj-ji. When I saw him, he said, "Won't you help them?"

I was supposed to be a devotee of Hanuman, who loves and serves everyone as God. Hanuman wouldn't have a Keep Out sign. But I was struggling. One day, when we were all supposed to take the bus to Kainchi, I arrived at the bus stop a couple of minutes late, only to find that the satsang had left me behind. "They don't even care!" I fumed.

Maharaj-ji had said, "A saint should not touch money," so I'd stopped carrying it, relying on an easygoing Canadian who agreed to be my bag man and pay for daily expenses like bus fare. Now I was so angry I couldn't talk to him.

I decided to walk the seven or eight kilometers to Kainchi, over the hills, through the forest and the tiny farm villages that dotted the countryside. It is a beautiful and idyllic walk, and although it soothed me, I was tired by the time I got to the ashram. When I entered, another Canadian intercepted me to offer a leaf plate of prasad, because they were already in the middle of lunch. He was being perfectly nice and accommodating. But as he handed me the pooris and potatoes, a wave of anger broke over me. I took the food and shoved it in his face.

"Ram Dass!" Maharaj-ji yelled across the courtyard. Throwing prasad was definitely a sacrilege. "What's the matter?"

I ran over to him. The other westerners sat on the opposite side of the courtyard, looking stunned. I said, "I'm angry at those people. They're all *adharmic*, bad people." I looked over and saw them all in their badness. They were whiny, selfish, needy.

I also knew I was responsible for most of them being there. I hated myself for that too. By then I was crying. "I hate everybody, including myself," I blurted out. "I hate everybody but you."

Maharaj-ji sounded sympathetic. "Oh, Ram Dass is angry," he said. Then he looked at me. "Ram Dass, love everyone. Love everyone and tell the truth."

I said, "Maharaj-ji, the truth is: I am angry."

He leaned over and looked me in the eye, practically nose to nose. He said, "Tell the truth. And love everyone."

I knew in that moment I had to choose whether to hold on to my righteous anger or surrender to Maharaj-ji. It's a rare moment when your guru gives you a direct command. Not to be taken lightly.

I knew what Maharaj-ji really meant. If, from my soul, I saw someone as a soul, I could love him or her as a soul, as part of God. On
the other hand, if I remained mired in my personality and my anger,
I could be stuck on the karmic wheel of birth and death for many
more lifetimes.

Maharaj-ji called for someone to bring a cup of milk, which in India
is always warm milk, usually with a little sugar, almost like mother's
milk. He handed me the earthen cup. I drank some of it.

He said, "Give up anger. If you try to give up your anger, I'll help
you with it."

For me to give up the anger, I had to give up my whole position, all
my reasons for being angry. My pride. But it's hard to be angry, drinking mother's milk from the guru. I looked over again at the western
satsang. Now they weren't whiners. They were luminous beings with
light coming out of them, and I loved them all. What was in that milk?

Maharaj-ji had done it to me again, confronting me with my negative emotions, anger and jealousy and self-righteousness, which were
keeping me separate from him and everyone else and from God. I'd
been wallowing in self-pity—not to mention self-hatred and unwor-
thiness, which of course I was projecting onto everyone else. Maharaj-ji
just sat there twinkling, an unflinching mirror.

I knew I had to make amends to my satsang brothers and sisters.
Maharaj-ji's essential teaching is to feed everyone and love everyone.
I took an apple and cut it up. Then I went from one member of the
satsang to another. Maharaj-ji said you should feed others with love;
if you feed someone in anger, it's like giving them poison. I looked
each person in the eyes, until I could see the place in them where we
are love together, and then I fed them each a piece of apple. It took a
while. The whole situation was Maharaj-ji's lila, his play, from start
to finish.

Over the years, Maharaj-ji's satsang has expanded to many thousands of devotees, people who were with him in the body and people
who weren't. But there's a special photo from that year, 1971, which
we call "Nainital High" because it looks like a school graduation
photo. We hired a photo wallah from one of the tourist shops, who
showed up at the hotel with a big ten-by-twelve-inch plate camera

from British times. He set up the camera under a big black cloth. The lens had no shutter. To make the exposure, the photographer took off the lens cap and counted. Anyone who moved came out blurry.

It's a treasured image because it represents a shared moment basking in Maharaj-ji's unconditional love. For most of those in the photo, that time is a deep fountain of faith and solace. Since those days together, there have been illnesses and deaths, terrible accidents, painful divorces and infidelities, problems with kids and careers, addictions, and now the depredations of age. Each of us, in our unique way, confronts the existential elements the Buddha laid out, of suffering, impermanence, and the ego delusion of any permanent self. But behind it all, still, is Maharaj-ji.

Love everyone, serve everyone, and remember God.

CHAPTER 22

BE HERE NOW

In the spring of 1971 the first copies of *Be Here Now* arrived in Kainchi. I couldn't wait to show Maharaj-ji. After all, this was his book. But after someone read it to him, he called me in and said, "You're telling lies."

I was taken aback. It turned out that I'd written that Hari Dass "went into the forest," that is, left home to become a sadhu, when he was twelve. Maharaj-ji called a devotee in and said, "Do you know Hari Dass?"

"Yes, Maharaj-ji," he replied. "He was my clerk in the forestry department office for a long time." Instead of going to the forest, Hari Dass had worked in the Indian Forest Service. He had been a tenant in a house owned by K. K. Sah's family. And he had not left home at age twelve; Maharaj-ji had. I had mixed up their stories. Maharaj-ji asked me to fix the inaccuracy. "You're printing lies," he said. "If you don't know, it's all right," he said. "But if you know it's a lie, and you print it, it's bad karma."

By this time, Hari Dass was visiting at the Lama Foundation in New Mexico, which I had arranged as part of his first trip to America. He was already revered and beloved by all the Lama Beans. I had to call from India and tell them to take out the part about Hari Dass, while he was there—a cosmic irony typical of Maharaj-ji. I hitched a ride from Kainchi to Nainital on an army truck so I could telegraph Steve Durkee. This was long before satellite phone connections, cell phones, or email. Lama had one phone partway down the mountain. Calls from India to the States could take a week to get through.

In his return telegram, Steve said the second printing of the book was already on the press. It would be hard to stop it and would cost a lot of money. We would have to throw out the whole printing.

I showed Steve's telegram to Maharaj-ji. The printing was already underway, I said, and changing things would cost thousands of rupees. He said, "Money and truth have nothing to do with each other. Change it."

The next day, I got another telegram from Steve. He'd driven three hours down the mountain from Lama to the printer in Albuquerque. He arrived to find that the printer had the book on the press, all ready to go, but at the last minute, they'd discovered that a page was missing. The original layout for the page was also missing, so they couldn't reproduce it. They had to take the job off the press.

The missing page had a picture of Maharaj-ji on it.

As fall chill turned into Himalayan winter, Maharaj-ji would leave the hills for the plains. At the other ashram he had in Vrindavan, we would also see him. Maharaj-ji had us stay at a traditional dharmsala, a pilgrim guesthouse, called Jaipuria Bhawan. Long since renovated, back then it had wood beds secured by rope "springs," in the old Indian style. At night, bedbugs emerged from the wood joints, and if you weren't vigilant, monkeys would make off with your sandals, eyeglasses, fruit—anything not locked down.

We'd go on excursions to the bazaar for milk sweets called *barfi* and *rabri*, to the garden where Krishna and Radha danced together under the moon, to the Yamuna River, and to the ecstatic puja at the Bankey Bihari Temple. Vrindavan was saturated with the *bhava*, the mood of the bhakti *marg*, the devotional path.

We weren't the only westerners in Vrindavan. A. C. Bhaktivedanta Swami Prabhupada, the founder of the Hare Krishna movement, had returned to India with a group of followers. They planned to build a big temple in Vrindavan. The Hare Krishnas got into a dispute over a ride fare with one of the cycle ricksha wallahs, who were the primary transport around town. Every ricksha wallah in town went on strike, refusing to carry any westerner. We had to walk everywhere until the Hare Krishnas made peace.

I also met Doug Uttal and three of his friends who had been followers of Prabhat Ranjan Sarkar, the founder of Ananda Marga, "path of bliss." Ananda Marga was supposedly about devotion and service, but Sarkar had recently been arrested for murder. They were eager to meet Maharaj-ji. Maharaj-ji gave Doug a new name: Jai Gopal. He is well known as the kirtan singer Jai Uttal in the West.

Maharaj-ji sent us to see Anandamayi Ma, an incredible saint whose name means "bliss-permeated Mother." Anandamayi, whose ashram was nearby in Vrindavan, radiated a deep maternal peace. She and Maharaj-ji were like a spiritual mother and father. Together they were like Shiva and Shakti, purusha and prakriti, the male consciousness and the maternal creative energy. We heard that when they were together, he called her Ma, and she called him Pita-ji, an affectionate term for "father."

It was quiet when we arrived, not a big crowd as there often was. The scene around Anandamayi was more orthodox Hindu than the one around Maharaj-ji, and the people who surrounded her were often Brahmins who didn't like westerners getting too close to her. (In the caste system, foreigners are *mlecchas*, lower than untouchables.) That day, though, the phalanx of her protectors was not much in evidence. After the darshan, there was kirtan, with Anandamayi chanting "Jaya Bhagavan." I loved the sound of her cracked, aging voice. Listening to her chant, I felt cradled by the Mother.

Anandamayi Ma also had an ashram at Kankhal, near Haridwar. Danny Goleman and I decided to visit, and when we arrived, we found Ma on the steps of the little temple, talking to the vice president of India. A couple of hundred people surrounded them. When the vice president left, Anandamayi retreated into one of the rooms. Occasionally we'd catch glimpses of her, dressed in white and walking from one building to another, almost as if she were floating. As dusk fell, we could smell food cooking. A conch and bells sounded for the evening temple puja.

Someone came to tell us the temple was closing. As we got up to go, Anandamayi came out a side door and walked across the courtyard, right in our path. She looked as if she were sleepwalking. She walked past us, hesitated, and stopped just in front of us so we could touch her feet. She was completely ethereal, hardly there. It was like meeting a startled deer in the quiet of a deep forest or having a bird land on your shoulder—a precious instant when you connect with something pure and elemental, untouched by the mundane.

It was a mysterious and intense moment. Anandamayi continued on, and we left the temple. There was no recognition; she didn't look at us, it was a darshan, a glimpse of something holy. We had touched love.

Maharaj-ji could be like that too. He wasn't ethereal like Anandamayi, but he lived in a state of sahaja sthiti samadhi, embodied and absorbed in the formless at the same time, here and not-here simultaneously. Sometimes, one of his eyes would be focused here on something or someone, and the other eye would be looking off in a different direction, gone.

On two occasions, once in New Delhi and another time in a village, Maharaj-ji walked right past me without acknowledging my presence. Not a flicker of recognition, no acknowledgment of any connection between us. Nada. He could be completely impersonal, which undercut any sense I had of being important or really of being anyone at all. It caused me to consider my personality in a different light. I would be carrying on an ordinary conversation with him, then realize there was no one there. Sometimes, talking to him was like engaging with a tree or a rock.

Yet, as with Anandamayi, I still touched love. I felt more love from him than I'd ever felt from anyone in my life.

In December 1971, a war erupted between Pakistan and India. India supported East Pakistan, soon to be Bangladesh, in its fight for independence from Pakistan. Pakistan launched preemptive air strikes against India. India retaliated with its own strikes. News headlines were filled with stories of bombings, killings, and rapes.

While the Soviet Union supported India, the US stood by Pakistan, then its ally in the Cold War. Americans quickly became unpopular in India, and many westerners left. Our satsang was at Allahabad, at Dada's home, for winter camp, where about thirty of us were sleeping on the floor in a vacant home owned by a devotee family. I told Maharaj-ji I wanted to drive our VW van to Bangladesh to help alleviate the bloodshed. I had the romantic idea that I could use it as an ambulance.

Maharaj-ji told me not to go. He said, "Don't you see, it's all per-fect?" He was telling me not to get caught by my view of the suffering. Not that there wasn't horrific suffering. It was awful. But it was also part of God's perfection, of the One. As humans we just want to alleviate the suffering. Understanding that suffering is part of divine perfection, that in the bigger picture it is all in the plan, was hard to accept.

To get us away from the war, Maharaj-ji sent us on pilgrimage to various holy sites. Maharaj-ji told me to visit Rameswaram, at the tip of the Indian peninsula, so I set out on the train with Ramesh and Lakshman Markus. In the Ramayana, Rameswaram is where Ram builds a bridge, with the help of Hanuman, to cross the ocean to Sri Lanka to rescue Sita, his wife, from the demon Ravana. It's one of the holiest places in India.

It took us three days to get there. By the time we arrived, I had a high fever. My pee turned dark brown, and my eyes turned yellow, both definitive for hepatitis A, which many of us got in India from the impure drinking water (no vaccine back then). I figured Maharaj-ji knew what was going on with my health and that when I got to the temple, the temple would heal me.

From a medical standpoint, that's what you'd call "magical think-ing." We were also on a train, and there wasn't much I could do. At Rameswaram, we hired a guide, a Brahmin pandit, who took us on a tour of the temple. Rameswaram has sixty-four *tirthas*, or wells of holy water; twenty-two of those are within the temple. Each tirtha repre-sents a place of holy pilgrimage somewhere in India; if you bathe in the water, you receive the blessing of that other place. As we went through the temple, at each tirtha the attendants pulled up a bucket of water and poured it over us. Even with a high fever, I felt it as an amazing darshan. The weather was quite hot, but by the time we finished, in place of fever I had a chill. I recovered quickly from hepatitis.

The war lasted only two weeks. When hostilities ceased, in mid-December 1971, we returned to Maharaj-ji in Vrindavan. I had been in India just over a year by then, and my visa was about to run out. Several others in our satsang were in the same boat. We appealed to Maharaj-ji. Since we regarded him as not only omniscient but omnip-otent, we figured he'd help us with this trivial bureaucratic issue.

This wasn't simple-minded guru worship. Politicians, judges, and military officers from all echelons of government sought out Maharaj-ji for blessings and counsel. From time to time, a motorcade of government cars would pull up at the ashram gates, lights flashing, fender flags flying, security guards in tow. His devotees included important people in the governing Congress Party, like Prime Minister Indira Gandhi's personal secretary. A simple note or word from Maharaj-ji, and visas would be taken care of at the highest level.

Instead, Maharaj-ji sent us to see a low-level officer in the Foreigner Registration Office in New Delhi. His firm opinion was that nothing could be done and we had to leave the country. We didn't know whether Maharaj-ji issued any instructions to him or whether he actually had the power to do anything.

We took the train back to Vrindavan and gave Maharaj-ji our disappointing news. He sent us back to inquire anew. For a couple of weeks, we shuttled back and forth between Maharaj-ji in Vrindavan and the FRO in New Delhi. Then we all received the dreaded "Quit India" notice from the central government. If you didn't obey the exit order, you could never reenter the country again. Maharaj-ji said, "It's time to go."

In March 1972, along with a few other soon-to-be-exiles, I booked a flight to London. Others in the satsang left by alternate routes. A few wouldn't take no for an answer and took other measures to get visas renewed, some outside of government protocol.

I was determined not to be emotional. Maharaj-ji wasn't much for Jewish good-byes, and anyway, I felt he was coming with me. He was my soul companion. I was established with him, and his loving presence was, and is, part of my world.

The last time I saw Maharaj-ji, he was sitting outside at Kainchi on the tukhat on the veranda, looking at the mountains. He looked far away but also completely in the moment. The form and the formless.

Be Here Now made quite a splash. Some two hundred thousand copies sold in the US in the first year, even though I was in India and the book wasn't promoted or reviewed in any national publication. Tapes of my lectures continued to play on FM radio, with transcripts printed in underground papers. Meanwhile, the Pentagon Papers were leaked, revealing that the government had deceived Americans about the nation's involvement in the Vietnam War. President Nixon declared a "war on drugs."

More than ever, young people were searching for meaning. Many wrote to me asking for wisdom and advice. Even in India, as far away as I was, I received about a hundred letters a week. I wasn't sure what the scene would be like when I returned home, and I was afraid it might overwhelm me. So I put off coming home, staying in London for six weeks. I didn't tell anyone I was coming back except for my father.

I shouldn't have worried. When I finally landed in Boston, there was no one waiting at the airport to receive me—not even Dad, who was out of town and didn't get the cable about my flight. This gave me some time to figure out my next steps. Maharaj-ji had told me not to have ashrams or students or to stay anyplace longer than five days. He also said to love and serve everyone. I needed to figure out what my service should look like.

Slowly, I took on engagements. I was invited to speak at Spring Grove State Hospital in Maryland, which had a center for psychedelic psychotherapy. My audience was made up of spiritual seekers and psychologists. We discussed the nature of consciousness. Researchers there had led studies on the effect of psychedelics on schizophrenia and then adapted their efforts to examine LSD's therapeutic effects on alcoholism, heroin addiction, and terminal cancer. One significant contributor to the research was my old associate Walter Pahnke. So were Stanislav Grof and his then wife, Joan Halifax, who together would write *The Human Encounter with Death*. We became lifelong friends, even after they divorced. The Spring Grove Experiment is still the largest study on psychedelics ever done.

In early 1973, Paul Gorman invited me to do a series of late-night shows on WBAI-FM with him. We were on from midnight until 6 a.m., and a surprising number of people tuned in, even from their beds. I read from the Ramayana and other texts, and Bhagavan Das, who had just put out a kirtan album, led chanting. Listeners called in from all over. It was radical radio satsang.

The WBAI series was such a hit that it evolved into a six-record boxed set. We recorded at a media commune upstate called ZBS, then distributed the box ourselves at just above cost. The albums included favorite readings from the Third Chinese Patriarch of Zen, chanting the Hanuman Chalisa—for probably the first time in the West—and even some of the call-in questions. Inspired by Maharaj-ji's simple, repeated instruction, we titled the box *Love Serve Remember*.

In September 1973, I was at Willenrica when my father told me I had received a telegram from India. It read: "Maharaj-ji has dropped his bojay." Dad asked what it meant. "Bojay" was a typo for "body." Maharaj-ji had died.

The satsang gathered at my family's farm. Many were crying about losing their guru, but to my surprise, I wasn't inundated with grief. I thought I might be in denial, but after sitting with it for a while, I realized this was different than when I'd suppressed my grief on losing Mother. My connection to Maharaj-ji was soul to soul. The body was gone, but the soul was still there. Curiously, my connection to Maharaj-ji was now even more direct, and I was held in the aura of his love.

Thirty of us took a Pan Am charter flight to New Delhi. We got on a bus to the Vrindavan ashram, where we found a still-smoldering heap of Maharaj-ji's ashes. Larry Brilliant took some of the ashes; later he gave me an amulet containing some. The ashram held a big *bhandara*, feeding thousands of people, a traditional way of marking an important event.

Afterward, we traveled up to Kainchi. While it felt eerie without Maharaj-ji shouting orders and throwing fruit and keeping the whole show in motion, our Indian family was as loving as ever. Maharaj-ji's energy was very present.

When Maharaj-ji left Kainchi for the last time, to go to Agra, his blanket had slipped to the ground as he was getting in the car. "Leave it," he had told the devotee who picked it up. "One shouldn't be attached to anything." Near the end of the train ride, he complained of chest pain and then was taken to the hospital in Vrindavan, where, according to the doctors, he fell into a diabetic coma. When he woke up, he pulled off the oxygen mask, ripped out the IV, and said, "Useless stuff." Then he said, "Jaya Jagdish, Jagdish Hare!" (Hail to the Lord of the Universe!) three times, each phrase quieter than the last.

Maharaj-ji's death was a shock. I thought he would never go anywhere. I anticipated returning to his warm, spontaneous giggle, his endless river of prasad fruit and sweets and tea. But he pulled a fast one, a disappearing act. He absconded; he fled the scene. Now there was no body, no form. As he left Kainchi, he said, "Now I am leaving central jail."

When we'd left India the year before, we passed the impound lot of the Indian customs department in New Delhi. Collecting dust in a corner were two vehicles I recognized. One was the Land Rover I'd driven with David. The Indian government had seized it because no one could figure out the paperwork to get it out of the country. The other was our VW van. After serving the satsang so well, it too succumbed to red tape, languishing in bureaucratic limbo. There they both sat, hubcaps slowly sinking into the Indian earth. Maharaj-ji left his body with even less trace.

In ten days we were back in the US. It was the shortest trip I ever took to India. And, just as I had walked away from those two old cars, now I felt as if I was closing another chapter. Everything outside was the same, but my perception shifted within. Maharaj-ji brought me to India; now he was sending me back to America again. One door closed; another door opened.

PART III

SERVICE CENTER

See God
in everyone.

MAHARAJ-JI

CHAPTER 23

ALL DOING TIME

Sri Ramakrishna relates a story from the Ramayana where Ram, who is God incarnate, asks Hanuman, the embodiment of service, "O monkey, who *are* you?" Hanuman responds, "Lord, when I don't know who I am, I serve you. When I know who I am, I *am* you."

That's the ultimate statement of service. Maharaj-ji's temples in India all center on Hanuman, and when I kneel in front of his murti, I remember that love merges into oneness, because Hanuman embodies such complete devotion to God. Out of that love, Hanuman performs his *seva*, his selfless service, as a pure expression of God.

In the Bhagavad Gita, service as a spiritual practice is called *karma-yoga*, serving the One so that servant and service are all One. In the West, most of the models I knew for helping were about doing good, getting results, using social and political activism to reform old structures. Hanuman's seva, or the selfless service of the Gita, means giving up the fruits of action, letting go of how it all turns out and serving God. As with Hanuman's devotion to Ram, seva is intimately connected to surrender.

When Maharaj-ji gave me the name Ram Dass, "servant of God," he began to awaken a Hanuman quality of service in me. I'd done plenty of studying and teaching, but not much hands-on service work. Now I felt called to find places where I could be more helpful to others. I was again shifting my perception to align with Maharaj-ji, to come closer to him by following his instruction to "love everyone, serve everyone, and remember God."

I had noticed that after *Be Here Now* was published, I started getting a lot of letters from prisoners, mainly drug offenders, probably because of my own past drug associations. The government's war on drugs was putting many people in jail for nonviolent offenses. I felt deep compassion for inmates, because society ignored and ostracized them.

In my replies I encouraged inmates to see their prison sentences as an opportunity for spiritual growth. In many ways, the austerity of prison life is like the austerity of an ashram. If they could do the work of forgiveness and love in spite of the harsh conditions, they could purify a tremendous amount of negative karma over the course of their sentence. No one was irredeemable.

There were a lot of letters to keep up with, and I was feeling overwhelmed. In December 1973, I spoke at Duke University, in North Carolina, and met a couple named Bo and Sita Lozoff. They'd both read *Be Here Now*. Bo's brother-in-law was in prison for smuggling marijuana into the States from Jamaica, and they told me they felt drawn to serving inmates. I said, "Why don't you take these letters?"

With that, the Prison-Ashram Project was born. I created the Hanuman Foundation to help fund it and to be an umbrella for social action efforts integrating spirituality and service. Money from my speaking engagements would go to the foundation, which in turn would help seed spiritual service projects. Besides replying to inmate letters, we went into prisons to teach yoga and meditation. We created newsletters for prisoners and sent them free spiritual books and tapes. With Bo, I visited prisons around the country. I remember walking through San Quentin State Prison in California and seeing inmates typing their appeals in their cells. I led a meditation over the PA system.

The idea was to prepare inmates for a life of service, whether they got released or not. I often told prisoners we are all doing time, even those of us not behind bars. And we all had the same task: to grow spiritually. "Imagine a cellblock in which the prisoners think they are in an ashram and the guards think they are in a prison," I would say. "Who'd be doing time then?"

Bo wrote a manual, *We're All Doing Time*, about how to turn prison life into spiritual life. He and Sita sent it free to inmates who requested it. It's now in its twenty-first printing and has been translated into several different languages. Eventually, the Prison-Ashram Project grew so large that Bo and Sita formed their own foundation, the Human Kindness Foundation, which has grown into the largest interfaith prison ministry in the world.

Maharaj-ji told me, "Birds and saints don't collect," and not to stay anywhere for more than five days. So I bought another VW bus and drove from lecture to lecture. I outfitted the van with a bunk bed, yellow curtains, and temple chimes. I taped an image of Maharaj-ji's feet to the ceiling. When I opened my eyes in the morning, that's what I saw. The royalties from *Be Here Now* were all going to the Lama Foundation, which in turn sent me what I needed to cover expenses on the road.

After returning from India, I'd been invited to speak at an April 1973 Dharma Festival in Boston. I lectured on gurus to three thousand people in the Boston College gym. Allen Ginsberg and Bhagavan Das led chanting onstage. Some of the satsang came to the festival too. They stayed with Dave and Mary McClelland, who had turned their Cambridge home on Washington Avenue into a spiritual and intellectual crossroads, with all kinds of teachers, anthropologists, artists, psychologists, and physicists coming through.

At the Dharma Festival, I overlapped with Chogyam Trungpa Rinpoche, who gave a lecture on Tibetan Buddhism and American karma. Trungpa was a *tulku*, or reincarnation of a high lama, who had fled Tibet and received an education at Oxford, arriving in the US in 1970. He wrote a number of books, of which the best known is *Cutting Through Spiritual Materialism*. He wore suits instead of robes and kept his hair short instead of having long hair or a beard. He smoked and drank in public. He was always late.

Trungpa also stayed at the McClellands. At one point he sat in Dave's favorite rocker, rocking until it tipped over and broke. He was heard to remark, "You can't change someone's karma." He openly seduced women. I heard he asked one young woman in our satsang to take off her clothes as "a gesture of openness."

Chogyam Trungpa and I had met before. When I was in New York, I'd heard there was a lama speaking one evening at 7:30 at an apartment in Brooklyn, so I took the subway to see him, missing supper to be on time. When I arrived there was a crowd of people, but no lama. We waited and waited and waited . . . and waited. No one seemed surprised or agitated about sitting around for so long. Just me.

At 9 p.m., a full hour and a half late, Trungpa came in, disheveled and drunk. He looked wild to me. He sat on a dais and proceeded to give an absolutely clear lecture about Buddhist principles. I was riveted. Afterward, I went up to meet him. I was holding my mala beads, and as we were talking, my mala slipped from my fingers and fell to the floor. He picked it up and gave it back to me, smiling. There was a certain gamesmanship to this—I was embarrassed, the sloppy bhakti meeting a high lama. He was enjoying himself.

Our second encounter was in Vermont, where Trungpa opened a retreat center known as Karme Choling, or Tail of the Tiger. I came up from New Hampshire to visit my friends Mirabai and Krishna Bush, who were living in a camper van. We decided to attend a talk Trungpa was giving. We got there early, and we were lying in the van, smoking a joint together, feeling pretty good. There was a knock on the van door. "Trungpa wants to see Ram Dass," came the voice from outside. I was surprised anyone even knew I was there.

His student walked me to the main building, showed me to a door, and said, "He's in there." Chogyam Trungpa was sitting in a chair behind a desk. There was no other furniture in the room. He didn't get up. I stood in front of him. He looked at me and said, "Ram Dass, we have to accept responsibility."

With that, he dismissed me. He didn't say responsibility for what. The dharma? By saying "we," he was bringing me into his sphere, telling me to take responsibility for students and uphold the dharma. I didn't know how to take it. Was he serious? Was he building up my spiritual ego? Was he guilt-tripping me? Or, as seemed most likely, was he just playing with my mind? Trungpa was, after all, a tantric, whose essential practice is to use external energies.

I attended the lecture with Mirabai and Krishna. It was about Carlos Castaneda and his first book on his spiritual experiences with the Yaqui shaman Don Juan. Trungpa sat on a chair, and everyone else sat on the floor. He gave a wonderful lecture. Then he took questions. There were some references to drugs, because that was part of Castaneda's journey. As questions about the mind and psychedelics came up, Trungpa would defer to me. "That question is difficult," he would say. "I think Ram Dass can answer that." Then the next question would come. "My, that's a difficult question," he would say again. "Maybe Ram Dass will answer that."

I hadn't expected to speak. I was sitting at the back of the room, unshaven and not very neat. Each time, I went up to the front of the room to answer, then I'd go sit again. By the fifth or sixth repetition of this act, I said I thought Trungpa was taking on the Don Juan role and that he was making me into Castaneda. Everyone had a good laugh, including Trungpa.

The questions got more and more technical. I was in over my head. I was getting into my professorial mind, which made me uncomfortable. Trungpa was playing with me. There was only one microphone, at his sitting height, and some kind of a flowering bush next to him that I was allergic to. Each time I stood next to him and bent down to the microphone to answer, I sneezed.

Later that week, I got a little package in the mail. In it was a small Tibetan endless knot design in gold, with a note from Trungpa that read, "This augurs well for our work together in the future."

I thought, "Well, that's interesting. I didn't know we had any work together."

In retrospect, this was Maharaj-ji's doing: after Muktananda, Chogyam Trungpa was my second teacher when it came to power. Like Muktananda before him, Trungpa wanted me to become part of his burgeoning scene. His version of Tibetan Buddhism was what he called "crazy wisdom."

I can't say I wasn't interested. Trungpa appealed to my desire for power. By the time we saw each other again, in Boston, Trungpa had become a mentor to my old friend Allen Ginsberg. Before Maharaj-ji died, I learned from Allen that Trungpa planned to open an institute for Buddhist studies, the Naropa Institute, in Boulder, Colorado. He wanted to create a place where students could learn Eastern and Western thought, as well as have meditation training.

They were launching it with a five-week program in the summer of 1974. Trungpa hired Allen to teach poetry. When Allen asked me to teach a course on the Bhagavad Gita, I agreed. It tied in with my own work about service and karma-yoga. I also liked that Naropa would be another opportunity to gather the India satsang. I made it a condition that I could bring a cadre of teaching assistants.

There was a certain playful competition between me and Trungpa. At the Dharma Festival, about twelve hundred people had attended Trungpa's talk, and about three thousand came to mine. Trungpa wanted me at Naropa because I was a big draw.

In early March 1974, responding to several invitations to college campuses, I drove to California. I expected to rest a bit after that, but a compilation of my lectures at the Menninger Foundation and Spring Grove State Hospital was released the same month as *The Only Dance There Is*. I received so many speaking offers, I had to hire a booking agent.

I led a retreat in Guerneville, lectured at the University of California in Santa Cruz, and helped pull together a marathon program at the Winterland Ballroom, my old psychedelic stomping ground in San Francisco. A satsang music group, Amazing Grace, performed, as did Bhagavan Das and my old friends the Grateful Dead. There was a puja table onstage and slide projections of Maharaj-ji. It was an all-night party.

Between gigs on "the holy man circuit," I spent time at a satsang house in the Berkeley Hills, where I'd see friends or young seekers and catch up on correspondence. In the mornings, I'd meditate, then study commentaries on the Bhagavad Gita, preparing for the summer course in Colorado.

Trungpa was a former Oxford don. I was a former Harvard professor. It was Oxford versus Harvard! By this time I'd stopped actually lecturing. Instead of using notes, as I'd done as an academic, I'd just get high and let Maharaj-ji come through. But this time I would be teaching in front of the intellectually rigorous Buddhists.

Trungpa's lama training included philosophical debating. I was in over my head, presuming to take on the Bhagavad Gita, which had thousands of years of Sanskrit commentary. My old performance anxiety reared its head. I was a terrified graduate student all over again, sure that everyone would see through my facade.

To prepare, I went on a desert retreat for two months, first at Organ Pipe Cactus National Monument in Arizona and then at Joshua Tree National Park in California. I lived in the van. I would study, outline my lectures, then try them out on an audience of jackrabbits. They were a little different from the Naropa students, though both turned out to be a bit obtuse.

After my retreat, I went back to Berkeley, where I ran into Joseph Goldstein, my friend and neighbor from the Goenka retreat in Bodh Gaya. He was stopping inside one restaurant after another on Telegraph Avenue, looking for a restroom. I was eating in the last one he came to. I invited Joseph to be meditation instructor for the Gita course. It was his first teaching gig.

I gathered my satsang troops—thirteen of my guru brothers and sisters who had been in India—and in July, we met up in Boulder. We hadn't seen each other since Maharaj-ji's passing and were happy to be reunited. My "teaching assistants" would lead music and chanting, teach yoga classes and Vipassana meditation, and coordinate public service projects. I actually felt ready and thought we would have a ball. K. K. Sah even came from India, his first time in the US.

Naropa's lecture hall was a former bus depot in downtown Boulder. They put down some industrial carpet, erected a stage, and called it a lecture hall. More than fifteen hundred students sat on the floor, six times what was anticipated. Besides Allen Ginsberg and his partner Peter Orlovsky, other faculty included Gary Snyder, William Burroughs, Joan Halifax, the poets Anne Waldman and her spouse, Reed Bye, avant-garde composer John Cage, and novelist Norman Mailer.

I alternated in the lecture hall with Trungpa. He was onstage on Monday, Wednesday, and Friday talking about "The Tibetan Buddhist Path." I spoke on Tuesday, Thursday, and Saturday. He taught about meditation and emptiness, and I taught about devotion and the guru. He spoke alone. I was accompanied by our satsang crew, who led ecstatic chanting. On several occasions, we went onstage together. Trungpa kept a glass and a pitcher of what looked like water on a table next to him, but was sake or vodka. He'd get sloshed, yet give absolutely pellucid lectures on Buddhism.

Students soon started crossing over between our classes. Between the Buddhist focus on paradox and the mind and my focus on service and the heart, the students going back and forth felt like they were in a Ping-Pong match. Trungpa's students who attended my lectures asked wiseass questions. The Buddhists called us "the love-and-lighters." They weren't having any of this gushy heart stuff. They thought we should cut to the chase and go for Nirvana.

But that summer we inhabited the Bhagavad Gita—at least, I know I did. We brought to life all the forms of yoga. Joseph Goldstein taught Vipassana meditation, we set up service projects in the community to practice karma-yoga, Krishna Das and Jai Uttal led kirtan, we did hatha yoga in the big hall, and K. K. Sah spoke of saints and bhakti yoga.

Around us that summer, the country was embroiled in the Watergate scandal, the botched burglary of Democratic headquarters by Nixon's "plumbers." We were living in the middle of an actual Bhagavad Gita battle for the soul of America. Nixon resigned the following month. The message of the Bhagavad Gita could not have been more appropriate: to stay in the present and cultivate your heart. The service projects were teaching us compassion. Each of the Gita lectures closed with kirtan or meditation. At the end of the course, we had a fire ceremony. Everyone symbolically incinerated their attachments, and we chanted "Om Namah Shivaya" all night.

Trungpa's talks were more the yoga of the intellect. Between his Tibetan monastic training and his Oxford education, he was a master of philosophy. Trungpa's lineage is tantric, using the energies of the outer world to go inward, and he took his students through their karma via gambling, sex, and alcohol. I couldn't tell if he actually helped release their attachments or reinforced their desires. Or he may have done these things because he liked doing them himself. The older students all swore his teaching was classical Vajrayana tantra and that it led them to greater internal freedom. I couldn't tell; it may have been wishful thinking.

Except when we shared the stage, Trungpa and I rarely saw each other. I heard gossip about what he was saying about me in his lectures. I wondered whether he heard what I said about him in mine. In our onstage dialogues he was friendly and convivial, and I held my own.

He trained in debate in Tibet and at Oxford; I was trained in bhakti yoga by Maharaj-ji and taught at Harvard. Intellectually he had the edge.

I couldn't decide about Trungpa. His students imitated his crazy wisdom, but they weren't tantric masters. Between his philandering, his drinking, and his crystal-clear talks on tantric practice, I couldn't reconcile Trungpa's behavior with his high state. Finally I gave up and took it all as a teaching.

Later I asked Kalu Rinpoche, the Sixteenth Karmapa's meditation teacher, about Trungpa's unusual teaching. He said, "If you go to the top of the mountain and a bird flies off the mountain, don't think you can too." Kalu also said, "Ram Dass, there are three things you have to do. Cultivate emptiness, cultivate compassion, and honor your guru." He was right. Those are the elements of my spiritual work.

Trungpa was an exquisite though uncomfortable teacher. The way he used existential conditions at Naropa to illuminate my ego was true tantra. Trungpa's students were also on my case, and though I was uncomfortable about falling into professor mode, they pushed me to be more coherent in my teaching.

The confluence of Buddhism, Hinduism, and American culture in Boulder that summer was chaotic but profoundly unifying. For me, the gathering began a crucial convergence of Buddhism and bhakti yoga, of wisdom and devotion. When Sharon Salzberg heard her friend Joseph Goldstein was teaching Vipassana at Naropa, she joined us, camping out in his apartment. Trungpa hired another Vipassana teacher, Jack Kornfield. The three of them formed a deep friendship and in 1976 took over a former church retreat and founded the Insight Meditation Society in Barre, Massachusetts. IMS is still one of the best places in the country to learn and practice meditation. Naropa itself is now an accredited university that exquisitely integrates arts and spiritual disciplines.

Trungpa and I had quite a dance that summer. For all our sparring, we enjoyed our interaction. We happily teased each other onstage. I think he felt the diversity of views was good for his Naropa students. The students were probably more factional. At Naropa, that summer was known as "the Holy Wars."

As the course ended, Trungpa invited me to a farewell dinner at his house with about twenty of his students. Before we sat down, he pointed out a painting of two white flowers, one over the other. He said, "I just painted this for you and me." I thought, "Why is one flower over the other?" He never let me forget the power dynamic.

As we sat down to dinner, the students were all looking at us, and he said, "I'd like you to join me at Naropa." They were preparing for the fall classes. Allen Ginberg was going to take up permanent residence; he and Anne Waldman were starting the Jack Kerouac School of Disembodied Poetics at Naropa.

For all the fun I'd had with my bhakti brothers and sisters, my mind and heart were not in it. With sudden clarity I knew I was done with this chapter. I attribute this thought to Maharaj-ji. His death had pushed me inside, to connect with him in a more profound way. Maharaj-ji was reminding me of my spiritual side and to surrender it all to him. I'd been in an ego fog of my old academic mind. But Maharaj-ji pulled me out of it. I could hear him inside, and I could touch my soul again.

I told Trungpa I didn't feel a need to stay on. I thought I should get back to India.

On my drive east to pack up for India at the family farm in New Hampshire, I stopped to sleep at a motel in New Jersey. When I woke up, there was someone sitting on the end of the bed. It was Maharaj-ji. The apparition said, in perfectly good English, "You don't need to go to India. Your next teachings will be right here."

CHAPTER 24

BROOKLYN DETOUR

I n the Indian way of thinking, you have one true guru, or *satguru*, but you may have other, lesser gurus along the way, who are called *upagurus*. These beings may give you significant help or teach you important lessons at critical moments on your spiritual path. They are vehicles for your awakening who may themselves be realized or not. They serve as teachings to propel you along your way. Some are teachers, all are teachings.

I feel Maharaj-ji put me with certain upagurus to burn out my desires for power. His power-and-love curriculum came in a succession of three very different power-oriented teachers. They all wanted me to become their follower or collaborator. They didn't think of me as an equal, but they knew others trusted me as a teacher and that I would give them legitimacy.

The first of these teachers had been Muktananda. The second was Trungpa. I was about to meet number three.

After the long cross-country drive from Colorado, I stopped in New York to get realigned by my favorite chiropractor. As I waited in his office, I called Hilda Charlton. Her weekly séance-like gatherings were continuing, and at Naropa I'd told students from New York to go see her. She treated me as somewhat of a junior on the path, but with great deference and affection. Hilda respected my connection to Maharaj-ji.

Hilda was a bhakti with a great sense of humor. She was a very loving and giving person, conducting astral healings with her council of disembodied saintly beings and helping her students cope with life in very down-to-earth ways. After *Be Here Now* came out, I connected her with WBAI-FM for some interviews. At times I think she kept a good part of Manhattan on spiritual life support.

After Hilda picked up the phone, she said, "There's a woman I want you to meet. She says she has your guru in her basement."

Maharaj-ji had always encouraged me to take teachings wherever I could find them and to trust my heart to discern between the useful ones and the irrelevant or harmful ones. "Take what you can use and lose the rest" is my motto. This time it occurred to me that Maharaj-ji had a teaching for me on my homosexuality and had sent me a woman teacher. I can't explain this thought, only that it entered my head.

The next day, I drove Hilda to a suburban-looking house in Brooklyn. It was home to a housewife named Joyce Green, who was calling herself Joya Santanaya. On the way, Hilda told me Joya's story. She had gone into some kind of samadhi state during a yoga class at a Jack LaLanne health club. Later, she was lying in the bathtub, and Christ appeared to her. She was a homegrown mystic.

Joya was also a Brooklyn-style entrepreneur. She peddled black market perfume at traffic lights, a line of hair care products, and occasional specialty items, like electronics that "fell off a truck." Her husband, Sal, had a Coca-Cola delivery business and low-level Mafia connections.

Hilda knocked on the door. When no one answered, she opened it and called out, "Joya? Where are you, dear?"

The first floor was empty. Hilda said, "Maybe she's down in the basement." We walked down the steps. The basement was smoky with incense. The lights were off, and candles flickered all around. On the floor was Joya, sitting in the lotus position. Hilda urged me to go over to her.

Joya's eyes were closed. She was a Kali-esque figure, with long, black hair, bright-red lipstick, and red nail polish. I sat down in front of her. Hilda came over and grasped a heavy gold necklace Joya was wearing around her neck. "Come down, Joya!" she said. "Come down!"

Joya opened her eyes and said to Hilda, "What the hell are you doing here?" Then she looked at me. "Who the fuck are you?"

Hilda said, "This is Ram Dass, dear."

Joya pointed to a corner of the basement. "Is that guy with the blanket yours?" she asked me. I looked at the corner and saw nothing at all. She turned to the side as if someone was talking to her. "Who's talking? What's your name? Padma what? Padmasambhava?" I recognized the name of the great yogi who introduced Buddhism to Tibet. There had to be a crowd of astral beings only she could see.

For all the weird kitsch of this scene, there was power, shakti, surounding Joya. I could feel it. Was this who my vision of Maharaj-ji meant?

Driving back to Manhattan, Hilda suggested the three of us teach a class together. She phoned Joya to get her consent. I decided to forgo New Hampshire for the moment and stay in New York.

Before Hilda, Joya, and I could start, I got a call from California. It was the counterculture political agitator Jerry Rubin. He was calling about Tim Leary.

After being arrested for drug possession again, Tim had been sentenced in 1970. It turned out the California prison system used the personality test Tim had written to evaluate prisoners, so Tim got himself assigned to a low-security prison. With the help of the radical leftist group, the Weather Underground, he escaped. He and his wife, Rosemary, fled to Algeria, where they joined up with exiled Black Panthers, and then moved to Switzerland. Eventually, Tim split up with Rosemary. He was traveling through Afghanistan when he was apprehended in Kabul and flown back to the US.

Nixon, faced with the Vietnam crisis and the spectre of impeachment, was obsessed with Tim, who he called "the most dangerous man in America." With much fanfare, in 1973 Tim received five years for his prison escape, added to his original ten-year sentence. He was sent to Folsom Prison in California and put in solitary confinement. I waited by the prison in Vacaville, California, to see him when he was transferred. I managed to wave to him as the car drove by.

Later I was invited to lecture at the prison, but a few days before my visit, Tim was transferred to federal custody. In the hopes of getting an early parole, he had agreed to turn over all his research records.

It was looking like he would give evidence on several lawyers who had helped defend him and others on the West Coast. Jerry Rubin and Allen Ginsberg felt strongly these lawyers should be protected, so they planned to stage a press conference in San Francisco in September 1974. The intention was to publicly discredit Tim's testimony. Jerry was calling to ask me to join them. As Tim's former partner in psychedelic research, I had some credibility.

I didn't wish Tim any harm, but there were a lot of people he could damage. I agreed to appear, along with Jerry, Allen, and Tim's son, Jack, who by this time was twenty-five. During the three-hour press conference, we raised doubts about Tim's veracity and sanity.

I didn't enjoy doing it, but no one was prosecuted on the basis of Tim's testimony. "This gathering can't have helped but to make your heart as heavy as mine," I told reporters.

Back in New York, Hilda, Joya, and I started teaching together in a hall on 72nd Street, on the Upper West Side. Sometimes we also taught at Joya's house in Brooklyn. While her husband was at work and her kids were in school, she would teach yoga in the backyard, on the deck around her aboveground pool.

Joya treated me as an honored guest, and there was energy in this new spiritual triumvirate. My participation and the added attraction of Maharaj-ji's supposed presence, a little more than a year after his death, was enough to pull others from our satsang.

Joya went into trances and delivered beautiful, erudite teachings. She put people in altered states just by touching them. She told everyone she was brahmacharya, celibate, and she required strict celibacy of all our students. She used sexual innuendo in a way that felt tantric.

Joya was a complex, many-leveled being, but she hadn't integrated the different levels. There was the spiritual side of her, which I think was genuine. There was also the Brooklyn housewife and her affinity for astral beings: American Indians, Hindu gurus, and deities. That was more suspect and anyway of less interest to me, though sometimes it felt like an unseen crowd was in the room. She learned a lot of that from Hilda, who sometimes got distracted by astral-plane stuff.

Joya was supposedly a manifestation of the Divine Mother who needed to be protected and maintained. When Joya would go off into so-called samadhi, Hilda had us all meditate to pull her back down to the physical plane by drawing off her shakti. Jewelry was another way Joya kept grounded. People bought her lots of gold bangles to help her stay in her body. I remembered Maharaj-ji warning us about "women and gold," although at the time I thought it was a metaphor for lust and greed.

Even Hilda got sucked in by the hypnotic drama. Joya could put a whole roomful of people into a deep meditative state. When I sat with her, at times I would get into a cold, formless space. I talked about bringing the head and the heart together, but that was not really what was happening. It was more about her power, her shakti. I felt like she was taking me deeper, but it was not into a heart place.

There was constant melodrama with Joya. She was like a tornado, calling me at all hours. I slept two or three hours a night. She would call and tell me my attitude on something was giving her a terrible headache, or I'd receive a desperate call from an attendant saying my resistance was causing Joya to bleed copiously from the mouth.

One time Joya, upset about something, came to confront me in the apartment where I was staying. She sat cross-legged on the doormat outside the front door while some of her people tried to get in the service entrance. She was so loud that the superintendent called the police. When the cops arrived, she was in a samadhi trance, so they called an ambulance. It was all very intense, but I felt like all I could do was give up on it all.

Joya told me she was going to help me through my homosexuality. Being brahmacharya at Kainchi hadn't been too hard for me. It was freezing cold, and there was no one else around. Now that I was back in the West, I was struggling with my bisexual urges. Maybe Joya could finally show me how to be free.

We taught together once a week. After speaking for a while, Joya instructed everyone to meditate on the Divine Mother. The satsang soaked it up. Up front were strong meditators like Bhagavan Das and Krishna Das. Everyone had their eyes closed. Joya would motion to me, and we'd head for the back door behind the stage. We'd leave the hall and go to her sister's apartment a couple of blocks away while her sister was at work. She'd put music on, and we'd make love.

After everyone had been meditating for a while, we went back to the class. I figured this was sexual tantra, Maharaj-ji taking me through my sexuality. That may have been true, but I could feel Joya also had her own desires. More to the point, I was lying to our students, whom we'd told to practice celibacy. Joya denied our affair, and I denied it too. Maharaj-ji said, "Love everyone and tell the truth." I was caught in a web of hypocrisy.

I've always been honest about my work on myself. I can talk about anything with anyone. I knew eventually I would have to come clean. Maharaj-ji also said, "They killed Christ because he told the truth." I was hoping that was not the relevant teaching here.

I also loved Joya. It was romantic and playful and exciting. I loved her mostly on the spiritual plane; the physical and emotional part seemed like a teaching. Her role, Joya liked to say, was to pave the way for me to become a world spiritual leader. And my main attraction was to her power—her shakti. She used and misused that power, sometimes for her ego to get what she wanted. Sometimes she was very innocent, other times completely calculating. I felt like I was in a blender.

I rented an apartment on West 100th Street between Broadway and Riverside Drive, where I taught classes in the living room. I used the apartment as an office, to write and to run the Hanuman Foundation. One satsang member, Anjani O'Connell, acted as secretary and ran the foundation. Rameshwar Das also lived there for about six months, working on a book project.

One afternoon, John Lennon and Yoko Ono came to visit from their apartment at the Dakota over on Central Park West. The red phone in the apartment, which was Joya's special line, rang almost as soon as they walked in. Joya demanded to speak to Yoko, whom she proceeded to accuse of destroying the Beatles.

Yoko turned red. She walked out, and John followed. I was angry at Joya for wrecking the visit and disappointed I didn't get a chance to talk to John. Later Joya boasted about telling Yoko off.

My doubts began to mount. The esoteric astral teachings and secret sex, amplified by all the melodrama and deceit, felt like a three-ring circus. I was bored by the astral stuff and by Joya's constant manipulation. The sexual relationship no longer seemed like a great tantric teaching, nor very loving. And it wasn't addressing my homosexuality.

I felt like I'd been taken for a ride. And not only me, but all the satsang who were there because of me—I was Maharaj-ji's Good Housekeeping Seal of Approval.

This is not to say Joya was a fake. She had siddhis, powers, and meditating with her could induce a feeling of great shakti and being transported into another state. It could be intoxicating. But, as with Muktananda and Trungpa, ultimately that's not why I was there. I was there to get Maharaj-ji's teaching, to bathe in his love. That came from inside, even while I was teaching alongside them. Ultimately I really didn't want the power. Maharaj-ji's love was still the strongest power.

After fifteen months of teaching with Joya, I announced I was leaving. I told the satsang Joya was no longer my teacher. It was a big upset, and in the immediate aftermath many opted to stay with Joya. Confused and hurt, I fled to the family farm in New Hampshire with only a couple of students.

In subsequent years Joya divorced her husband and moved to Florida, where she set up an ashram dedicated to Maharaj-ji. She took on a new name, Ma Jaya. She made a trip to India with a number of her students, including some of the satsang. They visited Maharaj-ji's temples and met with his devotees, including K. K. From what I was told, Joya was her usual brash self, giving gratuitous advice to Siddhi Ma, Maharaj-ji's great devotee, who was now overseeing Kainchi. She got into a screaming match with Ramesh when he refused to throw his Nikon cameras in the river to get rid of his attachment. I'm glad I wasn't on that trip.

Disillusioned and abashed by my own gullibility, in November 1976 I came clean publicly. I wrote a mea culpa titled "Egg on My Beard" in *Yoga Journal*. "I easily let myself be convinced," I wrote. Joya had been exciting, unpredictable, simultaneously powerful and emotionally dependent. But then "the incredible tapestry of half truths and lies began to unravel."

It was an unsparing takedown of Joya and my own involvement. I feel bad for rejecting Joya so abruptly, although there was no other way

to break free cleanly. She believed in the things she did, however mis-
guided or bizarre some of them were. And we had a real relationship,
spiritual, physical, and emotional. Maharaj-ji said, "Love everybody,"
and that included Joya.

CHAPTER 25

DYING PROJECT

I was done being resident holy man for Joya and Hilda. For a while it fed my spiritual vanity. My ego inflated with the idea of being a great world teacher.

The way a teaching works is that it reflects your desire back to you and shows you where you're at—or where you're not. Joya was a strong teaching about the seduction of astral realms and the misuse of power. Astral planes and psychic powers are just subtler forms of separation. The fantasies of becoming an esoteric world teacher were seductive and inflated my spiritual ego until I realized they were all built on separation. In Maharaj-ji's sub ek, in oneness, there is only love.

I assumed the vision of Maharaj-ji in the New Jersey motel room came from him. In retrospect, I suspect Hilda had something to do with it. Perhaps my longing for Maharaj-ji's form in the wake of his disappearing act left me vulnerable. Perhaps I suppressed some of the emotional fallout as I was feeling my way into living without his physical presence.

Joya had a murti of Maharaj-ji made for her new ashram in Florida. She also invited some of the Indian devotees, like Dada Mukerjee, to visit. I was embarrassed by her use of Maharaj-ji's name. I felt she was using him for legitimacy, the same way she'd used me.

Publicly admitting I'd been sidetracked by my own desires was embarrassing, but I discovered that it connected me to others. We need to know not only the signposts on the path, but also about the detours and pitfalls. Openly sharing my mistakes was part of my sadhana, part of Maharaj-ji's instruction about truth telling. The more open I was, the more others felt loved and served. Using myself as an object lesson in my talks and writings kept me honest and kept my ego out of the way. As long as I stayed in my heart, Maharaj-ji's message came across.

After leaving Joya, I started to reexamine my commitment to service and look again at how it could actually manifest. I needed to get back to Maharaj-ji's basic instruction to love everyone, serve everyone, and remember God.

Service as a spiritual path lacks glamour. I liked moving in and out of planes of reality, esoteric teachings, secret mantras, meditations in caves, experiences of bliss. Those experiences of different planes originated in my use of psychedelics, and I'd grown attached to those experiences. It was another subtle trap that I created for myself, another kind of spiritual ego.

I had romanticized and idealized my spiritual path—so much so that I distanced myself from the nitty-gritty of life. I wanted to transcend this earthly plane, with its imperfect humans caught in their greed and ambition and selfishness, including me. Serving God was an ideal. Serving God in the form of other people, with all their vagaries and flaws, politics and personality quirks, was a whole other kettle of fish.

I saw my aversion to my human incarnation. I'd lost track of the Buddha's admonitions about suffering, impermanence, and the illusion of a self. It was hard to fulfill Maharaj-ji's injunction to see God in everyone, especially, sometimes, in myself. My path as a renunciate, while bringing some new insights, was not bringing freedom. It was only making me more uptight. My lust had not subsided; half the time I was a horny celibate. I remembered Hari Dass writing, "When you dam a river, it builds up force." Only when I could face my incarnation and accept its contradictions and unique karma would I be free. Catch and release: see the patterns to let them go.

Maharaj-ji told me to be like Gandhi. Now I realized that meant fully participating in the human condition. But what did that look like? Others were better trained to alleviate suffering, like nurses, doctors, and political activists. They manifested compassion or fought injustice in their own ways. As I pondered Maharaj-ji's instructions, I realized my ability is to serve as a spiritual friend to help others see what lies at the root of suffering and help them to awaken. I could help people get free to serve others.

In Zen Buddhism, they say death is one of the Great Matters. I'd been thinking a lot about dying. Being with my mother as she was dying, I realized that, as the transition from the ego to the soul plane, death is a major rite of passage. When I thought about how Mother died—isolated in a hospital bed, surrounded by denial and the well-meaning hypocrisy of the medical profession—it was clear that few people in the West had any idea how to do this spiritual work. As with prisons, American society at the time largely avoided the subject of death.

The shift to my soul that Maharaj-ji had triggered changed my perspective from seeing myself as a purely physical being. The soul point of view now permeated how I saw the mystery of death.

When I first visited Benares with David Padwa in the Land Rover, I was so utterly horrified by all the sick people wandering around, carrying the coins for their funeral pyre, that I couldn't even look at them. But after months at Kainchi I stopped in Benares again. This time what I saw was entirely different. I was able to look in people's eyes. What I saw there was not hopelessness and despair but pity—for me.

To die in Benares is the highest aspiration of a truly spiritual Hindu. It's a way to go consciously to your death. When you die in Benares, Shiva whispers Ram, the name of God, in your ear, and your soul is liberated. Those people knew they were in the perfect place to die. They understood the symmetry of the cycle of life and death. Benares held incredible human suffering, but it was also a city of incredible joy.

In the West, meanwhile, I saw that death still provoked tremendous fear. The hospice movement was just coming into being, thanks in large part to the psychiatrist Elisabeth Kübler-Ross. A pioneer in near-death studies, she'd recently published her groundbreaking book *On Death and Dying* and was teaching around the country. She wanted to help people die well, sharing her model of the five stages of grief and working to create supportive environments for the dying. Elisabeth was among the first people to really talk openly about death in our society.

Like her, I wanted to offer new ways to view death, to bring a more open and loving approach to dying to our culture. In New York, a friend introduced me to a medium named Pat Rodegast, whom I'd heard speak on WBAI-FM. Pat channeled an astral being named Emmanuel; radio listeners called in with questions, and Emmanuel would answer. When I met Pat, we sat drinking tea in her living room while I asked questions of Emmanuel. His perspective on dying was especially refreshing. "Death," he said, "is absolutely safe." It was as much a part of the soul's incarnation as any other life experience. Death was like "going out the door of a rather stuffy room" or like "taking off a tight shoe."

I felt that broader view of dying could bring profound transformation to America. I was often asked to sit with the terminally ill, and I was learning what a gift it was to guide someone through the dying process. As with Mother, the most important part was simply being present. In Los Angeles, I went to visit a dear friend who was dying of a cancer of the nervous system. She was an intellectual, sensitive person who had no interest in reincarnation. Her pain was very severe. She was writhing in bed from the intensity of it. Words were of no use to her, so instead I sat next to her and began doing the Buddhist meditation on the decaying body.

This is a formal meditation that one does on the stages of decay. I sat there, eyes wide open, just noticing the pain and letting my emotions flow but not clinging or judging. Just noticing the laws of the universe unfold, which is not easy to do with someone you love, because of your emotional attachment. I sat there, watching the suffering, and I began to feel a vast, deep calm. The room became luminous. In that moment, my friend turned to me and whispered, "I feel so peaceful." Though her body was racked with pain, in this meditative environment, she was able to move beyond it. We created a space that we could be in together. It was bliss.

I was invited to work with a lawyer who had cancer. He lived in a fancy place by the ocean, and when I arrived, he was surrounded by friends and family. They were all drinking and laughing too loudly, trying to ignore the matter at hand, his death. I sat looking at the ocean for a bit, then I turned to him and said, "I understand you are going to die soon."

72

73

TOP   With Steve Durkee, Lama Foundation, circa 1974
ABOVE   Meditating in the dome at Lama

TOP LEFT Tellis Goodmorning, a Native American mentor for the Lama Foundation
TOP RIGHT Little Joe Gomez, an elder in the Native American Church, Lama Foundation
ABOVE The Blue Bus, still used as a residence at the Lama Foundation

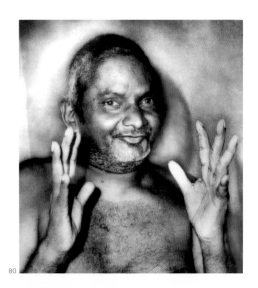

TOP Bhagwan Nityananda, Muktananda's guru
ABOVE Muktananda holding Satya Sai Baba at their meeting in Whitefield, near Bangalore

82

83

OPPOSITE The venerable VW van, en route from Nainital to Kainchi
TOP Coming down from PCP, Kausani, 1971
ABOVE LEFT Anandamayi Ma at her ashram near Haridwar
ABOVE RIGHT Maharaj-ji with Dada Mukerjee, Kainchi, 1971

88

89

90

TOP Along the Yamuna River in Vrindavan
ABOVE LEFT Bhagavan Das and Hari Dass, Haridwar, 1970
ABOVE RIGHT In Kainchi, 1971

Maharaj-ji with the first printing of *Be Here Now*

92

93

94

95

96

TOP With teaching assistants outside the "lecture hall," Boulder, Colorado, 1974
ABOVE Chogyam Trungpa Rinpoche, Boulder, Colorado, 1974

97

98

TOP Teaching on the Bhagavad Gita at Naropa
ABOVE Hanuman, the embodiment of service and devotion
for whom Ram Dass is named, at Kainchi

TOP LEFT Joya in Brooklyn
TOP RIGHT Joya in the Himalayas, 1977
ABOVE With Joya and Hilda Charlton, circa 1975

102

103

TOP Lama Foundation, view from the kitchen
ABOVE Anti-nuclear demonstration I attended in NYC, 1982

A young Maharaj-ji with an ancient Hanuman

105

106

TOP At Neem Karoli Baba Ashram, Taos, New Mexico.
Hanuman is adorned for the 2018 Guru Purnima festival.
ABOVE Barbara Durkee with her children at Lama Foundation, circa 1970

You could have heard a pin drop. I had said the thing that nobody ever says, and it changed the space completely. We got into a discussion about death with his family and friends, and we meditated on the ocean. We were in the moment to moment of the waves; we felt the immediacy and the oceanic vastness; and he was not alone.

From such experiences, I began to think about creating a center for conscious dying. Aldous Huxley came up with the idea in his final novel, *Island*. It would be a place near the mountains or the ocean, where the beauty of nature could offer a sense of the eternal. People could come there to die, supported by staff and volunteers who were not alarmed by death. Perhaps the Hanuman Foundation could start something like an ashram where people could come to die or to confront their own fear of death by helping other people die.

In June 1976, I led a retreat in Rhode Island, which Elisabeth Kübler-Ross attended. She was fiery, a real get-up-and-go type who smoked cigarettes like a chimney. I invited my friend Stephen Levine to teach meditation. Stephen was a poet and editor who'd helped found the underground newspaper the *San Francisco Oracle* before becoming involved in Buddhist meditation. Elisabeth had a center outside San Diego, and after I introduced them in Rhode Island, she invited Stephen to lead meditation at her dying retreats.

Stephen taught with Elisabeth for a year or so. Then she shifted to a psychodrama approach, which ran counter to his meditation practice, and they parted ways. I saw Stephen in Santa Cruz and floated my idea for the Dying Project. He liked it immediately, and I asked him to be the director. Though the Hanuman Foundation didn't have the funds yet to open a center, we came up with the idea of a free twenty-four-hour telephone hotline. People who called could have someone to talk to or to visit with them while they were dying. I nicknamed it Dial-a-Death. Stephen and his wife, Ondrea, ran it together. They were often on the phone for eight to ten hours a day. They corresponded with hundreds of people all over the country seeking support.

Stephen continued leading retreats and workshops. Eventually, with thousands of people writing letters and calling in, I became more involved myself, as did the executive director of the Hanuman Foundation, Ram Dev, aka Dale Borglum. Dale led meditation at

Stephen's dying retreats, and all three of us gave talks and workshops on conscious dying all over the US. Stephen and I also collaborated on *Grist for the Mill*, a book about awakening to oneness published in 1976.

The best preparation for death is to live in the present moment. If you are living in this moment, and in this moment, then when the moment of death comes, it is just another moment. But you can't tell someone else to live in the present moment unless you live here and now yourself.

Every dying person with whom I shared time helped me, probably more than I helped them. Dying is a collaborative dance, an opportunity to do the work within, whether as the one facing death or the one sitting at the bedside. It was a privilege to share those moments. I came to see death, not as an end point, but as a process of transformation.

As I was finding new direction, so were others in my spiritual family. The Lama Foundation in New Mexico was experiencing growing pains. Steve and Barbara Durkee divorced in 1971, and after leaving for the Middle East, Steve converted to Islam. He returned as Shaykh Abdullah Nooruddeen. In 1971, he had created an Intensive Studies Center for retreats at Lama, which he now converted to an Islamic Studies Center. I continued to teach at Lama, including at the ISC, but things grew so tense between the zealous Islamic adherents and the eclectic Lama Beans that in the spring of 1977, I was called upon to throw Steve out. Steve, now called Noor, ended up building a mosque at Abiquiú, between Taos and Santa Fe, a beautiful place. And the founding members of Lama agreed to leave the land, entrusting the foundation to a younger generation of residents.

Lama survived, and Barbara, who now goes by Asha Greer, still maintains a connection to it. More than fifty years after it was founded, what started as a simple, profound idea for spiritual community remains strong.

That same spring, a group of thirty or forty Maharaj-ji devotees gathered in upstate New York for a bhandara, a holiday feast. Most of the satsang who'd stayed on with Joya had left after a year or so, and it was a time of joyous reconnection. I proposed that we commission a murti of Hanuman in India and create a temple in the US. In short order, a family of traditional murti makers in India began work on a sixteen-hundred-pound marble statue of the monkey god, holding Ram's ring in his hand. The same sculptors had carved the murti of Hanuman at Maharaj-ji's ashram in Vrindavan.

The murti wouldn't arrive until the following year, in 1978, and some time would pass before we found a place for it, on a farm in Taos that we converted into an ashram. But now, after our difficult season with Joya, the murti symbolized a hopeful turn in our collective path. I spent the following summer on Martha's Vineyard further renewing satsang and family ties and recharging my spiritual batteries.

That October, I was invited to a reunion of another kind: a weekend seminar at the University of California, Santa Cruz, called "LSD: A Generation Later." Many of us from the psychedelic revolution were there, including Albert Hofmann, who gave his first public account of the discovery of LSD. More than four thousand people attended, many squished into the auditorium, others pressed against windows. Allen Ginsberg and my old Harvard Psychedelic Project colleague Ralph Metzner were there, as was Tim, who'd been granted a pardon by Governor Jerry Brown in 1976 and was no longer behind bars. He understood why I had denounced him, and we hugged and swapped stories. Tim was tickled by reports of the CIA's involvement in LSD research with its MK-Ultra project, which had just become public. "I'm all in favor of central intelligence," he joked.

I told the audience I didn't care if I ever took LSD again, but that I hoped serious research on it would resume someday. If there was anything our lives had proven thus far, it was that we were *not* psychotic.

In the spring of 1978, I got a call from Allen Ginsberg, who was still teaching at Naropa Institute. He knew I was scheduled to give a lecture in Boulder that April. "The day after you're lecturing," he said, "there's a demonstration to block the railroad tracks into the Rocky Flats nuclear weapons plant, outside Denver." He continued, "A group of Buddhists are going to sit and meditate there. I was going to lead them, but I have to be in New York. Would you go in my place?"

The Rocky Flats Plant produced plutonium triggers for atomic bombs, and there were reports of radioactive contamination in the area. Allen, along with Daniel Ellsberg, who had leaked the Pentagon Papers, civil rights leader Stokely Carmichael, and several others, planned to block the entrance to the plant to bring attention to the contamination issue.

I thought for a minute. From what I'd observed, a lot of social action came from the emotions of the people doing it, and I didn't want to get sucked in. On the other hand, I knew I needed to walk my talk, to bring my social action into line with seva, the selfless service of the Baghavad Gita. Seva as social action was different from practicing devotion in the Himalayas or giving talks in New York. Again, I saw how necessary it is to bring social action and spiritual work together to truly deal with our own and others' suffering.

The activism of the 1960s had led to deep divisions between radicals and hippies over how to effect change. Radical activists saw the hippies as self-involved hedonists; the hippies dismissed the radicals as angry and violent. And changing oneself was even harder than effecting political change. If I embraced my radical side, I feared getting lost in my anger and righteousness, as many did. There must be a way to embrace political action that would come from a deeper place in myself than "I should get involved." As Tim Leary would say, "I'm tired of being should upon." I wanted my action to emerge from an intuitive sense of rightness.

Nuclear warfare was collective insanity. I knew I was going to get involved, but I'd been waiting for the right moment. Now, Allen was on the phone. I thought, "I'll be in Boulder anyway. The handwriting is on the wall."

April 30, 1978, it was raining gently. More than five thousand people showed up, twice the number anticipated. It was the largest antinuclear protest in the country to date. Thirty-five of us sat in a circle on the tracks and meditated. As my meditation deepened, the leaders of the demonstration, including Ellsberg and Carmichael, gave rabble-rousing speeches from a platform. The meditators represented peaceful dissent, so I kept the group together. Mostly I just sat, then periodically walked around the perimeter, encouraging people to stay calm.

One of the most forceful speakers was the antinuclear campaigner and Australian pediatrician Dr. Helen Caldicott. Her passionate voice imparted a mother's outrage and a scientist's apprehension. I heard her playing on the fears of the audience with her urgency. I thought, "Haven't we gotten to a place in social action where we can inform and trust each other, instead of trying to manipulate people emotionally?"

I notice how many angry people there are at peace rallies. Social action arouses righteousness. But righteous anger can close your heart. If I want to be free more than I want to be right, I have to let go of righteousness. For social action to be done with love, the spiritual work has to come first. I work on myself to perform social action from a place of true compassion. Compassion and love are both in the soul. If my social action is not directed by the soul, it comes from the ego.

But even if I find myself afraid, or not feeling peaceful, or less than fully loving and compassionate, I must act. You can't wait around to be enlightened. There's no way *not* to act while you're in physical form. Krishna says as much in the Bhagavad Gita. As long as you're incarnate, you're acting. You can't *not* do anything—if you don't get out and vote, you're still affecting the outcome. Silence may itself be an acquiescence to injustice or unnecessary suffering.

Since I must act, I do the best I can to act consciously and compassionately. I try to make every action an exercise in liberation. Because the truth that comes from freedom, the power that comes from freedom, and the love and compassion that come from freedom are the jewels I can offer to my fellow sentient beings to relieve their suffering.

Although the Tao Te Ching says, "Truth waits for eyes unclouded by longing," I still desire peace. I don't want the world to end. I desire, I desire—all these desires cloud my mind so I can't hear as God hears. All I can do is keep working on myself.

A few years after Rocky Flats, in 1982, there was an antinuclear demonstration in New York. Almost a million people marched. The end of the march, in Central Park, felt more like a celebration than a political protest. No violence, no complaints, not one arrest. We were in the right place at the right moment doing the right thing. After that, I went to protests in a much lighter, more joyous way. After all, if you oppose something or someone in anger, all you proliferate in the world is more anger.

As the Dying Project progressed, Stephen Levine, Ram Dev, and I began to talk about having a physical space where we could invite people who had life-threatening illnesses to live and die consciously. We found a house in Santa Fe, New Mexico, and a satsang member graciously stepped up to purchase it. Ram Dev moved there to run it, and a wonderful woman named Diane Haug, who had worked with Stan Grof on pioneering end-of-life psychedelic treatment, came to help. I think the Dying Center was the first residential facility in the US to approach death in an open, graceful way as a spiritual rite of passage.

The Dying Center was so loving and supportive that it didn't work. It was a beautiful place, the food was great, and the staff were loving and deeply compassionate. Nobody wanted to leave. The first six months nobody died. After about three and a half years, the owner of the house needed the space. Ram Dev moved to the Bay Area and started the Living/Dying Project, a nonprofit that helps dying people and their caretakers in their own homes. Stephen Levine wrote *Who Dies?*, on how accepting death consciously is the perfect preparation for a meaningful life. With Ondrea, his wife and collaborator, he wrote several other books, including *A Year to Live*, about living each moment as if it were your last. In 2016, Stephen followed his own advice and passed peacefully on to his next adventure. He was a deep, poetic companion on the path.

I met Peter at a dying and meditation workshop in Santa Cruz, California. He was in his twenties, a painter and musician who played the guitar and harmonica. He was a free mountain spirit who had been living outdoors, except he was neat and clean and had a car. Peter was beautiful.

I felt a strong attraction to him. It didn't matter that I was in my late forties. "I wasn't expecting a guy like you at a Stephen Levine workshop," I said to him. Peter said he'd met someone at the beach who had told him about it. Later I learned that, when he was sixteen, Peter had taken an acid trip. The next day he'd found *Be Here Now* in his friend's apartment and started reading. He and his friend then went to a bookstore in Santa Cruz and, looking into the reflection in the store window, Peter had a vision of his future. He saw himself with me.

I was living in Soquel, near Santa Cruz, where I was sharing a house with Ram Dev and another satsang member. Peter and I started to meet at the beach and surf together. He was a great surfer. We went out for meals. Soon he was staying over.

Joya had claimed she would help me with my homosexuality, as if it needed fixing. Peter completed the sexual part of my being. We found an intimacy that flowered into a loving relationship and helped me bring together the physical and spiritual parts of my being. Sometimes I saw Peter as a lover and sometimes as a soul. When we entered that soul space together, it was unconditional love. The rest of the time we were two guys living life together.

Friendship, sex, and intimacy are all powerful teachings about love and attachment. Love wants for nothing, but sex, with its attendant lust, animal drives, and Freudian fantasies, reinforces sticky attachments and can create more karma. If you can focus on the love and bring it all into loving awareness, then you can truly enter into the spirit. My relationship with Peter started with attraction, moved into friendship and intimacy, and flowed into the spiritual.

At the same time, we were vastly different personalities. I liked being in control. I had a public life, going out on speaking tours, and a spiritual practice. Peter, meanwhile, needed stability. He was a good artist. I encouraged his art and helped him get exposure, and I supported him so he could focus on his work.

Our intimacy was nurturing. I could unwind with Peter after my hectic travel schedule. We would drive along the coast, north to Bolinas or Point Reyes or south toward Santa Cruz. We hiked beautiful trails, like Alamere Falls Trail near Point Reyes, around lakes with lily pads. We took mushrooms. We were in a bubble together.

Peter helped me bring mundane reality into spirit. From Santa Cruz on, I felt Maharaj-ji's presence in our relationship. Curiously, having that anchor for the restless sexual and emotional part of my being gave my spiritual life more space. Slowly we were both being absorbed into oneness.

CHAPTER 26

HOW CAN I HELP?

In December 1978, I had an opportunity to deepen my service and grow my compassion. Larry and Girija Brilliant, the satsang family members who were instrumental in smallpox eradication in India, invited me to Ann Arbor, where Larry was teaching public health at the University of Michigan. He and Girija wanted to start a nonprofit dedicated to alleviating suffering in the world.

Inspired by Maharaj-ji's teachings about service, they chartered a new foundation called Seva. *Seva*, of course, is the Sanskrit word for selfless service. It also stands for Society for Epidemiology and Voluntary Assistance, though hardly anybody ever used the long version. They convened a circle of friends and colleagues to launch the nonprofit and serve as the founding board at a conference center near Ann Arbor called Waldenwoods.

A winter storm arrived on our heels, and we were snowed in for several days. I didn't know many of the other people, and the blizzard gave us the time we needed to connect with one another.

We were a strange collection. There were doctors from the World Health Organization and the Centers for Disease Control in Atlanta, along with Larry and Girija's extended families from the Hog Farm commune and the Maharaj-ji satsang.

Across the table from me sat a doctor in a three-piece suit with an attaché case. Attaché Case, aka Dr. Steve Jones, stared in disbelief at my full beard and casual attire and at my neighbor, Wavy Gravy, aka

Nobody's Fool, the clown prince of the Hog Farm, sporting a red clown nose and a beanie with a propeller.

Also across the table was Dr. Nicole Grasset, a noted epidemiologist who had overseen the smallpox eradication push in Southeast Asia and had been Larry's boss. Next to her sat an ophthalmologist from South India, Dr. Govindappa Venkataswamy.

Dr. V., as everyone called him, was a devotee of the Indian saint and revolutionary, Sri Aurobindo. Dr. V. had founded Aravind Eye Hospital in the ancient temple town of Madurai, performing thousands of cataract surgeries every year, mostly for free. He appeared unassuming, but I felt an immediate spiritual connection.

The first order of business was to decide what suffering to tackle first. The first proposal was diarrhea, one of the biggest killers of children. Wavy spoke up, envisioning a fundraising campaign called "No Shit." Nicole Grasset produced an alternate proposal for a "two-year blindness campaign in Nepal."

Nicole had done her homework. Blindness in Nepal can be a death sentence because of the mountainous terrain; a person who goes blind has a life expectancy of less than two years. In Nepali, the term for blind person translates as "mouth without hands," useless to a family surviving on the edge of subsistence. Larry and the Hog Farmers had gone trekking and seen the heart-wrenching consequences of blindness in Nepal. I knew nothing about blindness, but Nicole was a dynamic and persuasive advocate. We quickly agreed Seva's first project would be to eliminate preventable blindness in Nepal.

My doctorate was in psychology, not medicine, and my efforts to alleviate the world's problems were limited to charitable giving and attending antiwar or antinuclear protests. I was impressed we were going to take on such a huge and tangible problem.

I had no medical skills, but I did know how to fundraise. Before long, I was explaining cataract surgery at all my lectures. Along with telling Maharaj-ji stories, I began talking about Seva and blindness prevention. We estimated each Nepal eye operation would cost five dollars. In fundraising terms that was powerful: for the cost of a movie ticket, you could restore a person's sight. Wavy took charge of "fun raising" for Seva. He gathered performers from among his rock musician friends to do benefit concerts around the country. The Grateful Dead, Bonnie Raitt, Jackson Browne, Joan Baez, David Crosby, and Dr. John all pitched in to perform in Seva's Eyeball concerts. We raised a lot of money and had a lot of fun.

Seva called itself "a conspiracy of friends masquerading as a foundation." From the beginning, the Seva circle was familial: we shared a lot, knew everything about one another, and made decisions together. We instituted regular circle sharing, which didn't always go smoothly. Wavy Gravy helped keep things light with a pair of tacky clown glasses with Groucho Marx eyebrows. If anyone uttered the word "serious," also known as "the S word," the meeting came to a complete stop while the offender donned the funny glasses. We avoided taking ourselves too seriously, even as we addressed deep suffering. (Wavy and his wife, Jahanara, named their son Howdy Do-Good Gravy, although as soon as he was old enough, he changed it to Jordan.)

Larry was the first chairman of Seva's board. He raised $10,000 from friends and satsang, and after he wrote an article about the new foundation in the Theosophical Society's magazine Quest, readers contributed another $20,000. Larry got a grant from the World Health Organization to write a book about the smallpox program, and put that money into Seva too.

The following year, in December 1979, we met for the second time, at a retreat center in Marin, California. While the first meeting had happened in good faith, no one knew what would come next. This was it.

Larry had invited a young entrepreneur who arrived late. Steve Jobs was a few years into a tech start-up called Apple. Years before, Steve had read Be Here Now and, inspired by the book, made a pilgrimage to India. He arrived at Kainchi a short time after Maharaj-ji left his body. Steve had come to the Seva meeting straight from an Apple board meeting, still wearing his three-piece suit (he had not yet adopted his famous black T-shirt uniform). He'd gotten stuck in traffic in his new Mercedes.

Steve had contributed $5,000 to help the fledgling foundation get rolling. As he entered, the discussion turned to getting the word out about Seva. Steve thought the board was clueless about marketing and recommended using Apple's marketing consultant. Although the gathering had begun as a convivial one, Steve, still stressed from his business meeting, grew abrasively insistent. Larry finally told him to cool it and walked him out. Steve cried for a while in the parking lot, then returned, apologized for his behavior, and left.

It was not the only early conflict in Seva. From the beginning, there were differing visions. The medical folks wanted simply to alleviate suffering. I and a few others wanted social service to also include spiritual practice to cultivate wisdom and compassion. Our view was, if we did not work on ourselves and teach others to do the same, our service would only contribute to more suffering.

This philosophical divergence became a core conflict within Seva, between what I came to call "the be-ers and the do-ers." To me, Seva was a laboratory for spiritual social action. By performing seva as selfless service and not being attached to the results, as the Bhagavad Gita taught, people would evolve spiritually while helping.

By the third board meeting, the do-ers were burning out. Nepal's bureaucracy was an endless hassle, an ingrained culture of influence and corruption that led to anger and frustration for those navigating it. "I'm confused," I said. "I thought this was going to be about conscious service, service for the liberation of all beings. *How* we are doing it is as important as *what* we are doing. I'm not really interested in being part of just another do-good organization. I want to be part of a fresh statement for the world."

I was spokesperson for the be-ers, and Nicole for the do-ers. I wanted the Nepal staff to work on themselves as well as cure blindness. Nicole was focused on helping blind people. Her public health approach leaned toward speed and efficiency. She was a smart, sophisticated, deeply committed medical professional. At one point, she asked, "Would you let a person be needlessly blind for one extra day?"

I replied, "Yes. There are worse things than being blind." It took us a year to come back from that one statement. It ripped the organization apart. Others referred to our philosophical impasse as the Battle of the Titans.

Several times, I sought to leave the board. My approach relied on faith, trust, and openheartedness, not always a fit for administering an increasingly large nonprofit. But every time I thought about quitting, I came back to the fact that we were, in fact, doing something new. Seva *was* dedicated to relieving suffering from a spiritual angle and doing service as karma-yoga. The board members were all compassionate and dedicated. I could not elevate spiritual values over managerial efficiency—they had to work together.

It was an essential debate. I don't think Nicole really understood my position at first, and I needed to appreciate the urgency of the frontline workers. We all had more work to do on ourselves.

We stayed in the fire together. Over the years, the self-awareness component, working on oneself spiritually while serving, has waxed and waned at Seva, depending on who is in command. But we all grew profoundly through that dialogue. I understand better how to serve and what alleviating suffering is about in myself and others. The do-ers understood that the point of view from which you serve, whether it truly comes from the heart, influences the outcome.

Everything we do to work on ourselves—going on retreat, meditating, opening our hearts, quieting our minds—transforms our being. However we serve, as a physiotherapist, or a bus driver, or a parent, is an expression of our being.

I use social action as a vehicle to work on myself and offer my being for the relief of others' suffering. If I go to an antinuclear rally, it is an exercise of my own consciousness. When I work with a dying person, it is a manifestation of my own heart. Those actions keep feeding back to my awareness so that I become clearer, quieter, more present, more spacious. Gandhi said that any good you do in the marketplace will seem insignificant, but it's still very important that you do it.

The less attached you are to your own desires, the more you can hear what other human beings need, and the less you project your own needs. Your response is more compassionate and appropriate to the need at hand. That doesn't mean you don't have desires. The paradoxical question is, how can we be fully engaged in life yet not be attached? Translating the inner work on ourselves into action is a subtle art!

Seva broke new ground in the world health arena by bringing together very different kinds of people and introducing cross-cultural service. It challenged institutions, like WHO and CDC and many NGOs, to deliver public health in ways that build indigenous capacity. Aravind Eye

Hospital eventually set up an institute for international training. Its eye care model has been replicated all over Asia and Africa.

Seva was my deepest dive into social action. Although the spiritual component was often a small part of the overall effort, it contributed subtly to how the people doing the work engaged with service and how donors viewed Seva as a spiritually oriented service group. It's still unusual in that respect.

I went on several multicity tours for Seva called "Spirit of Service," staying in Days Inns and Motel 6s. One tour, in 1986, took in ninety cities and grossed over $650,000. Sometimes it got to be a grind. I'd be onstage, lecturing about eye operations, and I'd think, "God, what am I doing here?" The audience had come to hear about consciousness and love, and here I was discussing blindness prevention.

Not unexpectedly, climbing into the role of social activist brought up my emotional past. I heard myself echo my father raising money for Jewish refugee children. Dad played on people's sympathies and guilt. He was good at it too. Was I doing anything different?

I hoped so. The point was to combine social action with the spiritual path, to challenge people to see the importance of working on themselves while helping others. My models were Hanuman and Gandhi serving God in the form of other people. Such service arises from spiritual roots, which *was* what people came to hear about.

Larry and Girija moved to Kathmandu for a year to study the incidence and causes of blindness in Nepal. They logged the data on an early Apple II computer donated by Steve Jobs. Seva started running eye camps in Nepal to test treatment strategies. Doctors trekked to mountain villages, set up camps, and treated the surrounding population. Western ophthalmologists volunteered to train Nepali physicians.

Dr. V. was intent on bringing Western technology and efficiency to Indian eye care. He wanted Aravind Eye Hospital, and Seva for that matter, to become a McDonald's of eye care. He passionately believed sight-restoring surgery should be available to everyone. I traveled with Dr. V. in Nepal, bumping along in a jeep through Himalayan hinterlands to a Seva-sponsored eye camp. We watched cataract surgeries performed in a field tent. I saw villagers have their bandages removed and see for the first time in years. Their joy was a gift.

I knew definitively then my fundraising lecture marathons for Seva were worth it. The question I had asked myself—"What am I doing here?"—was answered in that eye surgery tent.

I was becoming better acquainted with my compassionate side. Hanuman, who serves God with such love, was insinuating himself into my very being. Was this why Maharaj-ji named me Ram Dass, the servant of Ram?

Dr. Venkataswamy embodied my ideal of seva. He represented the bridge between the spiritual and the medical arms of Seva Foundation. He appealed to the medical activists, and at the same time he was a devoted spiritual practitioner who was deeply surrendered to his guru. His aspiration to systematize eye care and replicate it worldwide came out of a true spiritual commitment. I've met a lot of doctors and public health people who are deeply altruistic. But Dr. V. embodied true seva on a level rarely seen.

I visited Dr. V. at Aravind Eye Hospital in Madurai. From his origins in a South Indian village, Dr. V. had built an eye care empire. I saw how he treated his patients. Wearing an open-neck shirt, he was chatting with villagers with an easy familiarity. He talked and looked like them. He was already elderly but still doing delicate eye surgery. He used instruments made especially for his hands, which were twisted from rheumatoid arthritis.

Named for Dr. V.'s guru, Sri Aurobindo, Aravind Eye Hospital provides eye care on par with the world's best. The financial model is Robin Hood. Well-off patients pay a premium for personalized care, and the paying customers support free treatment for thousands of villagers, brought in to the hospital by the busload. Aravind performs more cataract surgeries than any other institution in the world. Western ophthalmologists go to train in Madurai because they can do more surgeries there in a month than in a year in the US.

Dr. V. took me on an overnight pilgrimage to Sri Aurobindo's ashram in Pondicherry. He suggested I meditate in Sri Aurobindo's room. As I began to sink into the silence, I heard somebody behind me. I opened my eyes, looked around, and saw a sadhu smeared in ashes sitting cross-legged on the floor, an old, old baba. He was blessing me in some way. Then he dissolved just like a cloud in the sky. When I related the experience to Dr. V. and his friends, none of them seemed the least surprised.

Back in Madurai, Dr. V. sent me to visit the ancient Meenakshi Temple that occupies the center of the city. The temple is an ornately carved medieval compound teeming with devotees and priests offering incense and flowers. Dr. V.'s family is well known, and I was brought into the charged inner sanctum where they worship the Goddess. It was another reflection of the spiritual side of Aravind.

Dr. V.'s family were all involved in one aspect or another of the hospital. His sister and brother-in-law were ophthalmic surgeons, his nephew was the chief hospital administrator. Family members still work there, spanning multiple generations.

Partnering with Seva, Aravind brought intraocular lens implants to India and later to Nepal, an indigenous manufacturing capacity for Indian eyes that serves many other developing countries as well. Seva continues its support, and even after Dr. V.'s passing in 2006, Aravind maintains its profound spiritual roots.

I think my own attitude toward service was at first rooted in fear. I observed this with clarity at a service program I helped lead in the mid-1980s at the Cathedral of Saint John the Divine in New York. Paul Gorman, my former WBAI-FM radio host, was now in charge of community programs and outreach at the great Episcopal cathedral. He invited me to teach a course in compassionate action.

Some two hundred people gathered, and we agreed to serve the homeless as part of the course. Some of us helped in shelters or soup kitchens; others worked with mental patients who had fallen through cracks; others organized street people to bring politicians' awareness to their plight. We kept diaries and shared our experiences at an open microphone.

One woman reported on her interaction with a neighborhood homeless man. "I realized," she said, "that though I gave him money, I had never really acknowledged his existence as a fellow human being.

I was afraid. I was afraid that if I opened up to him, he'd end up living in my apartment."

Her words captured exactly what I had been feeling. I'd been afraid to open my heart to the suffering of others because I feared I would be consumed, unable to set limits.

Over the years, as I have slowly opened to real love for my fellow beings, the connection between spiritual growth and relieving suffering has become clearer. By doing the inner work, I find my compassion deepens and my actions are more effective.

Paul and I wrote a book, *How Can I Help?* A few years later, sponsored again by Seva and the cathedral, we extended our focus on homelessness with an initiative called Home Aid. It included a retreat with Buddhist teachers and homeless activists, as well as an outreach program. In November 1988, we organized a Home Aid concert featuring David Crosby and Graham Nash, Carly Simon, Laurie Anderson, Paul Simon, Mickey Hart, Dr. John, and Sweet Honey in the Rock. Ben & Jerry's donated gallons of ice cream, and actors and activists showed up too: Robin Williams, Willem Dafoe, Allen Ginsberg, Susan Sarandon. We raised $50,000 to aid the homeless. I remember Robin Williams remarking on the harmonic connection among all living things.

At the same time, the AIDS epidemic was erupting in full force. A few years earlier, in 1983 or 1984, I'd heard from a guy who must have been one of the earliest cases. He had Kaposi's sarcoma, the purple skin lesions that were an indicator of full-blown AIDS. I called Dr. Larry Brilliant to see if he knew about it. At that point, no one understood what the disease was or what caused it. There was no cure.

As the disease struck seemingly everywhere, a feeling of dread gripped the country. Within a few short years, as many as ten million people worldwide were infected with HIV. (AIDS has since killed more than thirty-nine million.) Early on, it was known as the "gay disease," with all sorts of associated stigma, even within the gay community. People of color, who had less access to services than white people, were dying disproportionately. AIDS soon became a leading cause of death for women of childbearing age too. Everyone lived in fear of any lesion on the skin.

Given my own sexuality, I felt called to help. Half a dozen of my gay friends had AIDS, and there was a feeling of "There but for the grace of God go I." At the hospice centers, I would sit at patients' bedsides, holding their hands. We'd talk psychotherapy or spiritual stuff, but mostly I'd simply sit, offering my presence.

The fear around AIDS cut people off from the human contact they needed, so I touched and hugged people and helped other caregivers overcome their fear. I worked with dying patients in New York and Boston. I went on rounds in the AIDS program at San Francisco General Hospital, which was run by a friend of Larry Brilliant's, Dr. Richard Fine. I also worked with the Zen Hospice Project, whose first director was Frank Ostaseski, a Buddhist teacher mentored by my old friend Stephen Levine. Zen Hospice had a healing center for AIDS, where I sat with patients and helped with group counseling. When I wasn't traveling, I was there twice a week.

The AIDS work started me thinking more about Gandhi and karma-yoga. He famously said, "Work is worship." My view of the *nishkam karma-yoga* of the Bhagavad Gita, working selflessly with no thought of gain, was still a bit removed until I got down in the trenches with AIDS. It was the first time I experienced death on that scale. Seeing the terrible progression of HIV as it tore apart people's lives ripped open my heart too. I found myself committed on a more emotional level than before to help in whatever way I could.

I was with several patients as they died. In particular I remember one guy whose parents had rejected him. His finances were in ruins. He had sores all over his body. As I entered his room, I said something like, "How's your incarnation doing?" He was very caught up in his immediate predicament, and I was upleveling it to many lifetimes. We both laughed, and I shared being stuck in my own incarnation. In that moment we were souls, witnessing our incarnations.

Throughout these many opportunities to enter into the world's suffering—death, blindness, homelessness, disease—I tried to bring together the spiritual and action-oriented parts of my being. I'm sure I never succeeded entirely. This was far afield from what I had thought of as becoming a yogi. Maharaj-ji named me for Hanuman and told me to love everyone, serve everyone, and remember God. The key is always love.

It's a delicate balance: wisdom and compassion, detachment and devotion. Those twin lessons from the battlefield of the Bhagavad Gita still apply. Detachment is giving up how it turns out, and devotion is surrendering into love. The practice is to keep an eye on both and maintain the balance.

Whenever I could, I attended retreats at Insight Meditation Society in Barre, Massachusetts, with Joseph Goldstein and Sharon Salzberg. I liked drawing from a wide variety of spiritual practices to keep the balance, and both Joseph and Sharon are wonderful teachers. So when they invited me to Burma in 1985 to study with *their* teacher, a senior Burmese monk named U Pandita, I quickly agreed.

We traveled to a monastery in Yangon (Rangoon) to meditate for three months. The days were simple and rigorous. The first meditation sitting began at 3:15 a.m. The rest of the day, until 11 p.m., I meditated in an alternating sequence: sitting an hour, then walking an hour. There was nothing to read, no conversation. I was allowed six interruptions: for a couple of meals, for a nap, for an evening teaching, for laundry, and for an interview with U Pandita. Sometimes, in the afternoons, Joseph and I surreptitiously exchanged chocolate M&M's.

I felt like an amateur in the company of these big league meditators. Sharon got instruction in the practice of *metta*, or lovingkindness, while the rest of us focused simply on deepening our meditation. This was basic Buddhist practice: no Western embellishments or comforts, no talking, no mind games, just sitting. Like Theravadan Buddhism itself, it was bare-bones simplicity. I was trying to perfect meditation as a method.

It also deepened the fusion of Buddhism and bhakti yoga that remains a primary current in my practice and teaching. The combination of mind and heart, adapting the Buddhist insights of suffering, impermanence, nonself, with the practice of compassion, is a path we can relate to in the West. The dissatisfaction inherent in materialism, the constancy of change in our lives, and our identification with thinking—awareness of these qualities brings us into this moment. Compassion, the practice of seeing that others are the same as us, the heart of the wisdom of oneness—all contribute to our sense of inter-dependence and harmony.

Maharaj-ji instructed us to "bring your mind to one point and wait for grace." The time in Burma with Joseph and Sharon increased my concentration and one-pointedness. I felt like I was cheating, because one-pointedness is a key to my bhakti practice. What Maharaj-ji said isn't Buddhist doctrine, but it works for me. The state of being I associate with Maharaj-ji is my source of grace, unconditional love, and oneness. The language and concepts of Buddhism are different, but beyond language and concepts, beyond *nama rupa* (name and form), consciousness and love are the same. I can't picture the Buddha and Maharaj-ji arguing.

In retrospect, at every point in my sadhana, Maharaj-ji has given me exactly the tools I need. Meditation quiets me and focuses my attention. Then, when I put my mind to Maharaj-ji, the intense concentration opens a doorway to him, to his no-form, to his unconditional love. The combination of Buddhist meditation and bhakti devotion is still my practice. Integrating Buddhist wisdom with the opening of the heart feels like a completion of both.

The early weeks of the meditation practice in Burma were extremely difficult. My head filled with thoughts of all kinds. By the end of two months, my mind began to quiet. I was filled with peace and joy.

And then a cable arrived at the monastery. It was from my step-mother, Phyllis. "I am sorry to disturb your meditation," it read. "I am being operated on for cancer on Tuesday. I thought you should know. Love, Phyl."

CHAPTER 27

IT'S ONLY LOVE

I'd only just reached a space of quiet clarity in Burma. U Pandita urged me to continue deepening my practice, but I knew I needed to go back. It was a seeming dilemma between the inner pull of the spirit and the outer pull of love, my karmic commitment to Phyllis. I cut the meditation retreat short.

U Pandita spoke for the Noble Eightfold Path of Buddhism, saying, essentially, "This is your chance at enlightenment, don't blow it." On the other hand was love. Maharaj-ji spoke about how love between individuals, even between a guru and devotee, engenders attachment. He said, "Attachment grows both ways." It's inevitable. For incarnate souls, it's part of the package. When I got the message from Phyllis, I could hear Maharaj-ji inside. Choosing love wasn't even a choice.

A few years earlier, Dad and Phyllis had moved to a house in Cohasset on the South Shore, east of Boston. Phyllis loved the ocean, and the house was just blocks from the beach. When Dad started to lose strength, Phyllis asked for help in caring for him. Though I traveled constantly, I always returned to Massachusetts. Dad and Phyllis hired an excellent caregiver, a student of mine named Ken, to live with them. I was their safety net, overseeing their affairs. I turned their basement into an apartment where I stayed whenever I was in town.

For the next six months I helped care for Phyllis. Dad, eighty-eight by this time, was increasingly frail and quiet. I'd always been close to her. Phyllis was the only one in the family who'd shown genuine inter-est in my spiritual life. Now she asked me to share in the decisions about her medical treatment.

The meditation practice in Burma had brought me deep clarity and serenity. But Phyllis's cancer truly awakened loving compassion. As her cancer metastasized, devouring her body, I found myself afraid of losing her. At her bedside, I learned to keep my heart open, even when it was breaking.

As Phyllis lay dying, I sat with her, holding her in my arms. She was in a lot of pain, and we worked together on assessing the right levels of medication. Though she could get angry and depressed, we had many conversations about her spirit and how it would soon free itself from her sick body.

One day, she said to me, "Richard, sit me up." I did as she asked, placing her legs over the edge of the bed. To keep her erect, I put one hand on her chest and the other on her back. To steady her head, I put mine against hers.

Then Phyllis took three long, slow breaths, inhaling and exhaling, and died. This is how the great Tibetan masters have always done it: they sit up, take three long breaths, and then they're gone. I don't know how Phyllis knew to do that. Those of us who had been caring for her at her bedside felt a great sense of blessing and peace.

We buried her ashes at the Ramakrishna Vedanta Society ashram, which was still under the leadership of Gayatri Devi, who had been part of our early psilocybin work at Harvard. Phyllis's death engaged my heart. I didn't need to be so afraid of grief; it didn't separate me from the spiritual dimension. In fact, it put me more in touch with the soul plane. And knowing that grief is an experience shared by all humanity let me see myself as just one wave on a great sea.

After Phyllis's death, I became more of an active presence in Dad's care. The time with him was unexpectedly sweet. Most of my life was an implicit rebellion against everything he'd stood for or wanted me to do, his concepts of success, wealth, and power. When you rebel against parental projections, they're just as much a part of you as part of the parent. As a Harvard professor, even as I was rebelling, I was still competing with my father.

Still, he was proud of me: He had a framed cover of the *New York Times Magazine* with a beautiful photo of me on Martha's Vineyard. The article was negative, but Dad hung it on the wall anyway. Once during my years with Joya, I was speaking at a church on the Upper West Side, and he and Phyllis came to listen. I was wearing my whites and playing the tamboura, and behind me was a mural of Christ washing the disciples' feet. Dad leaned toward Phyllis and said, "God, I feel like the Virgin Mary." I loved that.

Dad was withdrawn and barely spoke, but I was glad for the opportunity to care for him. At first I did it grudgingly, looking for praise for being a good son. Later, as I worked to make my father happy in his final years, I felt like I'd been given a gift. In India, I saw how family roles give form and meaning to life. Now I understood this for myself.

I began to appreciate my father's legacy in a new light. When he raised funds for the American Jewish Joint Distribution Committee, Dad's service was meant to further his own social climbing, but he was also reaching out from his heart. In spite of, or perhaps because of, his poor upbringing, he had a very generous side. Dad always treated everyone when we went out to restaurants; a bit like Maharaj-ji, he enjoyed feeding people. I realized he'd given me a sense of idealism around compassion and service that deepened when I met Maharaj-ji and through him Hanuman. In Dad's and Maharaj-ji's memory, I pick up the check when I go to a restaurant.

Living with Dad, I learned the value of slowing down. I was aging myself, in my fifties by this time. Getting into the car, climbing the steps to the house, settling in his armchair—he gave each small movement great attention. "There we are," he would say, satisfied.

In New Hampshire, some years earlier, I remember looking out the window with him at the sunset over the lake. I said to him, "Isn't it beautiful?" He replied, "Yes, it's just perfect." I realized he was admiring the newly mown grass on his three-hole golf course. Now we sat in Cohasset holding hands and watching the sunset together. He smiled beatifically and said to me, "Isn't it just beautiful?"

I took him for a ride to Holliston, a town outside Boston where his grandfather had owned a farm. When Dad was a boy, he and his family would take the train to Holliston on the weekends. His grandfather would meet them at the station with a horse and buggy and drive them to the farm.

We went for so many family drives in my childhood, I thought Dad would enjoy revisiting a route from his youth. After studying maps and calling the town hall, I figured out where the farm had been. We drove from the train station along the old road. When we arrived at our destination, Dad had grown quiet and looked lost. I was disappointed. I'd worked hard to recreate a memory, but it had backfired.

Suddenly I realized we'd traveled from the station at the speed of a car, not of a horse and buggy. I decided to make the trip again, this time inching along at the speed of a horse and buggy. All of a sudden, Dad came alive. His memory was waking up. "Here's where we used to get apples!" he exclaimed. Then he shared story after story.

From this I realized old age and childhood offer a kind of spacious time other seasons do not, less filled with busyness and rushing around. This quiet openness allows the soul to enter, not unlike quieting the mind in meditation.

Dad and I developed a deep friendship. Friendship had never been part of my relationship with either of my parents, but with death beckoning, we were able to enter a shared heart space. When their bodies were falling away, I was able to see the spirit without the parental trappings. We were souls hanging out.

I had lots of time to reflect on those family dynamics. In my family, love was used in the service of wealth and power. That strengthened identification with our roles as separate egos and reinforced manipulation in relationships. Ultimately, when we die and return to our souls, we understand the separateness of ego is a delusion.

My blood family lost track of love in their need for power and control. I got lost in it too. We enjoyed Sunday dinners and holidays together, but sometimes we were just occupying a house together. We were not a family of the spirit but individuals with our own power needs.

Mother and I had a constant push-pull of power and love. She with-held her love to control my behavior. Her maternal ambiguity did a lot to condition me, especially my sexual ambivalence and my own need for power. Inside I yearned for real love, free from conditions.

On one of my lecture tours, I had a strange experience that gave me new insight into that dynamic. I was leading workshops on Oahu, Maui, and Kauai when I received a note that read, "We are a group living and meditating together upcountry on the Big Island of Hawaii, and we invite you to visit with us." I figured it was a spiritual com-mune. I had never been to the Big Island, so I decided to sandwich in a stopover.

They met me at the airport in Hilo in their Bronco pickup, an older man and a young couple. On the drive up the volcano to the old planta-tion where they lived, I was being my usual Ram Dass self, the charming spiritual friend. They were silent and almost unresponsive.

We arrived after an hour-long drive up twisting roads. They put me in a beautiful outdoor room with bougainvillea. The older man suggested I rest and come to his office down the path when I was ready.

After my nap, I knocked on his door. We had an intimate discus-sion about our lives, and together we watched a magnificent sunset. While we were sitting there, a young woman arrived with a platter of fresh tropical fruit. After a while, the man said, "Well, would you like to meet the rest of us?" I said, "No, not really."

But he pulled open a curtain and revealed about thirty people facing us, like an audience waiting for me to speak. They had been there the whole time, listening to us from behind the curtain. It was like a creepy horror movie. I started to feel like I had been had.

Their letter had said they were meditators. I figured I was supposed to give a talk, so I started to speak and tell stories, to do whatever it is I do. But as it turned out, they were actually a New York therapeutic community. They were interested in me because of my history with psychology, psychedelics, and spiritual stuff.

After a few minutes, a young woman near the back of the room raised her hand. She said, "Ram Dass, your book *Be Here Now* was very helpful. Why aren't you like your book?"

Her remark was like a bucket of ice water in my face. My defensive hackles rose. A fellow on the right said, "Ram Dass, my heart hurts from what you've been saying." Others spoke up in the same vein.

I began to freak out. They were all acting like enemies. I went on the attack: I was fine and openhearted, and it was they who were screwed up. This went on until around midnight, with one person after another criticizing me. Finally, the older man, who had been mostly quiet throughout the evening, said, "I think we've gone about as far as we can go tonight. Why don't we continue around seven thirty in the morning?" Everyone dispersed silently. I was left to return alone to my sleeping space.

I had expected to share a meditative evening. So much for expectations. I wanted to leave the next morning, but we were way up on the volcano and I had no transport. I was physically trapped in their psychological universe.

I lay in bed looking up at the stars. As I quieted down, I realized they were right. I was still a phony. I had been relying on my charm and stories to cover up my vulnerability all evening. I felt intensely embarrassed and humiliated.

Next morning, after breakfast, we gathered in a large room. I opened by telling them my insights of the previous night. They had been right in their accusations, I told them, and I wanted to ask for their help. The older man said, "Ram Dass, your brother that you told me about yesterday"—in that intimate talk!—"the one who is in the mental hospital? He's the only one who retained any power, who truly escaped from your family and got free." That comment upset me right off the bat, because Leonard was really crazy. He thought he was Christ.

The man said, "Why don't you lie down in the middle of the floor, and we'll all put our hands on you?" They ushered me to the middle of the room and put a mat out. I lay down, and they gathered around me, putting their hands on various parts of my body. The older man was over in the corner, telling me to relax and breathe.

All at once, I am back in my childhood bedroom, in my crib, the sun streaming in through the bars on the window. I am having a temper tantrum, wailing and feeling my own deepest pain, fury, and powerlessness. I am screaming with rage. I am alive, and the feeling is deeply sensual. I see my mother standing over my crib, red-faced and angry, pushing me down with her hand firmly on my chest, demanding I stop.

Then she's grabbing my arms and staring down at this male child, this part of herself that she cannot control, glaring at me with scorn and rejection. I am fighting her with all my power, but she just grips my arms and looks at me coldly. It is that look of cold anger that turns the tide. If I lose her love, I lose everything. My will flickers, then I am overcome with a paroxysm of defeat as I relinquish my power. It is as simple as that.

I quieted down and came back into the room with those thirty people in Hawaii. Though lost from view in the abyss of my unconscious, I realized the memory was true. It took thirty of them and being imprisoned in this contrived social situation to uncover that three-year-old child. What years of analysis, drugs, and meditation had been unable to do, they had done. I still didn't like them. But I was thankful to them for liberating this early, almost preconceptual, personality calcification hidden within me.

Other memories flooded back over time. I realized, from that very early traumatic experience, that I had power only when my mother gave it to me. Her intensely intimate love often combined with that implacable control, forcing me to focus on pleasing her. Later that pattern of submission extended to the other power figures around me.

I felt as if a part of me that was dead had come back to life. I felt revitalized, a new sense of peace about who I was and about my family—a peace that translated into forgiveness when I cared for my father.

We think of nature and nurture, heredity and environment, as different. But from the standpoint of reincarnation, it's all part of the subtle continuum of an incarnated consciousness. The organic complexity of biology and awareness—our bodies, minds, and environment—are all integral. They're all part of the karmic stew. As I identify more with my spiritual self, I see more of the framework of karma and reincarnation. From a calm place within, I observe the karma that defines this incarnation, constantly bringing it into awareness.

Karma, the result of past actions and our conditioned desires, keeps us turning on the wheel of birth and death. Our reality is a projection of desire on many levels, from gross to subtle. Coming into a body, incarnating into a human birth, brings all the drives for physical survival, sex, nourishment, safety, security. Above all, it brings the need for love. Love is different from other emotions because it can take us out of our instinctive drives and fears and connect us to our soul.

Each family member has their own karmic knot to untie. The family unit and its dynamic create the perfect vehicle for each member to burn off their karma. No matter how dysfunctional it appears from the outside, that's what family is about. Maybe the shared family karma will be complementary; maybe it will conflict. Seemingly random associations in a family are in truth a constellation of souls with interlocking karma that can be either reinforced or released. The poet e. e. cummings says, "let all go / dear / so comes love."

Maharaj-ji once said to me, "Your mother is a very high being" (*mahatma* in Hindi). I said to the translator, "Didn't he say she *was* a great soul? Because she is dead now." And Maharaj-ji said, "No! No!" I was remembering her as Mother. He saw her as a soul. She is a soul who, this time around, took birth as my mother. As I pondered his words I began to see our relationship as sharing a spiritual journey.

As my point of view shifts to Maharaj-ji's perspective, I imagine him seeing Mother's many incarnations simultaneously, a parade of all her lifetimes of spiritual evolution. Maybe my mother *is* a high being who took birth as a Jewish mother for my benefit—and hers, too. We both had our roles, as if we were onstage. As I live more in my soul, I realize Mother was spiritual. She was my first upaguru.

Dad died of pneumonia in September 1988, at age ninety. He made me executor of his estate, though I didn't take any of the money, per Maharaj-ji's instruction. I distributed it all to my family members. I didn't tell them I wasn't taking a share.

My lack of attachment to Dad's money had a positive effect on our relationship before he died. I think he could sense I didn't want anything from him. In the end we were just two people—father and son, yes, but more than that, two souls exchanging love.

After Dad died, I moved back to Santa Cruz. While I was in Massachusetts, I'd maintained a long-distance relationship with Peter.

In the time spent reflecting on my family, I was more aware than ever of the inner conflict I'd always felt between power and love.

With Peter, that internal struggle between power and love finally subsided. He and I moved in together, renting a guest house in Marin owned by Larry and Girija Brilliant. It featured an octagonal hot tub we called the Noble Eightfold Bath. When I wasn't on the road lecturing, Peter and I traveled together, sometimes on vacation as far away as Tahiti or to the beaches of Baja California.

Peter and I were together almost nineteen years, through many changes. What started as physical attraction grew into emotional interdependence, a deep love, and a spiritual bond. The karmic sandpaper of existence, time, and experience ground down separations and resistance to love, until we saw through to what is beneath, to the soul. Eventually it was as much a soul relationship as a physical one.

Being in relationship is its own kind of crucible. It forced me to confront desires and emotions I might not have gone through otherwise: lust, jealousy, dependency, emotional peaks and crashes. Peter came along years after Maharaj-ji left the body. Maybe earlier I was not ready to integrate those different levels of my being.

Maharaj-ji said a man could be brahmacharya with one woman. He meant that marriage could also be a spiritual route to God. Many of the westerners took that to heart. Of course he didn't say anything about a man being with another man. I think it applied to me and Peter.

I didn't hide our relationship, but I didn't publicize it either. I felt protective of Peter, who was not a public figure. And though I had struggled early on with my sexual identity, at that point labels like bisexual, homosexual, or gay didn't seem helpful. I had no interest in making my sexuality into a statement as my friend Allen Ginsberg had done. To identify myself with any movement felt limiting. Souls have karma that manifests as gay or straight, female or male. But souls themselves are neither female nor male. My focus is to connect with others as souls and to allow other souls to be who they are. And as Maharaj-ji said, "All love is pure."

CHAPTER 28

LOOKING INWARD, REACHING OUT

I first became involved in Seva Foundation to fulfill Maharaj-ji's injunction to serve; I emerged with a much deeper sense of interconnection with other people and cultures. By the late 1980s, Seva's focus had expanded from blindness in Nepal and India to other projects, like working with the homeless and funding a clinic on the Oglala Sioux Pine Ridge Reservation.

At the end of the Cold War we were living in a newly globalized world. With greater international awareness came more need to respond to global problems—famines, AIDS outbreaks, wars, and environmental degradation. Seva took on reforestation projects in Costa Rica, supported women in Afghanistan, and aided redevelopment in Guatemala and Chiapas in southern Mexico.

I became board chairman for Seva. My trusted satsang sister Mirabai Bush agreed to step in as vice-chairwoman to run the organization while I continued to tour. Mirabai headed up Seva's program in Guatemala, and in 1988 I went with her to see the villages decimated by conflict. The military government had killed rebel guerillas in the countryside, and the indigenous peoples were caught in the cross fire. Mayan people in the Altiplano of northern Guatemala had just emerged from *la violencia*, when the army came through burning villages, killing the men and raping the women. The women and children who survived had nothing—no seeds, no fertilizer, no money, almost no food.

Our first aim was to help restore the livelihoods of women who had been widowed by the political violence. We provided them with goats, seeds, training, funds to start microbusinesses, and access to co-ops where they could sell indigenous crafts. Mirabai and I traveled from village to village, meeting people and learning their stories. We were continually exhausted, living on tortillas and salt with our hosts, traveling off-road in jeeps. At one village there was a long introduction to everyone, then equally lengthy good-byes, all part of the social ritual. I was so tired that, as we were leaving to go to the next village, I said, "Can't we just throw the money out the window?" Classic bad development!

Instead I learned the power of connection. The deprivation opened my eyes and heart. The happiness of the women who received the goats was deeply moving. They were so poor! Yet their sense of community and gumption in the face of overwhelming oppression and suffering was inspiring. Their villages had been destroyed, but they still felt united. We reached one area with nine villages and explained that we could only fund one village at a time. The elders replied, "We'll spread the money to everyone, or we just won't take it." Community was more powerful for them than money.

Those Mayans lived deeply connected and spiritually rooted to the earth. We were invited to meet the shaman for the nine villages. At his house, where he was going to perform a *costumbre*, a blessing for the project, he sat on the floor with his altar behind him, candles and incense, and two stones. Trying to be the gracious visiting spiritual leader, I asked if the stones were deities. The shaman said, "No, they're stones."

He started chanting a blessing, and he wanted to know the names of all the board members to include them. When he got to Wavy Gravy, his pronunciation ("Waaby Graaby") was so funny we broke out laughing. These people didn't fit my spiritual world view, but they sure opened my heart. I had never spent time with rural people with no food or medical care, whose children were so malnourished and dirty.

The depth of need and the suffering were enough to bring us to tears—and they did, often. There was so much we couldn't change: inadequate government services, army brutality, the widespread trauma and grief. We were opening ourselves to the reality of suffering, keeping our hearts open in hell.

Compassion is seeing others as ourselves, expanding our identity to include the other person. When I sit with an AIDS patient, I know it could be me. When I sit with a dying person, I know that I too will die. Sitting with the women in Guatemala, their suffering was also mine. Behind our suffering, we share love.

Despite the cultural gulf, we became friends. Over the ten years that Mirabai oversaw Seva's Guatemala program, their kids grew healthier. We helped with agriculture, health, community structures, midwife training. We worked with indigenous agencies, training villagers to train others.

Seva's work in Guatemala was helped by Threshold Foundation, a social change philanthropy collective started in 1981 by Josh Mailman. Their approach was to seed social and environmental justice organizations. Josh invited me to provide a spiritual context for Threshold. Later, along with Calvert Funds founder Wayne Silby, Josh started Social Venture Network (now Social Venture Circle), businesspeople and investors changing how America does business. The circle included entrepreneurs like Ben Cohen and Jerry Greenfield of Ben & Jerry's Ice Cream, Paul Hawken of Smith & Hawken, and others who grew up in the sixties with progressive values. They advocated building a just and sustainable economy with a "triple bottom line": people, planet, and profit. I advised Social Venture Network too. It was a way to bring spiritual values into the business world. Dad would've been proud.

At home with Peter and with satsang, I also had a community of older friends in Marin from my psychology and psychedelic days. Post psychedelics, a new field called transpersonal psychology emerged to integrate spiritual and transcendent human experience into psychology. Transpersonal psychology was inspired by William James and Carl Jung and advanced by psychologists like Abraham Maslow and psychiatrist Stan Grof. Stan and his wife at the time, Joan Halifax, were friends going back to their pioneering psychedelic research at the

Spring Grove clinic in Maryland. Maslow and Grof helped launch the *Journal of Transpersonal Psychology* in 1969. I supported it through benefit talks and donated proceeds from one of my books. My friend and student Dan Goleman wrote extensively for *JTP*; another former student, Jim Fadiman, helped found the California Institute of Transpersonal Psychology in Palo Alto. Roger Walsh and Frances Vaughn, a psychiatry professor and psychologist, hosted a salon at their beautiful house in Marin.

We met every few weeks to discuss psychology and spirituality. Stan Grof came, as well as the cultural anthropologist Angeles Arrien and Huston Smith, then teaching religion at UC Berkeley. Huston and I were the elders. We were all good friends, peers, and an extraordinary sounding board for one another. I was having an uphill climb translating my path of the guru's grace and bhakti devotional practice for the West. Buddhist mindfulness was an easier sell. Our exchanges helped me crystallize what I wanted to get across.

Another Marin neighbor, Sat Santokh Singh Khalsa, a former Grateful Dead road manager, was a Sikh follower. Originally from the Bronx, he was an antiwar activist at San Francisco State during Vietnam. One day, his daughter, Snatam Kaur, then fourteen, brought some friends home from school to ask her dad about environmental issues. Headlines of the time charted human impacts on the ozone layer and the Chernobyl disaster; they would soon report the disastrous *Exxon Valdez* spill in Alaska. Snatam hoped her activist dad could help her and her friends make a positive impact.

The teenagers began meeting at school, and as word spread, they included kids from other schools. Sat Santokh set up a weekend workshop and invited me to participate. The kids didn't know anything about a "Ram Dass." Sat Santokh really got through to them. I asked him what his secret was, and he said, "I don't have a secret. I just treat them as people."

Weekend workshops grew to include a summer camp. Sat Santokh set up a nonprofit called Creating Our Future. Besides me, he brought Joanna Macy and Randy Hayes on board. Joanna is a renowned environmental author and scholar of Buddhism and deep ecology. Randy "Hurricane" Hayes was a founder of the Rainforest Action Network.

Both are environmental heavy hitters. Grateful Dead members performed benefit concerts to support the kids.

The weekend and summer camp programs of Creating Our Future became supportive environments for the kids to go through intense openings. The focus was environmental but also centered on the kids' own lives in their crucial teenage years. Joanna designed a deep check-in to use at the outset of each meeting. Some kids had been abused and in the safety of the circle were able to start clearing their trauma. Many became activists. One girl, Abby Reyes, went on to organize a recycling program for the state of Virginia.

In 1991, to help connect inner work with the outer world, I organized a ten-week course on compassionate action in Oakland. We called it Reaching Out. A thousand people showed up for weekly town hall meetings at the Scottish Rite Temple. The meetings were to catalyze service, whether feeding the homeless or protecting the rain forests. We explored questions like, "What keeps us separate and what can we do about it?" We engaged with some people who were waking up to compassionate service and others who wanted to become more conscious of why they were serving in the first place. Amid Reagan-Bush era cutbacks in social services, the savings and loan scandal, Desert Shield, and reverberations of the end of the Cold War, Reaching Out was designed to help people find joy in service and support those serving to avoid burnout.

At Seva Foundation, we were also considering how to help environmentalists connect between spirit and activism. Convinced that contemplative practice was critical, I helped Mirabai Bush and others develop a series of retreats we called Sustaining Compassion, Sustaining the Earth.

We held the first Seva retreat in July 1991 in Sharon, Massachusetts. It was cosponsored by Seva, Insight Meditation Society, and the Cathedral of Saint John the Divine. That sounds like a high-level collaboration, but really it was a small group of friends—Paul Gorman, Sharon Salzberg, Joseph Goldstein—bringing together frontline social activists and spiritual practitioners.

Eddie Hauben, a longtime IMS meditator, set it up. We rented a Salvation Army retreat center. Eddie told them it was a meditation retreat. The Salvation Army's idea of meditation is reading the Bible in silence. When they saw what we were doing, they wanted to shut down the retreat. The woman who ran the center was a captain in the Salvation Army. She called the general, but we were already there. And we had a contract.

We recruited a hundred New York City political and social activists to attend. The group included many people of color, and it was a potent brew of passionate individuals meeting on an unfamiliar playing field.

Paul Gorman and I started with a talk about spirituality and social action. It didn't go over well. We were two white guys, and I quickly realized my version of spiritual didn't resonate for many of the people who had deep roots in Christianity. Our world views collided. We misunderstood one another's cues and intentions. For example, activists were annoyed that meditators closed their eyes. They thought they were going to sleep.

It was hard for activists to sit quietly, much less meditate. It soon became apparent how difficult it is to be silent unless you feel that your voice has been heard. The activists resisted the meditations, led by Joseph and me. At first we were stunned, but Joseph was so open to the moment and such a good listener that his patience helped with the misunderstandings. The second day of the retreat, there was a revolution. The refrain was, "You brought us all the way here, and now you're lecturing us on how we should see things. No way!"

We reorganized the whole agenda around listening, with people in circles for different issues we called "fishbowls." One person sat in the middle, and others sat outside the circle, positioned as "allies." Despite my closeted upbringing and resistance to labels, I got into the middle of the gay fishbowl. It was the first time I'd talked about my sexuality in such a public setting, and it was a big thing for me. I got a lot of support.

With my participation, the activists' perception of me changed. It made a huge difference to some people there that I was open about being gay. By the end of the weekend, the interactions among people had become unbelievably loving. While there were still conflicts, a new communal atmosphere contained it all. The retreat ended with extended listening sessions, from which everyone emerged with deep appreciation. I was deeply inspired.

As an event, it was also a real seedpod. The activist and social entrepreneur Charlie Halpern attended, who was then executive director of the Nathan Cummings Foundation. Charlie later teamed up with Mirabai Bush to create the Center for Contemplative Mind in Society, which since 1995 has been bringing meditation and contemplative techniques into academia, law, philanthropy, corporations like Google, and the US Army.

An informal group also emerged from the retreat, which we called the Wisdom Party. It had no formal agenda but was a trusted circle for sharing personal transformation. We reflected together on the nature of social change and spiritual understanding and explored the deeper motivations for our work.

Out of my long collaboration with Mirabai Bush came a book, *Compassion in Action*. We wanted to put in writing what we had gleaned in the face of so much need in the world. Out of compassion comes action that may truly relieve suffering. We said that compassion is beyond sympathy or even empathy. It literally means being with another's suffering. It includes the wisdom of impermanence and the understanding that personal narratives are not so important in the larger scheme of things.

The two components of selfless service, detachment and devotion, are a curious combination. Psychologically these qualities at first glance seem quite opposed to each other. But this is the prescription Krishna gives in the Bhagavad Gita. He's basically saying, "Do your dharma, do your work in harmony with the laws of the universe, and don't worry about how it turns out. Just surrender it all to Me with love." That's what Maharaj-ji meant when he said simply, "Love everyone, serve everyone, and remember God." This is the true path of action, the nishkam karma-yoga of the Gita, acting without attachment, doing karma-yoga without creating more karma.

PART IV

THE WHEEL TURNS

Hold on to
nothing.

MAHARAJ-JI

CHAPTER 29

THE NEW OLD AGE

y 1991, some thirty years had passed since my ouster from Harvard and about a quarter century since psychedelics became illegal. I had just crossed sixty. As my generation was entering this new stage of maturity, the cultural attitude toward "entheogens," as psychedelics were now called, was finally evolving. Psychoactive drugs were still considered dangerous, but there was a revival of interest in mind expansion, helped in part by a growing awareness of the usefulness of substances like MDMA, also known as ecstasy or molly, and the South American jungle vine ayahuasca.

Research was resuming, despite opposition from some government agencies. MDMA studies were happening at the University of California, Los Angeles, and work with DMT at the University of New Mexico. In Santa Cruz, Rick Doblin founded the Multidisciplinary Association for Psychedelic Studies (MAPS), a nonprofit dedicated to research and education about psychedelics. The idea was to renew the exploration of these drugs with an honest view of their risks, emphasizing legitimate medical benefits, supporting researchers, and training therapists.

In April 1994, I was invited to speak at A Gathering of the Minds, a conference devoted to psychedelics held in Orange County, California, one of the most conservative corners of the country. Just the previous summer, the fiftieth anniversary of the discovery of LSD was celebrated in Santa Cruz. But this gathering was significant for its lineup:

fifty speakers from a vast variety of spiritual, pharmacological, psychological, shamanistic, and academic backgrounds. Fifteen hundred people showed up to listen. "Today is an omen of the rebirth of the counterculture," declared *The Realist* editor Paul Krassner, who acted as master of ceremonies.

Ironically, a day earlier, President Richard Nixon, who'd died at eighty-one, had been laid to rest a few miles away, in Yorba Linda. Nixon launched the war on drugs and once called Tim Leary "the most dangerous man in America." Yet here was Tim, ebullient as ever, talking about consciousness and chaos. Ralph Metzner spoke about the connection between psychedelics and ecology.

Tim and I experienced our own full-circle moment a decade earlier, when we were invited to a reunion of the Harvard Psilocybin Project organized by a graduate student, Joseph Kasof, who was interested in psychedelics. The two of us spoke to a packed audience on campus. Our old boss, Dave McClelland, moderated the conversation. It was the first time Tim and I had shared a stage since the sixties, and it was the first time Tim had been on the Harvard campus since our departure. After prison, he'd lectured around the country with G. Gordon Liddy, his prosecutorial nemesis at Millbrook. Tim befriended him in prison after Liddy was convicted for his role in Watergate, and on the lecture circuit they staged witty, spirited debates about politics and drugs. Tim also remarried, to filmmaker Barbara Chase, and raised her son, Zach, as his own. Though Tim and I periodically crossed paths, this moment in Orange County felt symbolic, recognized by media outlets like *Time*, *Newsweek*, and the *New York Times*, the same ones that years before had sensationalized our academic downfall.

In the days of the Harvard Psilocybin Project, Dave had worried about the permanent effects of psychedelics and argued that the use of cannabis in India made it a decadent society. But in the intervening years his travels in India, as well as exposure to Eastern philosophy, had altered that stance. He and Mary had even gone to visit Maharaj-ji themselves—she made a sketch of him—and in retrospect Dave felt differently about our drug experiments and our expulsion.

Mary died of stomach cancer in 1980. Her passing left a profound gap for me. I could only imagine the great gulf in Dave's life.

But apart from Mary's absence, this was a jovial Cambridge reunion. Neither Tim nor I harbored ill will toward Harvard. I told the audience that the past twenty years had been the happiest in my life; I didn't regret being kicked out, because of the path it put me on. Tim, never one to hold a grudge, expressed admiration for Harvard's history of transcendental thinking and its place at the cutting edge of drug research. Ralph Waldo Emerson and William James, he said, were the true inspiration behind his famous call to turn on, tune in, drop out.

Now, at the psychedelic conference in Orange County, Tim put on a multimedia light show that was reminiscent of the old days at Millbrook. He'd recently taken an interest in the new frontier of the Internet, which he saw as the next communal consciousness. He was developing video-art and electronic-dance-music shows with young cyberpunks and giving college lectures touting the digital future as "the LSD of the nineties" for the massive cultural shift it would bring. Onstage with the art heiress Aileen Getty, who ran an AIDS hospice in LA, he spoke about technology and chaos while music and visuals ran in the background. He was, by this time, seventy-three. "I've discovered the greatest drug of all," he declared. "Senility is much like the effect of good sinsemilla."

As ever, Tim was the social engineer and game theorist, fascinated by the consequences of how people interact with one another. I shared that I still tripped every once in a while, partly to keep my membership in the psychedelic club, but found the experience less important than contemplation, service, and compassion.

I did share my experience with a psychedelic I'd tried for the first time the previous summer: toad slime. It was an intense and scary experience; I took such a big hit that I went into breathing distress, and Peter had to help me. On the brief, intense trip, I turned into a large black woman surrounded by beings who were children, all suffering, hungry, frightened, sick. I opened my arms to draw them all into myself, gagging on the shared agony, the deep, hungry cry of life itself. Yet I was also in ecstasy: the ecstasy of bearing the unbearable, of being part of the total dance of life, of not looking away from anything.

A year later Tim reached out. He told me he had late-stage, inoperable prostate cancer. Ever the optimist and showman, he called it "wonderful news," and he was happy for the chance to face his death with intention, designing this final experience with curiosity and the help of friends.

I knew something about being with the dying by then. Since our early days with the *Tibetan Book of the Dead*, Tim and I had spent many years considering death. I was glad to sit with him for this last stage in our long and sometimes fraught friendship. Tim announced the news far and wide in the media, and when a filmmaker named Gay Dillingham heard about it, she proposed she film our discussion around death. Her idea was to recreate, in a way, our notion of set and setting, providing a warm and relaxed atmosphere for us to reminisce about the past and consider the great transition.

The ensuing conversations were lovely and loving, even at argumentative moments. (Robert Redford, who narrated the documentary Dillingham eventually produced, sat in my living room at one point and asked for advice on psychedelics.) Tim had experienced deep personal pain in recent years. His daughter, Susan, had died by suicide after a long struggle with mental illness. His son Jack was estranged, wounded by the many years that Tim had been too busy for his children. Tim was close with his son Zach, but his wife Barbara had left him. We both enjoyed having the space to consider our own complicated history with clarity and compassion. I felt real affection for him, even when he dismissed my spiritual ideas. We laughed a lot.

As psychedelics were slowly coming out of hiding, our long-ago experiments at Harvard were also being reconsidered. Rick Doblin, the founder of MAPS, had conducted a follow-up to the Good Friday Experiment as an undergraduate project. His study, published by the *Journal of Transpersonal Psychology* in 1991, found that the effects of the psilocybin experience at Marsh Chapel lasted, for a majority of the seminary students, throughout their lives.

Tim and I and Walter Pahnke had set out to test whether psychedelics could facilitate a true religious experience in a religious setting. The results appeared to bear out, with subjects recalling, more than twenty-five years later, how the sense of timelessness and light had permanently transformed their spiritual understanding. "We took such an infinitesimal amount of psilocybin," said one participant, who went on to become a minister. "And yet it connected me to infinity."

Doblin's work caught the attention of Michael Forcier, a researcher with experience doing research for the Massachusetts Department of Correction. He reached out to Doblin about replicating our other famous effort, the Concord Prison Experiment. Though many of Tim's files had been destroyed over the years, Forcier was aware of a collection of papers that still remained from the project. He and Doblin set about trying to reproduce the results. Unlike with the Good Friday Experiment, they discovered that Tim's original claims that the recidivism of inmates was greatly reduced after psilocybin didn't stand up to rigorous analysis. By crunching the numbers and following up with some of the prisoners, Doblin and Forcier found that a majority had, in fact, returned to prison.

As Tim's health declined, Doblin arranged for two of the original Concord convicts to visit him in January 1996. It was an emotional reunion, all three of them reflecting on the effects of psychedelics on their lives and the lessons they had learned. Both former prisoners had vivid memories of their trips, and both felt they had benefited. Tim acknowledged that his calculations for the study had been faulty. But he also recalled just how revolutionary it had been to share power with prisoners, erasing the line between researchers and subjects and promoting a shared vulnerability. It had been meaningful to him, he said, to bring mental freedom to people behind bars.

When Doblin asked Tim what he might have done differently to ensure more accurate results, Tim noted what we knew even back then: follow-up. Tim and others in the study had in fact devoted great amounts of time to follow-up, but what was really needed as a therapeutic intervention, Tim said, was a halfway house. That had simply been beyond our means.

In his report, which he published in the *Journal of Psychoactive Drugs* in 1998, Doblin noted that the failure of the Concord Prison Experiment to generate a reduction in recidivism rates "should not be interpreted as proof of the lack of value of psychedelics as adjuncts to psychotherapy in criminals." Rather, he continued, the failure of the experiment "should finally put to rest the myth of psychedelic drugs as magic bullets, the ingestion of which will automatically confer wisdom and create lasting change after just one or even a few experiences."

Tim died five months after the reunion with the Concord ex-convicts, on May 31, 1996. He'd intended to create an event around his death and have his brain cryogenically frozen. In the end, he departed with little fanfare, in his sleep. His last months served as a continuous wake, with dozens of friends coming and going. There was no big funeral. Instead, in keeping with the explorer he'd always been, some of his ashes were shot into space.

Gay Dillingham's film of our conversations, *Dying to Know*, came out years later. It captured what I remember best about my last visits with Tim: his strong presence, his iconoclastic humor, his insouciant curiosity, our loving connection. I was grateful to have Tim as an upaguru. As with psychedelics, we faced the next round together with a joyous sense of adventure. When you lose your fear of death, you gain a love of life.

All of us were growing older. The baby boomers were fast approaching their fifties. I was in my sixties. After years of travel and not paying enough attention to my body, I was starting to feel the consequences: achy joints, less flexibility, extra weight. Once, when I was introduced before a lecture, I bounded from the floor to the stage. I banged my knee so hard it began to bleed. I proceeded with my lecture, bleeding knee and all, rather than acknowledge my frailty.

In our youth-oriented culture, aging is a profound source of suffering. I'd been thinking about this since seeing Dad through his physical decline. On one of my trips to India, a younger relative of K. K.'s greeted me with, "Ram Dass, you're looking so old. You're so gray!" My first reaction was to take immediate umbrage at this perceived insult; then I heard the tone of great deference and affection that came with it. In traditional India, respect for elders is deeply ingrained. Not so in the West! Aging, too, is a state of mind.

For many years I'd been talking about dying consciously. I thought, "Shouldn't aging consciously be just as important?" If my life was my message, it was time to engage with age, both for the integrity of my own being and to scout this late-in-life frontier for my boomer followers.

Just as I had friends who shared my interest in conscious dying, like Joan Halifax and Frank Ostasteki, so too there were wise friends thinking about conscious aging. One of them was Rabbi Zalman Schachter-Shalomi. An ordained rabbi in the Hasidic tradition, he and I first met in the sixties, when I was still at Harvard. He wanted to try psychedelics. He and I danced while high on psilocybin swathed in his tallith, or prayer shawl. We had an amazing talk about God. He was the first truly spiritual Jew I met.

Zalman remained committed to Judaism, to restoring its legacy of mysticism and helping young people find renewal. He was the most joyous celebrant of Judaism I've met. I appreciated how he infused love into the rituals I found so empty as a boy.

Zalman was also considering aging from a spiritual perspective. In 1992, we were both keynote speakers at a two-day Conscious Aging conference in Manhattan sponsored by Omega Institute. Another was Maggie Kuhn, the elder rights activist. It was one of the first major efforts to bring together a spectrum of ideas on growing old with awareness. Fifteen hundred participants came from all over the country. Zalman spoke of conscious aging as laying the foundation for a new role in society: spiritual elder.

The baby boomers' retirement years were nearly upon them, and more than previous generations, they had the freedom, financial means, and the numbers to extract meaning from these later years. The don't-trust-anyone-over-thirty generation did not intend to, as Dylan Thomas wrote, "go gentle into that good night."

Later that year I was invited to speak on Jewish spirituality at the University of Judaism in Los Angeles. Until then, I'd avoided Jewish settings. Some traditional Jews blamed me and others for leading young people away from true spirituality. Others wanted to bring me back into the fold. I felt no need to be anyone else's spiritual project.

However, I saw this invitation as Maharaj-ji's hint that it was time to reckon with my family karma. I've said that the religion you are born with frequently becomes more important as you see the universality of truth. Once you learn to go beyond your negative experiences as a child, you can return to your roots with new eyes. Once, when I was in Jerusalem, I passed two Hasidic Jews coming across a square. They were wearing the usual black hats and black coats, and I heard one of them say, "That's Ram Dass! He's the one who got me into this." They had taken drugs and read *Be Here Now*. In Burma, I met two westerners who were studying to be Buddhist monks. "Your book started us on our Buddhist path," they told me.

Now, here I was, and I had yet to fully engage with one of the formative circumstances of my own life. I was born into Judaism. I needed to find ways to honor that. To prepare for the lecture, I read the Torah and bought wisdom books by Jewish writers such as Abraham Joshua Heschel, Martin Buber, Adin Steinsaltz, and Elie Wiesel. I wanted to study the tradition I came from and not embarrass the memory of my father, a founder of Brandeis University.

Loving God is central in Judaism, but I didn't get any of that growing up. Only later did I encounter the mystical, joyous side of Judaism with Zalman. And only when I met Maharaj-ji and opened to my own spiritual heart could I appreciate loving God. As I prepared for the talk, I thought about what it might feel like to be a Jew who truly loves God. I thought about lineage and community and about how all the mitzvahs are techniques for remembering God. When I finally delivered my talk, to more than nine hundred people, I spoke appreciatively about Judaism's inherent spirituality.

From a Hindu perspective, you are born into what you need to deal with, your karmic predicament. If you try to push anything away, whatever it is, the reaction against it creates more attachment, just like getting pulled into it: it's got your mind. It was no accident that I was born into a Jewish family, and I finally was able to appreciate its mark on me. Only when you honor your karma fully can you begin to be free.

———

Around this time Peter, my partner, went to visit my brother Leonard. After leaving the mental hospital, Len had left Boston and was living in a San Francisco singles hotel in the city. He still played the piano for people, whatever songs they requested.

I learned years later that Dad gave Len an ultimatum: He told him that if he went as far away as he could and kept his distance from the family, he would continue to support him. If he didn't, he would cut him off. Len loved his daughters and still had a relationship with his wife, Sylvia; he didn't want to leave. But he had no real option. His instability made it hard for him to support himself. If I had known the reason for Len's isolation, I might have reached out.

When Dad died, Len got back in touch with his kids. But even this was fraught, because in his will, Dad had given Leonard's inheritance to his daughters. He didn't want Len using the money for drugs. Len asked his daughters for the money anyway, and they gave it to him. This pissed off my brother Bill, who remained angry at Len for taking money from his own children.

In his later years, I think Leonard was in a spiritual state not unlike those of Meher Baba's *masts*, beings who are absorbed in other planes and too confused to function much in the physical world. In our culture, we hospitalize people like that. In San Francisco, Leonard got into heroin, and it put him over the edge. With his mental instability, his mix of mysticism and power needs, and his hidden sexual life, drugs were just too much. He became disruptive and destructive in his relationships, including his relationship with me.

Peter went to see Len at his hotel without telling me, undertaking the visit on his own as a kind of diplomatic peace mission. They had a lot in common: love of music, artistic sensitivity, emotional intensity. But the visit did not promote any great reconciliation.

There was no breakthrough, but I was grateful for Peter's attempt and felt more at peace with my own feelings about Len. As I was learning, we all carry the imprint of the past in emotional memories. Part of conscious aging is to reflect on and finish the business of our past, to dissolve the karmic knots by bringing them into awareness.

If we hold grudges, if we don't practice forgiveness or work on releasing our unfinished business, our karma will play out in other ways or just leave us more stuck. If instead we cultivate being in the present, the awareness of this moment is stronger than the memories of the past and brings a spaciousness that can surround and dissolve old traumas.

Speaking of the past, a flood occurred in the basement in our house in San Anselmo, where I was storing boxes of my papers and mementos. A lot of them got soaked, and we had to throw out the molding paper trail of my life. These artifacts of my past had been following me for years, and they represented an anchor of sorts.

I almost never opened these boxes. About a decade earlier, realizing the incongruity of having shelves full of boxes while supposedly living as a wandering sadhu, I'd actually burned many of my papers and memorabilia, saying good-bye to each memento before placing it in the fireplace. The flood finished what I had begun.

Not that we should dismantle our past. But we need to be aware of clinging, when identification with the past obscures our ability to be present. In teaching others to be more conscious of aging, I knew I often mined my own biography for entertainment value—whether it was stories about my mother, or my adventures in psychedelics, or my hair-raising moments flying airplanes. When I did, I noticed I got pulled into identifying with who I was in the past. We hold memories, yes, but we are not those memories. We are who we are, *today*.

I decided to write about what I was saying about conscious aging. My manager, Jai Lakshman, negotiated a book deal, with a two-year contract and a deadline in October 1996. The first year, I was too busy teaching to write much, but the second year, I wrote steadily. I turned in the manuscript on time. Soon after, my editor called up in tears to say she'd been fired. The publisher was unhappy with what we had turned in. They had expected something more optimistic and uplifting, like "Seventy is the new fifty!"

They hired a new editor to help rework the book and gave me another six months. I had already scheduled the coming months, so this brought a level of stress I hadn't counted on.

The projects included a long-cherished talk-radio show called *Here and Now with Ram Dass*. I continually got letters from all over the country, asking, "When are you coming back to Cleveland? When are you coming back to Florida?" But I was sixty-five by this time, and constant travel was getting hard on my body. I hoped to use the radio program to connect with people over the airwaves.

I did seven pilot episodes, which aired in Los Angeles and the Bay Area. We planned to take it nationwide the following year.

I enjoy live radio—this was before podcasts. We featured call-in questions and had real conversations—not "the expert tells us how it is," but "we're in this together." I wanted to create a safe space for everyone to talk about everything: drugs, relationships, sexuality, politics, whatever.

I've always been open about my own trip. My imperfections are my assets. By sharing my balding, aging, neurotic self along with my soul connection to Maharaj-ji, I would remind listeners that we are all fellow human beings walking each other home.

But I still had the book to finish. One afternoon in February 1997, I was at home reworking the manuscript, thinking about ways to conclude the book. My editor, Amy Hertz, helped me understand the draft was weak because it didn't engage deeply enough with the visceral experience of aging. Somehow I needed to reckon more authentically with the frustrations and indignities of a slower, weaker body.

After working for a while, I turned off the light and lay on the bed. I tried to imagine what life would be like if I were really old—not an active sixty-five-year-old, but a man of, say, ninety, with failing eyesight and unsteady limbs. I imagined how that old man might think and speak. Perhaps I was dreaming . . . I must have fallen asleep.

The phone rang, and I woke from my reverie. As I rose from the bed, my left leg gave out beneath me. I crumpled to the floor. "Strange," I thought. "My leg must have fallen asleep." I reached up to grab the phone on the table by the bed. I couldn't reach it, though I must have knocked it off the cradle. Somehow I got the insistent dial tone to stop. The phone rang again later, and I managed to get it. I was still on the floor.

It was Jai Lakshman, my manager, calling from New Mexico. I tried to say hello, but I couldn't get any words out.

"Ram Dass? Are you there?"

CHAPTER 30

STROKED

A re you sick?" Jai asked. When I couldn't articulate a response, Jai said to tap with the phone, once if I was okay, twice if I needed help. I kept tapping. He immediately called my secretaries, Marlene Roeder and Jo Anne Baughan, who lived nearby. Before I knew it, Marlene was standing over me, calling 911. I was having a stroke. It was scrambling my words and my thoughts.

This was about five in the afternoon. Marlene had called earlier but the phone was busy. She had actually gotten in the car to drive over but didn't want to disturb me and had turned around. I must have been lying on the floor for some hours.

When the paramedics arrived, I observed their actions from my witness place: lifting me onto the stretcher, loading me into the ambulance. Was this part of my old-man dream? It felt as if we were all actors in a movie. I watched with fascination. It was as if I wasn't having the stroke, but the stroke was having me!

The paramedics took me to the Kaiser hospital in Marin. As I was being wheeled in on the gurney, I was looking up at the pipes on the ceiling. Entering the emergency room, I thought, "This is a critical moment, and my mind isn't on God!" Here I was, Mr. Spiritual, having a life-and-death experience. I should've been merging with God, with Maharaj-ji, not watching the pipes on the ceiling.

If death is one of the great matters for spiritual work, I flunked the big test. I was disappointed with myself. But that's my judging mind looking back. Why wasn't I saying my mantra or concentrating on Maharaj-ji? If I was truly identified with my soul, that's what I would do. Instead, my consciousness was captured by the hospital melodrama. I couldn't walk my talk. In fact, I couldn't walk at all. Or talk. My time sense of those events is skewed, and a lot of the memories are lost in the fog of the stroke.

The medical diagnosis was a massive brain hemorrhage. Though I was somewhat coherent when I got to the hospital, the doctor explained that the most life-threatening moments were yet to come, because of how the brain swells in the first days after a stroke. (Nowadays they give a lot of salt to reduce the fluids.)

I knew this was a big deal, but it didn't really occur to me I might be dying, that this might be all she wrote for this body. As I looked from the paramedics to the doctors, I could see they all thought I was dying. But inside I wasn't dying. My consciousness was alive. I wasn't thinking straight because of my scrambled brain. Maybe I was in the witness place. But clearly I was still here.

When they realized I had had a serious stroke, they transported me to a special Kaiser stroke facility south of San Francisco. They gave me a 10 percent chance of survival. But survive I did. I was in the ICU for four or five days and then was moved to a rehab center. I don't remember much of those first days.

Since I understand this reality as a projection of mind, my immediate reaction to the stroke was that I had created this medical disaster as an exercise to finish the book. Was this reality, or was it my projection? On some level both were true. But the arrival of the paramedics and my not being able to talk or move the right side of my body was a potent sales pitch for reality.

As I had trained myself to do with any bad trip, I settled into witness consciousness and watched it all go by.

The brain hemorrhage paralyzed the right side of my body and left me with complete aphasia, total inability to speak. Trying to make sense of my incapacity, I felt frustration and despair. The clinical psychologist in me noticed the growing emotional fallout and the effects on my thinking and mental process. Even so, the profound mental and physical nature of the stroke hadn't fully registered.

The hospital scene was disorienting, not least my interactions with visitors. I remember my brother Bill came to see me from New York, but he wouldn't talk to my partner, Peter. Larry Brilliant, our satsang doctor, sat at my bedside looking very serious, sadder than I felt. But I was in a lot of physical discomfort.

I was working on a book about aging—and now this wave of incapacity was my own next chapter, perhaps the final one. The physical shock of being stroked, the arrival of the paramedics, and the inability to move or speak or think clearly made the drama of sickness and old age very palpable. I was suddenly old and disabled. Wherever I was, it was not in a fantasy.

Truth be told, I'd ignored the signals that my body had been sending me for some time. I was too invested in my spiritual teaching—too busy traveling, writing, and serving—to pay attention. In the previous months I'd collapsed on a dance floor at a wedding reception, lost my hearing on one side while scuba diving in the Caribbean, and had dizziness and then a fainting spell—in retrospect, all stroke precursors.

I knew I had high blood pressure, and my doctor had prescribed medicine for it. But I shrugged it off and stopped taking the medicine, in part because blood-pressure meds suppress sexual activity. I started taking Chinese herbs instead, but I wasn't taking them regularly. Now I don't remember all the details. A lot of my memories from that time were erased by the stroke.

Lying in the hospital, I was frustrated on many levels. I can usually extricate myself from thoughts and emotional upheaval, but this time I was really stuck. I was angry at myself for being sucked into the melodrama and frustrated I couldn't do anything to get out of it. I couldn't formulate ideas. I couldn't move. I couldn't speak.

My satsang friends put up a picture of Maharaj-ji on the wall of my hospital room, but then I thought the stroke must have happened because of my lack of faith, and I became deeply depressed. Strong faith would have avoided this. Once again I told myself I'd failed the test.

Of course, the truth is that we all keep failing tests until we don't. That's a definition of the spiritual path. Eventually, surrendering to my damaged body, I had to surrender my judging mind too—the attachments, the motivations, how I thought it should be or how I should be.

But at that point, I had fallen off the path. My faith was shaking like a leaf in a high wind. I would look at the picture of Maharaj-ji and say, "Where were you when I had this stroke? Were you out to lunch or something?" Depression barely begins to describe how I felt. My emotions were in a deep hole. I thought Maharaj-ji had abandoned me, that he had withdrawn his grace because of my lack of faith.

And now I had no more faith left. That was a terrible feeling—the very worst part of my illness—because life under his blanket had felt so graced until then. I experienced a mix of violent emotions, anger and despair. My reference points were all gone. The interface between my consciousness and the world was ripped out.

One day, some of the satsang members brought another picture of Maharaj-ji and one of Hanuman to the rehab center, thinking it would help. I lost my temper. I was emphatic they should take them out. Someone else brought some of Maharaj-ji's ashes, but I didn't want those either. I thought the pictures were inappropriate in the setting and that the doctors might think Hanuman too weird. I was angry because I couldn't control anything. More than that, I was angry at myself for losing faith. In the end I let the pictures stay.

At the hospital and rehab, a lot of people came and went, doctors and nurses and friends and relatives. They all had long faces that said, "You poor guy, you've had a stroke!" The whole view of a stroke as a medical disaster was continually projected onto me. And by absorbing their mindsets, I started to think of myself as a "poor guy," another stroke "victim."

Only the cleaning woman didn't project despair onto me. Whenever she came into my room, she was totally present, just . . . cleaning. She knew. She didn't see me as a medical disaster. She saw me as a fellow soul.

I had to ask everyone to leave because their minds were so negative. I probably let them know I needed to rest. I started talking to Maharaj-ji's picture again. It was hard because my mind was still scrambled. But I'm a bhakti yogi, and I was able to come into my heart. I quieted down, sitting up in my bed. I was talking to him in my mind. I said, once again, "Where were you when I had this stroke? Were you out to lunch?"

This time, I heard him laugh, the slightly high-pitched "He, he, he!" that was so typical. I didn't know what he was laughing about. But inside I got the message: "I am with you. Just wait and see."

That was when I began to turn the corner. The connection to Maharaj-ji wasn't completely restored—it would flicker for a while after that—but it was there. Maharaj-ji's giggle laughed off my depression; I was done thinking about the stroke. Everyone around had been making me into a disaster victim. Now my faith came back, and I could speak to Maharaj-ji inside. I remembered he once said, "If you want to find God, go to the hospital."

I found myself back in soul land, an instant but subtle shift in point of view from ego to soul. I went from not feeling his presence at all to again dwelling in the place in myself where he lives. It was like getting beamed up to another plane. The rehabilitation exercises and speech therapy were hard work, but I was making new neural connections, forging new ways of relating. I was starting to repair from the inside.

I started thinking about this seemingly catastrophic event in a different way. I thought, "Well, maybe I had this stroke so my soul will learn from it. What if this is a blessing in disguise?"

As I looked at the devastating effects of the stroke, there were few that couldn't also be seen as positive. My aphasia, my newly hesitant speech and searching for words, made me quiet a lot more of the time. Meditators think it's good to quiet the mind. Aha! The stroke had made my mind quiet. Good.

My physical limitations made me dependent on others. I'd been such a helper—that was my thing! I'd written about service with Paul Gorman in our book *How Can I Help?* Now I had to ask, "How can you help me?" I had enjoyed driving my car; now someone else would have to drive me. This also meant I could enjoy the trees and the sunset, and I didn't have to look at the road. I was seeing the world anew.

As Maharaj-ji had told me to do, I waited. As the silence of my mind deepened, I saw how the intervals in my broken speech allowed others to become quiet too. Humiliation at my new dependency turned into humility in the face of the love coming from my caregivers. Embarrassment at my helplessness became gratitude for their help.

As my needs for power—for independence, for the witty, eloquent speaker I'd once been—calmed, I began to merge more deeply with Maharaj-ji, shifting perspective from the mind to the soul. From that vantage, I could feel the service and love and compassion that is his real being, that is all of our true nature, and feel the joy, peace, wisdom, and bliss emanating from that core. K. K. Sah wrote to remind me that Maharaj-ji had said about me, "I will do something for him." He was doing it.

Rehab was hard. I was relearning how to walk and how to feed myself, brush my teeth and hair, bathe myself—things I'd done habitually but couldn't do anymore. The hardest part was being in the role of patient. To the rehab people I was my body. I wasn't thinking that way, and I felt distant. I was straddling two planes of consciousness, one witnessing the other as an impatient patient.

I had to accept the karma, the fierce grace of my situation. And I had to work with my therapists. One part of me watching the lila, the dance of consciousness, and the other part of me working like hell to get my body functions back. My relationships with the physical therapists were warm, and they were wonderfully skilled. So I did as instructed, witnessing from the inside and doing the exercises outside.

We were enjoying one another's company. They were gentle and helpful. When therapists are souls, there's a kind of intimacy. Other times, when someone had to move me around and position my body, I felt like a sack of potatoes. At those times I felt like an old man, because of the mind of the helper. We go in and out of being able to share our souls together. When we're in the soul, we just hang out.

The self-critical me kept creeping in with the extreme effort required to make any progress in rehab. My paralyzed leg was heavy and unresponsive. My ego saw that as laziness, even though I was overcoming physical obstacles daily just to exist. The subtle transition from witnessing to judging was a slippery slope, happening constantly. Accepting the karma of the stroke and witnessing it from the soul was one plane of consciousness. But for the exertion of will and hard work, my ego needed to take over. Maintaining the inner perspective was, in its way, as challenging as the grueling physical therapy.

When I could return to my witness place, I was not in the stroke. The therapists were insistent I do the exercises, even when I couldn't control my body, and kept pushing me to try harder. From the witness perspective, I could love the therapists giving me such a hard time. I was a soul in a body—but I wasn't the body or the stroke. The witness didn't fit into the medical system, but it rescued me from always thinking, "I have a stroke" and alleviated some of the mental suffering. It was still hard work.

Witnessing is movie-like, and because the witness is from the soul, it takes me into love. That loving awareness is the connection to Maharaj-ji, to the One. There were times when it merged into a flow of oneness and love that was more seamless, with less back and forth. Then I could play the game better, because the witness perspective is Maharaj-ji playing the game with us while saying, "Ram" all the time.

At times I could even find a degree of contentment. I remembered contentment was part of the *yama/niyama* practice of yoga, called *santosha*, one of the mindsets you use to direct your consciousness toward oneness. Contentment is a practice. It's not a feeling of accomplishment from doing something. Contentment is just being complete in the moment. In the moment, there is just presence, no future or past, just happy to be here in the moment. Contentment is an attitude of the soul.

By the time I got out of rehab, I could manage a halting walk with a cane. Aphasia was still the hardest aftereffect to deal with. I depended on my verbal facility—lecturing, storytelling, and being a spiritual raconteur. A speech therapist came to the house in San Anselmo to help me relearn how to speak from scratch. I struggled to express ideas again. It was weird, I knew what I wanted to say, but I couldn't find the words. It was as if words were clothes hanging in my closet and I was searching through the closet, trying to find the right outfit for the occasion. It was slow going. As Wavy Gravy, my old friend, quipped one time, "Ram Dass used to be the master of the one-liner. Now he's a master of the ocean liner."

I went to LA for experimental therapy in a hyperbaric oxygen chamber. My old friend Laura Huxley, Aldous's widow, helped arrange it. The course of treatment lasted several weeks. I would lie in the chamber for half an hour at a time. It was warm, like a mild pressure cooker.

I couldn't tell whether it improved my cognitive facility, but I had nice meditations.

The more I thought about it, the more I realized the stroke was just a stroke. My *reaction* to the stroke was something else: that was my work on myself. The saving grace was being able to see it from the soul perspective. Instead of saying, "Oh, no, I've had a stroke!" and going through the whole cascade of medical disaster and despair, I came around to, "Well, let's see what's graceful in this stroke." I began to treat it as just what was happening in the present moment.

When Marlene called my book editor, Amy, with the grim news of the stroke, the first thing Amy asked was, "What about the book?" The due date for my new draft had originally been set for a few weeks after my stroke. We all agreed the book was even more important to finish. So I continued writing, this time with the help of Mark Matousek, a gifted writer and teacher who was both workmanlike and wonderfully patient with my aphasia. He listened deeply and helped me express what I needed in order to complete the book.

By the time *Still Here* came out in 2000, it joined a chorus of other books on aging. My friend Rabbi Zalman had come out with a book on the topic, *From Age-ing to Sage-ing*. I felt I had something important to add now, because now I was coming from an intense life crisis. Before, I had been *thinking* about aging and death; now I was reporting on it. I had to revisit my words from before the stroke. What I most wanted to explore was the dependency the stroke had created, because independence is so prized in our society.

The cosmic irony of working on a book about aging and then having to finish it as a disabled old person is stunning. Of course, if I had to describe Maharaj-ji's humor, cosmic irony would be central. Like a Greek tragedy, it was a matter of hubris. I had the chutzpah to write a book about using aging as a spiritual practice when I hadn't experienced it.

I still wonder to what extent I imagined myself into becoming disabled with a stroke. That is magical thinking; nevertheless, how our mind creates our reality is powerful. Wherever it came from, the stroke—and the crisis of faith that it precipitated—was a deep teaching. Faith seems fragile and intangible when it disappears. Yet it has been the most powerful wellspring in my life and a source of strength since it returned. Maharaj-ji said, "You may forget me, but I never forget you. Once I take hold of a devotee's hand, I never let go."

The stroke stripped me of many things on the outside: physical strength, the ability to drive, play my cello, fly my plane, have sex. I'm dependent on others, and I feel vulnerable. My mind and speech are slow; it's hard to find words. But since the stroke, I've been more with Maharaj-ji than ever.

CHAPTER 31

LONG ROAD BACK

efore I launched the *Here and Now with Ram Dass* radio show, Peter and I went on vacation to Baja California in Mexico. We stayed at a hotel on the ocean, just south of the California border. I remember walking naked on the beach and passing a white heron or egret perched atop a hill. Peter and I had sex on the beach. As it turned out, it was the last time we were physically intimate.

The stroke turned our relationship upside down. Instead of me supporting him and his art scene, I was the one who needed care, and I needed it around the clock. The assumptions of my active life and of our life together were blown away. Peter spent many hours at the hospital as I emerged from the fog of the stroke, dealt with depression, and faced the daunting journey of rehab. He rose to the occasion. When I was able to come home, he enlisted a friend, Rolando, who proved an able caregiver. Rolando was very empathetic, and with his aid, Peter and I began to patch together a semblance of normalcy.

My work life fell by the wayside. We cancelled the radio show. I could no longer travel or lecture. The stroke ended my fundraising, which complicated things for Seva Foundation. Money, or the lack of it, opened me up to an even deeper dependence. Before I'd devoted my energies to raising funds for others; now I became a recipient. Jai Lakshman took charge of my support, helped by members of the satsang. Friends from the Threshold Foundation, Social Venture Network, and others helped with contributions and connections. Together they provided financial support for Peter and me to move to a more wheelchair-friendly house in Tiburon, California. It was smaller but more practical than our San Anselmo digs.

Peter put together a studio in the upstairs bedroom and started painting again. He and Rolando created a healing environment, and I had a slew of therapists every week: physical, occupational, speech. After years of ignoring the physical plane, I now had to care for my body with great purpose, addressing muscle spasms with massages, practicing basic speech and motor skills, soothing my uncooperative limbs in the hot tub. It was a full-time job.

A parade of friends visited, loved, and encouraged me. My dear friend Joan Halifax brought Laurance Rockefeller to visit. He and I had met in the early nineties, and I'd stopped in a couple of times at his Park Avenue apartment in New York. He attended a lecture I gave at Memorial Sloan Kettering Cancer Center about dying. His enthusiasm helped get the doctors to pay attention too. For a man of his wealth and position, Laurance was a pretty enlightened being, whose great generosity came from his heart.

When Laurance heard about my stroke, he contributed to the fund for my rehabilitation, my endless stream of therapists and handicap adaptations. It was wonderful to see him. In the past, we'd smoked pot together and played verbal consciousness games. Now I wasn't so verbal, but we did have a convivial smoke. He parked his Cadillac limo outside our little Tiburon house and had a vegetarian lunch with Joan and me. Before leaving, he bought one of Peter's paintings for an overly generous amount.

Another friend was Mickey Lemle, a documentary filmmaker who had made a wonderful film about the Dalai Lama. Mickey asked if he could document my stroke and recovery, which he saw as a story of spiritual redemption that would inspire people dealing with similar terrible mishaps.

It was Mickey who challenged me to start lecturing again. His idea was that speaking in public would force me to find the words. He was right. After about six months of rehab, I started traveling to speaking engagements. I gave workshops at Omega Institute in upstate New York and Breitenbush Hot Springs in Oregon, old stomping grounds

PREVIOUS AND ABOVE Martha's Vineyard, 1976

109

110

TOP   George Alpert, circa 1985
ABOVE   With Dad and Phyllis, Gay Head, Martha's Vineyard

111

112

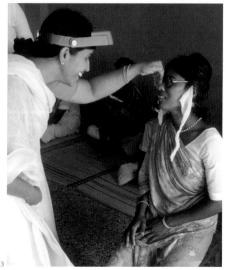

113

TOP Seva Foundation board meeting in Ann Arbor, 1987
ABOVE LEFT Govindappa Venkataswamy, aka "Dr. V."
ABOVE RIGHT Dr. Natchiar, Dr. V.'s sister, Aravind Eye Hospital, Madurai, South India

114

115

TOP Larry Brilliant plotting the rates of blindness in Nepal on an
Apple II donated to Seva Foundation by Steve Jobs, Kathmandu, 1980
ABOVE Laurie Anderson performing at the Home Aid benefit,
Cathedral of Saint John the Divine, New York City, 1988

TOP LEFT With Timothy Leary and Ralph Metzner at the Harvard Psychedelic Project reunion, 1996
TOP RIGHT Together with Tim, California, circa 1996
ABOVE Hawaii, circa 2005

119

120

TOP Siddhi Ma, Kainchi, 1990s
ABOVE Viewing the new temple site with Gopal Singer, Taos, 2005

Maharaj-ji's empty chair, Kainchi, 2004

122

123

124

125

Maui Retreat, 2018

126

127

TOP Meeting my son, Peter Reichard
ABOVE With Peter, his wife, Linda, and my granddaughter, Emily

With Roshi Bernie Glassman, Peggy Hitchcock, Dr. Raj Rajan,
David Padwa, Joan Baez, Dassima Murphy, Roshi Joan Halifax,
Krishna Das, Eckhart Tolle, Andrew Weil, Oprah, and Sharon Salzberg

135

137

139

140

141

142

TOP In the beach buggy at Kihei
ABOVE LEFT At home on Maui, 2017
ABOVE RIGHT A reunion with my brother Leonard, 2005

143

144

My two families: The Alperts, circa 1961,
and Maharaj-ji's Western devotees at Kainchi, just after his death

145

146

147

Inauguration of new temple at Neem Karoli Baba Ashram in Taos, New Mexico, July 2019

where I had held retreats for years. I went to Kripalu in Massachusetts and taught at Hollyhock in British Columbia. I did a retreat up on the mountain at Lama Foundation. These were mostly one-man shows, except for a few times when Krishna Das came to chant kirtan with me. Marlene Roeder and Jo Anne Baughan organized the gigs and traveled with me. Mickey came along to film a couple of the lectures. Travel was more difficult. I was mostly wheelchair bound and needed a lot of help.

The intentional dilemma of lecturing left me no choice but to speak. I still had aphasia, and I had to work hard. Onstage, with a microphone and an expectant audience, I was forced to confront the painstaking process of constructing sentences. My talks came from a different place than before. Gone was the glib storyteller, the charismatic ex-professor. The survivor on stage was a loving soul whose faith had been shaken. Maharaj-ji was still with me, though, and his presence came through the broken sentences and the silence. And that's what people came for, a spiritual hit. It was clearer than ever that I was only the messenger.

I said I didn't want anyone feeling sorry for me. I instructed people to meditate on the gaps between my words. I'd say, "I know the concepts I want to share with you. Allow the silence to be the space around them." If they started feeling sorry for me, I told them, it was just a thought form to let go of.

Many people were interested in what had happened. The same year as my stroke, Allen Ginsberg died of liver cancer, followed by Bill Burroughs, of a heart attack. The sixties wise men and upstarts were feeling the passage of time, changes in our bodies and in our culture. The dot-com bubble was forming, and the online world was redefining daily lives. There were mind-boggling technological advances, like gene therapy and hybrid cars and space telescopes. But for all the technology, we were still saddled with our very human reality. The discomfort of my body constantly intruded in my awareness, and my own mortality and that of others was poignant and ever-present.

My audiences listened intently to my insights from the stroke and how I was dealing with pain. I wasn't the only one going through life-threatening physical challenges. Now that I'd entered the portal of the medical system, it felt like I, along with many others, had signed up for an intensive in Buddhist suffering. After seemingly endless months of rehab, I was able to meditate with others once again, together as souls.

Not being able to function within my habitual verbal facility and dancing rational mind created an opportunity for me to explore what I call soul land. As I lived more in the soul, I saw what Maharaj-ji had meant with, "Love everybody and tell the truth." The stroke took away my fascination for outward things, and I delved more deeply into my inner life. Desires were still desires, but my mind and sensory equipment no longer grappled with everything as they used to.

Slowly, the strain of loss and disconnection from the stroke started turning into love and appreciation for other souls. In the process of connecting, the subtle ego tentacles, the almost impreceptible judgments and likes or dislikes about another person, remained suspended. I was just a loving awareness. The witness place in me was changing. In my witnessing, the loving heart of the soul was becoming more dominant than the impartial observer of my Buddhist meditations.

I noticed a change in my awareness. It happened in a moment, and it surprised me. The whole universe became lovable. I loved everything that came in through my eyes, nose, ears, and skin. It all delighted me. It all made me happy. Not just the parts I used to love, like my partner and good food and my sports car, but everything. I began to live in love as a state of being. It was as if love was no longer a verb with an object. In that state, I simply became a loving being, an emitter of love. It's a two-way street: as you become a loving being, the Universe is loving you. You are at home in the Universe. hOMe, hOMe on the range.

Before the stroke, my talks were a mix of heart and intellectual. Now, that professorial speaker was gone. Now I expressed the meditative, quiet parts of my being, feelings of love, joy, and peace. Before, my lectures had been filled with words; now they were filled with love, closer to Maharaj-ji. I would stumble over my words, get lost, have to start over, pause for long stretches. And yet afterward, people would come up and say, "That was such a wonderful talk. It was so spacious. It gave me time to think about each thing you said." Aha!

I was forced to be less of a giver and more of a receiver and to really see people. Once, for example, I was wheeled by an airport attendant from the terminal gate to the outside entrance of the airport. I was left to catch my ride, but I found myself stuck at the curb, unable to get where I needed to go. I couldn't make headway, and nobody would help me. Finally a couple came along who helped me find my transport. I realized, in that moment, that when I see the people who help me as souls, I mirror their souls for them, much as Maharaj-ji did for me. Even a moment of that shared state of soul love can be transcendent.

I began using the term "fierce grace" to describe what I'd gone through. After losing my faith in the hospital and then regaining it, I had come to see the stroke as Maharaj-ji's doing—a loving pat on the head, a fierce grace that served to strip away my outer trappings. Bereft of the things I'd thought still defined me—my wit, my loquacity, my love of driving—I was pushed into a new humility. This, it seemed to me, was a gift.

When Mickey finished his filming, we decided to title his documentary *Fierce Grace*. I felt the stroke didn't matter, because of my connection to Maharaj-ji. I didn't identify myself as a strokee or as crippled by the stroke. The feelings of depression had turned around, as had the mindset of everyone seeing me as "Poor Ram Dass, he had a stroke." I felt my life was the opposite: full of grace. Fierce grace—not that it was going to be easy!

In 2000, I went to Montana and spoke at the annual summer gathering of the Rainbow Family, a hippie collective from the seventies. Every year, the group staged Rainbow Gatherings around the US, which attracted people with a spiritual focus and an interest in promoting peace, love, and unity, often with psychedelics. The largest of these gatherings could bring together some twenty thousand people.

The Rainbow Family has no official leaders, but one of its main figures was Michael John, known as "the washing machine hash king" for his method of processing marijuana. Michael John was also a professional flight instructor, and he asked me if I wanted to come along to the gathering. He flew me to Montana in his Cessna, wheelchair and all. I remember we flew right into a thunderstorm, hoping to see rainbows, which was both thrilling and terrifying. At the gathering,

I sat for several days, answering questions from many of the hippies. Though my words were halting, they listened with interest. At the end, they presented me with a brass pipe full of ganja.

Afterward, Michael proposed that we live communally. I liked the idea; the Tiburon house was small and starting to feel cramped. We rented a house in Woodside in the hills west of Palo Alto. Peter, Ronaldo, and I moved in with Michael and his girlfriend. At first, we all enjoyed it. Michael, who'd been caught with psilocybin on his plane and was out on bail on drug smuggling charges, continued making hashish. I used it to treat my chronic pain, which was still severe after the stroke. (His hash wasn't that strong; I only got minimally stoned.) Pretty quickly the scene grew chaotic. Peter had an affair with another guy, who he invited to live with us. Other Rainbow Gathering people kept stopping by and staying over. There was friction between everyone.

Living up in the hills, I was farther away from my spiritual satsang family. Marlene and Jo Anne and others were back in Marin and Berkeley. It was as if I had fallen back into Richard Alpert. To the Rainbow Gathering crew, I was a psychedelic elder. I was enjoying being good old hedonistic Richard after the rugged rehab routine. Smoking hash alleviated the physical pain. But the living scene was beginning to resemble the Bowling Alley experiment at Millbrook. Things were slipping downhill.

In April 2001, my seventieth birthday rolled around, and I invited friends to a party. The scene that greeted them was of drugs and unrestrained intoxication. My satsang friends from Marin were appalled. They'd brought along my guru brother K. K. Sah, who had come all the way from India to see me. He was really upset.

To my satsang family, I'm not a psychedelic elder. To most I'm their first connection to Maharaj-ji. And under Maharaj-ji's blanket, we are one family. K. K. was vehement that I should clean up my act. Listening to them, seeing their faces, I realized that these were people who loved me, with whom I had the deepest of associations. Their presence reminded me poignantly of my connection to Maharaj-ji.

They saved me from myself. Some kind of choice occurred then, an internal farewell to my Richard Alpert identity. After that party, the lingering tendrils of my Richard karma faded. This feeling was helped when *Fierce Grace* was released in theaters the month after my birthday. I did some live appearances with the film openings.

During the filming, I'd gone to see a Chinese acupuncturist in Santa Cruz. He was very sweet to me. He got me up on my feet, and I was able to walk with one of those four-pronged canes. But I had to really work at the exercises, walking with a person on each side. I hadn't sustained the effort. Now, this doctor came to an opening for the film. Afterward, I invited him to promote his acupuncture treatment for the audience. He soon became an honorary member of the satsang.

I was feeling my way back.

Months after *Fierce Grace* came out, someone showed it to Siddhi Ma in India, Maharaj-ji's great devotee who was running Kainchi ashram. She sent a message to me in the US: "Maharaj-ji would never give you a stroke." It was not fierce grace, she said: the stroke was part of nature. I took that to mean that it was a consequence of my karma.

I realized then that the grace was not the stroke itself but the ability to see the stroke from Maharaj-ji's soul perspective and to have tools to work with it. Maharaj-ji's presence had never really left me. I had just been overwhelmed by the physical pain, confusion, and the weight of medical pessimism surrounding me. The grace came afterward, when I was dealing with the effects of the stroke. That was when I delved into my being for strength and wisdom. Maharaj-ji helped me with that. *That* was the grace.

That fall came 9/11. The collective trauma at Ground Zero, followed by pervasive fear and reactionary xenophobia, convulsed our collective emotions and political lives. Suddenly, everyone was searching, hungry for answers and meaning. A year earlier, the dot-com bubble had burst, evaporating trillions of investment dollars. Everything felt unstable. I could feel how people needed to reconnect through love across the chasm of fear and separation.

Though having a stroke is different from these sorts of geopolitical and cultural shifts, my experience gave me deep compassion for those being whipsawed by bewilderment and loss. I returned to my lecturing, speaking to audiences all over the country about what I'd learned:

about surrender, about not being afraid, about letting go of the future and the past, and about living in the truth of the moment.

In September 2004, Rameshwar Das took his wife and two young kids, ages five and seven, to India to stay at Kainchi. Given my post-stroke physical limitations, I thought I would never make it back to the land of my spiritual roots. But if Ramesh could do it with two little kids, I could do it too.

Peter and I, along with a dozen of my old students, left for New Delhi, wheelchair and all. Though we had traveled many places, Peter and I had never gone to India together. Taking off in the airplane with him, watching California recede into the blue Pacific, felt nothing short of miraculous.

CHAPTER 32

MAROONED ON MAUI

Kainchi ashram is not wheelchair accessible. But when we arrived, after riding in a small bus up the twists and turns of the Himalayas, the people at the ashram were kind and accommodating. They had built ramps and made things as easy as they could for me. Peter and I were given a new ground floor room at the ashram, so I wouldn't have to move around much.

In 1967, when I first arrived at Kainchi, I was in my thirties. Now I was white-haired and seventy-three. Kainchi had changed, and most of the devotees there now had not been with Maharaj-ji. Still, the ashram was full of his presence. Kainchi recharged my batteries. It helped restore part of me I had not even known was starved for that immediate connection to the guru. Once again I touched the feeling of being home in the heart.

In the months I'd spent at Kainchi training as a yogi, I had numerous astral visions or flashbacks of meditating cross-legged in the jungle. On several occasions, Maharaj-ji referred to me as Samarth Guru Ramdas, a renowned Maharashtra yogi and hermit sage of the 1600s. Though he was implying that I was Samarth Guru Ramdas in one of my past lives, he referred to me, not in the past, but as if *I am* him. Where was that yogi within me now?

Samarth Guru Ramdas's incarnation was deeply immersed in God consciousness. In contrast, Richard Alpert learned from birth to be an individual and to achieve in ways that emphasized separateness, wealth, and power. In the rooms at Kainchi where I'd meditated and first felt the possibility of merging into oneness, I thought about the intervening years. Teaching and teachers, traveling and writing, relationships, the stroke—had all changed me, yet the simplicity of this connection to oneness through Maharaj-ji was still here, underlying everything, present through it all.

The Mothers, Siddhi Ma and Jivanti Ma, took me into Maharaj-ji's back room, where he had lived and slept. The Ma's told me stories about their lives with him. Before moving to the ashram, Jivanti Ma had been a schoolteacher. Siddhi Ma was a housewife who raised a family. Once Maharaj-ji entered their lives, these two friends became totally devoted to him. When Siddhi Ma's husband died, she and Jivanti Ma left everything and went to live at the ashram.

Being with the Mothers was Maharaj-ji's darshan, a blessing received via a spiritual encounter, but from Maharaj-ji in a nurturing female form. These Ma's had been so focused in their devotion to Maharaj-ji for so long, they had become part of him. The whole atmosphere of Kainchi is permeated by Maharaj-ji's memory and presence: the pine-forested mountains surrounding the valley, the temple bells and the kirtan chanting, the prasad, the food, all create an atmosphere that carries Maharaj-ji's blessing. I watched as Peter and my students drank it in.

Siddhi Ma told me that if I recited a Hanuman chant called "Bajrang Baan," it would help the symptoms of my stroke. "Bajrang Baan" is a powerful prayer to Hanuman. It is specifically for the destruction of negativity and protection from fear. Sadhus sing it in the jungle when they are afraid of wild animals and evil spirits. I tried to learn it, and Krishna Das tried to teach it to me, but the aphasia made it too difficult.

Maharaj-ji had set up his temples and ashrams and institutions and let them run. But some of the people on Kainchi's board didn't particularly like westerners, because we didn't conform to Hindu traditions. Now the ashram was more formal than in Maharaj-ji's time, with posted rules. At one point, I was massaging Peter in our room, and the people in the room next door, who were new devotees of Siddhi Ma, must have thought it sounded sexual. They complained to me about it. The restrained welcome was a reminder to the Western satsang that

Kainchi was not our home base. Maharaj-ji had always said as much. The time was spiritually fulfilling and renewed a connection for all of us, but when the day came, I was ready to go.

Peter stayed behind, as did some others, so they could see more of India. I took a flight from New Delhi to the US. Adding the daylong road trip to Delhi from the hills to the airport and layover time, we were in transit for thirty-six hours across the Pacific. On arrival I was exhausted. Two days later, after barely regaining my California equilibrium, I headed to Maui. My old friend Sridhar Silberfein had invited me to lead a retreat there. About twenty-five people had signed up. My tired body was disoriented, but it was time to serve as Ram Dass again.

Stretches of emerald green, an explosion of flowers, the infinite expanse of the Pacific sparkled before me. Trade winds rustled through the palms and the pines; afternoon showers painted rainbows in the sky. The smell of the earth and the crash of the waves filled my senses.

Maui was a kaleidoscopic treasure. Much as I'd sensed the embrace of nature as a boy at Willenrica, here, too, I felt enveloped by beauty and timelessness. I understood in my bones why Samarth Guru Ramdas always took refuge in the jungle. While Maharaj-ji had made it clear Kainchi was not my home, the island felt peaceful and welcoming.

Unfortunately, I wasn't feeling well. So many unfamiliar maladies exist in India, I might have brought one back. Not wanting to disappoint the retreatants, I pushed along. Sridhar had rented a house for me to stay in, and in the afternoons, I invited retreat participants to my living room, where I could give dharma talks and answer questions as the tropical rains drizzled outside. We talked about death and dying, about finding home. It was lovely.

But by the end of the retreat, I was running a fever of 103. Sridhar took me to the emergency room, where doctors diagnosed a urinary tract infection that had spread to my kidneys and into my bloodstream, causing sepsis, a systemic infection. The bug responsible was resistant to common antibiotics and if not controlled could be life threatening. All this talk of dying and home—was Maui my Benares?

Word reached Ramesh and the others still in India, who in turn told Siddhi Ma, giving her regular updates on my condition. Through my fever haze at the hospital, I felt the flow of blessings and love coming in my direction as a healing force. Day by day, I began to recover. I received such loving care from the nurses, attendants, and doctors that the hospital felt like a vacation.

After a month in the hospital, I was released, though I was too weak to travel home to California. Sridhar arranged for me to stay at a friend's house just off Hana Highway, along Maui's north shore. Questions loomed: How long would I stay on Maui? How would I support myself? Through all my years traveling and lecturing, I had given away the proceeds or put them into nonprofits like the Hanuman Foundation and Seva Foundation. With my itinerant speaking on hold, my rainy-day fund rapidly depleted. I was broke on an island in the middle of the Pacific.

Friends stepped in to help, making the journey from the mainland to rotate as caregivers, run my household, and help organize my finances. Wayne Dyer, an inspirational speaker who lived on Maui and thought of me as a mentor, sent an email appeal to his thousands of followers, who together donated $300,000 to help me. One of my students from the India trip, a human resources executive named Kathleen Murphy, retired from her job in Philadelphia. She moved to Maui to serve as my assistant, stayed, and is now Dassima, mother of service.

Too frail to leave, I moved into a rented home and made Maui my new address. After a few years, a wonderfully openhearted supporter, a Florida cardiologist, Dr. Raj Rajan, bought a spacious house for me to live in. Others helped install lifts and a pool and we paid the mortgage as rent. It became the Maui office of the foundation distributing my teaching. An amazing network of health practitioners, allopathic and alternative, worked to keep me healthy. Several Maui doctors became close friends, including Michael Klaper, ER physician Mark Haddad, and Joel Friedman, who plays the didgeridoo. A former student of mine at Naropa, Malik Cotter, became my dietitian, Chinese herbalist, chiropractor, acupuncturist, and island guide. A remarkable osteopath, John Impey, eased my paralyzed limbs. I also had a team of physical therapists and massage therapists who did their best to keep me mobile, and a consortium of specialists, organized by Chuck Blitz, consulted every week on my treatment.

Peter came to visit me while I was in the hospital on Maui. I told him I wasn't coming back to California. We'd been together for almost two decades, the longest relationship I'd ever had. He returned to San Francisco, but we spoke on the phone, trading life details, consoling each other over difficulties, exchanging stories about our cats. In many ways, the evolution of our relationship was a direct reflection of my own internal evolution, from the outer work of traveling and lecturing to a quiet deepening of awareness and love.

In the wake of my new limitations, I have had to move from doing, from acting and serving in the external world, to being love and awareness just where I am. This is my karma-yoga, doing work from the soul perspective. You work with what life presents you with, but you convert your life activity into your individual spiritual path, into grist for the mill of love and awareness.

Gradually, I settled into a life on Maui. Where once I'd traveled to see and speak to everybody, now people came to me. There were old friends from my psychedelic days, like Peggy Hitchcock, Stan Grof, and Ralph Metzner. There were Buddhist teacher friends, like Roshi Joan Halifax, Sharon Salzberg, Joseph Goldstein, Jack Kornfield and his wife, Trudy Goodman. There were satsang brothers and sisters, like Krishna Das, Rameshwar Das, Mirabai Bush, Danny and Tara Goleman, Larry and Girija Brilliant, and Lama Surya Das. K. K. Sah made the long trip from India several times. When visitors came, the breakfast routine at the house sometimes trailed off into long silences, as we would gaze together at the ocean, drift into meditations.

Lots of younger folk came too, like Tim's son Zach Leary and Benjy Wertheimer, a composer who is the son of my old Wesleyan professor Michael Wertheimer. Some stayed and worked as caretakers. As my stroke-weakened body slowly atrophied, I needed more help. Dassima presided over the household and kept track of my helpers, doctor appointments, the twice daily pills, and supplements. She turned out to have a green thumb, too, turning bare lawns around the new house into lush tropical gardens, growing spectacular blooms and local fruits that tasted like perfume. As my mobility decreased, they got me a balloon tire wheelchair for Mondays at the beach. The Maui satsang posse would rendezvous to swim on the other side of the island in calm surf. Afterward, I would take everyone to lunch, a pleasure that reminded me of Dad.

I felt a deepening bond with my friends and caretakers. Just as my relationship with Peter changed from an outside focus to an internal one, so too did my other interactions. My limbs were atrophying. I fought regular infections. But all this brought me deeper inside. When I spoke and laughed with others, when I meditated with my visitors, when I sang kirtan with my caretakers, the love I experienced was soul to soul.

One day, I was transferring myself from an armchair to my wheelchair. I didn't focus my full awareness on what I was doing, and I fell. I crashed onto my hip, and there it was . . . a broken hip. I am old, so this comes with the territory. The broken hip was my fault, for not paying attention.

This is increasingly my dilemma. If I pay attention full-time to my body, then my consciousness strays from my soul, because I am attending to my body. But as I continue to age, my body demands focus more and more.

These bodies really capture our consciousness. As our parents impressed upon us, if you're not careful, you are going to hurt yourself! But from another point of view, the workings of the body are a vehicle to get to the soul.

It's tough work. I was in the hospital getting my hip repaired. The hospital is the body shop. To most of the staff, I'm the old guy in room 322 with a broken hip. But don't I also have a spiritual identity? Aren't I also a soul? I am in this incarnation to learn about my true self. Along the way, I am also learning about strokes and broken hips.

I like to think of my body as a coach, with horses and a coachman. My soul rides inside the coach. The horses are desires, the coachman the ego—the "I" that controls the desires and watches where he's going . . . and makes sure the foot doesn't go in the wrong place.

Now and then my coach needs a grease job or a new bearing or a hip joint replaced. But my soul, inside the coach, rides along, merrily, merrily, merrily. I am still here. Just hipper than ever.

After my illness on Maui I couldn't travel physically, but I could travel electronically. Technology meant that, even from Maui, I could serve not just folks in my immediate vicinity but those far away. I couldn't lecture in halls full of people, but I could teach, and the Internet allowed me to do what I do best: connect soul to soul with individuals.

In 2009, the satsang put together a new foundation, Love Serve Remember, to support this teaching. My satsang brother Raghu Markus undertook running it. As a way of sharing wisdom with new generations, the foundation began to archive and digitize my lectures and writings, to make them more widely available. Sometimes I thought back on my days at WBAI-FM and how radio connected so many of us, and I would marvel that now we were watching one another's facial expressions on a screen, staring into one another's eyes. We have Facebook and Instagram. My lectures live in podcasts on the Be Here Now Network. A new era!

I gave talks, interviews, and seminars via the Internet all over the planet. I held online dialogues with other teachers. In 2004, the same year I arrived on Maui, my old friend Frank Ostaseski, from the Zen Hospice Project, founded the Metta Institute to educate end-of-life caregivers. He invited me to be an online faculty member. Frank taught with another old friend, Roshi Joan Halifax, whose annual Living with Dying workshops at Upaya Zen Center in Santa Fe, New Mexico, probed the spiritual mystery of death. Dying, we liked to say, is not a medical problem but a ceremony, a rite of passage.

Love Serve Remember created a guesthouse near my home, where I could supervise people on individual retreats. I taught locally at a lovely old church between Paia and Makawao. Twice a year the foundation organized larger retreats at Napili Kai Beach Resort on the southwest part of the island. Four hundred people came from all over to sit for five days with a host of teachers, with Krishna Das leading kirtan each evening. The combination of bhakti devotion and Buddhist insight we brought to the retreats must have struck a chord. Retreat spaces sold out within minutes.

I love that the resort shares the same initials as Neem Karoli Baba, NKB. I think of it as the Neem Karoli Baba Resort, though I haven't told the management. Two women from a Hawaiian spiritual lineage, Lei'ohu Ryder and Maydeen Kuuipo Iao, open and close the retreats with blessing rituals using ti leaves, making offerings to the island spirits and singing prayers. They invoke the gods of the island, the volcanoes, the ocean, the plants and the jungle, the crops and the rain. Lei'ohu says the rain is tears from heaven to bless and cleanse us. At one retreat we were swimming together in the ocean, and a full 180-degree rainbow arced directly over us. I thanked Maharaj-ji. Lei'ohu said the island gods welcome us.

Lei'ohu was a student of Auntie Mahi Poe Poe, a respected Hawaiian priestess and teacher. When I broke my hip, Auntie was hospitalized in the room beneath mine, and she died there. She had come to one of my talks, and afterward she wrote a beautiful blessing prayer for me. Lei'ohu said that it made no difference to Auntie that I was a haole, or outsider. I felt deeply honored, because Hawaiians hold their customs close.

My stroke, my health, my being at such a physical distance from my audiences—all these things could have left me isolated. Instead, I discovered I could still serve in deep ways. My physical frailty allowed me to feel the pain of others more acutely. Though I couldn't work directly with the homeless or others in need, I could still serve by offering a spiritual perspective. I could help change the world in more subtle ways.

Gandhi said, "When you surrender completely to God as the only Truth worth having, you find yourself in the service of all that exists. It becomes your joy and recreation. You never tire of serving others." Billions of acts create suffering in the world—acts of ignorance, greed, violence. But in the same way, each act of caring—the billion tiny ways that we offer compassion, wisdom, and joy to one another—serves to preserve and heal our world. When I help someone change their perspective on their individual problems, I also change society.

Meher Baba said, "Love is like a disease. Those who don't have it catch it from those who do." Love is transmitted from Maharaj-ji's heart to my heart to your heart and to the next heart, one to another.

That's my social action. It happens one heart at a time. Maharaj-ji and other great beings—and I include Christ and Muhammad and Buddha here, also Meher Baba and Anandamayi Ma—spread that heart-to-heart soul love. They are examples of what it means to live in the spirit. Maharaj-ji's tender care for the devotees, feeding them, finding them jobs, comforting them in death and disease, dealing with their family problems, was an amazing lesson in how to tend to material needs while also transmitting spiritual teachings.

Maharaj-ji didn't lecture; he didn't have academic training or great eloquence. Most of the time, he simply sat on his wooden bed, wrapped in his blanket. And yet he directed political leaders, helping them orient their decisions. He told a hippie doctor to go to work for the World Health Organization's India smallpox program, to help eradicate this ancient plague (which they did).

After that hippie doctor, Larry Brilliant, sat in front of Maharaj-ji, he said, "It's appropriate that he loves everyone—he's a saint. The real miracle is that I love everyone when I am around him." Maharaj-ji broadcast love. When I first met him, the realization that he loved me unconditionally, with all my imperfections, changed me. I actually began to love myself too. Not in the self-aggrandizing ego-inflating way, but by seeing myself as a loving being, as a soul. Once I could forgive my imperfections, the same guilt and shame for which he had forgiven me, I could begin to love and forgive others as well.

As I settled into this quieter life on Maui, I cherished Maharaj-ji's example. My practice became simply to love people, to bring love into everything I did. When the transmission of love spreads from heart to heart to heart, one soul to another, it is irresistible. I first felt this kind of group energy at Harvard, when we started living communally, insisting on connection and openness. Maharaj-ji created a field of unlimited love wherever he was. I remember sitting next to him and feeling more love than I had ever felt from anyone. When I looked up, I realized everyone there was feeling the same.

When we gather for spiritual retreats, the dominant feeling is love. As the social and political environment becomes more and more polarized by economic inequality, racial conflicts, and inflammatory rhetoric, I see spiritual work as an antidote. Social action from the inside out, when we serve others in love, doesn't create opposites.

A loving community is a powerful force for change, whether at a retreat, a neighborhood gathering, a local meditation circle, or a group of social change philanthropists or entrepreneurs or environmentalists. When Jesus and Gandhi and Martin Luther King Jr. spoke from their souls, they galvanized love and truth in others. As Maharaj-ji said, love is the greatest power.

CHAPTER 33

ONLY SON

I n 2009, when I was seventy-eight, I received an odd letter. "I believe you may be the father of my older brother," it read. The writer explained that he and his younger brother looked a lot like their father, but their older brother did not share the resemblance. He did, however, look a lot like me. The writer had seen a photo of me on the Internet and was struck by the resemblance.

The letter writer mentioned that his mother, Karen Saum, once let slip that his brother might have a different biological father. This had made a connection for him. I thought for a minute, scanning my past. I'd had different partners over the years, certainly. But a child? Not that I knew.

I never had the desire to form my own nuclear family. I enjoyed communal living in many configurations, to be sure, often with satsang and their offspring. I enjoyed baking bread and taking care of the kids. But I had enough to sort out with the Alpert clan and satsang relationships.

Maharaj-ji uses everything, including sexuality, as part of my spiritual development. I thought maybe Maharaj-ji arranged for me to have homosexual inclinations in this incarnation so I wouldn't get attached to a wife and family. And now, I might have a son after all?

I didn't know what to make of the letter. I wasn't sure how or whether to respond. A short time later, when an old friend from the Threshold Foundation, Chuck Blitz, came to Maui for a visit, I decided to mention it. We were at dinner with a few friends at an upscale hotel restaurant when I brought it up. At first, my companions wondered if it was a scam. Chuck pulled out his smartphone. He searched the name of my supposed offspring and came up with a photo. Round face, same eyes, same hairline. The resemblance to a young Richard Alpert was uncanny.

Karen Saum, a fellow graduate student at Stanford. We had a passionate fling for weeks. Back in 1956, we'd slept together one last night before she graduated and left for the East Coast. The memory was distant but unforgettable. She married her former history professor soon afterward, but they'd agreed to an open relationship until the wedding. I never heard from her after that.

Intrigued, Chuck volunteered to be the middleman. He reached out to the letter writer, who had not told his older brother about his inquiry. When he broke the news to his astonished sibling, we agreed to arrange for a DNA test. Chuck received our cheek swabs and sent away for the test. After a week or two, the results came back.

A positive match. I was a father.

Karen, I learned, had discovered she was pregnant soon after getting married. She was honest with her new husband: she could not be sure whose baby it was. He replied that it didn't matter. He would raise the child as his own.

Their son—our son—Peter Reichard was born in February 1957. By then I was consumed with teaching at Stanford, barely staying ahead of my students. I was oblivious to much else. Harvard was on the horizon.

If Karen suspected I was the father, she never reached out. She and her husband went on to have two more boys, who grew to be about five foot eight, like their father. They also took after him physically. Meanwhile, Peter grew to be almost six foot two, my height. His features and disposition were also different. Karen told everyone he took after her side of the family.

I was astonished by the news. I had explored spiritual love for decades, but the direct emotional connection between parent and child was outside my experience. Child development had been part of my psychology training, of course. I'd also served as a parent figure, from caring for Tim Leary's kids in Newton and at Millbrook to watching our satsang children grow up. I was even a godfather to several. I thought of myself as a spiritual uncle, a loving elder. Now here I was, a blood father to a fully adult human being.

This was an unforeseen turn on the path. Wow.

Peter was fifty-three. He was married to Linda, a yoga teacher, and they had a daughter, a teenager named Emily. I was a father *and* a grandfather! This whole revelation was as discombobulating for them as it was for me. I wondered about my feelings. Should I expect a surge of recognition or of love? I didn't. I'd missed all the years of primal bonding and intimacy and teenage hormonal chaos. When Peter was a toddler, I was experimenting with psychedelics. By the time he was a teenager, I was leading the life of a yogi. I wondered how parental I would feel if we got to know each other. I hoped to find out.

Curiously, and similar to my leaving the nest, once Peter left for college, he never returned home. It was not until later that he formed real bonds with his family. Haltingly at first, Peter and I began talking on the phone every Sunday, feeling our way. I learned that, as a son of academics who moved around, he'd had a somewhat chaotic childhood. His parents eventually split up, and Karen had found a new life with a female partner. Peter pursued a career in real estate private equity. Though he loved his father and brothers, he never felt fully aligned with them. They have a tendency toward depression; he has a sunny, relaxed outlook. He's active in Democratic state politics and loves connecting with people. He smokes cigars and plays golf and loves to cook—just as I once did.

Though Peter claimed not to be spiritual, he had found a peaceful place, as I had decades ago, in Quaker meeting. He had no idea what a Ram Dass was, but he was open to learning. We discovered we had qualities in common, like our humor and compassion and a certain lightheartedness.

Some months after our introduction, Peter came to visit me in Maui and later brought Linda and Emily too. I worried at first what they might think of my home setup. I didn't want my altars with all the pictures of Maharaj-ji and Hanuman around the house to weird them out. But they all took it in stride. Dassima and I took them to the beach, on a helicopter ride, to favorite restaurants. I even managed a ride on the golf cart with Peter for nine holes. I connected with Emily about school and with Linda about yoga.

Our DNA surprise package was turning into an actual relationship. For a while, we kept it quiet, but word soon got out. For those who had known me for decades, my becoming a dad was a delightful sensation. People got a kick out of quoting back my own words, "If you want to see how you are doing on your spiritual path, go spend a week with family." Chuck arranged a New York cocktail reception for Peter to meet East Coast friends, and I introduced him to Alpert relatives, including Aunt Edna, the family elder and keeper of history. She introduced Peter to his Boston cousins. Peter had grown up believing he was a descendant of the Pennsylvania Dutch who'd fought in the American Revolution. Now, he learned, he was third-generation Polish American Jewish.

Once our initial rush of discovery dissipated, Peter and I settled back into our respective lives. I was nearing the end of my life; he was actively leading his. I couldn't take a very vigorous role. But we continued to visit on the phone, and once a year, he brought Linda and Emily with him to Maui for a visit. Linda, as a yoga teacher, attended one of the spring retreats. Peter came a day or two later and played golf. They stayed for a few days at the house, and Peter's younger brother came out to visit too. Emily and I talked about her aspiration to become a physical trainer; she even called me "Grandpa."

At first, I struggled to see Peter beyond the father-son labels. The soul-to-soul bond is the glue for most of my ties, and I wondered how we would get there in this case. For Linda, a yoga teacher, the idea of connecting as souls wasn't all that foreign. But for Peter it was. He told me he didn't really go into his spirituality. Eventually, when I reminded him of his Quaker traditions, that helped shift our point of view to the soul. "There's a piece of the spirit in each individual," he said. "I can do it on my own terms."

Later he said getting to know me had shined a deeper spiritual light into his life. Among personal traits that we shared, he recognized an ability in himself to connect with and read people that he now realized came from being in touch with his core spirit, much in the way he and I connected.

We are still puzzling out our relationship, but our bond grows stronger, warmer, and more affectionate. I continue to delve into newfound feelings of attachment and wonder. I can feel the glow of the proud parent. Peter and I meet as father and son, but underneath we're two souls. I'd like to get beyond the roles with him, but I am not pushing anything on anybody. I can only work on myself. In Maharaj-ji's universe, everything happens for a reason. Peter and his family have their own karmic trajectory, as do I.

This enigma of DNA and karma, the biology of the West and the inner sense of the East, fascinates me. How these waves of incarnations, and the winds of grace, shift our lives! I love that I am a father. It has given me the opportunity to cultivate part of my being I didn't think would be touched in this life. In the context of my karma, Maharaj-ji is giving me this chance to work intimately with parental love. I see, more and more, how interpersonal love and soul love are part of the same fabric. They aren't separate. I see how love for a child can become soul love.

Peter called me on Father's Day. He greeted me with, "Namaste!" the Hindu greeting. It was a genuine gesture from the heart. I was touched and delighted.

After Maharaj-ji left his body, we discovered that not only was Maharaj-ji guru to thousands of devotees, but unknown to almost all of them, he had simultaneously been fulfilling his family responsibilities to his wife and three children. He had been married at the age of twelve, as was the custom in rural India, and had run away from home. After about a decade, he'd returned to carry out his duties as a husband and father.

He was a good father, and though frequently away, his now adult children said he was always there when they needed him. He was also the headman of the village where they lived, adjudicating community disputes and helping people with their problems. Both lives, guru and father, apparently occurred more or less in plain sight, though only a few devotees and family members were aware of the connections. How this sleight of hand occurred was a mystery.

Maharaj-ji was a family guru. Most of his Indian devotees are householders with families, living the constant drama of secular lives.

Unlike most gurus, Maharaj-ji ate and slept in his devotees' houses and in that way brought unconditional love into the home.

In India or in the West, family life can be a powerful sadhana, or spiritual path. Sometimes it seems like you can't get away from it. It can be difficult and intense and all consuming, and it can also be very loving and joyful. Each individual's karma in a family complements and compels the evolution of the others. Only rarely do any of us catch glimpses of this from within our family dynamic. The veil of unknowing that comes over us at birth hides this knowledge. We constantly get lost in our existential situation. If not, how could we participate in the lila, the dance of life, and take it seriously?

It is a grace when we can think less about our roles—mother, father, daughter, son—and see our kids as souls and see one another as souls, one at a time and all together.

Family is such a part of our incarnation. The next incarnation is a whole new family.

I had the opportunity to ponder this myself anew when my brothers came to see me on Maui. Leonard came first, in 2005, with his daughters Kathy and Cindy. He had done a lot to rehabilitate himself and to restore his relationships with his children. He was not paranoid or delusional, and we had a sweet time with the girls. Still, it was a difficult visit, with much left unsaid. We didn't address any of the unresolved issues between us: familial, spiritual, sexual.

Bill came to Maui on a cruise ship. He was a widower by this time; his wife, Helen, had died in 2001. After being an active fundraiser for breast cancer research at Albert Einstein College of Medicine, she got breast cancer herself and died from it rather quickly. Crazy karma! Like Mother, Helen had been the queen bee. I remember when she first came to Boston as Bill's new bride. She and Bill stayed at our house in Newton, and Mother nicknamed her "the Princess" because she stayed in bed late while everyone was doing housework. Helen was the strong one in her family, and her death decimated Bill.

Bill learned to hula on the cruise ship. When he came to see me, we went to eat at Mama's Fish House, an iconic Maui restaurant, and Bill gave a hula demonstration next to the table. Some other women came over to dance with him. As far as Bill was concerned, I had it made.

I was living in a big house on a tropical island, with people taking care of me: I was a complete success on his material value scale. I found myself reacting to his judgments as if he were Dad, back in our old family patterns, but then I took a step back. Here we were, two old guys hanging out, him doing the hula, our sibling rivalries dissolving in the river of time. It was hilarious.

Leonard died in 2007, in a veteran's hospital after a hip operation. His mystical and creative side will always remain a warm current in my being, even though he had a hard time living in the world. Billy died in 2015. He was in his nineties and had dementia. My son, Peter, went to see him, and they had a wonderful visit. Bill kept thinking Peter was me, because he resembled the earlier me. Bill and I kept in touch thanks to his daughter, my niece Trish, who was taking care of him. In his confusion, Bill would ask me about Leonard, and I'd say, "He's dead." Bill would invariably respond, "Lenny's dead? Why didn't I know that? Nobody told me!" We'd talk about other things, and afterward, he'd still ask, "So, have you heard from Lenny?"

Our minds go, our bodies go. Our souls remain. Years after meeting Maharaj-ji, I see my parents and brothers, not through the lens of power I grew up with, but through the lens of love. I have my mother's photo on my altar, alongside all the saints. I was at my doctor's, and at the end of our session, he put me into a state of deep relaxation by playing his didgeridoo. The instrument comes from Aboriginal peoples, and it makes a deep vibration. In my trance, I had a kind of visitation from my mother. I felt her presence, and as a soul, she spoke to me. "I'm proud of you now," she said. "Why not accept my affection and let go of the resentment from the past?" It was a big shift in our relationship—almost love! She was tough, but I'm no longer afraid of her.

Sometimes I regret not living more with my family—not helping Leonard enough or being in California when Mother died. Family photos bring uncomfortable memories of my childhood. But it's interesting to think of all of us incarnating to play our roles for one another. More and more, I see my family members as souls.

We think of karma as a kind of action and reaction, cause and effect, but karma is organic and very subtle. I don't know how well we can understand it from within our incarnation. Even the view that everything happens for a reason treads the slippery slope of fate or predestination versus free will. Both are true!

As I turn toward Maharaj-ji within, my understanding of family changes. I see the work each soul has to do when it takes birth. When I think of my years as a therapist, I would work a little differently now. From Maharaj-ji's long view, a person is not just a bundle of adult needs and childhood traumas, the building blocks of personality. It is a much subtler picture of karma working out across incarnations.

We may have regrets about our family, or, as I did for many years, avoid or resent them. But the soul demands that every moment-to-moment experience of living be meaningful, fulfilling, and real. The soul's game is not about reorganizing external life. It's not about getting a new job, friends, lifestyle; making more money or getting a new car; finding a new partner or a new therapist—or ignoring the family history.

It's about inner reorganization, reorienting toward your soul. The battle of the Bhagavad Gita is not about dropping out or leaving the family. Where can you drop out to that your soul is not present? No, this life is about finding a way to *be* in the world that connects you to your soul.

PART V

OCEAN VIEW

I am always
in communion
with you.

———————————

MAHARAJ-JI

CHAPTER 34

HEART 2 HEART

I'm an island boy now. Monday is my regular beach day. We pack the car with life jackets, floats, towels, and the amphibian wheelchair, and off we go to a spot where the Pacific surf is usually gentle. I love swimming in the ocean. Sometimes I go when my caretakers think the swell is too big. I still love taking risks.

Maui does not get old. We go out on the whale-watching boats or visit the neighboring island of Lanai. Lei'ohu Ryder, my Hawaiian priestess friend, has taken us up to a sacred spot on West Maui and to the Iao Valley, another sacred place. We've been up the ten-thousand-foot Haleakala volcano peak to watch the sunset, and we've driven the rough perimeter road around the back side of the island.

On Maui I don't feel the pull to return to India. There's something of India here on this sacred island. I sense oneness in the wind, the birds, the sky, the waves. Floating on the ocean swell, I begin to dissolve into the oneness with nature, with Maharaj-ji.

I let my mind dissolve into the ocean of love in my spiritual heart. As the mind quiets, the spiritual heart is the gateway to the soul, the place where we are one without distinction.

I associate that place with Maharaj-ji's being. He exists on the threshold of self and no-self, of the individual soul and God. As we come together in the spiritual heart, there's just pure *being*, no experiencer, no subject-object. Just the vast oneness. Sometimes, imagining what it's like at that edge, I go out, into sleep or samadhi or some other state. When I reenter my personality, my conceptual mind, my ego, I have no words to describe where I've been, a place beyond form where I *am*.

For years I've taught others how to shift from identification with the thinking mind to the spiritual heart, from discursive thought to simple awareness, from the multiplicity of experience to the ground of being, from the ego to the soul. That shift is at the core of what came from Maharaj-ji. It is the greatest teaching and the most subtle.

Perception from the soul plane is all in the moment. *Be Here Now* is an expression of that. When I am fully in this moment, it is timeless.

Especially when I am by myself, I can slide into the soul rather than be distracted by my body and the barrage of the sensorium. The soul doesn't *do* anything; the soul is not a *thing*. The soul just *is*. The witness function, the calm, nonjudgmental observer, comes from the soul.

Since I am a *bhakta*, a devotee on the path of love, from the soul perception I see the world around me as love, as the Beloved. The trees moving in the wind are love. The universe is love. I am a loving point of awareness in the vastness. This consciousness is part of the One. The One is another word for God. God uses your consciousness or my consciousness to talk to himSelf or herSelf, to ourSelf. We are writing this book and reading it to ourSelf.

Before meeting Maharaj-ji, I didn't comprehend the unity of these planes. Psychedelics took me up and down through planes of consciousness, but I was still perceiving and experiencing them as a separate ego. Psychedelics traverse the astral planes of visions and vivid dreams and colors and archetypal beings. Then there's the causal plane, where you see how it all works according to the laws of the universe. Beyond all that is the soul plane and the One.

Psychedelics led me through the astral plane, to an encounter with the soul. The first glimpses of being beyond time and space on the soul plane, at home in the heart, were what propelled all my spiritual journey.

Then I met Maharaj-ji, who lives on the cusp of the soul and God, the *jivatman* and the Atman. That's what a Siddha, a perfected being, is. For him there is no discontinuity, no going up and down between planes, no going, no coming. He kept saying, "Sub ek," it's all One. An integrated whole.

I still shift between my ego and soul. I get irritated, impatient, and all the rest. I am often in pain. I have diabetic neuropathy in my toes, which costs me sleep at night. I have to deal with the discomforts and dependency of poststroke paralysis.

But mostly I live in the soul. There's a story about a woman who came to Maharaj-ji who was very sad. She said, "My life is so much suffering." Maharaj-ji said, "I love suffering. It brings me closer to God." The place in me, in us, that is Maharaj-ji loves everything.

Like the sun, Maharaj-ji radiates love. Like the waves, he washes us in love. It's a state of being rather than an interpersonal relationship. But it's not a fixed state, it's ever-changing as are we. Maharaj-ji is in my soul, and he's here on Maui. He once said he would come to America and wear a suit. I haven't seen the suit. Would I recognize him in a suit? Did he mean a bathing suit?

Being with other people is sharing Maharaj-ji's unconditional love. Every week I have online counseling appointments with individuals. It is one of my favorite things. I call them Heart 2 Heart sessions. I speak with people from all over the world. We meet on the screen. There's a long waiting list. People ask me their questions, and I answer by getting quiet and listening to them and to Maharaj-ji inside.

I use the light of the computer camera as the person's third eye, so I can make contact with their soul. I transmit love into that third eye, and this brings us into our shared identity, behind thoughts, behind roles, into our souls.

Working one-on-one is deep work. A person's karmic movie emerges as we witness our life issues together, soul to soul. Sometimes I can be a soul mirror for them, just as Maharaj-ji is for me, a mirror of love. When someone reveals a problem, I listen for where in their being the question comes from. I try to address that place in their inner being. Depending on the need, I offer a psychological or spiritual approach.

These are soul-to-soul meetings, but my psychology training as a therapist mixes with the soul view. Psychology shows me the layers of emotions and motives, self-imaging, and relationships. I look intuitively at how the mind has fastened on the person's situation, where they are clinging. Of course, I know the limits of psychology.

Psychedelics first showed me that. My yoga training also shows me planes of consciousness.

At the beginning of a session, I ask, "What is your sadhana, your path?" We may go into that spiritual history. I enjoy solving the puzzle of another's mind and body and soul.

Maharaj-ji said, "I hold the keys to the mind." Me, I'm kind of figuring it out as I go along. I have a whole ring of keys, from psychology, psychedelics, and spiritual practice. I try them out until I find one that fits.

Sometimes I can tell if the person I am interacting with is part of Maharaj-ji's satsang, connected from past births. Mostly I don't know. I am just listening, intuiting what is needed in the moment, hearing what resonates behind the talk, the flavor of the soul behind the personality.

I also look at where I may be stuck in relation to that person. I work on what keeps me from seeing them as a soul. If I'm getting trapped in our individual differences, I use humor as a tool that opens the way. Or we look into each other's eyes through the e-thers. Because the eyes are windows of the soul, I feel Maharaj-ji's love when we see eye to eye. I just turn it over to Maharaj-ji until there's only one of us.

I use my bag of therapist tricks to help people work with their mind stuff. I look at the attachment, the place where they are holding on or wanting it to be a certain way. That can be like Vipassana or going back to Freudian fixations. I see where a person is in their inner journey.

I go into my soul to mirror their soul, to help them free up their attachments and come into the heart. That's what Maharaj-ji did for me. I don't feed my personal curiosity about their issues; I look behind the eyes, behind the thoughts flickering between us. I tune in to Maharaj-ji, and I say what comes into my mind. As both of us become aware of the karma of the situation or how they are holding onto a particular point of view, a moment of letting go can happen.

When we go back to their questions and look at them from that witness point of view, the person may no longer identify so much with the difficulties and obstacles that caused distress. Problems become impersonal phenomena; often they just dissolve.

Even without being in a body, Maharaj-ji's presence comes through to those who need it. What he transmits between beings and across generations is soul love.

Nowadays the mantra I give everyone is "I Am Loving Awareness," which is my own simple practice. The love is bhakti, the awareness is Buddhism: awareness and love, wisdom and compassion, formless and form, consciousness and love.

Awareness and love are like two sides of a coin. Awareness is not aware of itself, it's just aware. In that sense, the entire universe is aware. A spiritual master with siddhis knows the universe from inside itself.

The poet Rainer Maria Rilke described a quality he called "in-seeing," which is changing one's point of view to inside another being. "This describes my earthly bliss: 'in-seeing' in indescribably swift, deep, timeless moments." That's when your awareness merges into Awareness. Then you are inside everything as well as outside, because it's all One. That's why it's called the Universe. This is the mystical root.

Maharaj-ji said, "You can plan for five hundred years, but you don't know what will happen the next moment." Giving up experiences of the past or expectations of the future leaves only this present moment. Everything is present in this moment—everything! When I burrow into this moment, there is nothing else. If I am fully in the moment, my own death or someone else's is just another moment. The spiritual journey is less about our timeline from birth to death than from separation to oneness. Rather than a small being soon to be extinguished, I am simply a spark of an infinite awareness.

Maharaj-ji's unconditional love lives in each ordinary instant, love without expectation, without desire, without need of an object. The vastness of emptiness is completely full of love. To be here now in this vastness, I have to let go of the desires and expectations that keep me time bound. This is the essential surrender of the bhakti path. Letting go allows the self of everyday experience, my ego, my thinking mind, to merge with my higher self—my true nature. To merge with the Beloved, I have to let go of my experiences, of even being an experiencer. That is how this jumble of my thoughts and sensations and emotions is forged into one, in the fire of love.

The nineteenth-century Indian saint Ramakrishna likened himself to a salt doll melting into the vast ocean. That ocean is pure consciousness and love. Though I have only one arm that works to swim, I love to float in the Pacific. On land, my paralyzed body is a burden to be carried around, but once in the water I am buoyant and free, and I can be that salt doll.

Surrender is difficult for westerners to accept. We see ourselves as rugged individualists whose creative energy and willpower and constant striving make our lives better and the world a better place. We think our power is the power of our minds to conceive new ways of manipulating objective reality. Our minds are our very being—or, as Descartes said, "I think, therefore I am." What we think of as reality is a conceptual thought of how we think it is. We're afraid that if we give up thinking, we give up our power and free will, and we may succumb to someone else's power and lose ourselves forever.

That's the fear. But it turns out giving up conceptual thinking is not so scary after all—in fact, it's a relief! I keep telling people, "You are not who you *think* you are!" So-called objective reality is only relatively real compared to the deeper reality of the Self.

Mindfulness is an easier sell in the West, because people think it's about controlling thoughts, which are at the foundation of our Cartesian reality. The paradox is that to really practice mindfulness, you have to let go of thinking. The mind is a wonderful servant but a terrible master. Our attachment is to the thinking mind, which dies with the brain and the body. Getting past the thinking mind allows the essence of our deeper being to shine forth. The soul is beyond conceptual thinking, beyond space and time. When you give up thinking you are catapulted into *being*.

Surrender on the bhakti path is a different proposition from giving up ego power. It is the surrender to the Beloved that is no surrender: first, because the attraction to that state of being is so blissful that it subsumes all else; and second, because who or what one really surrenders to is no other than our own being. Call it our true nature, the Self, God, Krishna, nonduality, or in Sanskrit *sat chit ananda*, existence-consciousness-bliss.

Maharaj-ji represents that kind of surrender for me. He's the direct reflection of my innermost being and the purest expression of unconditional love I've found. In that oneness, there is such peace, joy, and bliss that even the idea of surrender dissolves. Who is there to surrender what to whom?

As the inner guide, Maharaj-ji is overseeing my transformation in the most minute detail. From the moment I met him, I never questioned that I was on a spiritual path or that he was directing it. To my amazement, I just flowed into it; I just changed. His love is the ground for that change. You can surrender to love, even if surrendering to another being is scary.

My personality is still here. What has really changed is my point of view. Maharaj-ji reflects pure being. He is a mirror for the soul, and in that mirror, I began to see myself as he sees me, as a soul, a part of the one. That subtle shift in perception alters the entire universe.

Maharaj-ji said, "Love is the greatest power." That conversion, from power to love, is perhaps the most significant transformation of my human existence, and yet when I met Maharaj-ji I barely noticed his love because I was so fascinated by his power. This is not something that happened once upon a time. It's continual. Love is a verb: it's changing and present; it's both transitive and intransitive. It's a state of being, but an active state. Maharaj-ji doesn't love me or you. He *is* love.

I'm not a finished being, a Siddha like Maharaj-ji. As the allure of desire subsides and the dissolution of this body approaches, I live in the heart more and more. Maharaj-ji is taking me under his blanket. My mind is quieter. Words are fewer. Love blankets everything like a warm mist.

CHAPTER 35

MAHARAJ-JI'S LILA

A s I see it now, Maharaj-ji has been directing the cosmic play of this life since before my conception. He was there when Mother and Dad conceived me. He was there when I was born. He directed the course of my education and my career. He will be here when I die. I know this sounds crazy, but on the subtle level, behind the scenes, this is how it is.

Instead of creating my own show, I am an actor being directed in a play, listening within for cues and scene changes. In India, that inner director is called *antaryamin*, the indweller or knower of hearts, the knower of the soul. The guru in form is an externalized part of my deeper Self. You find me referring to Maharaj-ji both as my internal guide and as my guru in human form, which seems contradictory. He is both. Maharaj-ji is a paradoxical being with one foot in this relative reality, the other in the formless One. Either way, I am a mere player in the mystery play of the universe.

As an actor, I accept Maharaj-ji as the director. But don't I still make my own life choices? If I see it from where Maharaj-ji sits, what appears to be a dichotomy between my free will and a kind of determinism or fate is just a shift of perspective between levels of awareness.

I imagine he sees, not just this life, but the parade of incarnations, births, deaths, and brief flashes of in-between. A being like Maharaj-ji intersects our time-bound, linear reality at a kind of metaphysical perpendicular. His eternal present is another dimension coinciding with our past, present, and future. Like the story of a two-dimensional

Flatland seen from our three dimensions, Maharaj-ji sees time from outside.

Western psychology and philosophy don't have much to say about consciousness after death and even less about it before birth. In a materialist world, we come from nowhere when we're born, and we return there when we die. Death is not part of life but the end of it.

Reincarnation explains some of that mystery. From my own life—taking psychedelics, meditating, sitting bedside with the dying, studying wisdom books like the *Tibetan Book of the Dead*—I've developed a perspective on death and reincarnation. Between death and the next birth, it seems, each soul goes through an interval, something like what the Tibetan Buddhists call the *bardo*, an in-between state, intermediate between death and birth. I think of it as "soul land," a place where one meets one's guru, or inner guide, between incarnations.

Most of us eventually reincarnate to fulfill our karma. We take birth to live out the lingering tendencies from past births. In the Eastern view, the newborn is not a blank slate but a soul wrapped in a karmic bundle of its own desires. From birth to birth, we carry our sanskaras, the subtle traces of past incarnations. Sanskaras manifest in the circumstances of a birth, in heredity and social environment, nature and nurture, DNA, family dynamics, the whole ball of wax. Sanskaras are the subtle tendencies that attach us to the wheel of time, of birth and death.

Taking birth in a family, entering with the innocence of infancy into an existential situation of parents and siblings, is the perfect recipe for karmic stew, for cooking a soul. The permutations of relationship and personality, prosperity and poverty, ease and difficulty, joy and sorrow, success and failure are the ingredients.

Tibetans think a human birth is a great blessing. A human birth is precious because, of all the visible or invisible realms, it has the perfect mix of pleasure and pain, the best balance with which to work toward liberation. Think about it. If you're in a heaven realm experiencing seemingly endless bliss, what's the incentive? Conversely, if you're in a hell world, all you can think about is suffering.

But in that in-between of soul land, before you reincarnate, you may not want to come down to the human realm. Let's face it, being human can get pretty depressing. Your guide, a being of light, helps you see that you need a human birth to work out your karma. This being shows you your previous incarnations, helps you reflect on your past lives. With your guide, you consider your karma and the environment needed to liberate your soul from those bonds.

I imagine communing with my guide (in my case, Maharaj-ji) as only souls can, hanging out in intimate delight. There is no real separation. We are together in the ground of being, the unthought "I" in the spiritual heart, the loving awareness of the soul. In that place between death and birth, we are no-bodies, but souls intuiting directly, without the mediation of thought or senses. There are no words, nor can words convey this relation between beings beyond form. We simply are. Souls recognize other souls, and such is the recognition of our love that there is barely any difference between lover and beloved.

Between death and birth, we are beyond time and space in any earthly sense, existing neither now nor later, pure presence. We float on a peaceful sea of love, an infinite silence beyond sensation, perception, or thought. Our conversation is not really a dialogue but, rather, an internal process of reflection. It is really between parts of the soul: the Atman, the universal aspect of soul, and the jivatman, or individual soul, the essence that will enter into a particular incarnation.

In a glow of omniscience, Maharaj-ji shows my soul its seemingly endless cycles of birth and death. We review the subtle traces of karma over many reincarnations. He sees what I have come through and what I need. As souls we see beyond roles, gender, circumstance, or environment.

Then guide and soul choose a new birth. Imagine that they look at images of alternate incarnations. One of the future incarnations will match the karma of the past, like continuity in a movie. It can be in any time and any culture or family or body, perhaps even a different plane of consciousness, a god or goddess plane, or on a different planet.

As Maharaj-ji and I review the parade of my incarnations, we consider how this next birth will wear away the lingering sanskaras and how it will propel my soul along its arc by resolving my need for love or my desire for power. Maharaj-ji shows me what I need to work out, what will best serve my soul.

Together, we look at families, heredities, genetic molecular soup to find the right combination. We see new lives spring from sexual passion, sperm and ovum playing hide and seek, generating precious human births for evolving souls. Childhoods, careers, accolades, accidents, tragedies, wartime and peacetime, privation and wealth, exultation and depression, praise and blame, the great karmic time machine, the wheel of birth and death, are all in this panorama.

I see my next life overlayed with power needs from my previous births. Those power needs come from fear: of not getting enough, of losing control, of not being loved, of death. Fear comes from the ego, from separateness. I see how this coming incarnation will give me the opportunity to break through my fears.

Maharaj-ji shows me my new Alpert family. Maybe George is smoking a cigar and Gertrude is gossiping with her sewing circle. We see the family joys and flaws, all the karmic stuff they're working out with one another and how it fits with mine. It's all there, the richness of experience, the subtlety and unpredictability of life, anxiety and joy, subconscious urges and intuitive flashes.

Soon I will enter my mother's womb and be born, bawling and helpless, through the shimmering flesh of her canal, and I will start over again with the seemingly clean slate of a newborn.

Enlightened beings say that when we take birth, a veil of unknowing covers our soul, lest the knowledge of our previous incarnations distract us from our work in this life. The veil is part of maya, the illusion of separateness that accompanies incarnation.

The first part of my life will be about clearing the way and cultivating the qualities to become Ram Dass. The rest will be Maharaj-ji's turn. Maharaj-ji lets me know that when the time is right, he will awaken me from my movie role. He will pull me once again into the unlimited love of the soul.

My work in previous incarnations was about power. In this incarnation, it is about shifting the power orientation to love. Not just worldly power but also spiritual power. I was attracted to Maharaj-ji's spiritual power. At first the power outshone the love, but the love has worked on me. I came to Maharaj-ji with a strong Western ego. Ego and soul are a balance, as are power and love. The balance has shifted from ego power toward soul love. I can still get lost in power, but then I think, "What the hell am I doing here?" because those thoughts are constricting, and I feel my heart close. Then I reorient toward the soul and to love.

Maharaj-ji's unfettered love continues to carry me through. Just knowing that a being like that exists and that he is actually within me generates a kind of inner faith. Knowing that state of full consciousness, love, and compassion actually manifested in that man wrapped in a blanket gives credence to the possibility I might also come to live in that state.

Even after I understood the need to disentangle from my attachments to get there, it has not been an easy or rapid process. Instead of the instant enlightenment I envisioned from psychedelics, it has required years of incremental practice to even begin to get free of the conditioned feelings, habits, and unconscious urges that keep rising to the surface. And it's not that they have gone or will go away, but how I identify with them as I shift more toward the soul that Maharaj-ji reflected back to me.

I was born right after the Great Depression, and in World War II I saw what happened when people seized power over others. The evolution of my soul took place concurrently with a spiritual awakening in the seventies, a call to service in the eighties, a hunger for dignity in the nineties. This was the stage set for my incarnation.

Tim Leary and I didn't just share psilocybin and LSD, we shared an amazing cultural moment of transformation, a collective internal journey that played out on a national stage. The real change that came from psychedelics was not hippie drug culture but opening people to their inner nature, to their soul. Psychedelics were a gateway drug all right, but not to more drugs. They were an opening to the living spirit beyond the materialist and existential constructs of the 1950s. Because of that opening, Eastern philosophy and inner exploration have penetrated deeply into our culture. *Karma* is now part of the English language, meditation is an accepted practice, and there are yoga studios on every street corner. Kids learn to cultivate awareness as part of social-emotional learning in school, and spiritual practice is a wide-spread lifetime pursuit.

Psychedelic research has been revived and is becoming scientifically respectable again. A 2006 study at Johns Hopkins found that magic mushrooms can induce mystical experiences with long-lasting effects; a 2008 study discovered the therapeutic value of MDMA for post-traumatic stress disorder (PTSD). In September 2019, Johns Hopkins opened a new privately funded institute for psychedelic research. The first LSD studies in decades have patients, including terminal cancer patients, reporting benefits from treatment. Microdosing with LSD for creativity and focus is gaining traction. Under the leadership of Rick Doblin, MAPS, the Multidisciplinary Association for Psychedelic Studies, has continued to advocate for research and sponsor FDA-approved studies on psychedelics for end-of-life care, depression, addiction, and trauma therapy. The Drug Policy Alliance and NORML, the National Organization for the Reform of Marijuana Laws, are pushing successfully to end the draconian drug laws that put Tim Leary in jail. All this makes me feel like a grandfather, as do other movements I have been a part of that are now accepted parts of our culture: hospice, conscious aging, environmentalism, and of course yoga and meditation.

When I hear about today's spectrum of gender choices, gay marriage, and the transgender movement, I applaud the removal of that stigma I struggled with so much. Sexual confusion, especially in the teenage years, is more natural than I knew. I take comfort in younger generations that celebrate the rainbow of sexual expression.

But what matters is getting to soul love. More and more, I don't need any labels at all. Whatever I am, I just am. As I age, my sexual drive has slowed. I still have occasional sexual thoughts and fantasies, but the less I identify with my body, the further my lust evolves into love. From my soul, I look at people I would have been sexually attracted to in the past, and I just love them. I don't think about their bodies. I see where they are in their journey or in their relationships. When I can just *be* with someone, it allows them to come into their soul too.

How does my incarnation look through the eyes of the guru, those eyes of love? Those eyes see beyond bodies, births, and deaths. They see beyond the jigsaw puzzle of so-called objective reality.

Maharaj-ji entered my life at a moment when I was preoccupied with power. His love was the entryway to the soul. He gave me a new name, and he gave his ashirvad, his blessing, for the book *Be Here Now*, which precipitated a shift in my public role from psychonaut to spiritual teacher. He gave me a new family, first the Indian satsang and then the Western satsang of his devotees—one family, really, a cross-cultural bridge.

In my lifetime I've seen how subtle but profound inspirations from people like Mahatma Gandhi or John F. Kennedy or Martin Luther King Jr. caused big changes. I feel blessed to have lived at the fulcrum of a change, a rising wave of sixties consciousness and love, for which I am endlessly grateful.

Each incarnation, each turn and return of birth and death, is grinding and polishing my karmic rough edges, wearing away my attachments. Slowly, I home in on the depth of the soul. I am only the ventriloquist's dummy—my work in this incarnation has been to convey to the West the infinitely loving state of soul awareness that Maharaj-ji showed me.

From my vantage now, near the end of my story line, it's amazing and joyful to contemplate how everything interconnects in the moment, every instant flashing into and out of existence, every breath the first and last. It's all here, the Great Perfection and the toilet backing up, together in this moment! The reality is that we are interdependent, interconnected on every level, from quantum soup to planetary survival.

The emotional bond, the very feeling of that interconnectedness, is love. Love holds the universe together. Love is the emotion of connection and merging. Viewed from the soul, this world is a manifestation of love. Love is the bridge, the transfer of energy between form and formless, matter and spirit.

Half a century after meeting Maharaj-ji, I remember his unconditional love, his lila, the way he played with us, and the stillness that was behind the play. Now I recognize that the only real power, my only real power, is love.

CHAPTER 36

CLOSER TO HOME

I've been reading about near-death experiences. It seems that after death, there are memories and perceptions, even when the brain is dead. In *The Last Frontier*, Julia Assante notes, "When people are out of body, mental faculties and perception do not just continue; they are enhanced practically beyond imagining. One of these faculties is super-vision. People often take in supernormal amounts of information in 360-degree Panavision."

These are the experiences of people who come back and report. The afterlife is still a perceptual realm of sorts. I've read accounts of blind people who can see after death. In life, the brain transforms and translates sensory input, thoughts and emotions, for this physical plane. At death, the ego relinquishes its hold, the breath stops, the thinking mind ceases, and the soul essence takes over. The soul still perceives. As the barrage of physical and temporal stimulation recedes, there is an opportunity to go more deeply into soul land. The death experience varies from illumination to true transcendence.

Scientists go to the brain to get to the mind. But neuroscience has never been able to adequately define consciousness. It's like the guy who loses his keys and is looking for them under a streetlight. Someone asks him where he lost them, and he says, "Back in the alley." The person asks, "So why are you looking here?" And he says, "This is where the light is."

Neuroscientists may make the case for love and compassion and peace originating from the brain because that's their field of study.

They don't distinguish the two planes of consciousness within us: our head and our heart, ego and soul. The thinking mind is a plane of consciousness connected to the body. When the soul leaves the body, consciousness shifts from the mind to the heart, from the ego to the soul, and ultimately to the Atman, the universal soul. But, while these are useful descriptions, none of these planes or states are truly separate or discontinuous.

At the moment of death, a pure soul can be liberated and get off the wheel of birth and death, leave all attachment behind to merge with the vastness of consciousness and love. My friend Lama Surya Das says that in the Tibetan tradition, when you die, your guru calls you to awaken by your dharma name, your spirit-essence name. If you don't awaken immediately to the clear light of liberation at death, you try to realize it in the bardo after dying. As the *Tibetan Book of the Dead* suggests, when you die, you are received on an astral plane by loved ones who have died before you: parents, friends, lovers. If you don't go into the clear light in the bardo, then you are pulled on to the next incarnation.

If you're reading this, you didn't make it into the clear light last time. Or if you did, you decided to come back as a bodhisattva to help other sentient beings. A bodhisattva refrains from merging, chooses to remain in the fire of service and love until all beings are liberated.

In some ways, my spiritual progression in life was like this afterlife transformation. Meeting Maharaj-ji was the ego death of Richard Alpert and the spiritual birth of Ram Dass. I gave up on trying to figure it all out in my mind and became immersed in Maharaj-ji's unconditional love. My intuition tells me I will meet Maharaj-ji on the soul plane when I die, and I'll have an opportunity to merge into him.

Almost everyone in the West who reports a near-death experience tells of a loving, light-filled return to the source, the home of the soul. They report an experience of wholeness outside time and space. Recently, my old friend Mirabai Bush and I collaborated on a book, *Walking Each Other Home*. In it we share a conversation about this last frontier. I imagine that death is like finally coming home to an old friend who has always known me and loved me completely.

In that view, death is no big deal. It's like taking off a tight shoe, as my astral friend Emmanuel used to say. It is not to be feared. If I see death as the moment when I engage the deepest mystery of the universe, then I am prepared for that moment. That's what the Eastern traditions are about: preparing for death, so that you'll be open, curious, equanimous, not clinging to the past. You'll just be present, moment by moment.

For me the question around dying is about identity. The crux of the mystery of death is, who dies? Will my thoughts and personality persist? Would that be disappointing? What about my soul? My awareness? Who is here to enjoy it? Is there still an experiencer to experience death?

The other day, somebody offered me a big dose of psilocybin. I was afraid to take it. I was not afraid of dying. I feared losing my connection to Maharaj-ji, as I did after the stroke. That attachment will last right up to death's door. As attachments go, a realized being like Maharaj-ji is not a bad life raft.

Loving Maharaj-ji is my route to oneness. As I approach death, my perspective is shifting from my Richard Alpert or Ram Dass personality and the limited view of myself as a deteriorating body package. I go from my individual view to Maharaj-ji's universal view, of life and death as a seamless whole in the vast ocean of love. As my mind dissolves increasingly into the heart, I go from thinking about love to being love.

In July 2019, I took a last trip to the mainland. I flew to New Mexico for the inauguration of a new temple to Hanuman and Maharaj-ji at the Neem Karoli Baba Ashram in Taos. What once was farmland, where the Hanuman statue commissioned from India was kept on an altar in an adobe milking barn, is now a place of pilgrimage.

Although I'm the official president of the Neem Karoli Baba Ashram in Taos and I participate in all the board meetings online, I hadn't been there in more than ten years. The new temple took us thirty years to design, raise money for, and build. It blends in with the adobe style of Taos. Hundreds of satsang members, Indian devotees, and Taos locals congregated over Guru Purnima, the full moon festival of the guru in July, to celebrate, have a picnic feast, sing kirtan, and enjoy one another's company. It was a hard trip on my body, but I was ecstatic to help celebrate Hanuman's new home.

Maharaj-ji has no lineage. He didn't inherit his dharma from anyone, and there's no one to succeed him. This is it. Maybe his lineage is Hanuman, the monkey god. But there is no replacement for Maharaj-ji. Siddhi Ma, the mother who ran the ashrams for so many years, was so deeply merged in Maharaj-ji in her devotion, there was not much difference between them. She died in December 2017. Maharaj-ji's lineage is a mystery. I call it the nonlinear lineage.

In any case, the guru is not about continuity but presence, the subtle moment-to-moment essence behind this reality. The Taos ashram is part of Maharaj-ji's lila, his dance, his play in the world. We're still the actors, and at times the ashram seems like a stage for personal melodramas and spiritual politics. Everyone perceives a different Maharaj-ji, according to their needs. People express their devotion in all kinds of ways, by feeding people, chanting, meditating, working in the gardens, or serving visitors. Siddhi Ma, in India, once said that the ashram is the body of the guru. All those expressions are ways of serving the guru.

I returned to Maui from Taos joyful but tired. I was reminded of when Maharaj-ji left the ashram at Kainchi for the last time and said, "Now I am leaving central jail." He dropped the blanket he wore constantly and handed the diary in which he wrote two pages of Ram mantra every day to Siddhi Ma and said, "Now you will keep it." To someone else he said, "This body is all worn out."

Twenty-odd years ago, when I had the stroke and found myself confined to a wheelchair, I, too, felt like I was in central jail. I couldn't speak and could barely move. My right side is still paralyzed, and I no longer have the strength to transfer myself from the wheelchair to the bed or to the toilet. I have diabetes. With the help of my doctors and caretakers, I have cleaned up my diet; the prospect of insulin shots, amputation, and blindness are powerful motivators. I receive wonderful, loving care. But this body will not last.

I'm not an ascetic yogi. I tried that. Am I just an old fart in a wheelchair being sweetly cared for in old age? I am that too. Am I a teacher? I recall a story about Gandhi who, when asked by a reporter for a message for his people as his train was leaving the station, scrawled on a scrap of paper, "My life is my message." My train is leaving soon too.

I have been close to the edge in recent months. There have been times I could have gone either way. I thought I might lose my competence, my mental acuity, my conceptual mind. But some deep part of me brought me back. Some determination of my consciousness to stay in this body is still here. As I said to Mirabai Bush the other day, "I thought I was dying, but I changed my mind."

Maharaj-ji said no one can die a moment before his or her time or live for a moment past it. Sometimes I have to work to stay here. My real home, after all, is in the soul. Awareness of death is a way to awaken to this truth and to lead a happier life.

Souls are not afraid of dying, because souls have many, many incarnations. Each time we die, we go home. Much of my life has been about reconnecting with this home in my heart. I've seen it up close at times—through psychedelics, through meditation, through being with Maharaj-ji—but it has always been temporary. I will be home again soon. A new beginning awaits around the corner.

I've been working with a Sufi friend, Bodhi Be, to establish green outdoor funerals on Maui with simple burials or open-air cremation. I signed up to be the first customer. I'd like to lead the way with my death, but the Maui Health Department has not given a permit. Anyway, I will be a no-body at that point. The witness in me contemplates this body and mind from my soul. Body and consciousness may seem separate, but it's all one, sub ek. It's all under his blanket.

Other things Maharaj-ji said about Christ come back to me as I contemplate leaving my body. He said, "Christ died for the truth. He sacrificed himself. He loved God so much he gave up even his body. He never died, he never died. He lives in the hearts of everyone as the Atman." I realize that's how I understand Maharaj-ji, as Atman, the universal soul, God within me.

Before his death, I related to Maharaj-ji as a human being, the man in a blanket in India. I feel him now, not as a person, but as presence inside me. We converse in the soul. I get an intuitive feeling, and it's as if Maharaj-ji initiates the connection between us. I put my mind on him, and that connects us. It's not my mind doing it or him doing it, it's some combination, a merging of mind and Mind. He's my connection, the doorway to the soul.

Sometimes his presence has a playful lightness. I hear his all-knowing giggle that transects lifetimes. There's a story about Maharaj-ji with one of his longtime devotees. They were walking in the hills, and out of the blue, Maharaj-ji started laughing. The devotee asked him what was funny, and he said, "Oh, old Ma So-and-So just died." The devotee said, "Maharaj-ji, you butcher, she was one of your great devotees!" Maharaj-ji replied, "You want me to be like one of the puppets?"

His humor illuminates my life. He doesn't take me seriously. He helps me be more lighthearted about being an old man.

Someone asked me, "Do you talk to your dead guru?" I said, "Yes." He said, "That's just your imagination!" I said, "Yeah!" Maharaj-ji is in my imagination too. I no longer separate the person from the formless presence.

It is hard to express the experience of Maharaj-ji, because it is not a relationship in form; it is neither sensory nor truly thought based. It's not even an experience in the usual sense. The guru is ineffable, beyond thought, an upwelling of love, the source of consciousness. He lives in a unified state that encompasses all these levels simultaneously, the embodied mind, the jivatman, and the Atman. His presence surrounds and permeates mine. That sounds abstract, but it's real.

The clouds, the ocean, the trees, the wind—as I sit looking out at the Pacific these are my companions. The birds in the treetops, the rains of Maui. How quiet nature is most of the time. The conversations I have with these friends are inner and spiritual. I feel the Hawaiian spirits envelop me. We share this Middle Earth paradise. All these friends, sometimes they are the One, fashioned from love. Sometimes they're a representation of the forces of the universe.

The spirit of the island is my spirit. The Hawaiian deities are the same as the Hindu deities, but they have a fiery edge from the volcanoes. They yearn for peace.

My body is eighty-eight, but I am infinite. I love nature, and that love is a method, an entrance into the vastness. Love brings things together. Then I am the trees, I am the ocean.

Every so often, I notice my mind latch onto the birds singing or the sound of the mower outside. As the observer, the witness, I laugh when I see myself get caught. My mind is a funny place.

Before Maharaj-ji, I was the captain of my ship. Now he's the captain. His cosmic humor is part of the witness, like he is enjoying each situation along with me. It's serious and humorous at the same time. Maharaj-ji beckons me to come out and play.

This is his play, his lila, this dance of form and formless, body and no-body. The soft trade-wind breeze in the room is his breath. Maharaj-ji's unconditional love fills this instant, without expectation, without desire, without need of an object, without need of someone to love or to love him back.

There's a quote from Meher Baba I included in *Be Here Now*. "True love is unconquerable and irresistible," he said, "and it goes on gathering power and spreading itself, until eventually it transforms everyone whom it touches."

My evolution from an ego to the soul is about merging into love. Maharaj-ji said, "Love everybody and tell the truth." I live in that state more and more, though I am still learning and unlearning. I accept everything. I love the wall, I love my wheelchair, I love it all.

Maharaj-ji kept repeating, "Sub ek, it's all One." The original sign at Kainchi, the temple where I spent my first winter learning yoga, reads, "Sri Sankata Mochana Advaita Ashram." *Sankata Mochana* is the Remover of Obstacles, a name of Hanuman; *Ashram*, a place for practice; *Advaita* is nondual, not two. All One. The true yoga, the great integration of immanent and transcendent, existential and spiritual, is subtle.

Each moment now is part of the lila, the love play. The book you have just read is my love play with Maharaj-ji, the intermingling of lover and Beloved.

May you, too, be in Love.

RAM DASS:
HERE/NOT HERE

by Rameshwar Das

Iknew Ram Dass for more than fifty years, longer than practically anyone in my life. He was my spiritual friend. There
is a term for that in India, *kalyana mitra*, which means more
than a friend: a mentor, guide, inspiration for inner life.

I never knew Richard Alpert. As have you, I've gotten to
know Richard in these pages. I met him as Ram Dass at the
first talk he gave when he returned from India in 1968.

I was in my junior year at Wesleyan University in Middletown,
Connecticut, where Richard Alpert earned his master's degree. I
expected to hear about the annals of LSD from one of the intrepid
advance team of Leary and Alpert. Instead of the former Harvard professor, in walks a guy with a long beard in a white dress, barefoot in the
frozen mud of New England in March.

Forty or fifty people were sprawled around a lounge of the College of
Letters. At 7 p.m., Ram Dass started speaking about his transformation in
India. He had just spent six months learning yoga and meditation in the
Himalaya foothills, keeping celibate, mostly in silence. Through those
practices, he had built up a lot of spiritual energy. Ram Dass's words and
thoughts flowed like a spring freshet after snow melts and the ice breaks.
The concepts he wove were exhilarating, like shooting rapids in a canoe.

After a while someone turned out the lights, and there was just his
voice coming out of the darkness, responding to questions. Ram Dass
spoke until 3 a.m. Something shifted in me—the subtle sense of identity I had lived with since childhood, my self-image, my point of view.

That evening changed the course of my life. Truly, it was a stealth darshan of another reality. Whatever that state of unconditional love and unlimited awareness in which Maharaj-ji exists, it awoke in me that evening. Maharaj-ji came through Ram Dass as clearly as if he had reached through a space-time warp and pulled me through. I, too, was home, home in the heart.

On December 22, 2019, Ram Dass left his body on Maui. He would prefer that transitional expression instead of the finality that "he died." He was eighty-eight. It was the day after the winter solstice. Just as the earth was turning from the dark to the rising of the light, he passed over into the invisible light of the spirit.

Although there's been plenty of death in my life, it was the first time I've been with someone as they actually departed. Ram Dass's moment of death was more, as he described with others, a rite of passage, a cessation that took a few minutes as he stopped breathing. The breathing reflex continued with a series of gasps after his consciousness had left. That aside, it was a grace-filled exit, an intensely powerful space.

I felt mixed emotions: devastated at the culmination of our shared time, yet joyful that he had escaped the confines of his increasingly painful physical frame. Dassima Murphy, his chief of staff/personal assistant/house manager/medical advocate/garden designer and deep friend of many years, sat on one side of the bed. I sat on the other. Two of his longtime doctors, Mark Haddad and Malik Cotter, were there, as was Christopher Fiorello, one of his caretakers.

Ram Dass had stuck around for more than two decades after the near-fatal stroke in 1997 that wrecked his brain and body. Through the paradoxical forces of his will to live and the depth of his surrender to Maharaj-ji, he remained. I think he stayed on to serve others more than for himself.

When another health crisis stopped his travel fifteen years ago, he persisted, living on Maui in the middle of the Peaceful Ocean. As his body declined, he became an extraordinary lighthouse of love, a stationary beacon. People came from all over to visit, or waited years in the online queue for an interview, just to bask in that love.

Over the Maui years, despite zealous care by Dassima and a loving medical and support team, he suffered recurrent infections, constant

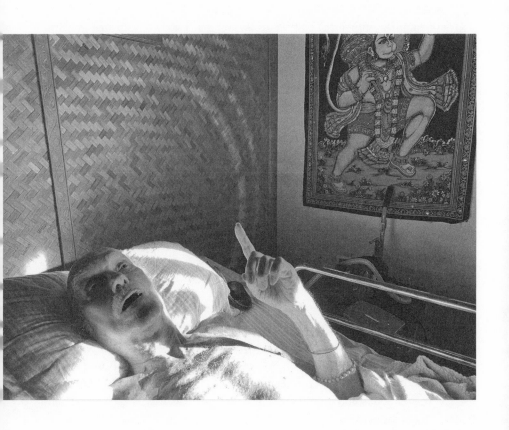

pain from atrophying limbs and diabetic neuropathy, and decreasing mobility to the point where he needed bodily help for the simplest of functions. He never complained.

I talked him into doing this memoir project in 2009 or 2010, after we had finished another book, *Be Love Now*. I wanted to write it with him more than he wanted to look back and reexamine his life. After all, his entire being has been about living in this moment. But after we came up with a frame, to see his life through Maharaj-ji's eyes, he grudgingly agreed.

We shared his understanding that Maharaj-ji is not a person or our dead guru who was that body, but a state of being or presence of infinite awareness and unconditional love. If we have to put a name on it, which we don't, it comes down to the equivalence made by Ramana Maharshi: that God, Guru, and Self are the same. Whether we fell short is for you to decide, but that is the point of view of the book, and the anchor for Ram Dass's life.

Though I can confidently say I have been inadequate to the memoir task, it gave me cause to spend thousands of hours with Ram Dass over ten years. I irritated Dassima, who didn't like my taking up so much of his time, nor my talking with him about his sex life and the drugs. Actually we talked primarily of his (ongoing!) transformation from ego to soul, from the head to the heart.

The foundation that supports Ram Dass's teaching has held public retreats on Maui since 2004. The 2019 winter retreat ended two weeks before Ram Dass's death. Already weak, he hardly spoke, though he waved gaily and beamed his oceanic love silently to a crowd of four hundred. In the closing ceremony each person came up and received prayer beads and a personal blessing. The next morning, he swam in the ocean with everyone.

I stayed on for a while to read this manuscript to him. He had started taking medication for yet another opportunistic infection, a strong antibiotic that made him groggy. We did little work. Krishna Das also stayed for a week, and we hung out sitting by Ram Dass's bed.

If there was ever someone without fear of dying, it was Ram Dass. He had considered death so deeply and often, had sat bedside with so many dying people, that he saw death as a release more than an end point. His last book, *Walking Each Other Home*, was an extended conversation about dying with our old friend Mirabai Bush. Ram Dass is home now, home as in no-body home, home in the soul, back home in the heart of being, the formless OM home.

Three weeks after Ram Dass's death we learned his guru-brother, Krishna Kumar Sah, who had been his translator with Maharaj-ji in 1967 and a dear friend ever since, had left his body in India. Peas in a pod, birds of a feather—K. K., like Ram Dass, no longer had a reason to linger.

A line from the Buddhist Heart Sutra that Ram Dass often quoted is with me constantly: "The form is the form of the formless; the formless is no other than form." Ram Dass is gone beyond form. He is the final Heart Sutra mantra, which he used to lead people in chanting: *Gate, gate, paragate, parasamgate, bodhi swaha!* "Gone, gone, gone beyond, gone beyond all going, offering the heart-mind to the fire of awareness!"

During the last year working together on his memoir, Ram Dass said something we didn't use, because it felt open to misinterpretation. "Recently I have had thoughts of suicide. It's not that I want to escape, so much as I am feeling pulled toward the Light. I want to go the spiritual route, without the burden of this difficult, compromised body. Like the Tibetan lamas who leave their bodies intentionally or the yogis who turn around three times, sit in the lotus position, and go out the crown of the head. That's not suicide. I am like a moth attracted to the flame of the spirit. This body is tired of being a moth. The pull toward my soul is like gravity."

Now as I watch the greening of the season through the sliding door of my basement office, I remember anew how we are each a momentary particle wave of the great harmonic life cycle. New growth is a slow-motion explosion, and I am again pulling weeds, feeding them to the compost to make soil, adding the ashes of winter's fires and the neighbor's chicken manure to this year's rose bushes and the tomato patch. As humans we may just be a warm slime on the biotic coating of life on the planet's surface, soon to merge back into the overwarming ocean we have skewed with our emissions. What of this flickering fiction of awareness, this sense of self we make so much of? Where will it go? Where did Ram Dass go? Is he still here now?

The answer comes when the questions stop, when the thoughts cease and the mind sinks into the sun in the heart.

ACKNOWLEDGMENTS

COMING FULL CIRCLE

I was not much interested in writing a memoir. My life has not been about collecting experiences. Since my first inkling of being home in the heart on psilocybin, then meeting the guru in India, my trajectory has been about becoming more present, not living in the past or the future. And I was wary of hurting anyone.

When Ramesh suggested looking back at my life through Maharaj-ji's eyes, it took me a while to come round to the idea. It has been a way to bring my karma into awareness and release it, and Maharaj-ji's view has burned through some of my attachment to my personal story line.

In my teaching and lecturing, I draw on my own experience. I hope this exercise may also prove useful to others on the spiritual path.

I always enjoyed living communally. While my life is the focus here, making the mystery of my-story into a book took a lot of people. Their contributions throughout have been a loving exchange. The flashes of insight and humor that surfaced in our work were a source of joy. I hope that comes through.

Once we completed a draft, Raghu Markus, who runs Love Serve Remember Foundation and ramdass.org, carried it to Sounds True. Founder Tami Simon and executive editor Jennifer Yvette Brown orchestrated an empathic symphony to transform a sprawling manuscript. Lee Eastman helped us with the contract.

Kate Rodeman and Amy Hertz of Tangerine Ink helped structure and edit the original manuscript. It was a feat to trim the ten years of material Ramesh and I had accumulated without throwing the baby out with the bathwater. Besides expert editing, Kate used her journalistic skills to fact-check endless details. Copyeditor Diana Rico helped our elliptical prose make sense. Sounds True's production, design, and marketing teams brought it to fruition. Monkstudio's Cynthia Daniels wizarded the audiobook into existence, editing individual electrons.

My extended spiritual family, especially Krishna Das and Mirabai Bush, recalled details lost to my holy memories—"holy" as in full of holes. My deep thanks to many other friends and family who gave of their time and love to get things right—too many to enumerate, but especially to my partner, Peter; and David Padwa, my fellow traveler to India; to Larry and Girija Brilliant; Rukmini Forrest (née ex-girlfriend Caroline Winter); Asha Greer (Barbara Durkee); Peggy Hitchcock; my son, Peter Reichard; Nena and Bob Thurman; Joseph Goldstein; Roshi Joan Halifax; and Radha Baum, for her diary of Maharaj-ji quotes. My Indian guru brother, Krishna Kumar (K. K.) Sah, who translated from the first time I met Maharaj-ji in 1967, has been a constant and devoted mentor. He kept every letter we exchanged over half a century. Siddhi Ma, the Mother of Maharaj-ji's ashrams in India, was an abiding reminder of his presence.

Birth of a Psychedelic Culture, a collection of interviews by Gary Bravo with me and Ralph Metzner, published by Deborah Snyder of the Synergetic Press in Santa Fe, was a vital sourcebook for the psychedelic time.

Our personal photography collections were amplified by my niece, Kathy Alpert, Dassima Murphy, Balaram Das, John Phaneuf, Perry Julien, Mohan Baum, Mary Godschalk, Larry Schiller, Lisa Law, Ahad Cobb, Hanuman Das Kane, and Gay Dillingham. The provenance of some images remains uncertain. We would be happy to attribute them in future editions if they can be discovered.

Ramesh's wife, Kate-Lalita, sustained and encouraged him through a decade of labor on this project with childcare, gourmet cooking, yoga practice, and sage counsel. The accidental death in 2013 of their fourteen-year-old daughter, Anna Mirabai, was a cataclysm that happened while Ramesh was on Maui working with me. Their son, James Dhruva, is his own miracle of love.

I have learned we are all blessed and guided from within even when we lose faith or feel lost. That guide, the real guru, is our own being, our true nature.

Namaste, Honoring the Light within each of us!

PHOTOGRAPHY CREDITS

Numbers in roman type refer to photographs in the inserts; numbers in *italic* refer to the book pages.

© Kathy Alpert/Alpert Family Archive: 1, 2, 10, 11, 12, 13, 14, 15, 19, 20, 42, 63, 64, 142, 143

© Love Serve Remember Foundation: 6, 44, 45, 46, 47, 48, 52, 57, 58, 59, 61, 62, 94 (unknown), 119 (unknown), 124 (unknown), *153*

© Rameshwar Das: 7, 8, 9, 18, 49 (K. K. Sah), 51, 54, 55, 56, 60, 65, 66, 67, 68, 69, 70, 71, 72, 73, 74, 76, 77, 78, 79, 80 (unknown), 81, 82, 83, 84, 85, 86, 87, 88, 89, 90, 92, 93, 95, 96, 97, 98, 99, 100, 101, 102, 103, 104, 106, 111, 112, 113, 114, 115, 118, 120, 121, 122, 123, 141, *144, 259, 321, 399*

© Timothy Leary's Futique Trust: 3, 7, 21, 22, 23, 26, 28, 30, 32, 33, 35, 38, 39, 44, 117

© Peter Simon/Ronni Simon: 17, 107, 108, 109, 110

© Dassima Murphy: 126, 127, 128, 129, 130, 131, 132, 133, 134, 135, 136, 137, 138, 139, 140

© Synergetic Press, *Birth of a Psychedelic Culture*: 3, 4, 5, 25, 27, 29, 31, 34, 116

© Don Snyder: 36

© Peter Gould: 37

© Andrea Rabinowitz, photo by Sara Karl: 16

© Rukmini Forrest: 40, 41

© Lisa Law: 43

© Lawrence Schiller: 24

© Balaram Das: 50, 53

© Ahad Cobb: 75

© Mohan Baum: 91

© Hanuman Das: 105

© Mary Godschalk: 125

© Perry Julien: 145, 146, 147, 371

The Log, Williston Academy Yearbook, 1948: 29

ABOUT LOVE SERVE REMEMBER FOUNDATION

Love everyone. Serve everyone. Remember God.

These are the three central tenets given by Neem Karoli Baba to Ram Dass, which informed Ram Dass's teachings over five decades and became the name of the nonprofit foundation dedicated to preserving and continuing his work and that of Neem Karoli Baba (Maharaj-ji).

Since Ram Dass's passing in 2019, the Love Serve Remember Foundation is fulfilling his wish to make teachings accessible to the next generation of seekers. RamDass.org and the Be Here Now Network have a rich library of online talks, videos, and podcasts, most of which can be streamed for free. Love Serve Remember Foundation also sponsors and produces books and films, online courses, virtual and physical retreats, collaborations with artists and musicians, and a fellowship community.

After meeting Maharaj-ji in India, Ram Dass returned from his first trip in 1968 and shared his experience through talks he gave across the US. The talks were compiled into his spiritual classic, *Be Here Now* (1971), which opened generations to the living spirit. When Ram Dass was asked why he talked about Neem Karoli Baba when he was told not to, he said, "How could I not share the jewel I had been given by Maharaj-ji?"

Loving everyone, serving everyone, and remembering God, together in this moment, is that jewel.

For more information, visit ramdass.org and beherenownetwork.com.

ABOUT SOUNDS TRUE

Sounds True is a multimedia publisher whose mission is to inspire and support personal transformation and spiritual awakening. Founded in 1985 and located in Boulder, Colorado, we work with many of the leading spiritual teachers, thinkers, healers, and visionary artists of our time. We strive with every title to preserve the essential "living wisdom" of the author or artist. It is our goal to create products that not only provide information to a reader or listener but also embody the quality of a wisdom transmission.

For those seeking genuine transformation, Sounds True is your trusted partner. At SoundsTrue.com you will find a wealth of free resources to support your journey, including exclusive weekly audio interviews, free downloads, interactive learning tools, and special savings on all our titles.

To learn more, please visit SoundsTrue.com/freegifts or call us toll-free at 800.333.9185.